The Surplus People
Forced Removals in South Africa

The Surplus People

Forced Removals in South Africa

Laurine Platzky and Cherryl Walker
for the Surplus People Project

Ravan Press   Johannesburg

Published by Ravan Press (Pty) Ltd.,
P.O. Box 31134, Braamfontein 2017

© Laurine Platzky and Cherryl Walker

All rights reserved. No part of this
publication may be reproduced, stored in a
retrieval system, or transmitted in any form
or by any means, electronic, mechanical,
photocopying, recording, or otherwise,
without the prior permission of the Copyright
owner.

First published 1985

ISBN 0 86975 255 3

Cover design by The Graphic Equalizer. Cover image
by Seton Bailey.

Printed by Galvin and Sales (Pty) Ltd., Cape Town.

Contents

List of Abbreviations	vi
List of Maps and Photographs	vii
Glossary	ix
Foreword	xvii
Preface	xx
Postscript March 1985	xxvi

Introduction — 1

1. Jamangile Tsotsobe — The Story of a South African — 3
2. From Kuruman to Kosi Bay : The Scope of Forced Removals — 7
3. Why Removals? Some Popular Explanations — 61
4. 'Land Divided by History' — Native Policies Before 1948 — 70
5. 'Pegging It Down' — Separate Development after 1948 — 95
6. 'Getting Them Away' — GG at work — 128
7. Communities in Crisis — Six Case Studies of Relocation in Practice — 189
8. Responses: The People Wish Unity — 279
9. 'Trying by All Ways and Means for Survival' : Conditions in Relocation Areas — 326
10. Siyabuswa : We Are Controlled — 369

Resources on Relocation — 401

Bibliography — 404

Index — 409

List of abbreviations

AFRA	Association for Rural Advancement
ANC	African National Congress
CNIP	Ciskei National Independence Party
CP	Conservative Party
DSG	Development Studies Group
ECAB	Eastern Cape Administration Board (now Development Board)
GG	Registration plate letters denoting state transport
HUCA	Huhudi Civic Association
MRA	Mgwali Residents' Association
NAUNLU	Natal Agricultural Union/Natal Landbou Unie (and reports)
NCAB	Northern Cape Administration Board (now Development Board)
OFS	Orange Free State
PFP	Progressive Federal Party
PNAB	Port Natal Administration Board (now Development Board)
RSA	Republic of South Africa; also used to denote 'white' South Africa outside the bantustans
SABC	South African Broadcasting Corporation
SACC	South African Council of Churches
SADF	South African Defence Force
SADT	South African Development Trust
SAIRR	South African Institute of Race Relations (and reports)
SAP	South African Police
SPP	Surplus People Project (and report)
SWAPO	South West People's Organisation
Tvl	Transvaal
UDF	United Democratic Front
WCAB	Western Cape Administration Board (now Development Board)
YB	Registration plate letters denoting Bophuthatswana police

Maps

Map 1:	Tomlinson Commission Consolidation Proposals, 1955	37
Map 2:	1975 Consolidation Proposals	40-41
Map 3:	Northern Transvaal	48
Map 4:	Western Transvaal	49
Map 5:	Eastern Transvaal	50
Map 6:	Natal	52
Map 7:	Orange Free State, Northern Cape and Western Cape	54
Map 8:	Eastern Cape	56
Map 9:	Natal Colony	77
Map 10:	'Die Beswarting van die Platteland' — Natal, 1960	121
Map 11:	KwaNdebele — 1975 Consolidation Proposals	180
Map 12:	KwaNdebele — 1983 Consolidation Proposals	181
Map 13:	The Tsitsikama Reserves	192
Map 14:	Klipfontein	231
Map 15:	Sekgosese	239
Map 16:	Areas Surveyed by the Surplus People Project	333

Photographs

between page 35 and page 36

1. Boy in Oxton, a Ciskei transit camp near Queenstown.
2. Woman in Emadakeni, an informal relocation area next to Sada in the Ciskei.
3. Family from Riemvasmaak in Welcomewood, a closer settlement near King William's Town.
4. Elderly woman evicted from farm. Zweledinga, near Balfour, winter 1979.
5. Children in Bendall, a Bophuthatswana closer settlement near Kuruman in the Northern Cape.
6. The road to Deerward, a closer settlement a few kilometres from Bendall.
7. Tseki. Qwaqwa, in 1980 : a typical new settlement.
8. Single sex hostels for migrant workers in Durban.
9. Phoenix, outside Durban, built to hold people uprooted by group area removals.
10-13 Crossroads 1983 : 'We demand passes and places to stay'.

between page 147 and page 148

14. A landowner stands in front of his numbered door in Steincoalspruit, a black spot in the Klip River area, Natal.
15. 'GG' trucks removing households from Kwapitela, a black spot near Himeville in Natal.

16. Houses under demolition in Kwapitela following the removal in July 1981.
17. The view remains, the people have gone: after the demolition in Kwapitela.

between page 234 and page 235

18-19. Two views of Elukhanyweni, a closer settlement in the Eastern Cape to which 400 families were moved from the Tsitsikama reserves.
20. Joseph Gqivana, a blind pensioner, with eviction notice in Kenton camp.
21. Residents of Klipfontein meet to discuss the impending removal.
22. Klipfontein residents leave the magistrate's court in Kenton at the end of the hearing which led to their eviction.
23. Glenmore, the transit camp to which the Klipfontein residents were moved.
24. A community meeting in Kwapitela, the Natal black spot near Himeville.
25. Kwapitela women after the move to Compensation, the closer settlement near Pietermaritzburg.

between page 325 and page 326

26. Rural scene in Wartburg, a black spot in the Eastern Cape where people are under threat of removal.
27. Family group in Mooiplaas, another threatened black spot in the Eastern Cape.
28. Resident addressing a community meeting in Umbulwane, a Northern Natal black spot near Ladysmith.
29. Produce offered for sale at a roadside stall by a woman from Reserve Four, Natal.
30. Signpost in Daggakraal, Eastern Transvaal black spot under threat of removal.
31. Elderly resident of St. Wendolins, a Natal black spot near Durban which has been partly reprieved.
32. Boys in Driefontein, the threatened Eastern Transvaal black spot near Wakkerstroom.
33. Unemployed man in Thornhill, a Ciskei transit camp and closer settlement near Tarkastad, Eastern Cape.
34. The face of unemployment in Nondweni, a Northern Natal closer settlement near Nqutu in KwaZulu.
35. Toilets dominate the landscape in Peddie, a Ciskei village and closer settlement near King William's Town.
36. Fletcraft housing units in Oxton, a Ciskei transit camp and closer settlement near Queenstown.
37. Old woman in Ndevana, an informal settlement in the Ciskei.
38. Emadakeni, an informal relocation settlement next to Sada, a Ciskei relocation township near Whittlesea.

A glossary of apartheid terminology

Categories of relocation

Relocation, Removals, Resettlement
All three terms are commonly used to describe both the overall policy and the processes involved in the massive, state-sponsored removals of people (almost all of them black) from one area to another that have characterised the apartheid system. SPP has favoured using either 'relocation' or the more descriptive 'removal' (or 'forced removal') in preference to 'resettlement' since 'resettlement' implies some accrual of benefit to the people who are moved and disguises the coerced nature of these population movements.

Consolidation
This is the official term used to describe the policy developed by the central government in the 1970s to reduce the number of separate, isolated pieces of land making up each of the bantustans (see below); it is part of the process of turning these areas into independent 'national states'.

Betterment planning
This refers to the schemes introduced by the central government in the African reserves since the 1930s and 1940s in an attempt to control land usage and thus improve and rationalise reserve agriculture. Under betterment, tribal areas are divided into residential and agricultural land and the people living on the land are moved into rural villages.

Black spot
See below.

Influx control
This refers to the network of legislation and regulations which controls African access to the urban-industrial centres situated in what is claimed to be white South Africa; it severely limits the numbers of

African people allowed to live and work there to those qualifying in terms of Section 10 of the Urban Areas Act of 1923, as amended.

Categories of Rural Land

Reserve, Bantustan, Homeland, National state

These are the terms that have been officially applied to the African areas by the central government at various stages of recent South African history. 'Reserve' dates from the pre-apartheid period; the last three terms represent stages in the evolution of the policy of apartheid and refer to the various ethnic political constructions that have been created on the basis of the former reserves : Transkei, Ciskei, KwaZulu, Qwa Qwa, Bophuthatswana, KwaNdebele, Kangwane, Lebowa, Gazankulu and Venda. 'National state' is the term most recently coined. SPP has chosen not to use either 'homeland' of 'national state' because of their unacceptable ideological bias. They present an image of these territories as economically viable, politically separate entities that are the only true and traditional 'homes' of the African people of South Africa, themselves divided along ethnic lines, and thus serve to justify the apartheid policy. Where possible we have referred to the various territories by name directly (e.g. KwaZulu, Ciskei etc.); otherwise, depending on the context, we have used 'reserve' or 'bantustan'.

Scheduled land

Land set aside in terms of the Natives Land Act of 1913 for occupation and ownership by Africans. The schedule to the Act was based on the existing African reserves and locations and amounted to about 8,98 million hectares.

Released land

Additional land set aside for African occupation and ownership, to be added to the scheduled areas, in terms of the Native Trust and Land Act of 1936. The total amount to be released in South Africa in 1936 amounted to about 6,2 million hectares. Some of this was land that was already occupied or owned by Africans; the balance had still to be acquired by the South African Native Trust (SANT, later SABT, then SADT) which was established at this time.

Quota land
The total amount of land to be added to the scheduled areas in terms of the 1936 land legislation was apportioned between the four provinces on a quota basis; that amount represented the maximum area that could be occupied or owned by Africans in each province. The total area of African land (scheduled and released) was thus fixed at a little below 13% of the total area in South Africa.

Trust land
Land purchased by the State in terms of the 1936 land legislation and administered by the SANT/SADT.

Black spot
This is an official term that is generally used to refer to African freehold land which was acquired before the 1913 Land Act and which lies outside the scheduled or released areas. It is one of the categories of land threatened with removal because it falls within what is considered the white area. In this book we have used this term to refer to all African freehold land that is under threat of removal, including land falling within scheduled or released areas that are to be moved in terms of the consolidation policy.

Badly situated areas
This is a term used by the authorities to describe scheduled or released areas (tribal and, in some instances, freehold) that are to be moved because of the consolidation policy. Officials often use this term and 'black spot' interchangeably and we have tried to avoid using the term altogether.

Excised land
Land which has been or is to be excised from the bantustans in terms of the consolidation policy of the government.

Added land
Land which has been or is to be added to the various bantustans, in compensation for the areas to be excised in terms of the consolidation proposals of the government, so as to keep the quota of land set in 1936 constant.

Categories of Urban/Residential Areas

Prescribed areas
Prescribed areas are proclaimed or deproclaimed by means of a notice appearing in the Government Gazette; they take in all the white urban areas and the presence of Africans in them is governed by influx control regulations.

Townships
Residential areas set aside for African, Indian or 'coloured' occupation, usually situated adjacent to or within commuting distance of a white urban area on which they are economically dependent. Conditions in these areas vary, but generally formal housing is provided for rent, and sometimes for sale. These areas are typically better off with regard to services and facilities than are the closer settlements described below.

Group areas
These are areas that have been proclaimed solely for occupation by members of a particular race group, either white, 'coloured', or Indian, in terms of the Group Areas Act of 1950. The Act also affects trading rights and inter-racial property transactions.

Informal settlements
Areas of settlement which are not planned or approved by the local authorities or the State. Housing is erected by the occupants of the land themselves, generally out of unorthodox building materials. The areas are often densely populated and generally poorly serviced.

Deproclamation (of a township)
The process by which the legal procedure for establishing an authorised African township is reversed. This is a necessary preliminary step before such a township can be relocated.

Closer settlement
The official term used to describe a type of settlement established for African people on reserve or Trust land that is for residential purposes only — no agricultural land is attached — and far more rudimentary in the type of facilities it has than a township. People who are removed off black spots and white farms are generally relocated to these settle-

ments. They are provided with temporary accommodation and are expected to build their own permanent houses. Facilities vary but generally (not always) include pit latrines and one or more communal water supply points.

Categories of people

Black, African, Indian, 'Coloured', White
In terms of the Population Registration Act of 1950, everybody in South Africa was classified according to their 'race' as defined by the Act; the four major classifications being established as 'white', 'native' (subsequently Bantu, subsequently black), 'coloured' and 'Indian'. This is another example of language being manipulated by the government to promote the ideology of apartheid. In this book the term 'black' is used to include all those who are disenfranchised and are not classified as white; it thus includes all the people who are officially classified as Bantu/black, coloured or Indian. However since the apartheid legislation affects these different sections of the black population differently in certain important respects, it is often necessary to distinguish between people along the official lines and in those instances we have used the terms 'African', 'Indian' or 'coloured'.

Labour tenants
These are African families living on white-owned farms who supply their labour to the landowner for part of the year (3–9 months) as a form of rent, in return for the use of some of the land for themselves. Historically the most widespread form of farm labour in the northern parts of the country, the labour tenant system was finally abolished by the government entirely in 1979.

Rent/cash tenants
The term 'rent' or 'cash tenants' has been used in the report to refer specifically to those African families living on white-owned farming land who have commonly been referred to as 'squatters', because they are not labour tenants or full-time farm workers, but who do pay a cash rental for the land. The term has been used to distinguish them from labour tenants. The government has over the years acted to eliminate this class of people.

Squatters
This is another ideologically loaded term. It is used in the report to refer to people living illegally on land without the permission of the landowner. The official use of the term is far broader and looser and it may be used to describe any black person whose presence on a particular piece of land is not approved of by the authorities, regardless of the nature of the agreement between the occupant and the landowner. It has been used to describe people living on white-owned land, on black-owned land, both within and without the bantustans, on tribal land and on state land.

Commuters
The term has been used in the report to refer to workers who work outside their place of residence but who are able to travel to and from work on a daily or weekly basis, i.e. as distinct from migrant workers (who only return home monthly or annually) or people working in the place where they live. We have not restricted the use of the term to workers travelling between bantustan settlements and non-bantustan centres of employment only, which is the official usage.

Sharecroppers
These are African families living on white-owned farms who worked the land while the white owners normally provided the seed. The crop was shared between the two, sometimes on a 50-50 basis, sometimes in greater or lesser proportions. In some areas sharecropping agreements included labour for a certain number of days on the landowners' fields, or forms of labour tenancy. Sharecropping or farming 'on the halves' gave Africans considerable security of tenure as landowners had an interest in the same crops and therefore would be unlikely simply to evict people.

General

Administration Board/Development Board
The organisation which controls specific areas in which Africans reside. There are fourteen administration boards throughout South Africa. Together they cover all non-bantustan areas. They are responsible to the Department of Cooperation and Development. Previously they were called Bantu Affairs Administration Boards (BAAB). This name is still

frequently used by Africans. The Minister of Cooperation and Development renamed them 'Development Boards' in 1982.

Ethnicity

In social anthropology an 'ethnic group' refers to people with a common languge, ideas, beliefs, and values. In South Africa government ethnologists have misused this concept in a sometimes arbitrary and nearly always inappropriate way to justify a policy of fragmentation of the African people into the so-called 'homelands' or 'national states'.

Foreword

January 29th, 1968, the day that the first people were loaded onto lorries at Meran and taken to be dumped at Limehill, is a date that is indelibly imprinted on my memory. Before that date I had lived for nearly ten years in African rural areas where I could not but witness, and indeed be virtually overwhelmed by, the poverty and suffering caused by apartheid. But from that date on I became increasingly aware of the all-pervasive and totally brutal nature of the control which apartheid imposes. It was my experience of the enforced removal of people which really awakened me to the enormity of the evil that is apartheid. I trust that *The Surplus People* will do the same for many, many more people. I am very honoured to have been asked to write the foreword to a work which is the product of a truly remarkable project. Such detailed research can surely leave no doubts about the nature and extent of the Nationalists' resettlement policy. It should, but unfortunately will not, be the definitive work on the subject. Doubtless there is even yet more to come.

Anybody who is tempted to believe the Nationalist government's propaganda that South Africa is peacefully progressing towards a more equitable and humane society, complete with a new, enlarged Constitution, needs only to glance at this book in order to be disillusioned. No amount of cosmetics can disguise the true face of apartheid which is revealed by the evidence accumulated by the Surplus People Project which forms the basis of this book. This evidence is more than a seemingly endless catalogue of human suffering designed to produce a purely emotional response of either breast-beating or almsgiving. It is a statement of the costs which black South Africans have had to pay, and continue to pay, for the economic prosperity of whites. It is not only white South Africans who are responsible for, and who benefit from, the imposition of these costs. Particularly guilty partners are those foreign investors whose capital-intensive and high-technology ventures are rendering more and more black workers 'surplus'.

The Nationalists and their allies are prepared to go to any lengths to retain political control and the concomitant economic privilege in white hands. On the one hand, Piet Botha is so 'enlightened' that he is prepared to enter into an accord with a black, Marxist-Leninist government in Mozambique; on the other, he sanctions the systematic and ruthless subjection of millions of black South Africans to the violence of being uprooted from their own homes. He is only able, of course, to do the former — and to increase South Africa's dominance in Southern Africa — because of the success of the latter in suppressing political activity among indigenous blacks. The more research is done into the resettlement programme the more clearly it emerges as a supremely effective form of control.

There are those who would dismiss such research, such interpretation of what is happening, as the idle pursuit of philosophers, whereas we should be busy changing things. It is very important, however, to know just what it is we are seeking to change. This prevents us from tilting at windmills and alerts us to the true nature of our task. In this instance, the windmills are the hardheartedness and racism of Afrikaner Nationalists.

Over 25 years ago members of the Liberal Party in Natal began drawing attention to the injustice and hardship being suffered by Africans who were being forcibly removed. Since that time, although most of the resettlement programme has been carried out far away from the public gaze, there have been fairly regular revelations of particularly horrific removals: Charlestown, Mondlo, Limehill, Stinkwater, Doornkop, Rooigrond, Crossroads . . . In every case there has been widespread condemnation and, often, very generous offers of help. The people of South Africa, and indeed of the world, have, therefore, known something of what has been happening. Now they have no excuse not only for not being fully aware of the enormity of what is being done but also for not understanding *why* it is being done. It is not the result of a sadistic aberration; it is not the expression of a pathological negrophobia; above all, it is not a mistake. It is being done because it *has* to be done if apartheid is to survive. The foundations of apartheid are not shaken by people sitting together on park benches, or eating together in multiracial restaurants, or playing together in 'international' sports. But they would be shaken by the absence from the 'white areas' of those blacks whose labour is needed there and by the presence in those areas of blacks who are 'superfluous'. The resettlement policy is the cornerstone of the whole edifice of apartheid. The Surplus People Project has amply demonstrated this and it is to be hoped that as a result there will be not only an increased concern for the victims of that policy

Foreword

but also a concerted attack on the cause of the problem.

In pursuing their resettlement policy with such vigour and with such disregard for the human consequences, the Nationalists are not only condemning themselves, they are also paying a compliment to black South Africans. They are recognising that it is only the victims of apartheid who pose any real threat to continued white supremacy. They pose this threat because they are the only ones who have no vested interest in maintaining the present system. It would be difficult to find anybody anywhere with less to lose than the inhabitants of the resettlement camps. But they are at the same time the main source of hope that change can, must, and will come. One of my first reactions, after having visited numerous resettlement camps, was to believe that the resettlement policy even if it was not designed physically to destroy people was bound to lead to their total demoralisation. On reflection I believe that the courage, dignity and will to survive of the people concerned are more a cause for hope than their misery is cause for despair.

There are little grounds for hope elsewhere. Although many people, both within and outside South Africa, would deny that they have any vested interest in the system and vociferously profess their abhorrence of it, most are either unable or unwilling to go beyond a purely verbal rejection of apartheid and a moralistic condemnation of the racism of its supporters. South Africa's military might and economic muscle is sufficient to defuse the threat which neighbouring States would like to pose. The West has no desire to pose any threat. The millions who have been or who will be resettled are sacrificial victims on the same altar as the millions of unemployed in Britain, the millions of victims of American imperialism and the potential billions of victims of the nuclear holocaust. That is no consolation to them; but perhaps those who have been rejected by the system can teach the rest of us how to reject the system — in South Africa, in America, in Britain or wherever profit takes precedence over people.

Cosmas Desmond
London, March 1984

Preface

This book has grown out of the work of the Surplus People Project (SPP). It has been written in an attempt to show how the South African government's policy of relocation — of the forced removal of millions of black people — fits into the whole apartheid system. It is an attempt to explain how the bantustan system, influx control and forced population removals are interwoven to maintain political and economic power in the hands of the white minority group. It is an attempt, too, to show the effects of relocation on the people and the communities who are the victims of this policy.

An understanding of the overall policy of apartheid is necessary for those who want to put a stop to removals — and to the apartheid system itself. Unless our action is informed by a thorough knowledge of the system and how that is changing, becoming increasingly more sophisticated, it will be misdirected. The relocation programme *is* shocking. It is cruel and inhuman. But anger at the enormous suffering caused to people who are removed is not, by itself, enough. The issues at stake do not concern simply the huge numbers of people who have been and remain to be moved. Neither is the main issue the appalling conditions under which relocated people must live. There is more to it than that. The relocation programme has to be understood and fought against as a central support in the structure of apartheid.

The government's policy of relocation is part of a policy of deliberate dispossession of black South Africans, of excluding them from their birthright. The people who are removed are, almost entirely, black. They are moved out of what is claimed to be white South Africa into small, impoverished and separate areas — the ten bantustans in the countryside and separate group areas in the cities. In the process they are being systematically stripped of their land and, ultimately, of their South African citizenship itself.

Forced removals are part of a cynical process of division of people as well. The government is deliberately building divisions among South Africans. While the majority of South Africans strive for unity and an end to apartheid, the government is desperately trying to find new ways of preserving and extending the life of minority rule. It divides urban people from rural, employed from unemployed, 'legal' from 'illegal', male from female, enfranchised from disenfranchised, white/coloured/Indian from African, and African people into ten different ethnic groups.

SPP was established in late 1979 as a national research project to investigate these issues. It was established by a group of people who felt the need to focus attention on forced removals throughout the country. They felt that an update of Cosmas Desmond's pioneering study of removals in the 1960s, *The Discarded People,* was due.

At the time Gerhard Maré was compiling *African Population Relocation in South Africa* for the South African Institute of Race Relations. His book raised the general issue of relocation, drew together the available secondary material on the subject and suggested further areas of work. Removals were also in the headlines at the time. Black residents of the illegal squatter settlement of Crossroads outside Cape Town were struggling for the right to remain in the Western Cape. Their struggle became a national and then an international cause. In April 1979 the newly appointed Minister of Plural Relations and Development promised not to remove the community of Crossroads by force. Many opponents of removals and of apartheid were euphoric. However, some people who had been involved in the Crossroads support group were unconvinced by minister Koornhof's deal. They also felt it was important to broaden the scope of the debate. While Crossroads had been the focus of attention from the churches, liberal organisations and those in opposition generally, it was by no means the only community under threat of removal. But because the focus was on an individual community rather than on the policy itself, the government was able to continue implementing removals outside the major urban areas without scrutiny or outcry.

What drove this home was an obscure report in the press in which Dr Koornhof confirmed that large-scale removals were to take place in the Tugela Basin in Natal. This followed within days of his announcement of a reprieve for the Crossroads community — yet it received barely a mention in the press, compared with the headlines about Crossroads.

At the same time influx control laws were being tightened in the wake of the Crossroads reprieve. Officials made it clear that the reprieve, limited as it was, was to be an exception only. Just how limited an exception has been clearly demonstrated in the course of writing this book. Today, only four years after the reprieve was announced, the residents of Crossroads are once more threatened with removal. This time it is not Crossroads alone. The whole African population of Cape Town, a quarter of a million people, are under threat of removal to a planned township called Khayelitsha ('new home'), 30 km beyond the city. It is indeed ironic that the community in crisis which sparked the establishment of the Surplus People Project should once more be in the centre of resistance to removal in the Western Cape.

As a result of these concerns and after consultation with various community workers and academics, it was decided to hold a seminar of interested people to see if a national project to investigate relocation and raise the issues in public could be launched. The first meeting was held in February 1980. It was attended by 23 participants, most of whom became the core of the project, which subsequently adopted the name the Surplus People Project.

The original concept that the project was investigating, as reflected in its name, was broadened as a result of fieldwork and the realisation that people were not only moved to suit the economy's needs. It is clear that the changing nature of capitalist development in South Africa has resulted in an increased demand for skilled workers. As a result of increased capitalisation of industry, agriculture and mining, relatively fewer unskilled workers are demanded by the economy. The ruling class is attempting to consolidate an urban black population with a stake in the system. The government is determined to rid white South Africa of the unproductive, the unemployed, the disabled and those too young to work. From surveys and fieldwork it became clear that there are thousands of people who will never gain access to employment in urban areas. Unless they are prepared to work for R1 a day on rural white-owned farms, where there may still be some work, they have been made redundant permanently. These surplus people will never enter the wage labour market under the present economic system.

However, while the relocation programme has been aimed mainly at these redundant people, large numbers of the employed, including skilled workers, have been relocated under the group areas and urban relocation policies, for instance. At the same time, the removals linked to consolidation planning of the 1970s have had a major political component to them. The title *The Surplus People* describes the political plight of these groups of people more accurately than their economic position.

SPP members felt that the project should concentrate on developments

in the 1970s, since the publication of Desmond's book. The objects of the project were established as follows:
1. To co-ordinate and initiate research projects into population relocation in South Africa, and anything which has a bearing on such relocation.
2. To work in conjunction with other groups and individuals who are engaged in similar work.
3. To publish the results of the research in any manner that is decided by the management committee.
4. To engage in any activity which is deemed by the management committee to be necessary to the adequate fulfilment of the above objects.

Initially the project was intended to last one year, but this never looked like being long enough, and while funds were raised for that period, they were stretched to cover three years. The Interchurch Co-ordination Committee for Development Projects in the Netherlands helped finance the project.

The state intervened at various stages. Guy Berger, an early participant, was jailed (under the Terrorism Act) for other activity. Cedric de Beer and Auret van Heerden were detained for over ten months and were released without being charged. A number of other participants were detained for shorter periods in connection with other alleged activities. Fieldworkers were harassed at various times.

In June 1983 SPP published its five-volume report, *Forced Removals in South Africa*. The first volume provides a brief general overview of the policy and the findings of the project from a national perspective. It contains an historical background to the policy, a detailed section on removals and the law, and a section on the questionnaires used in the SPP fieldwork. The remaining four volumes deal with the implementation of the policy in the various regions of the country. It is here that the substance of the report is contained. Volume Two covers the Eastern Cape and concentrates on the Ciskei where some of the worst conditions in the country occur — extremely high unemployment, little economic activity, a very dense population and a particularly reprehensible bantustan administration. Volume Three covers the Western Cape, Northern Cape and Orange Free State: thousands of people are endorsed out of the Western Cape alone every year in an attempt to implement the Coloured Labour Preference Area policy. Volume Four covers Natal where farm evictions and group area removals have already been very extensive, but removals for the consolidation of KwaZulu have barely begun. Volume Five covers the Transvaal with its six bantustans. Here the situation is often so confused that in some areas the people are not sure in which bantustan they are living.

Within six weeks of publication, some volumes were already sold out and a second print run became necessary. While a five-volume report is useful for both researchers and community workers who need detailed information about removals, by itself it is of limited significance. Because many people who live in relocated or threatened areas are illiterate, or have had very limited opportunities for formal education, the report could not reach those most deeply affected by the policy. For this reason SPP has tried to find other ways of spreading its information to these people and to the 21 communities in which it undertook detailed household surveys. It developed a slide-tape show for communities threatened with removal. This show has been seen by other audiences as well. SPP has tried through field trips and meetings to report back to those communities. In this process other organisations such as AFRA (Association for Rural Advancement), the Black Sash Rural Development Project, GRC (Grahamstown Rural Committee), and RAP (Rural Action Project) have helped.

At the same time, SPP wanted the issue of forced removals in South Africa to be brought home hard and clear to the general public. Therefore it was decided fairly early on that the general report should be followed by a much briefer, more generally accessible account of the findings of the project. This book is the result of that decision. Its two authors — Laurine Platzky, who co-ordinated the project nationally and Cherryl Walker who co-ordinated the project in the Natal region — were asked to write it on behalf of the project as a whole.

The book is not intended to be an academic study of relocation, although it is hoped that academics will read it and extend the analysis with further research of their own. It is an attempt to extract the main issues at stake in relocation in South Africa from the mass of detail contained in the original SPP report. It is intended for a general readership: literate people in the areas investigated, community workers and concerned outsiders in both rural and urban areas. It is hoped that those who read this book will want to contribute to and expand the campaign against removals. For this reason there is a list of resources and useful organisations at the end.

Unless sources are stated, the material used in this book comes from research conducted by SPP. The research was carried out between early 1980 and mid-1983. Where possible the information gained in the early stages of the project has been updated but it is inevitable that in a study of this kind some of the factual information may be out of date. It is a time of flux in South Africa and the implementation of policy with regard to removals (like many other aspects of the apartheid policy) is not standing still. New developments are expected even in the time between the finishing of the writing of this book and its publication. (See postscript.)

Where non-SPP sources of information or opinion are used, they are identified in brackets inserted in the main text. In the case of a published book or article, the brackets will contain the author of the work, the date that it was published and the page in the work from which the information was drawn. For instance, if the source is page 46 of Cosmas Desmond's *The Discarded People*, the reference will be shown as: (*Desmond*, 1970, p46). In the case of a newspaper report, only the newspaper and the date of issue are given in the brackets : (*Rand Daily Mail*, 3 May 76). The bibliography at the back of the book contains full details of each work drawn on in the text — the name of the author, the title of the work, its publisher and the date of publication.

While it is difficult to offer the right proportion of thanks to organisations and individuals, AFRA in Pietermaritzburg deserves special mention for making the services of its co-ordinator, Cherryl Walker, available for research and fieldwork. Special thanks also go to the Rural Action Project of SALDRU at the University of Cape Town for allowing Laurine Platzky time to write her section of the book and for use of their computer. The churches, particularly the Church of the Province of South Africa, the Roman Catholic Church, the Lutheran Church and the South African Council of Churches, cooperated warmly. Without their network and contacts this project would not have been possible.

Sincere thanks also go to the Black Sash, the South African Institute of Race Relations, the Pietermaritzburg Agency for Christian Social Awareness and Action (PACSA), Diakonia and the Community Research Unit, both in Durban, the Legal Resources Centre in Johannesburg and Durban, the Centre for Applied Legal Studies at the University of the Witwatersrand, the Grahamstown Rural Committee (GRC), and many journalists and people from universities and institutions too numerous to mention.

Although the authors take full responsibility for the way in which the material has been presented and used, this book would not have been possible without the contribution of various members of SPP to the project over the past four years. We would like to thank the following people in particular for their much needed and appreciated encouragement, critical comment and general support during its writing and production: Jacklyn Cock, Josette Cole, Jenny Grice, Priscilla Hall, Gerhard Maré, Andre Roux, Judith Shier, Charles Simkins and Barry Streek. We would also like to acknowledge the following people for contributing photographs: Ben Maclennan for the photographs of the Eastern Cape, Jeremy Grest, Cherryl Walker and Ian Weir for the photographs of Natal, *Varsity* newspaper for those of Crossroads, Colin Murray for the OFS. The rest of the photographs were taken by Laurine Platzky. Finally, thanks to Seton Bailey, who designed the cover and undertook the task of standardising the various maps.

Cape Town, February 1984.

Postscript, March 1985

Since this book was written the call to end forced removals has grown both within South Africa and abroad. The demand has come from quarters as diverse as the Afrikaans press, the business community and the UDF. This widespread call escalated as a result of the forced removal of the Mogopa people on 14 February 1984. Their relocation to Pachsdraai in Bophuthatswana against their will severely tarnished South Africa's reform image. The age of forced removals was, and is, by no means over.

A year later, on 18 February 1985, violence broke out in Crossroads in response to a statement made by the new Minister of Cooperation, Development and Education, Dr Gerrit Viljoen. He said that uncontrolled squatting in Crossroads would not be tolerated. At the same time a removal squad of non-Xhosa-speaking people had arrived from the Transvaal, to move people to Khayelitsha. In four days of conflict between residents of the Crossroads complex, residents of Nyanga and the police, 18 people were killed and more than 230 injured. This intensity of police reaction to those who resisted (even a rumour of) removal has not been seen since the 1960s, if ever in South Africa.

On 22 February 1985 the government announced that 99-year leasehold would be extended to the townships of Langa, Guguletu and Nyanga. Leasehold was an inadequate reply to the people's demands for freehold rights for all. In effect, 99-year leasehold meant that the qualified residents were no longer threatened with removal to Khayelitsha. While this was a victory for those who had resisted the removal of the townships, it was also an attempt to divide the united response of township residents and squatters. On 27 February the government announced the upgrade of 3 000 sites for 'legal' Crossroads residents. Approximately three quarters of the estimated 100 000 Crossroads and KTC residents would still be required to move. So, while the government conceded that (part of) Crossroads could stay, this concession, which divided the people into 'legals' and 'illegals', would force the majority to move.

Over the past year there have been concessions for Africans in the Western Cape. Firstly, a moratorium on the demolition of shacks was announced in mid-1984. This resulted in people streaming out of township backyard shacks to the Crossroads complex, in the hope of qualifying for rights and housing in Cape Town. Local control in Crossroads could not cope with the influx. Fights broke out between different groups as they competed for the same land which each group claimed had been allocated to it.

Secondly, in September, 99-year leasehold was extended to Khayelitsha and the Coloured Labour Preference Area was abolished. On the one hand, both these concessions angered rightwing whites who want the Western Cape free of a permanent African population. On the other hand, the concessions were too little, too late for Africans — they demanded freehold and the right to live and work where they choose in the land of their birth.

On 26 February 1985 the government announced small amendments to the Urban Areas Act to make the process of qualifying for Section 10(1)(b) more flexible.

Meanwhile, right across the country it has been a time of confusion and contradiction, repression and reprieves. The apartheid structure is in tatters. The bantustans are not viable. Even the highly-acclaimed decentralisation plans of 1982 are a failure. For example, it was recently reported that in at least two Ciskei factories workers only receive between R40 and R60 of the R110 cash paid per worker per month by the government (*Cape Times*, 8 March 85). The economy is depressed. The rand has fallen to a record low and the international community is threatening disinvestment. The UN Security Council has unanimously condemned South Africa's handling of the Crossroads conflict.

The main problem is that the government has responded to community demands with piecemeal suspensions, moratoria and dubious concessions, in some cases, and direct violence and repression in others. There has been no change in policy. Relocation sites continue to be prepared, despite Dr Viljoen's announcement on 1 February 1985 that he would suspend forced removals except for squatters and communities which agreed to be moved. The government is still trying to persuade people to move voluntarily. It is determined to find co-optable leaders. In Mogopa they found a headman who agreed to move although he was democratically deposed by the community. In KwaNgema in the Eastern Transvaal the community has recently lost a Supreme Court case against Cuthbert Ngema who claims to represent them. The law states that the government may recognise whoever it wishes. The government has chosen to recognise Cuthbert Ngema because he has agreed to move, against the will of the community.

Recently in Mathopestad some white farmers arrived, apparently to offer tenants work. Once outside Mathopestad, the tenants were transferred to GG trucks and taken to view the proposed relocation site at Onderstepoort. They were then returned to Mathopestad. This is another indication that the government has not abandoned its attempts to remove the people.

It seems that the government's attempts to move people are being intensified wherever there are divisions in the community or where people are unorganised. But it has had to back down on some of its more outrageous plans, such as moving the residents of the Cape Town townships or Huhudi. Organised communities realise they cannot afford to relax their struggle. They are suspicious of government promises. In 1981 Dr Koornhof said there would be no more forced removals. Since then there have been over 345 000 removals and a further two and a half million people are still threatened with relocation.

With the arrival of the new Minister of Cooperation, Development and Education in September 1984, came a further crop of new words. Instead of 'cooperation' and 'development' as in the Koornhof era, 'orderly urbanisation' and 'urban renewal' were the catchwords in the Viljoen era. In this new era everyone except for the extreme right-wing has called for the abolition of influx control. But the government, the PFP and the business community want 'orderly urbanisation' and an end to 'ideological removals'. Yet the people will settle for nothing less than complete freedom of movement.

Many urban South Africans fear that if influx control is scrapped, the towns would be 'swamped'. Certainly families would join their breadwinners in the urban areas. But people make economic decisions — they would move to where there is work. Then there should be no problem in allowing them to live with their families. The problem is to provide employment for all South Africans, wherever they live, under the existing economic system.

'Urban renewal' will not simply be accepted as a reason for relocation. Too many communities have experienced group area and urban relocation undertaken in the name of 'urban renewal'. First the government froze development, then declared the area a slum when it deteriorated. For those moved 'urban renewal' meant upheaval, dispossession, unemployment, high transport costs and often loss of South African citizenship.

Although the Orderly Movement and Settlement of Black Persons Bill was withdrawn, the penalties clause for 'illegals' in prescribed areas reappeared in the Aliens Act which became law on 18 June 1984. The penalties are applicable to 'aliens', i.e., eight and a quarter million Venda-, Tswana- and Xhosa-speaking South Africans.

The new tri-cameral parliamentary system became a reality in 1985 as a result of the implementation of the new 1984 constitution. Some Cooperation and Development department functions such as labour placement, courts and reference bureaux came under other departments: Manpower, Justice and Home Affairs, respectively. Administration Boards became known as Development Boards. (The name was changed in 1982.)

The Commission for Cooperation and Development has reported, but most of the findings have not been made public and will need further discussion, according to the Minister of Cooperation, Development and Education (Parliamentary Question 27, Col. 76, 12 Feb. 85).

As for the categories of removal discussed in Chapter 2, there have been changes in approach towards some. *Farm removals* remain the single biggest category moved and threatened with removal. A UCT economist, Charles Simkins, estimated that at least a further million farmworkers and their families are likely to be evicted during the next decade. Unless influx control is abolished, they will have no choice but to move to the bantustans. Already there is talk that sites prepared for black spot communities which refuse to move will be made available for ex-farmworkers. Ironically, this would be a better option than having to search for their own sites and shelter, but they would still have no land or access to urban employment.

The government claims that *black spot* removals and *consolidation* are suspended but they continue to prepare sites at Onderstepoort, Vaalkop, Uitvlugt and Waaihoek near Ladysmith and at Franklin near Port Shepstone. On 27 November 1984 the authorities moved over 250 people from the old mission farm of Stendahl in Natal to Waaihoek. They claimed it was a voluntary removal. The people had been told to leave the farm before the end of the year, but one month before the deadline they were taken by surprise and moved by GG trucks. The mission farm had been sold and the new owner evicted the people whose families had lived there since 1860. They had no choice but to go 'voluntarily'.

Since Mogopa was moved, other black spot communities have reaffirmed their determination not to move. Around the country, at Matiwane's Kop, Mgwali, Driefontein and elsewhere, there is strong resistance to being moved. Even the three Kwapitela landowning families are still on their land.

Those communities which have actively resisted for two or more years are strong and determined to win their struggle. Others which have recently begun to organise against relocation are experiencing the problems outlined in Chapter 8. The issues and strategies have not changed much but different communities are now moving through them.

In February 1985 Dr Viljoen announced that he was reconsidering the removal of some 67 black spots. But in Natal alone SPP identified more than 180 threatened with removal, according to the 1975 proposals.

One government strategy might be not to move the communities physically, but to incorporate them into the relevant bantustans. Mgwali is contesting in court the right of the Ciskei to administer part of South African territory. This manoeuvre may be the prelude to a 'reprieve' on removal — but incorporation of Mgwali into the Ciskei. This would anger the residents of Mgwali and other black spots because they neither want to move, nor lose their South African citizenship.

Meanwhile '*ethnic*' *conflict* increases. There have been serious fights between Tsonga and Sotho over the Gazankulu/Lebowa borders and a great deal of insecurity and bitterness over the consolidation of KwaNdebele, Venda, Lebowa and Gazankulu. Removals within the bantustans continue. They are difficult to monitor and virtually impossible to resist. The people are seldom given more than two to three days notice to move. They do not know if they have any rights. They are generally too frightened and isolated to resist. SPP has not managed to estimate the number of removals in this increasingly important category.

In the Eastern Cape, Oxton and Zweledinga have been moved to new sites within the Ciskei. People were moved from Blue Rock to Potsdam in mid-1983. Many had moved to Potsdam in the vain hope of becoming eligible for housing in Mdantsane.

The Glenmore people are no longer to be moved to Peddie. The S.A. and Ciskeian authorities plan to move them about 4 km away so that their present site can be used for agriculture.

Group area removals continue although there is much talk of a repeal of the Act. Early in 1985 Central Business Districts were opened to all races. But brutal response to group area victims continues. In February 1985 police used batons and teargas to disperse Atlantis residents protesting against planned evictions. Retrenchments have affected residents' ability to keep up rent and bond payments.

Urban removals continued in 1984. Among others, Luckhoff residents were moved to Onverwacht and at least 295 families were moved from Kleinskool to Motherwell outside Port Elizabeth. But owing to the staunch resistance of some communities such as the people of Umbulwane, Dr Viljoen included urban removals in his 1 February announcement. Only 25 to 30 communities would be considered, he said. Subsequently only the reprieve of Valspan has been announced. Meanwhile the people of Ekangala near Bronkhorstspruit in the Transvaal are angry. Ndebeles were moved into one part of the township which was to be incorporated into KwaNdebele. Into the other part the government moved people of different language groups. In early 1985 they announced that the whole township would be incorporated into KwaNdebele. Now, not only will people lose their South African citizenship when KwaNdebele takes independence, but the non-Ndebeles will no doubt be harassed out as the non-Tswanas were forced to move from Winterveld.

A brief update of the case studies of Huhudi and Valspan (pp201-221) illustrates the latest attempt to suspend certain categories of removal and to find other ways of getting rid of the people. The reprieve of Huhudi shows how dubious recent strategies to cause people to move are. Firstly, although the people of Huhudi had won the struggle against the removal with some support from the business community, when the government announced the reprieve on 16 October 1984, it credited the community council and the Development Board for spearheading the campaign.

Secondly, the government has said that it will need the 'cooperation' of the people to develop Huhudi. HUCA interprets this as the Huhudi residents having to pay for development a second time. From 1963 to October 1984, the period of freeze on development, residents continued to pay rents and increases in return for which there was no township development. Now they are unwilling to pay again. If the people cannot, or refuse to pay, this would become an economic rather than an 'ideological' pressure to move.

Thirdly, many residents who qualify do not formally hold Section 10 rights. Building at Pudumong continues. HUCA feels that, at some point, these unregistered residents will be labelled 'illegal', evicted and forced to move to Pudumong. HUCA is working to get all residents registered and trying to bring back those who moved to Pudumong against their will.

The government announced that people could buy and build their own houses on 99-year leasehold. The people demand freehold rights and adequate wages to enable them to take loans from the Development Board, rather than from their employers. Then they would not be tied to their bosses.

Huhudi residents are organising as workers, women and youth. The General and Allied Workers Union (GAWU), the Commercial Catering and Allied Workers Union (CCAWUSA) and the Domestic Workers Association (SADWA) are present. GAWU workers hold literacy classes. HUCA hopes that these will be broadened to include the rest of the community. HUCA has civic members among the migrant workers in the hostels.

HUCA continues to organise, not only against removals and registration of Section 10 rights, but also for old-age pensions, and it has started a brick-making project. This is to help those who want to build since the reprieve. It is also a project which gives work to the unemployed. The next community project is the building of a crèche.

It is clear that if Huhudi had not been organised it would not have won a reprieve, neither would HUCA be able to point out the weaknesses of the reprieve, or the loopholes for future removals. Constant vigilance will be necessary to win long-term security.

Further south, on the 27 February 1985 Valspan's remaining residents were told that they would not have to move to Pampierstad. However, those who 'chose to move' would receive 'all possible assistance and encouragement' from the government. Dr Viljoen went on to say that those who were locally employed would receive assistance in upgrading and development. (*Cape Times*, 28 Feb. 85).

Once again, this ambiguous encouragement leaves doubt about the future of the remaining one third of the Valspan community. The residents who refused to move argued, firstly, that although rents may be cheaper in Pampierstad, they fear losing their Section 10 rights and pensions. They argue, secondly, that their trilingual town has been divided: Tswanas sent to Bophuthatswana, Sothos to Onverwacht (from where they return every two months to collect their pensions) and Xhosas to Transkei. The reprieve, better late than never, is little comfort for the thousands forced out of their Valspan homes already.

In all the confusion surrounding plans to remove millions of people, the government has made it clear that it will not tolerate 'uncontrolled squatting'. The Minister refuses to deny that forced removals of 'illegals' will stop. He claims that the people will be consulted. And if the people still refuse to move? All legal loopholes for peaceful protest against relocation have been plugged. Interdicts are no longer possible. The Prevention of Illegal Squatting Act has been amended to prevent appeals to courts of law. Not even peaceful opposition is tolerated. While delays and suspensions will appease certain communities for a while, fear, anger and distrust will spark more violence, just as a mere rumour of removal did in Crossroads. At the time of writing there are twelve committees in the Crossroads complex and KTC. They have their differences. Some are fighting primarily for rights to be in the Western Cape; others, who have permits, demand houses. But the mere threat of relocation will unite them and the international limelight will settle on Crossroads once more.

The only real option for the government is to scrap influx control (and not rename it 'orderly urbanisation'), to stop all removals, and to accept that the days of white minority rule are over. Only when apartheid has gone can the reconstruction begin.

We record our warmest thanks to Priscilla Hall for editing, indexing and proof reading this book so thoroughly. For their patience and support, we thank her family too.

Cape Town
20 March 1985

Introduction

This book is an attempt to answer some basic questions on the policy of relocation in South Africa. The more frequent questions asked include:
- How many people have been moved?
- From where and to where have they been moved?
- Who are they?
- Why are they moved?
- How does the government go about moving people?
- What do people feel about removals?
- What are conditions like in relocation areas?
- Can anyone do anything about this?

These questions form the basis of the chapters which follow. To link answers to these questions and to add substance we include a number of case studies which are accounts of individuals and communities uprooted by the programme of relocation. The material presented indicates trends. The current situation is very fluid. There have been splits in the National Party, constitutional changes, proposals and counter-proposals. But most important of all is the growing pressure of urbanisation nationwide and the resistance of the majority of South Africans to being pushed around indefinitely. Patience is wearing thin. Further government attempts to refine methods of control are being met with increasing organised resistance.

Chapter 1 is a case study based on an interview with a man living in Glenmore, in that part of the Eastern Cape known as Ciskei.

Chapter 2 describes the extent of relocation in terms of numbers of removals, who the people are, where they are moved, how this varies across the country and what the effects are. Problems encountered in research are also described.

Chapter 3 gives some popular explanations of why there are forced removals. Both local people's perceptions and academic theories are presented.

Chapter 4 describes the history of relocation from 1652 to 1947, from settler attempts to control the local population through colonial and Boer efforts, to changing economic demands with the discovery of diamonds and gold, to the Land Acts of 1913 and 1936. It ends with conditions in the reserves after the Second World War.

Chapter 5 traces 'separate development' from 1948, when the Nationalist government came to power and began implementing apartheid: the Group Areas Act of 1950, the 1952 amendments to the Urban Areas Act of 1945, the overhauling of the migrant labour system, and the creation and control of the bantustans towards 'independence'.

Chapter 6 recounts the process of relocation: what actually happens. The stages of removal are described, as well as such matters as compensation, the use of the law, of the police and the army and other less direct forms of compulsion, and the role of bantustans.

Chapter 7 is a collection of six case studies of communities in crisis:
— people moved from Tsitsikama reserves to Elukhanyweni in Ciskei;
— the Northern Cape townships of Jan Kempdorp and Vryburg, under threat of removal to Bophuthatswana;
— the Klipfontein removal to Glenmore;
— the Kwapitela removal to Compensation in KwaZulu;
— Umbulwane, a Natal community threatened with removal to KwaZulu;
— the reprieved area of Sekgosese in the Northern Transvaal.

Chapter 8 describes responses of people to relocation, from silent resignation to fierce resistance. The elements and strategies of resistance and organisation are examined.

Chapter 9 outlines conditions in relocation areas from surveys conducted by SPP. Discrepancies in what is promised and what is actually provided in terms of facilities are listed. Unemployment, migrant labour, means of survival and attitudes to the plight of the relocated people are discussed.

Chapter 10 concludes by summing up previous chapters, pulling out the main issues and outlining expected trends in terms of restructuring apartheid: 'no more forced removals', bantustan consolidation, influx control, urbanisation and resistance.

CHAPTER ONE

Jamangile Tsotsobe — the story of a South African

We are sitting in a tiny, three-roomed, wooden house in Glenmore, on the edge of the Ciskei in the Eastern Cape. It is one of 500 structures that were erected by the government in 1979, in a fenced-off camp beneath the dry hills of the Great Fish River valley.

Glenmore is a relocation site — a settlement created specially by the government to house people whom it has forced to move from where they were living before. It is about 40 kilometres from Grahamstown and 200 kilometres from Port Elizabeth, where many of its people must go to look for work. The people living at Glenmore are black. They were brought there either because they had been living on land that the government said was for white people, or because their labour was no longer needed in the places where they had been living before. The houses that they live in are government houses — temporary wooden sheds lined with chicken wire; mud floor beneath and asbestos roofing overhead. They are cold in winter and hot in summer, leaky and draughty and cramped. When the people were first moved into them in 1979 they were told they would have to build their own houses to replace the government ones. Now, however, they are likely to be moved by the government again, because Glenmore is in the way of a large irrigation scheme that has been established next to it. So there is no point in the people building new houses or spending money on their present ones.

We are talking to an old man who is head of this house. His name is Jamangile Tsotsobe.* He is a small, neat man. Everything about him is tiny, neat, controlled. We are asking questions about his life — how he came to be in Glenmore and what that has meant to him. He sits with his feet crossed, answering questions but seldom offering us extra information. He was moved from a place called Colchester, near Port Elizabeth, along with 31 other families whom the authorities said were squatters.

---

*Other names are used here to protect identities.

On the floor at his feet sits his granddaughter. She is ten years old, very shy, with thin stiff limbs — an epileptic. Tsotsobe says many trucks came to fetch them at Colchester and brought them here but he cannot remember how many. His granddaughter spreads her hands on her knees and says 'Ten. The trucks and noise, much noise, and then the flames and people.' We ask: 'What did the people do?' 'The people scream', she says and then she runs out of the room. Tsotsobe says she is a great sorrow to him because she is clever and can talk many languages, but she is different from the other children and on that day when the trucks came, she ran between them and screamed and waved her arms and broke a leg. He tried to hold her, but he is an old man and that day there was a devil inside her. There weren't any flames, he says. We must not believe this child, because she is different. There weren't any flames, and yet she saw flames. Perhaps the flames were inside her head? He would like to know if such a thing is possible.

We ask him about his life before he came to Glenmore. He tells us that he was born in 1911 in Kinkelbos, a little village near Alexandria in the Eastern Cape. His father worked on a farm near the village — he milked cows and chopped wood. He was the eldest son. He had three younger brothers who are all here in Glenmore with him, and two sisters. He never went to school. When he was twelve he became a herdboy on the farm. This was against his father's wishes, but there was not much that either he or his father could do about it. For many months his father was angry and his parents talked about moving away. His father went to the farmer more than once and asked him to let him work in his son's place instead, to work double-time, because he did not want to see his son work. He wanted his children to play. But the farmer told him that he could leave the farm if he was going to be cheeky.

Tsotsobe says that life was bad. This man, this farmer, was cruel. He did not see them as human beings. The children who worked on his farm did not get paid. They did not get time off for lunch and breakfast. Once his father went to the farmer and said that his son had to eat — he would do the work while his son was having lunch. The farmer said that they could go if they were not satisfied with the arrangements. But they had nowhere to go. So in the end his father did not say anything more, but he was always full of anger against the white man.

Tsotsobe stayed on the farm and eventually he became a tractor driver. He got married when he was thirty-two, and then, he says, for him too there were no more thoughts of leaving the farm. The farmer's name was Dirk. He worked for Dirk for twenty-five years. Until his sixteenth birthday Dirk did not pay him at all. When he turned sixteen, Dirk started paying him ten shillings a month. After working for ten years for ten shillings a month, he got a raise of another ten shillings. He then earned a pound a month. His wife worked in the dairy and she got ten shillings a month. Dirk also gave them a quarter of a bag of mealies every month but that was not enough and they had to buy mealies from the farm as well.

Then, when he was thirty-seven and still earning only a pound a month and had three children, he went to Dirk and asked him for another raise. Dirk said he was cheeky, like his father before him, and he dismissed him.

Tsotsobe found work with a Mr Beale, at a farm called Hughenden. At first Mr Beale paid him four pounds a month, but every year he got a raise of another pound. His wife earned three pounds a month, so they were satisfied and happy on this farm. His children were not forced to work in the fields but could go to school. He was allowed to own goats and cattle, and he had a big wattle and daub house. He was able to buy furniture: a cupboard and a table and a chair for himself and a chair for his wife.

But then the farmer died and his son took over the farm. This son did not like goats and so they had to sell all their goats. He did not like the children to go to school, either; they had to work in the fields. So then they had to leave. They left for Colchester.

In Colchester they lived in a township with coloured people. There was nobody above them, they did not have to please anyone, and so they were happy. They lived there for thirty years. Jamangile found work as a gardener. Life was fairly good. They had enough food to eat and they were friends with their neighbours. When they arrived at Colchester they had six children. By the time they left, they had twelve.

But then everything changed. They were informed by the police and the Baab* that they were going to be moved to a place called Glenmore. They were told that there was work at this place for everyone — there were many industries — and that there were good houses which they could have for free. But they did not know this place, so they did not want to move. They were happy enough where they were, and

---

*Baab: the shortened name for the Bantu Affairs Administration Board.

they did not trust the police. They know that Baab would never give a black man a house for free.

But while they were still discussing these things, suddenly they were given seven days' notice. Suddenly they simply had to leave. It was so quick he still cannot believe it or understand it. Sometimes he wakes up at night, and he thinks about it, but he cannot understand it. He thinks about his life and he cannot understand how it is possible that a man is forced to leave his house and his work and his friends, that he is put on a truck, he and his wife and his children with his furniture and his pigs, and that his pigs die and his furniture gets broken.

He can only understand it if he says to himself that he is not a man. But then, what is he?

That day when they were taken to Glenmore, the trucks came very early, when they were still asleep. They had to collect their pigs. Some people left all their belongings behind. They were so full of grief that they could not pack their belongings properly. The officials were angry men who shouted at them to get out. There were buses for the women and the children. There was so much confusion. The houses were demolished before they could get all their belongings out. The men had to ride on the back of the trucks. Their furniture was broken. They left the place in grief and they came to Glenmore. The houses in Glenmore were bare, with draughty wooden walls they had to fix with mud.

Tsotsobe looks at us and says that now there is no hope. When he was young, he wanted to give his children and his grandchildren a different kind of life. Now he sees that there is no hope for his children. There is no hope for him or for his wife, and he doesn't understand why he had to live at all. He is now over seventy and he cannot say: This is my life. I have given my sons an education and they are now wealthy men, and my daughters are married to good men, and my grandchildren are healthy.

He can say nothing.

CHAPTER TWO

From Kuruman to Kosi Bay: the scope of forced removals

Jamangile Tsotsobe's story is not unique. There are millions of people like him and there are hundreds of places like Glenmore. One in five South Africans has shared or will share Tsotsobe's fate. Off the farms, out of the towns and cities, away from the borders of the country, more than three and a half million black people have been removed already and nearly two million more are threatened with removal. (And even these figures, as explained below, are incomplete.)

In 1969 Cosmas Desmond set out to 'illustrate what apartheid means in practice' in his book *The Discarded People*. Between May and September 1969 he travelled the length and breadth of South Africa in an attempt to document removals. His book, which described the horror of the policy, resulted in an international outcry. This forced the government to improve some of the appalling physical conditions in which relocated people lived and to soften some of the brutality of their methods of removing people.

Fourteen years later, however, the policy has not changed. Forced removals continue; they are basic to the establishment and maintenance of apartheid South Africa.

Equally pertinent in 1983 is a quote from Desmond's opening paragraph:

> I have seen the bewilderment of simple rural people when they are told that they must leave their homes where they have lived for generations and go to a strange place. I have heard their cries of helplessness and resignation and their pleas for help. I have seen the sufferings of whole families living in a tent or a tiny tin hut. Of children sick with typhoid, or their bodies emaciated with malnutrition and even dying of plain starvation.

The enormity of relocation only hits the traveller when driving through bantustans. Relocation sites are designed to be out of sight from all national roads. For example, driving from Bloemfontein to Maseru before reaching Thaba 'Nchu one passes within 10 kilometres of the Qwaqwa relocation settlement of Onverwacht. This has a population the size of the city of Bloemfontein, yet all one sees from the main road is a large signboard and a tarred road (stretching 4 kilometres before the dust begins) that leads apparently nowhere. Beyond the hill is the largest closer settlement in South Africa accommodating an estimated 200 000 people. Most of the people have been evicted from or have left white farms. While many relocation sites are kilometres away from national roads, hidden in desolate rural areas, many are urban, on the edges of cities and towns. People have been moved out of the centres of Johannesburg to Soweto, out of Cape Town to the Cape Flats, and out of Durban to Chatsworth, Phoenix and KwaMashu, etc.

Wherever one travels in the bantustans one comes across relocation settlements and displaced people. In parts of KwaZulu and Gazankulu one passes settlement after settlement, each village within a kilometre or two of the last. But the density of relocated people is nowhere more dramatically demonstrated than in the 'city-state' of Qwaqwa with its capital, Phuthaditjaba (formerly Witzieshoek). In 1980 the local magistrate estimated the 1978 population as 200 000. By 1980 this estimate had leapt to 300 000: a population density of 484 people per square kilometre.

With the 1980s came the phase of 'voluntary' relocation. In April 1981 Dr Koornhof, Minister of Co-operation and Development, said there would be no more forced removals. Forced removals changed from being blatantly forced (police, dogs, guns) to being indirectly forced with 'motivational action' and 'generous compensation' enabling relocated people to 'feel at home' and enjoy 'normal and happy lives' (Circular 2 of 1982 updating Circular 25 of 1967). The emphasis was on improving the image of the relocation policy, not changing it. Although government officials talk of voluntary relocation, the policy of removals itself has not been abandoned despite exposure of the process and conditions over the years.

In South Africa removals are part of the way of life of the black majority. Dispossession and exclusion lie at the heart of apartheid. This chapter looks at the dimensions of removals since 1960 — the numbers, who is moved, where they are moved to and how this process varies across the country.

Number of removals, 1960 to 1983

Precisely how many people have been affected by the relocation policies of the South African government over the past two decades will never be known. The removals that SPP have been able to quantify for the period from 1960 to mid-1983 can be rounded off to a massive 3 500 000. But even this figure, large as it is, is incomplete. Firstly, it does not include the bulk of people affected by influx control in the urban areas. Official figures on influx control are available for metropolitan areas only and it is difficult to estimate how many people are endorsed out of the small towns in terms of the pass laws. The number of arrests in the metropolitan areas increased from 117 518 in 1980 to 160 600 in 1981 (SAIRR, 1982, p278) and to 206 022 in 1982 (*Star*, 23 Feb. 82). This was an increase of 37% from 1980 to 1981, and an increase of 28% from 1981 to 1982. It is estimated conservatively that about two million arrests have been made over the past 20 years in terms of the pass laws. Not all these people were convicted or moved physically to the bantustans, but the numbers give an indication of how extensive this system of population control is. Most of those affected probably remained in urban areas risking re-arrest and deportation.

The second major category of relocation not included in the figure of three and a half million is those people moved within the bantustans for the implementation of betterment planning. Under betterment, tribal areas are divided into residential and agricultural land. Instead of living in scattered homesteads close to fields, people are clustered into villages on poorer soil such as hill tops, while the rest of the land is divided into fields suitable for growing crops, forestry (wood lots) or grazing. The number of rural people affected by this enforced villagisation is not known but it is thought to be massive. It is estimated that more than a million people have been moved as a result of betterment planning in Natal alone since the 1950s.

Detailed figures are set out in the tables below. (Explanation of the categories follows from page 30.) What these figures reveal is that farm evictions account for the single largest category of removals in South Africa. Group area removals have been the second largest category. However, if black spot, consolidation and urban relocation are added together, over 1,3 million removals have been implemented so far in direct enhancement of the bantustan policy. These three categories together thus account for the largest number of removals under apartheid.

The Transvaal, the most populous province, has seen the greatest number of removals. Natal, where very little of the proposed consolidation planning has yet been implemented, is faced with the largest number of threatened removals for those categories where projections of this sort can be made.

REMOVALS — NATIONAL FIGURES

The following tables set out the national figures on removals — past and threatened — compiled from fieldwork and research in the SPP study. Without extensive fieldwork it is impossible to uncover the numerous inconsistencies and inaccuracies that exist in the available literature, including official documents. The figures are estimates only. They indicate the general size and relative scale of removals — precise counts are impossible. Those figures followed by a question mark (e.g. 10 000?) are more speculative than the rest. It should also be noted that the figures listed here report the number of individual removals that have taken place, rather than the number of people who have been moved. In numerous cases an individual has been moved two, three or four times. These have been classified as three or four separate removals, as it is the effects of the policy that need to be shown.

Table I: Estimated Numbers Removed, by Category and Region, 1960-1983

	E CAPE	W CAPE	N CAPE	OFS	NATAL	TVL	TOTAL
Farms	139000		40000	250000	300000	400000	1129000
Black Spots* & Consolidation	10000? 9000		40000	40000 10000	105000	280000 120000	} 614000
Urban	151000?	32000	20000	160000	17000	350000	730000
Informal Settlements	12000	See A	50000	50000?	See B		112000
Group Areas	←—	See C 409000	—→	14000	295000	142400	860400
Infrastructl & Strategic	30000 50000 See E		See D	See F	18500	5000 }	103500
Totals	40100 & G A	32000 & G A	150000 & G A	514000	745500	1297400	3548900

*Black Spots — freehold land owned by Africans or missions in areas declared for white ownership and occupation only.

Note:
A Major category of relocation affecting many thousands but difficult to quantify how many moved
B Some informal relocation included in above categories
C Figures for the Cape to the end of 1982
D Already included under black spot/consolidation
E People from Glen Grey/Herschel to Ciskei
F Movement of Kromdraai people to Onverwacht included in previous figures

Table 2: Estimated Number of People under Threat of Removal, by Category and Region, 1983

	E CAPE	W CAPE	N CAPE	OFS	NATAL	TVL	TOTAL
Farms	150000						150000+
Black Spots & Consolidation					245000 300000	60000 450000	}1093000
Urban	38000						
Urban	84000+	250000	25000		61000	12000	432000+
Informal Settlements	170000+						170000+
Group Areas		23500 See C above		150	13000	17500	54150
Infrastructl & Strategic	33000					2500	35500
Totals	475000 & G A	250000 & G A	25000 & G A	150	619000	542000	1934650

Table 3: Total Numbers Removed and under Threat of Removal, South Africa 1960-1983

	REMOVED	UNDER THREAT
CAPE: E Cape	401 000	475 000
W Cape	32 000	250 000
N Cape	150 000	25 000
Group Areas	409 000	23 500
OFS	514 000	150
NATAL	745 500	619 000
TRANSVAAL	1 297 400	542 000
Totals	3 548 900	1 934 650

Note: This table summarises the information in Tables 1 and 2.

Three and a half million people have been removed. A further minimum of 1 934 650 people are under threat of removal, mainly in terms of the proposals for consolidation of the bantustans. Instead of leaving lots of little pieces of land occupied or owned by blacks, the government proposes to 'consolidate' the land into fewer and larger blocks. The people who are displaced have to be moved elsewhere into the bantustans. Their former land is then available for sale to whites. It is a massive and enormously expensive undertaking. Mr H van der Walt, then chairperson of the Commission for Co-operation and Development investigating consolidation, said in 1982 that R1000 million would be needed simply for the purchase of land and this amount would not pay for the removals or the development of infrastructure (*Star*, 15 Sept. 82).

Sources

To date literature on relocation has drawn mainly on a few limited sources, namely Desmond (*The Discarded People*), Baldwin ('Mass Removals and Separate Development'), Maré (*African Population Relocation in South Africa*) and the Black Sash publication, *South Africa — A Land Divided*. Works on various aspects of relocation such as betterment were published in the 1980s. In turn, most of these authors have drawn on each other, requoting sources to come up with sometimes the same, but sometimes different figures! Until the SPP reports were published in 1983 Cosmas Desmond's book was the only comprehensive first hand coverage.

The figures presented above are derived from a number of sources. They include official sources such as answers to parliamentary questions, unofficial sources such as informants familiar with areas in which they work and fieldwork conducted by members of the SPP. In a country where the government insists that its policy is correct but hides the effects of that policy, it is difficult to find out exactly what is going on. SPP fieldworkers had to travel long distances on poor roads in extremes of heat and cold. They found frightened people unwilling to trust strangers. It was a low-budget project so return visits were often not possible. To top it all, fieldworkers were harassed by security police and unhelpful officials.

Official figures frequently present a distorted picture. Figures may be contradictory, inconsistent or simply inaccurate. For example, in the House of Assembly in 1980 the Minister of Co-operation and Development said that a black spot known as The Swamp, near Himeville (Natal), had been cleared in 1976 and 125 people moved as a result (*Hansard*, Question 537, 22 April 80). In fact, it was not cleared until 1978 and the population was closer to 700.

Even where official information is available it is sometimes contradictory. For example, the number of black spots in Natal has been given as 76 in 1955 (Tomlinson Report), 210 in 1961 (*Bantu*), and 252 in 1962 (Minister of Bantu Affairs and Development, *Hansard*, Question II, 23 March 62) — the figures increase, despite the fact that removals of black spots in Natal were under way during the period. In 1964 the Senate was told by the Minister of Transport, on behalf of the Minister of Bantu Affairs and Development, that there were 199 black spots in Natal. Less than a month later in April 1964, the House of Assembly was told by the Minister of Bantu Affairs and Development himself that there were 218 (Senate Debates, Col. 2267, 17 March 64 and House of Assembly Debates, Col. 4854, 24 April 64).

At other times officials may deliberately overestimate numbers, if it suits them. For instance, at one point in 1979 in the negotiations for a reprieve of the informal settlement of Crossroads outside Cape Town, the Western Cape Administration Board claimed that there were more than 40 000 people living in the settlement. Up until then both sides had been discussing approximately 23 000 to 25 000 people. When challenged to release statistics gathered in their own survey, the Administration Board was silent. The Crossroads Committee hotly denied that thousands of people had poured into Crossroads since the talk of the reprieve.

The extent of population removals is deliberately hidden from the public and suppression of statistical data is one of the means of achieving this. Increasingly the responsible minister tends to avoid direct answers to parliamentary questions concerning relocation:

> The required information is not readily available. No special record in the form of a register is kept in this connection and the information required cannot be ascertained without performing a considerable volume of work. (*Hansard*, Question 231, 24 March 82.)

> Data regarding prosecutions in terms of the Group Areas Act of 1966 (Act 36 of 1966), are not kept. (*Hansard*, Question 566, 28 April 82.)

> Figures not readily available. (*Hansard*, Question 733, 11 June 82.)

Another example of governmental attempts to obscure the extent of relocation was given during a special debate on removals in parliament in February 1983. During his speech Dr Koornhof compared the numbers of blacks and whites moved between 1976 and 1982. He said that 34 000 blacks and 25 000 whites had been moved during that time (*Hansard,* Cols 843 & 845). However, in a press release dated 6 June 1983 he claimed the following numbers of removals:

Table 4: Persons and Families Moved from Black Spots & Consequent Development Costs

YEAR	PERSONS	FAMILIES	COSTS (Rs)
1975	19 603	2 800	1 173 200
1976	30 980	4 425	2 398 350
1977	63 694	9 099	5 959 845
1978	57 656	8 236	6 745 284
1979	61 780	8 825	9 036 800
1980	—	—	700 000
1981	420	60	96 000
1982	506	72	144 000
TOTAL	234 641(sic) 234 639(actual)	33 517	26 253 479

Table 5: Whites Bought out for Consolidation

YEAR	FAMILIES
1975/6	551
1976/7	506
1977/8	735
1978/9	599
1979/80	638
1980/1	786
1981/2	544
1982/25.1.83	662
TOTAL	4 981

In effect, he had compared the number of white *individuals* affected by consolidation with the number of black *families* moved over the same period, and then said that there should not be such a fuss when almost as many whites had been moved as blacks!

In terms of the ominous Laws on Co-operation and Development Act of 1982, more information will be withheld. Clause 1 of the Act provides for 'the preservation of secrecy in connection with matters dealt with by the Commission' of Co-operation and Development. Foremost among those matters, as the parliamentary debate made very clear, is the question of the consolidation of the bantustans. 'An overemphasis on the right to know', as Nationalist MP Val Volker put it, could endanger delicate negotiations between Pretoria and the bantustan governments.

Yet another means of obscuring information on relocation is the redefinition of parts of South Africa. Areas formerly part of South Africa are now defined as 'independent' and therefore different authorities control these areas. They are no longer accountable to the South African parliament, but to bantustan assemblies. In answer to a question in the House of Assembly, the Minister of Co-operation and Development said:

> The required information is not readily available and a census in loco will have to be conducted to ascertain the particulars concerned. Elukhanyweni is situated in the Republic of Ciskei and it is consequently not possible to furnish the information. (*Hansard*, Question 399, 21 April 82.)

Official definitions of land and people are not consistently applied either. 'Black spot' and 'squatter' are two particularly loosely applied and confusing terms. For some officials any area to be removed is labelled as 'black spot' and any person to be removed becomes a 'squatter', regardless of the actual legal standing of either place or person. In 1969 the Minister of Bantu Affairs and Development said that 'by black spots is meant land which is owned by Bantu and does not include small proclaimed Bantu reserves.' (*Hansard*, Vol.25, Col. 326.) However, various state officials, keen to move certain areas, have included in this definition non-freehold land and even state land on which Africans have lived for years. In April 1980 Dr Piet Koornhof included both scheduled reserves and state lands in his list of black spots in reply to a question in parliament.

Sometimes a place may be described as a black spot, at other times it is 'badly situated'. This can lead to double counting, unless one is familiar with the areas being discussed.

A further problem with official statistics is that owing to shifts in policy over the years, the places and people under threat of removal have not remained constant over time. A few of those who have been under threat for years may now find themselves no longer under threat because the consolidation plans for bantustans have changed. Similarly, communities that formerly seemed secure may now find themselves threatened by relocation.

Only when one moves out of the libraries and out of the cities and starts to explore in the countryside is it possible to start to get a full picture of forced removals in South Africa.

A process of exclusion and dispossession

> Pretoria has set in motion the implementation of its ultimate fantasy — a South Africa in which there are no black South African nationals or citizens; a South Africa that cannot be accused of denying civil political rights to its black nationals for the simple reason that there will be no black South Africans, only millions of migrant labourers (or guest workers, as the fantasy sees them) linked by nationality to a collection of unrecognized, economically dependent mini-states on the periphery of South Africa.
> (John Dugard, 'Denationalisation: Apartheid's Ultimate Plan' in *Africa Report*, July/August 1983.)

Almost all of those who are moved in terms of government policy are black, disenfranchised and dispossessed. They are moved because they are black, by a minority government which has made the maintenance of white supremacy the cornerstone of its programme. They are moved from white areas to those proclaimed for blacks.

The bantustan policy of the Nationalist government — basic to the system of apartheid — has developed largely as an attempt to appease militant demands from blacks for some control over their own lives and for a share in the wealth of the country. In place of rights in a common South Africa, it gives them 'homelands' where they are supposed to exercise political rights and build their own economies. Historically, as will be shown, apartheid has been the foundation for economic growth in serving the labour needs of the mining, agricultural and industrial sectors of the white economy.

Over the decades the bantustan policy has evolved into an extremely sophisticated (though increasingly cumbersome) system of control over the African population. It operates simultaneously at a number of levels — political, economic, ideological and demographic. Its basic premise is that South Africa must be divided into a white area consisting of the major urban and industrial cores, and a black area comprising a number of ethnically divided 'homelands' (called bantustans in this book). Whites, coloureds and Asiatics live in 87% of the country (in separate group areas). The African population — 73% of the total — has been divided into separate ethnic groups and confined as far as possible to the other less developed and overcrowded 13% of South Africa.

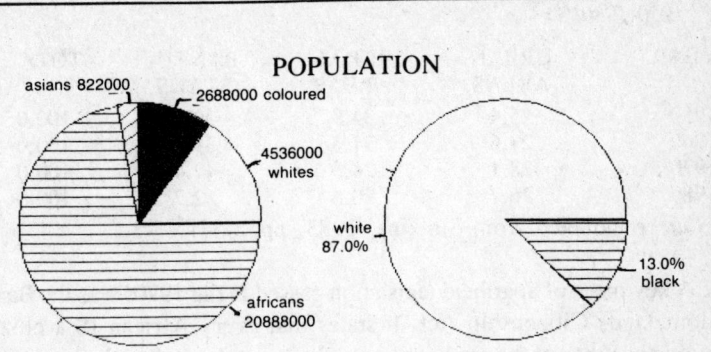

Table 6: Area, Population and Density of South Africa 1980

	LAND (km²)*	POPULA-TION**	POPULATION DENSITY
Gazankulu	7 730	514 280	66,5
Kangwane	3 000	161 160	53,7
KwaNdebele	1 970	156 380	79,4
KwaZulu	32 130	3 400 000	105,8
Lebowa	24 540	1 700 000	69,3
Qwaqwa	620	157 620	254,2
Ciskei	9 000	677 820	75,3
Bophuthatswana	44 109	1 323 315	30,0
Venda	7 410	315 545	42,6
Transkei	43 798	2 323 650	53,1
	174 307	10 729 770	61,6
South Africa (incl. Cis, Bop, Venda, Tkei)	1 221 042	28 783 510	23,6
		30 222 685	24,8***

* SAIRR 1982, p372
** SAIRR 1982, p45 (census figures)
*** Simkins estimates an underenumeration of 5% in the 1980 census bringing the total population of S.A. to 30 222 685 and density to 24,8.

In pursuit of the goal of 'no more black South Africans' (as Connie Mulder, Minister of Bantu Affairs and Development, put it so clearly in 1978) millions of South Africans have been moved. Between 1960 and 1980 the percentage of the total African population living in the bantustans rose from 39% to 53%. Population relocation and an increasingly stringent application of influx control were the two major mechanisms by which this 'reversal of the tide' was achieved during this period.

Table 7: Distribution of African Population in South Africa 1950-1980(%)

YEAR	URBAN AREAS	RURAL AREAS	BANTU-STANS	TOTAL
1950	25,4	34,9	39,7	100,0
1960	29,6	31,3	39,1	100,0
1970	28,1	24,5	47,4	100,0
1980	26,7	20,6	52,7	100,0

(*Source:* adapted from Simkins, 1983, pp53-57)

A key piece of apartheid legislation passed in the 1970s was the Bantu Homelands Citizenship Act. It states that every African IS a citizen of one or other of the ten bantustans. Its passage marked the beginning of a new phase in the bantustan policy. The government hoped that all ten bantustans would opt for 'independence', and by so doing assume responsibility for millions of rightless blacks, who according to this new law 'shall cease to be citizen(s) of South Africa'. The granting of independence and its resulting citizenship regulations ensure that those African people who cannot be removed physically are dispossessed of their claim to South Africa: they have become citizens of a foreign state.

CITIZENSHIP

In 1970 the South African government passed the Bantu Homelands Citizenship Act. The Act said that *every* black (African) South African *is* a citizen of one of the bantustans. This applies to everyone, even to those who have always lived in the white areas and have no knowledge of any 'homeland' or any relatives there.

When Transkei became independent in 1976, Bophuthatswana in 1977, Venda in 1979 and the Ciskei in 1981, the intention of the 1970 Act became clear. The Status Acts conferring independence on the bantustans say that every person who is a citizen of the bantustan in terms of any law 'shall cease to be a citizen of South Africa'. On the day that each of Transkei, Bophuthatswana, Venda and Ciskei took independence, all Xhosa, Tswana and Venda-speaking South Africans became foreigners in South Africa.

CITIZENSHIP

The claim to political participation

While people are citizens of a country, they have the right to demand a vote in the central political institutions of the country. Foreigners have no such right. No country in the world gives the vote to aliens working in the country. Black South Africans are being made alien in their own country and thus lose their claim to the vote in South Africa. They are supposed to vote only for representatives in the parliament of the bantustan they belong to.

The claim to a fair share of the economic wealth

While people are citizens of a country they have the right to demand a fair and just distribution of the land, wealth and resources of that country. Once the bantustans become independent, the people lose this right. They can no longer demand a just distribution of wealth as a right. They become beggars for the charity of the wealthy neighbour.

Rights of residence in urban areas

Those black people who are citizens of independent bantustans but who have Section 10 rights to be in town in white South Africa retain these rights after independence. Those who qualify for Section 10 rights have lived in one town since birth, or have worked for 10 years in registered employment in one town for one employer, or have had a permit to live in one town for 15 years. They and their wives and children have a legal right to remain in that town. They do not lose this right when their bantustan becomes independent, but the children who are born after the date of independence of the parents' bantustan have no such rights. They will only be allowed to remain in the town if they are given a Section 12 permit to be there. This section controls the presence of black persons from foreign countries in towns in South Africa. It allows for a permit and is not a legal right. The permit can be withdrawn at any time without reason being given and the person concerned cannot go to court to fight such a withdrawal because there is no LEGAL RIGHT involved.

CITIZENSHIP

Leasehold title in urban areas

Africans in urban areas can obtain 99-year leases on sites in black townships and may buy or build houses on those sites (except in the Western Cape, where they may only have 30-year leases). They have full ownership, can make wills and leave the houses to anyone they like. But heirs of citizens of independent bantustans born after the date of independence of the bantustan will not be allowed to occupy the house unless they have Section 12 permits to be in the towns where the houses stand, although they will have full rights of ownership.

Survival

1. Pensions

After independence citizens of the independent bantustans who live permanently in South Africa and are lawfully resident on white farms or in the towns will continue to get their pensions as usual from the South African authorities. Those who live inside the bantustans must get their pensions from the bantustan administration, which has full power to change the pension legislation and to increase or decrease the amount payable.

On relocation a pension paid to a person living in South Africa is cancelled and a new application must be made to the bantustan administration after removal. There is no transfer of a pension because different administrations are concerned. Pensions paid by employers and private pension funds will remain payable in the usual way irrespective of where the person is resident on retirement.

2. Unemployment Insurance

Unless the bantustan establishes a fund of its own, people who work within their borders have no protection against unemployment. 'Foreigners' permanently and legally working in that part of South Africa outside the bantustans will continue to be covered by the South African Unemployment Insurance Fund. Citizens of Bophuthatswana, Transkei, Ciskei and Venda who work outside those areas on one year contracts will cease to be contributors to the Fund when the contract on which they are engaged at the

CITIZENSHIP

time of independence expires. They will still be able to claim benefits from the South African Fund if they become unemployed within three years of independence day. After that they will be entitled to no benefits whatsoever, however much money they may have contributed to the Fund before independence.

This also applies to commuters. A commuter is a person who lives in the bantustan but who travels each day to work in white South Africa, e.g. workers who live in Mdantsane and work in East London. Because they are not resident in South Africa they will no longer be eligible to belong to the Unemployment Insurance Fund.

3. Workmen's Compensation
Workers who work outside the bantustan will continue to be entitled to Workmen's Compensation if they are injured at work. Those who work inside the bantustan will not be entitled to compensation unless the bantustan establishes a Workmen's Compensation Fund.

Deportation
All those black South Africans who cease to be South Africans on the day of independence become 'aliens' in South Africa. As such, they have no protection against deportation, even if they have Section 10 rights to be in town. Aliens can be deported from South Africa at any time without trial.

Renunciation of bantustan citizenship
There is a provision in law for citizens of independent bantustans to renounce their citizenship of the bantustan and to apply for South African citizenship. In no known case has the application been granted simply because the person wished to remain South African.

Identity documents
In theory all citizens of independent bantustans are supposed to be in possession of a travel document issued by the bantustan

> **CITIZENSHIP**
>
> administration within two years of independence. In practice this requirement has not been enforced and people who are resident in 'South Africa' continue to use Reference Books. However, children applying for a first identity document at age 16 years are refused a Reference Book and are forced to take a passport or travel document. Once their bantustan is independent black South Africans are refused a South African passport and told they must take a passport from their own country. But the rest of the world does not recognize the independence of the bantustans so it is difficult to travel on a bantustan passport.
>
> The bantustans encourage/insist that those living in the bantustans apply for such travel documents if they wish to go away to work. These travel documents are used in South Africa outside the bantustans in exactly the same way as a Reference Book and must be produced on demand.
>
> Exchanging a 'dompas' (the popular name for a Reference Book) for a passport has effectively lost the holder a claim to wealth and rights in South Africa.
>
> — adapted from Sheena Duncan, 'Citizenship — The Consequence of its Loss' in *Sash*, May 1982.

In this way about eight million South Africans have been stripped of their South African citizenship since Transkei became the first bantustan to take independence on 26 October 1976. Although not yet foreigners, the remaining 12 million African South Africans have been tied to six self-governing bantustans. Pretoria is applying pressure on these bantustans to take the path of independence. One of the pressures is financial: they have received less financial and developmental support from Pretoria than have the more pliable bantustan governments. Gazankulu with double the population of independent Venda claimed it received less than half the 1981/2 budget of its more compromising neighbour. KwaNdebele is scheduled to take independence next, judging from the facilities being provided by Pretoria.

While some bantustans have a policy of non-racialism, they cannot deny their reason for existence. The government established the bantustans as ethnic units. Their population is planned to be ethnically pure.

This is used as a means of dividing and controlling the black population.

Not only are Africans turned into non-South Africans. The bantustan policy is also designed to split them into separate 'nations' and thus divide them against each other. African South Africans are encouraged to think of themselves in separate ethnic terms as Zulus, Tswanas or Xhosas instead of as (black) South Africans. The bantustan policy is based on the manipulation of ethnicity. It thrives on the promotion of ethnic identity and ethnic conflict within the black population of South Africa. Scarce resources such as land, business licences, health and education facilities are granted to those who identify with and promote the ethnically separate states. Thus bantustan officials have a significant vested interest in the growth of ethnic identification amongst their citizens. In many cases this develops into ethnic conflict between people. Those bantustans which have opted for 'independence' are rewarded with an impressive building programme (roads, independence stadium, ministers' housing and offices, hotels and shopping centres); those that have not are not so favoured. Inevitably this leads to tensions and rivalries between the people of the various bantustans. This is the case with KwaNdebele and Lebowa. Prior to the formation of KwaNdebele few can recall tension between Pedi and Ndebele. In many areas there was extensive intermarriage. Tribal affiliations were loose and unclear. Now that KwaNdebele is preparing to take independence and Pedis are threatened with removal, however, people are identifying themselves ethnically — Pedis do not want to move, neither do they want to become part of KwaNdebele.

The last major proposal removing rights of Africans to participate in the economy and government of South Africa is the set of Bills introduced by Dr Piet Koornhof in parliament in 1982. The most contentious, the Orderly Movement and Settlement of Black Persons Bill, was withdrawn for redrafting in the wake of heated protest from communities, concerned organisations and the liberal business world. The Disorderly Bill, as it came to be called, made provision for tighter control in white urban and rural areas. Although the Bill was withdrawn, the Western Cape Administration Board circulated a warning to employers of Africans in the Western Cape. *(See next page).*

Administration Board of the Western Cape
Notice to all Employers of Blacks

The following very important points relating to the employment of blacks in the Western Cape are brought to your notice.

(1) The employment of Blacks without the necessary authority of the Board's Labour Officer is viewed in a very serious light.

(2) The policy in the Western Cape is that this area is a Coloured labour preferential area and as such, Coloureds are to receive preference above Blacks in regard to employment opportunities.

(3) The employment of Blacks illegally in the area causes serious social and economic hardships which affect all in the Western Cape especially the local Black population of about 145 000. Among these are the establishment of illegal squatting areas, housing shortages and the lowering of wage and income levels.

(4) Employers offering employment to Blacks unlawfully in this area encourage the influx of such persons to the Western Cape. This conduct is of such a serious nature that the Government has prepared draft legislation which, inter alia, provides for fines with a maximum penalty of R5 000.

(5) To ensure that you do not employ Blacks illegally you are advised to ascertain that all your Black employees are registered with the Labour Bureau at Langa and that you hold a BA1004 registration certificate in respect of each Black employee. This certificate is an important document and the ENGAGEMENT portion thereof should be completed, signed and returned forthwith upon engagement to the Administration Board.

The DISCHARGE portion of the registration certificate BA1004 must be completed and kept by you as proof of registration of your Black employee. This card must be kept in a safe place and produced for an inspection by an authorised officer.

When your employee leaves your service, the discharge certificate must be returned to this office immediately.

CHIEF DIRECTOR
15 September 1982

The removal of South African citizenship, the physical removal of Africans to bantustans and increased tightening of influx control through the 'Disorderly Bill' along with the new constitutional proposals which exclude Africans from any participation in South African government effectively make up the package which keeps power and resources in white hands.

The Orderly Movement and Settlement of Black Persons Bill
The New Influx Control

Together with the Black Communities Development Bill, this Bill is intended to replace the Urban Areas Act No. 25 of 1945. In terms of the Orderly Movement Bill Africans will be allowed to visit towns during the day. As long as they have their Reference Books (passes) or their bantustan travel documents, they will not be arrested. They are not allowed to work without permission. If found at work without being registered, both they and their employers can be fined or sent to prison.

Between 10p.m. and 5a.m. any African without a permit to be in that town who is found in the streets or in a house in a township or in a white suburb, will be arrested.

Urban Areas

Permanent Urban Residents will be allowed to stay in urban areas provided they have: a) approved accommodation, and b) authority to be in the area. Authority will be granted to those who qualify in terms of Section 10(1)(a) or (b) of the Urban Areas Act when the new Act comes into force, but the children of such people will only qualify if *both* parents were *born* in an urban area (i.e. not if they merely qualify in terms of the 1945 Act).

In terms of Section 6(1) 'a Black person who is a South African citizen' may become a Permanent Urban Resident i.e. it seems that no Ciskeians or Transkeians, Vendas or Tswanas will become Permanent Urban Residents, nor will the children of Permanent Urban Residents born after the date on which their 'state' became 'independent'.

Visitors may only stay in town after 10p.m. and before 5a.m. if they have permits to stay in approved accommodation. No one can have a visitor's permit for more than a total of 14 days in any one year.

Fines for employers illegally employing Africans will be increased to a maximum of R5000 or 12 months in prison or both for a first offence. If an African is found in an urban area after 10 p.m. and before 5.00 a.m. he or she can be fined R500 or 6 months in prison. Householders, black or white, who allow an unauthorised African to stay overnight may be fined R500 or receive a six-month sentence for a first offence, and a fine of R20 per day or 7 day's imprisonment for each day during which the offence continues.

Rural Areas
Africans may only be in white rural areas if authorised, and may only be in that particular place where they are authorised to be. They may have certain dependants living with them and they may receive visitors with the permission of the landowner.

Informal Settlements
Section 31 deals with squatters:

> If any Black persons settle in such numbers on a piece of land to which they have no right and reside on that land in such conditions from which it *appears in the opinion of the Minister that their conduct*
> (a) *is calculated to canvass support for a campaign for the repeal, or amendment, of any law, or for the variation or limitation of the application of the law.*
> (b) is calculated to endanger the maintenance of law and order
> (c) threatens their own health, social welfare, or health of the public in general:
>
> The Minister may by notice in the gazette order that every Black person who on, or after, a date stated in the notice, is unlawfully resident on that land . . . *may be summarily removed with his dependants (if any) to the area from which he comes in the opinion of the director general or to any other place or area indicated by the latter.* (own emphasis).

Thus no law need be invoked, not even the Admission of Persons to the Republic Act. There is no court jurisdiction — no warrant for arrest or removal — no chance of legal defence.

Section 42 states that any inspector or peace officer may *at any time call upon any black person* to produce for examination any authority or certificate granted or issued to such a person

> under this Act.
> For Africans all residence outside the bantustans is now subject to permit, not held by right. A Select Committee of parliament is considering amendments to the Bill in the wake of nationwide protests against tightening influx control.
> — adapted from two Black Sash mimeographs: "The Orderly Movement and Settlement of Black Persons Bill" by R N Robb, Mowbray, 2 July 82 and "The New Influx Control" by Sheena Duncan, Johannesburg, July 1982.

The South African government claims that the only way to secure a peaceful future for all is for the different racial groups to develop in their own areas. This policy of separate development is thus enforced by the white-elected government in every sphere of political, economic and social life. In reality it furthers privilege in each of these spheres for most whites at the expense of most blacks. Whites have been given 87% of the land area, free education and every opportunity, while blacks are permitted to leave their areas only to sell their labour on the white market. It is partly to justify dispossessing the vast majority of South Africans of their land and right to wealth that the bantustans are developed. R659 million was budgeted for assistance to non-independent bantustans while 'independent' bantustans received R302 million in 1982/3. Inclusive of costs such as secondment of officials, expenditure exceeded R1000 million for the 1982/3 financial year. This figure could have been spent providing housing, educational and health facilities for blacks in and around the cities of South Africa, where many of them could earn a living rather than queueing for the few contract jobs that the labour bureaux offer in the bantustans. Instead, they have ceased to be South Africans in the land of their birth. Ethnic conflict and divisions have escalated as groups are set against each other in competition for scarce resources. And finally, the 'Disorderly Bill' attempts to streamline influx control even further.

Who is moved

Broadly, people have been moved from white rural areas, from the urban areas and between and within the bantustans. They have also been moved to make way for dams, game reserves and agricultural developments, and to clear the borders of South Africa. The history and relationships between the various categories of removals are briefly described in Chapter 4.

General Circulars of 1967 and 1982 state clearly the categories of people who are to be relocated in terms of the policy. Extracts are quoted in the box below. It will be seen that all that has changed over fifteen years is the wording — the policy remains unchanged.

GENERAL CIRCULAR NO. 25, 1967
(Head Office File No. V. 164/1)
Settling of Non-productive Bantu Resident in European areas, in the homelands

1 It is accepted Government policy that the Bantu are only temporarily resident in the European areas of the Republic, for as long as they offer their labour there. As soon as they become, for one reason or another, no longer fit for work or superfluous in the labour market, they are expected to return to their country of origin or the territory of the national unit where they fit in ethnically if they were not born and bred in the homeland.

2 The Bantu in the European areas who are normally regarded as non-productive and as such have to be resettled in the homelands, are conveniently classified as follows:-

 (i) the aged, the unfit, widows, women with dependent children, also families who do not qualify under the provisions of Bantu (Urban Areas) Act No. 25 of 1945 for family accommodation in the European urban areas;

 (ii) Bantu on European farms who become superfluous as a result of age, disability or the application of Chapter IV of the Bantu Trust and Land Act, No. 18 of 1936, or Bantu squatters from mission stations and black spots which are being cleared up;

 (iii) Professional Bantu such as doctors, attorneys, agents, traders, industrialists, etc.. Also such persons are not regarded as essential for the European labour market, and as such they must also be settled in the homelands in so far as they are not essential for serving their compatriots in the European areas. Normally they are well to do Bantu and by settling those people with buying power in the homelands, a great contribution can be made to the development of those territories.

> *Circular 2 of 1982, which replaced Circular 25 of 1967, amended the wording to read:*
>
> 1. In pursuance of the Government's policy of developing national states and bringing them to full independence, the policy in practice is that Blacks should be able to live and work in such states to the maximum extent. Alternatively, Black families should as far as possible be resident in the national or independent states, the workers commuting between their homes and places of work in the White area. If owning *[sic]* to distance or other acceptable reasons, this is not feasible, workers' families may live in their own areas while the workers themselves are accommodated at their places of work in the White area on a single basis.
>
> 2. For convenience, the Blacks in the White area who are normally regarded as non-productive in the White area and should as such be given the opportunity of settling in a national state, are classified as follows:
>
>   (i) The aged, the disabled, widows, the women with dependent children, as well as other families who do not qualify in terms of the provisions of the Blacks (Urban Areas) Consolidation Act, No. 25 of 1945, for housing on a family basis in an urban Black residential area: provided that the aged and other disabled persons who qualify in terms of existing legislation to live in an urban Black residential area, may be admitted for care to homes for the aged or such other suitable institutions as may exist in such urban Black residential areas, unless, of their own free will, they prefer to join their relations in a national or independent state.
>
>   (ii) Blacks on White farms who become unfit for work owing to age, disability or the application of Chapter IV of the South African Development Trust and Land Act, No. 18 of 1936, as well as Black squatters originating from mission farms and Black spots that are being cleared.
>
>   (iii) Professional Bantu such as doctors, attorneys, agents, traders, industrialists, etc. *in so far such persons are not needed to serve members of their own national group in*

> *the white areas or to assist in their upliftment.* These people, although not regarded as essential for the White labour market, do fulfil an important function in regard to serving people of their own national groups and should be encouraged to settle, whether full-time or by extension, in the national and independent states so that in this way they will be able to make their expertise and capital available to their fellow nationals and for the development of the economies of the states concerned, respectively.

A. White rural areas

Over 1,1 million removals have taken place from white farms over the past two decades — about one third of all relocation during this period. This is the largest single category of removals. The process is by no means complete. Depending on the passage of the proposed Orderly Movement and Settlement of Black Persons Bill, many more thousands could be moved. No estimate of the numbers can be made until the final terms of the legislation are clear. Those affected constitute the most oppressed group of people in the country. They live in small isolated groups, often under appalling conditions and at the whim of the white farmer.

Individual evictions of unwanted farm workers are an ongoing feature of life in the rural areas. This has been exacerbated by the present serious drought. In the OFS, for example, farmers have sent their farm workers to a closer settlement at Brandfort. Here they will stay, rather than being sent to Onverwacht. When the drought is broken the farmers will be able to reclaim their workers easily, without searching among 200 000 residents of Onverwacht.

The people moved off white-owned farms may be divided into three main categories — tenants, full-time workers and those living without permission of the owner on the farms (generally called 'squatters').

There were two types of tenants — labour tenants and cash tenants. Labour tenants were people who supplied their labour to the land owner for part of the year (three to nine months) as a form of rent, in return for the use of some of the land for themselves. Historically this form of labour was most widespread in the northern parts of the country. In 1964 the 1936 Land Act was amended to abolish the system. The districts of Delmas, Groblersdal and Warmbaths in the Transvaal were the first to be declared non-labour tenant areas in June 1966.

The abolition was not uniformly accepted by farmers and tenants. Particularly in Natal the system suited both parties and it was only finally abolished in August 1980. Many informal, illegal operations still carried on after 1980 but the conversion from part-time to full-time labour on white-owned farms is nearing completion.

By 1979 Natal farmers, the last to comply, supported the government move to abolish all but full-time labour:

> Generally speaking the people kicked off are surplus to the needs of the farmer. I feel it is up to the Bantu Administration Board to ascertain where labour shortages exist and supply those areas from areas like the Weenen district where there are labour surpluses. (Donald Sinclair, Natal Agricultural Union, *Natal Mercury*, 12 Sept. 79.)

Throughout the country thousands of blacks paid rent on white farms. They rented land, mainly from big companies.

Increased mechanisation, use of pesticides and fertiliser, and advances in processing and distribution of produce all favoured the concentration of farms into fewer hands (from 106 000 farming units in 1960 to 78 000 in 1975 — SPP Vol.2, Table 2, p.21). That and real increases in farm wages over the past two decades resulted in fewer farm workers being employed, as farmers did not want to spend more on wages. Details of mechanisation are mapped out in Chapter 4. Farm evictions as a result of mechanisation are the most common form of removals in rural areas.

Local political and ideological tensions, and the growing security fears of white farmers over the *verswarting* (blackening) of the white countryside, particularly after the rural riots of the 1950s, increased the government's determination to limit and control blacks in non-prescribed white rural areas.

While the number of Africans in white rural areas has increased over the last three decades from 3 596 900 in 1960 to 4 310 000 in 1980, the proportion resident has dropped from 34,9% in 1950 to 20,6% in 1980 (Simkins 1983, p.58). The proportion resident in the bantustans for the same period grew from 39,7% in 1950 to 52,7% in 1980 (Simkins 1983, p.58).

Farm evictions normally take place on an individual basis. Farm workers and ex-tenants have least protection from the law, making any response let alone resistance to this massive programme of relocation almost impossible.

Yet others left the white-owned farms 'of their own free will' as SPP surveys show. But those interviewed added that poor conditions on the farms such as wages of R1,00 per day, half a bag of mealies per month and derelict housing, not to mention harsh farmers, forced them to leave.

> Is it not better to sit all day [in a relocation area] even if you are unemployed, rather than work every day from sunrise to sunset for a rude farmer and earn R1,00 a day?
> (Former farm worker, Pampierstad, 1981.)

In moving to the bantustans many ex-farm workers found their only way into the labour market — through migrant labour. However, many found themselves with passes stamped 'farm work only'. This excluded any possibility of urban industrial or mining recruitment. All they could expect was the odd poorly-paid migrant job in agriculture, probably on a seasonal basis only, according to people interviewed by SPP and reports from Black Sash Advice Offices.

'Black spot' removals are another form of relocation from white rural areas. Black spots are areas occupied and often owned by blacks in rural areas that have been declared for whites only. They will be examined later.

B. Urban areas

Influx Control

An increasingly tight network of laws operates to keep Africans out of urban areas. Officials can pressurise even those with rights to be in urban areas into leaving for the bantustans. As argued in Chapter 4, influx control is central to the establishment and maintenance of the apartheid system in South Africa.

Influx control, systematised through the 1952 amendment to the 1945 Urban Areas Act, was implemented in ways which will be discussed in the next chapter.

The notorious pass laws were the subject of widespread militant protest in the 1950s and early 1960s. Twenty thousand women marched to Pretoria in 1956 to tell the government they would not carry passes. But all non-parliamentary opposition was smashed by government repression and the pass laws were implemented. Since the early 1960s at least 100 000 arrests have been reported each year. In 1982 alone

206 022 Africans — one every two and a half minutes of the day — were arrested for pass law offences (*City Press*, 27 March 83). The cases are heard, often one a minute, in the commissioners' courts around the country. The convicted pay fines or spend time in jail, but most avoid the bantustans if they can. They know that little chance of a livelihood awaits them there.

In some cases people were physically removed in terms of influx control. The women of Crossroads report being put on trains out of Cape Town to the Transkei. Many, desperate to remain in Cape Town, jumped off the trains at Bellville and walked back to informal settlements to continue their furtive existence in constant fear of arrest. Others tired of the insecurity. They settled in closer settlements and rural townships like Sada and Ilinge, from where members of the household tried to obtain migrant labour.

Through relocation to bantustans thousands of people have been locked into farm labour or contract work. Only the lucky few who qualified remained to work in the cities and towns.

Deproclamation of Townships

In the 1960s there was massive relocation particularly in the Transvaal and OFS as a result of deproclamation of townships. Where a town was within commuting distance (up to 75 kilometres) of a bantustan, the African township was deproclaimed and the residents moved to a new rural township built in the bantustan. In some cases, such as Nelspruit and Lichtenburg, the whole African population was moved. The townships were demolished and the people moved to Kanyamazane in Kangwane and Itsoseng in Bophuthatswana respectively. In other cases only the unemployed, the women and children, the elderly and the disabled, were moved, leaving the workers to live in single-sex hostels and visit their families on a weekly or monthly basis. This was the fate of the Africans of Naboomspruit and Potgietersrus, for example.

The workers have been turned into commuters, if they live close enough to the city, or migrants if the distance is too far. The government has used the deproclamation of townships to sort the people into those useful in the white urban areas and those to be dumped in the bantustan. The costs of education, housing, job creation and health are paid by the bantustan, which is encouraged to take independence. Although indirectly Pretoria provides social services for the bantustans, in future it need not be obliged to pay for the social security of foreigners (or give them the vote).

Other townships have been incorporated into the nearest bantustan, e.g. KwaMashu outside Durban which is now part of KwaZulu. The boundaries of bantustans were drawn to include existing townships where possible. Others were planned as part of the bantustan to accommodate thousands of commuters, e.g. Ezakheni outside Ladysmith which has been included in KwaZulu.

In the 1960s and 1970s people were moved into the bantustans and forced into migrant labour. The South African economy needed a large number of unskilled and semi-skilled workers. Now in the 1980s there is a new strategy, that of limiting migrant labour (the number of migrant workers from the bantustans increased by 11,7% from 1979 to 1980, and by 9,2% between 1980 and 1981 — SAIRR 1982, p.86). The pattern is changing from migrant to permanent and commuter labour. As more townships were moved into bantustans, or the borders were redefined to include townships, people lost their rights to live and work in the urban areas. Now they commute as foreigners. The central economy needs fewer unskilled but more skilled workers. Those who live in the more remote rural areas have little chance of employment as recruitment has been stopped. The more skilled workers who are recruited and trained come from black townships in white areas, or those living close enough to commute to white areas.

Between 1976 and 1981 the number of commuters increased 6,7% per year (from 536 100 in 1976 to 739 700 in 1981 — *Cape Times,* 9 Nov. 82). This trend ties in with government decentralisation proposals which will be discussed later. The need to secure a stable middle and working class in urban areas has been recognised. The less-skilled surplus workers are moved to the bantustans. Qualified people will be able to live and work in the urban areas by permit, not right.

Informal Settlements
Over the past ten years informal settlements have mushroomed close to the urban areas of white South Africa. Only where they exist on bantustan territory have they been allowed to remain. The harsh squatter removals of the Western Cape are attempts to move people to faraway Ciskei and Transkei. Elsewhere, however, the borders of the bantustans come close to white urban areas, for example, near Durban and Pretoria. Being able to live close to work or potential employment is a high priority for low income people. Living there legally, even in overcrowded,

unserviced shanty towns, is equally important. So thousands of people — either forced out of white urban areas through influx control, or escaping from bantustan hinterlands — flock to places like Winterveld (outside Pretoria) and Inanda (outside Durban). There they build shacks on land, usually rented at high prices from 'squatter farmers' whose returns depend far more on rent than agriculture. They work in industrial areas within commuting distance. South Africa does not have to provide them with housing or social services, and the employers have all the labourers they could want.

Doubts and insecurity are emerging in the white community as tightened influx control and relocation into bantustans increase the pressure on the land. Unemployment, during a recession exacerbated by drought, has pushed a large mass of people into informal settlements in the bantustans on the edge of South African cities. In an attempt to control this movement various means such as removals, slum clearance and ethnic sorting are used. The non-Tswanas of Winterveld are sent to KwaNdebele, 75 kilometres east of Pretoria. In consultation with the Department of Co-operation and Development, the Urban Foundation is planning and laying out Inanda Newtown in an attempt to control urbanisation and channel development in a way acceptable both to liberal business interests and Durban's whites.

Even outside rural townships in bantustans, large informal settlements are appearing. Forced off farms and/or unable to pay rents in bantustan townships, many people with no access to land or even plots in tribal villages are forced to build shacks on the edges of townships. They may then have access to schools and shops in the townships while seeking work through the labour bureaux. These people face future relocation, this time by bantustan authorities wanting to expand the township, or clear unsightly shacks whose inhabitants are difficult to control.

Group Areas

Group areas removals are the single largest category of relocation within urban areas. 860 400 people, mostly coloured and Indian, may have been moved over the past 20 years in terms of the Group Areas Act.

Although the Act was passed in 1950, mass removals of coloureds and Indians only began in earnest during the 1960s, following the suppression of popular black organisation and resistance through widespread bannings and trials. Extensive urban removal was undertaken in terms of both the Group Areas and the Urban Areas Acts —

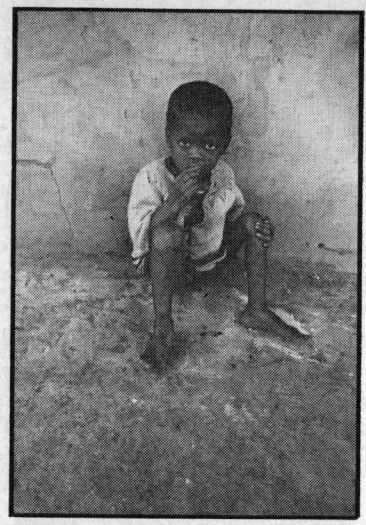

1 *Boy in Oxton, a Ciskei transit camp near Queenstown, 1981. (See pages 57 and 301.)*

2 *Woman in Emadakeni, an informal relocation area next to Sada in the Ciskei. Houses were built there by people evicted from white-owned farms. (See also photograph 36, between pages 325 and 326.)*

3 *Family from Riemvasmaak (North Western Cape reserve near Upington, cleared in 1973) in Welcomewood (closer settlement near King William's Town), 1982. (See pages 280 and 288.)*

4 *Elderly widow evicted from farm, with daughter's child. Tent provided by farmer. Zweledinga, near Balfour, winter 1979. (See pages xxxi, 57.)*

5 *Children in Bendall, a Bophuthatswana closer settlement near Kuruman in the Northern Cape. (See pages 55, 285, and 349-350.)*

6 *The road to Deerward, a closer settlement a few kilometres from Bendall (above). People were moved here from Di Takwanen, a well-watered, fertile scheduled area near Vryburg, settled in 1889. (See pages 55 and 285.)*

7 *Tseki, Qwaqwa, in 1980: a typical new settlement (post 1974). Most of the houses are occupied by former farm workers and their families.*

8 *Single sex hostels for migrant workers in Durban.*

9 *Phoenix, outside Durban, built to hold people uprooted by group area removals. (See pages 102, 339, 352, 355, 359, 373.)*

10-13 *Crossroads, 1983:*

'We demand passes and places to stay'.

the latter affecting Africans.

Removals continue. According to the Minister of Community Development, another 100 white families and 8 976 coloured and Indian families are destined to be moved (*Hansard,* Question 38, 21 Feb. 83). Most future relocation is scheduled for the Cape. The OFS has only 31 (white) families still to be moved. The remaining 32 families were moved from District Six in Cape Town in 1982. Nearly 11 000 families have been relocated to the distant townships of the Cape Flats.

> The Welgemoed Commission of Inquiry into public transport admitted that in terms of the Group Areas Act
>
> > 'large numbers of people were resettled, mainly from slums and as a result of slum clearance, in new areas, and in many cases this resulted in employees now living further from their jobs than had been the case before.
> > 'In such cases, it is obviously necessary to consider the subsidisation of bus transport.
> > 'To give these people the opportunity to work, transport services were instituted to increase their mobility.
> > 'However, owing to the long distances and transportation costs which may be high in relation to their earnings, the Government began to pay subsidies to these workers so as to enable them to be economically active while at the same time retaining their family ties, and so as to make sources available to the employers of the Republic of South Africa.'
> >   — quoted in the *Sunday Tribune,* 27 March 83.

C. Creation of the bantustans

Essential to apartheid is the creation of bantustans. Chapter 5 details the development of policy from reserves to bantustans to homelands and finally to 'independent' and 'national' states. This section deals with the process of creating bantustans, in which relocation plays a vital part. People are moved from areas declared for white use and occupation, to their relevant 'homeland' according to the language they speak, i.e. to which ethnic group they apparently belong.

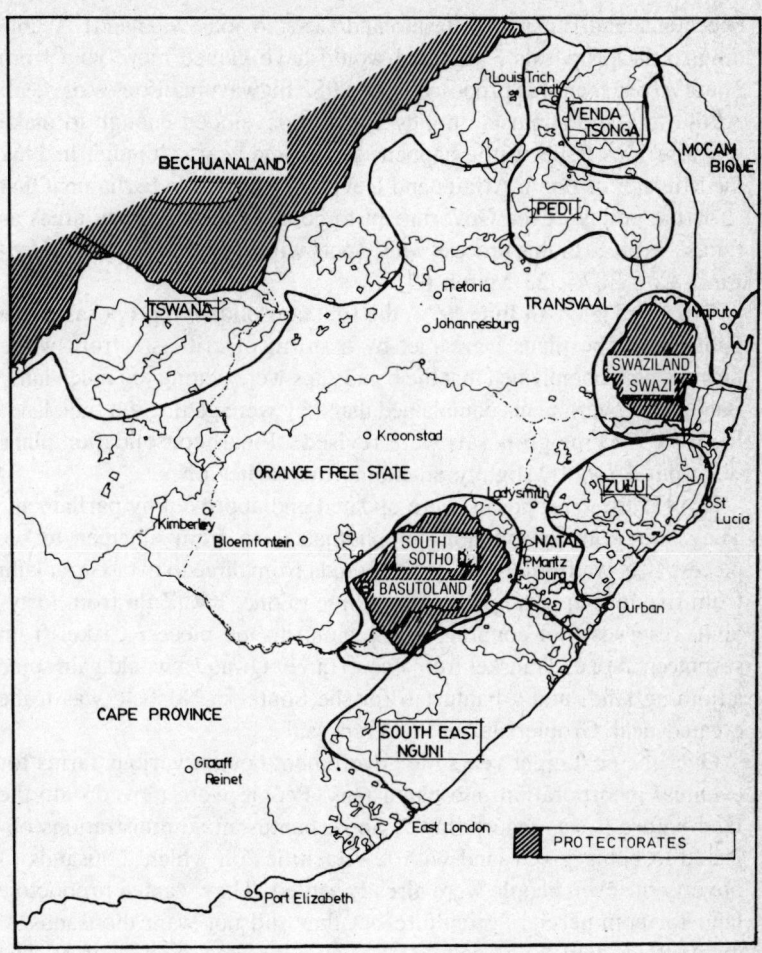

Map 1: Tomlinson Commission Consolidation Proposals, 1955

Consolidation
The creation of bantustans as ethnic units to accommodate blacks in a divided South Africa began with the report of the Tomlinson Commission in 1955 when it was proposed that seven blocks be established as 'heartlands' for black development: Tswana, Venda-Tsonga, Pedi, Swazi, Zulu, South-East Nguni, and South Sotho. Three would one day be incorporated into the neighbouring British Protectorates

(Bechuanaland/Botswana, Basutoland/Lesotho and Swaziland). According to the proposals Swaziland would have gained more land from South Africa than was proposed in the 1982 Ingwavuma/Kangwane deal. At the time the bantustan policy was not developed enough to make this a serious issue. Little happened for some years although in 1962 the Minister of Bantu Affairs and Development said in parliament that 'It is the policy of the Government to consolidate the Bantu areas as far as possible. In this process white spots will also be eliminated' (*Hansard*, Col. 3076, 23 March 62).

Ten years later, in June 1972, the first consolidation proposals were published. The plans were met by a storm of criticism from white farmers who complained that the bantustans were getting too much land. Bantustan governments complained that they were getting too little land. In April 1973 the proposals were revised. 'Final' consolidation plans were put forward, slightly amending the earlier ones.

In 1975 these proposals were updated and approved by parliament. They aimed at consolidating Bophuthatswana from nineteen to six pieces, Lebowa from twelve to six, Venda from three to two, Gazankulu from five to four, Kangwane from three to one, KwaZulu from forty-eight reserves (not counting black spots) to ten pieces, Ciskei from seventeen to one, Transkei from two to three. Qwaqwa would gain some adjoining land, and a bantustan for the Southern Ndebele was to be created near Groblersdal in the Transvaal.

Over the next eight years the government bought various farms for eventual incorporation into bantustans. People were moved onto the land before it was incorporated. Some bantustan administrations objected to being given land with few facilities on which thousands of poverty-stricken people were already settled. They wanted productive land for commercial agriculture but they did not want thousands of dissatisfied, demanding people who could threaten their security. The Transkei refused land unless it was fertile, well maintained and empty of people. Ciskei, on the other hand, has accepted, if not welcomed thousands of extra people. In 1976 Ciskei ceded 45% of its land area (Herschel and Glen Grey districts), containing a third of its people, to Transkei in return for less but better land in the Hewu and Stockenstrom districts. Showing them this fertile land, Sebe lured 50 000 political refugees back to Ciskei. Their three chiefs supported him in the last election before Ciskei became a one-party state under the CNIP. Ciskei also pays its chiefs according to the number of subjects in their districts.

The Scope of Forced Removals

The consolidation programme has faced strong opposition from various interest groups. Those under threat of removal to bantustans for the consolidation of their area have most to lose, and therefore try to resist removal. Dr Koornhof recognised this problem when he described 'the unwillingness of Zulu people to be moved' (*Natal Witness*, 14 May 81).

White farmers whose land was to be incorporated also opposed consolidation. Interest groups such as the sugar industry, wanting to maintain as much productive land in white hands as possible, joined the protests. Organised agriculture complained that too much land would be given to blacks, and was also dissatisfied with the amount and form of compensation offered. Farmers bought out between 1972 and 1977 had to take 60% of the amount in RSA registered stocks, redeemable 22 years after the date of issue, and only 40% in cash (*NAUNLU*, April 1982). There was talk of paying the full amount in cash, enabling farmers to buy other land immediately; but this will not be implemented, according to the Minister of Finance. Farmers bought out prior to 1972 or after 1977 were paid the full amount in cash.

Budgets for actual relocation dropped between 1981/2 and 1982/3/4 while the amount to be spent on purchase of land more than doubled in the last year:

Table 8: National Budget for Relocation (Million Rands)

	1981/2	1982/3	1983/4 ‡
Grant-in-aid to SADT Fund for purchase of land	67,0	64,0	141,84
Settlement (for consolidation)	14,0	12,7	13,0 (acquisition of township properties in 'independent' states)
Settlement of population (towards 'self-determination')	73,68	68,22	20,0
Totals	154,68	144,92	174,84

(*Hansard*, Question 995, 30 June 83)

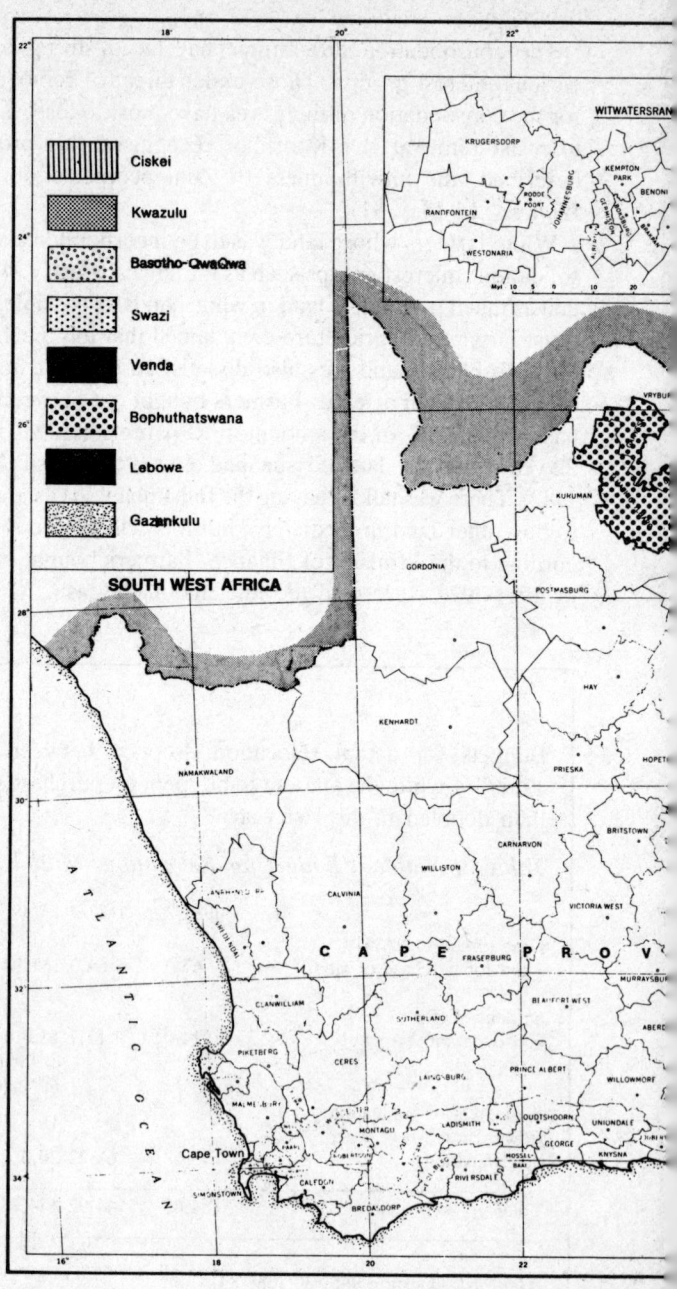

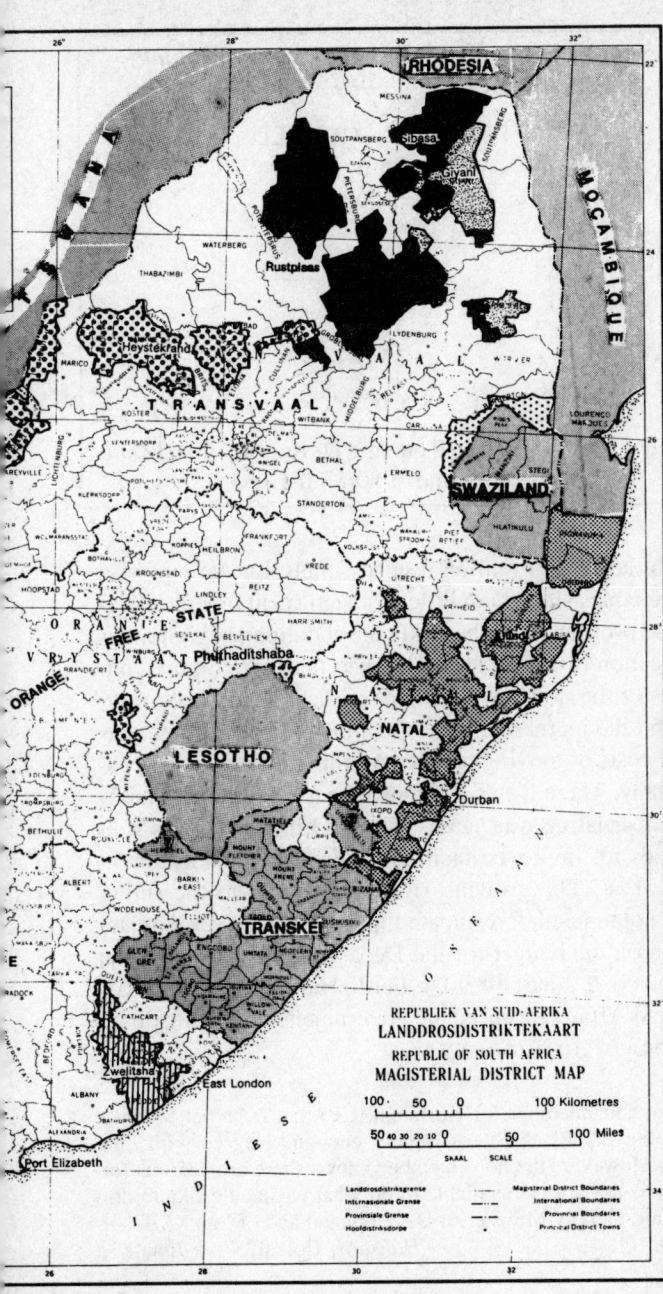

Consolidation Proposals.

Table 9: Allocation of Funds for Purchase of Land for Consolidation Purposes, South Africa 1974/5 — 1980/81 (Million Rands)

YEAR	FUNDS ALLOCATED
1974/5	25,6
1975/6	59,0
1976/7	53,6
1977/8	47,3
1978/9	40,4
1979/80	47,4
1980/81	57,0
	330,3

Sources: *Financial Mail*, 20 April 79 quoting Dr Koornhof, and *Daily News*, 18 May 80 (for 1979/80 and 1980/81 figures).

Compared with the R1 000 million needed simply for the purchase of land, the above tables show how little has been spent on consolidation relative to the programme. The land consolidation programme is a major reconstruction of land distribution and therefore highly contentious. Reasons for the slowdown include resistance from the various interest groups and the increasing cost of compensation to farmers as well as the actual costs of moving people. All this has slowed the programme considerably. There is fierce competition for government funds in the face of the escalating war against SWAPO in Namibia as well as internal demands for improved facilities, housing and education at home in South Africa. The growing right-wing threat to the ruling National Party is not to be underestimated, particularly in rural areas. During the debate on the budget for the Department of Co-operation and Development on 6 June 1983 Dr Ferdi Hartzenberg MP, CP spokesman on Land Affairs, accused the government of slowing down consolidation. The government reply was:

> I want to tell the hon. member for Kuruman (CP) that if he believes we are not developing the Black States rapidly enough, I agree with him wholeheartedly. However, the hon. member knows there are reasons for this. The money is not always available to do what we should like to do.
> — H van der Walt, Deputy Minister of Development and of Land Affairs,
> *Hansard*, Col. 8737, 6 June 83.

In 1979 the Van der Walt Commission (chaired by Hennie van der

Walt, Deputy Minister of Development and of Land Affairs) was requested to determine how consolidation could be speeded up. It was further required to reconsider whether the existing proposals could achieve the desired 'freedom' of all the peoples of South Africa. In making the announcement PW Botha said that consolidation would be considered not only from the 'geographical' point of view but also from the point of view of 'the consolidation of nations' and the 'economic consolidation of states'. (*NAUNLU*, May 1981). He also said that more land would be added to the bantustans if necessary.

Because consolidation has become an increasingly contentious issue, the report of the Van der Walt Commission has been withheld from the public by a process of delayed deadlines. It is understood to have been changed over the years as some proposals were too radical or would cause too much division within the National Party.

At various stages, Van der Walt consolidation proposals have been released. In July 1982 the plans for Venda (with some communities being reprieved) caused concern for Conservative Party members in and around Louis Trichardt as well as for Venda leaders who had claimed more land than was being offered. This is a clear example of the National Party dilemma. Loss of white voter support must be weighed against the credibility of an 'independent' bantustan. The government is also trying to keep the local black people who live close to border areas loyal - a buffer against insurgency. These people living on the borders of South Africa are moved inland so that the area may be more easily controlled.

Another of the Van der Walt proposals triggered the Kangwane/Ingwavuma fiasco in 1982. Pretoria tried to persuade Kangwane and KwaZulu that they should cede part of their bantustans to Swaziland. The Swaziland hierarchy seemed keen, but Kangwane and KwaZulu were adamant that their people would not voluntarily give up South African citizenship to join a poverty-stricken country almost entirely dependent on South Africa. They challenged South Africa in the Supreme Court. The crisis was averted by setting up the Rumpff Commission of Inquiry after successful court action and international outcry.

In June 1983 part of the Bophuthatswana consolidation plan was released. This time Conservative Party supporters clearly indicated their opposition. They held a protest meeting in Zeerust. The agriculture co-operatives in Zeerust and Swartruggens mobilised opposition. Conservative Party supporters accused the government of trying to obliterate the constituency of one of their MPs — Dr Ferdi Hartzenberg, MP for Lichtenburg, who had previously been Deputy Minister of Bantu Affairs and Development and who had played a central part in consolidation planning. The government had the option of incorporating either the Brits or the Zeerust corridor into Bophuthatswana. As the National Party is strong amongst Brits farmers, the government decided to incoporate the farms of the already alienated Conservative Party supporters around Zeerust.

While Conservative Party supporters are vociferous opponents if *their* farms are faced with expropriation and consolidation, they accuse the government of not implementing 'homeland policy' speedily enough. 'They are in the process of giving up', said Dr Ferdi Hartzenberg in the House of Assembly on 6 June 1983. Dr Koornhof said that he felt 'guilty' about the delay in the consolidation of Kwazulu. 'I would like to remove that sword hanging over them as soon as possible', he said in reply to probing. (*Cape Times*, 9 June 83).

Many people living in the bantustans of the Transvaal have little idea which bantustan they live in or will live in in a few years' time. Ethnic divisions are thus emphasised. Families may be split and communities divided as ethnic conflict grows. The story of the creation of Gazankulu, which is outlined later, is a typical example.

Mr Rex le Roux, MP, took over the chair of the commission on consolidation from Van der Walt, who resigned as Deputy Minister in August 1983. The commission is scheduled to release its report in 1984. Meanwhile 1 093 000 Africans live in dread of relocation as a result of consolidation proposals announced so far. Land deteriorates while farmers, both black and white, await their fates.

Black Spots
Since the 1950s the removal of black spots, in pursuit of the government policy that Africans should live in bantustans, has been a sensitive and stormy issue.

Here 'black spot' is used to describe African freehold land and land owned by church or mission stations leased to individual Africans; in both cases land falling within what the government has defined as the white area. In terms of this definition SPP estimated 363 black spots in Natal alone, 189 of which are still under threat of removal.

The removal of black spots is closely linked to consolidation; the elimination of all African-owned areas that fall outside the bantustan boundaries.

Completed black spot removals number some 614 000 people, while over 400 000 people are estimated to be under threat of relocation. The National Party claimed proudly that 231 641 people had been moved off black spots between 1975 and 1982 at a cost of over R26 million, and that more removals would follow — the black spot of Zwartrand/Mogopa near Ventersdorp in the Western Transvaal would be moved on 21 June 1983. This category of removals has attracted the most publicity in recent times, partly because the communities affected have frequently attempted to resist, and partly because of the freehold nature of the land. This carries a stronger emotive appeal in the press and tends to legitimise such opposition in the white public's mind more readily than in the case of removals off non-freehold land (evictions from white-owned farms, in particular).

Betterment
Integral to the creation and establishment of the bantustans as proposed by Tomlinson in 1955 was the idea of planning them to maximise agricultural development. Betterment planning schemes had been introduced into the African reserves in the 1930s and 1940s in an attempt to control land usage.

Over the last three decades there has been strong resistance to betterment planning in many parts of the country. In the 1950s and early 1960s there were rural riots in parts of Pondoland and Sekhukuniland. While betterment was forced upon people in some areas, other groups resisted successfully and continue to live in the traditional way. Grievances included having to walk long distances to tend fields. In the case of families of migrant workers, this often meant that women had to abandon agriculture. They were unable to leave household duties and children long enough to walk to distant fields. While people were not moved long distances, their lives were disrupted as they had to rebuild their homesteads and restructure previous land tenure agreements.

Despite planning and allocation of land for different functions, it is clear from trips through bantustans in the 1980s that more and more land is being used for residential purposes. Tomlinson had proposed that 50% of those living in the reserves in the early 1950s be moved off the land to allow the other half to develop into a class of small-scale subsistence farmers. (The commission in fact noted that to make a viable living from the land, 80% should be removed, but rejected this as involving the relocation of too many people.) The 50% were to be moved into rural villages, the forerunner of closer settlements, from where they would have to send breadwinners to town as migrant workers.

In many parts of bantustans such as Gazankulu and Lebowa one may drive only a kilometre or so between betterment areas and rural villages which have had to absorb thousands of landless people evicted from white-owned farms or former tenants of black spots. These people have no option but to seek a residential plot in a bantustan. Chiefs or headmen often have no option but to accept them, giving them plots on land planned for agricultural purposes. In other areas betterment schemes are strictly controlled and entry is restricted.

Although the percentage of bantustan land 'bettered' is no longer reported in official documents, in 1967 it was reported that 60% of Natal was planned while 77% of the plan for the Ciskei had been implemented, 76% for the Northern Territories and 80% for the Western Territories.

In more recent years betterment has been undertaken by bantustan authorities rather than Pretoria officials. Bantustan officials realise this is a sensitive issue. KwaZulu, finding betterment difficult to implement, has issued instructions against forcing people to move. Elsewhere, in Ciskei and Bophuthatswana, the authorities have chosen to ignore popular response. They bulldoze their plans for agricultural progress whatever the consequences.

Relocation for infrastructural and strategic reasons

Throughout the world people are moved to make way for infrastructural development such as the building of dams, highways or conservation areas, and for strategic purposes such as the clearing of border areas. South Africa is, however, exceptional in two respects. Firstly, the vast majority of people affected by these developments have no say in government — no vote and therefore no effective means of expressing their opinions in the matter. Secondly, because they are voteless they are not part of the interest group to benefit from developments such as improved water supply, transportation or national security. The removals are therefore forced and resented by the people.

Both infrastructural and strategic relocation occur throughout the three areas mentioned above — rural, urban and bantustans. They affect black and white South Africa, but more notice is taken when whites are to be moved. The establishment of two missile ranges illustrates this very clearly. At Lake St Lucia, north of Richards Bay in Natal, more than 3 400 Africans were moved off reserve land occupied by them for hundreds of years, as well as off state land, from 1974 to 1979. This removal went barely recorded in the press. By contrast, the proposal to establish a second missile range at the De Hoop nature reserve near Agulhas in the Cape, first published in 1983, has received wide publicity. The white farmers and fishermen objected to their removal and have received extensive press coverage.

> My great-grandfather and the rest of my family were all buried in the graveyard here. What will they do with the graveyard and the church once we have gone? We have no choice about the price they offer for our land. We will have to accept whatever they offer and then we will have to go. I have a farm called Hardevlakte in Moerasfontein where I could go, but I believe that land could also be appropriated. If that happens I don't know where I'll go. (Mr Hennie Groenewald, who owns the only shop in Spitskop, quoted in *The Argus*, 29 March 83.)

The people of Spitskop are more fortunate than the people of St Lucia who have been moved three times. But their worries and demands are similar. They too want to stay where their forefathers grew up. Most are direct descendants of shipwrecked settlers from 1860. They want to stay where they are. They are only interested in catching fish, not working for Armscor, according to Mr Groenewald quoted above.

Most strategic removals have taken place on the borders of South Africa. In 1977, 20 000 square kilometres were cleared north of Venda along the Limpopo River on the Zimbabwe border. The people were moved south into Venda. Similarly, along the Mozambique border from Kosi Bay to the Swazi border a strip of KwaZulu and state land was cleared of people.

In the Northern Cape many of the scheduled reserves and released areas excised were converted into military bases. An example is the Gatlhose-Maremane reserve from where 20 000 people were moved in 1977 to a collection of Trust farms north of Kuruman. The reserve is now the Lohatla military base.

Infrastructural removals have occurred both in white South Africa and in the bantustans. In some cases people moved into the bantustans by 'GG' truck have to move again as bantustan officials plan other uses for the land. This is the case at Glenmore, the home of Jamangile Tsotsobe. Four years after this camp was first set up the Ciskei government intends moving the people of Glenmore again, to make way for

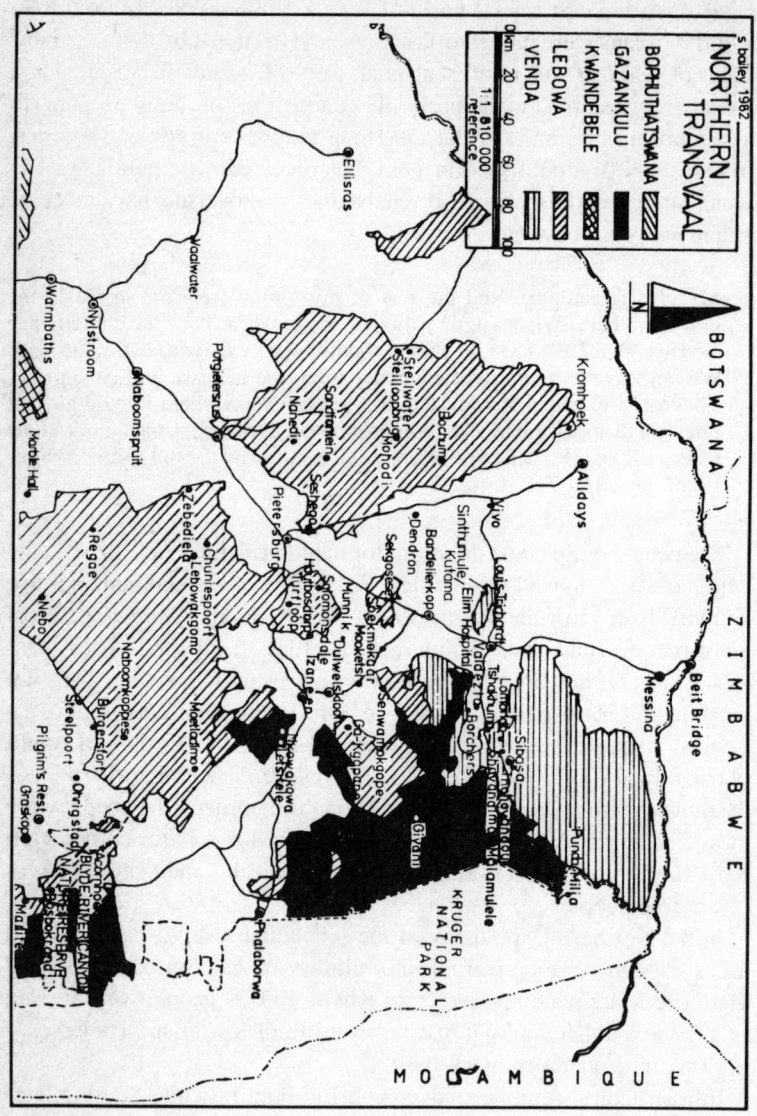

Map 3: Northern Transvaal

The Scope of Forced Removals

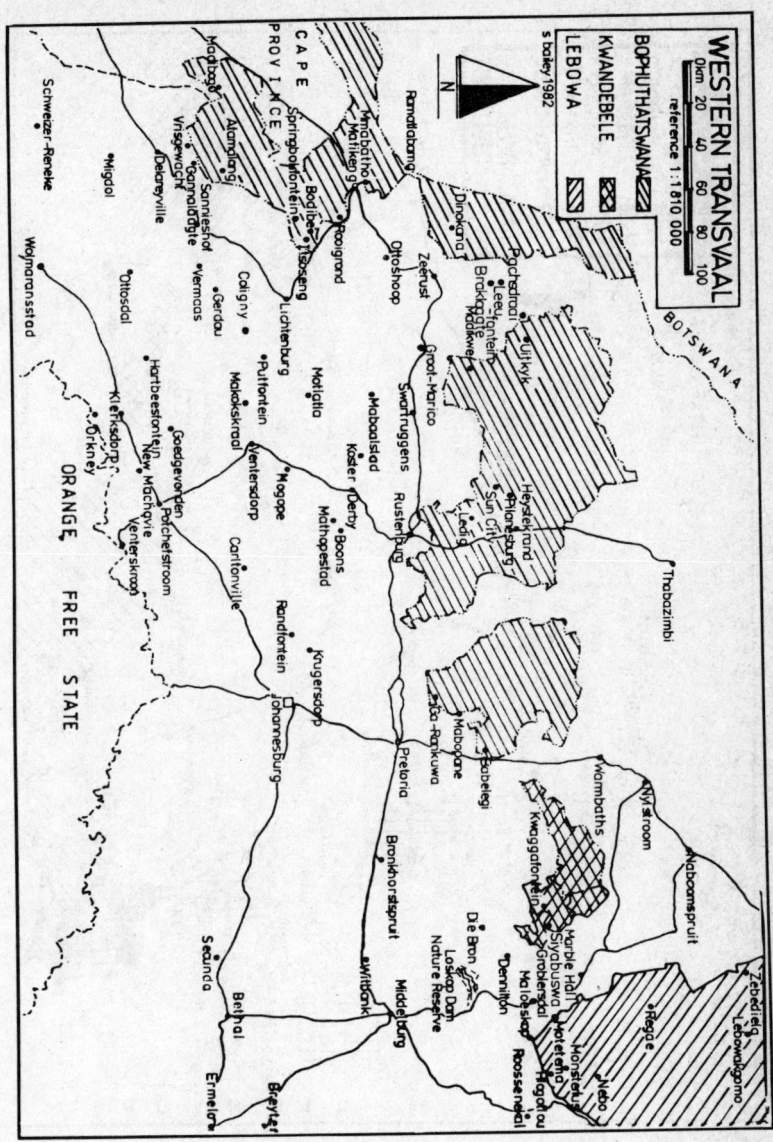

Map 4: Western Transvaal

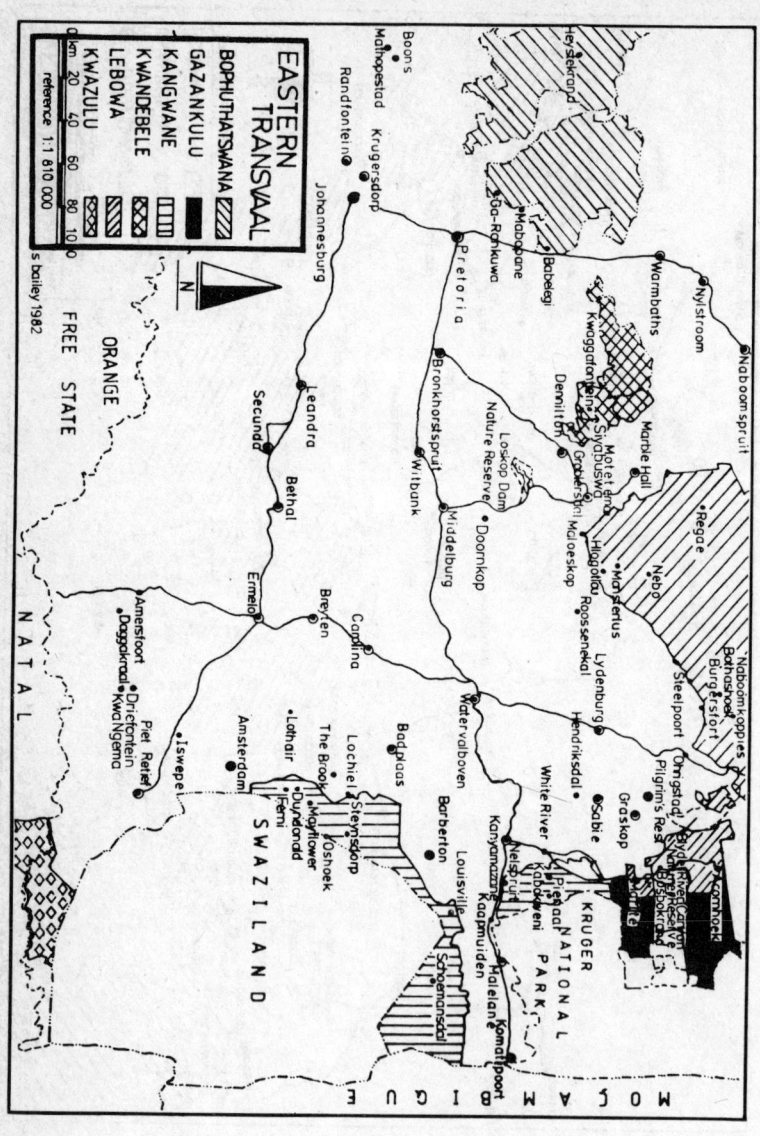

Map 5: Eastern Transvaal

the extensions of the Tyefu irrigation scheme.

The then Ciskeian Minister of Agriculture and Forestry, Rev WM Xaba, denied that there was anything inconsistent in refusing to accept responsibility for the people when they were dumped by the South African authorities:

> We objected in principle to the move to Glenmore and refused to take responsibility for the place. But we want the land and do not mind the people moving to Peddie as long as the South African government provides houses and job opportunities. (*Eastern Province Herald*, 19 Nov. 81)

'We will never get used to one place. We lead the life of a bird,' commented one young Glenmore mother of three on hearing the news that they were to be moved again.

Regional overview

The conditions under which people in relocation areas live will be discussed in Chapter 9. Overall conditions in the rural relocation settlements differ little from those in the bantustans generally. However, conditions do vary around the country. This may be due to natural factors such as climate, vegetation and fertility of the soil — KwaZulu is geographically favoured in comparison with Ciskei, for instance — as well as social and political factors. The proximity of urban areas, the degree of ethnic consciousness and the brand of 'development' present within each bantustan, are all factors that affect local conditions.

Transvaal
Nearly 1,3 million removals have taken place in this, the most populous province. A further 600 000 are presently under threat of removal, three-quarters of whom are scheduled for relocation in terms of the 1975 consolidation of the bantustans plan. There are no less than six bantustans in this region, all closely interlinked. Some borders are still undefined, and not one map, not even an official one, reflects the precise position. In some areas people are not sure whether they live in Gazankulu or Lebowa, in Venda or Gazankulu, in Lebowa or KwaNdebele.

Urban relocation has been implemented more thoroughly than anywhere else. Some townships have been moved in their entirety to the nearest bantustan from where workers now commute, e.g. White

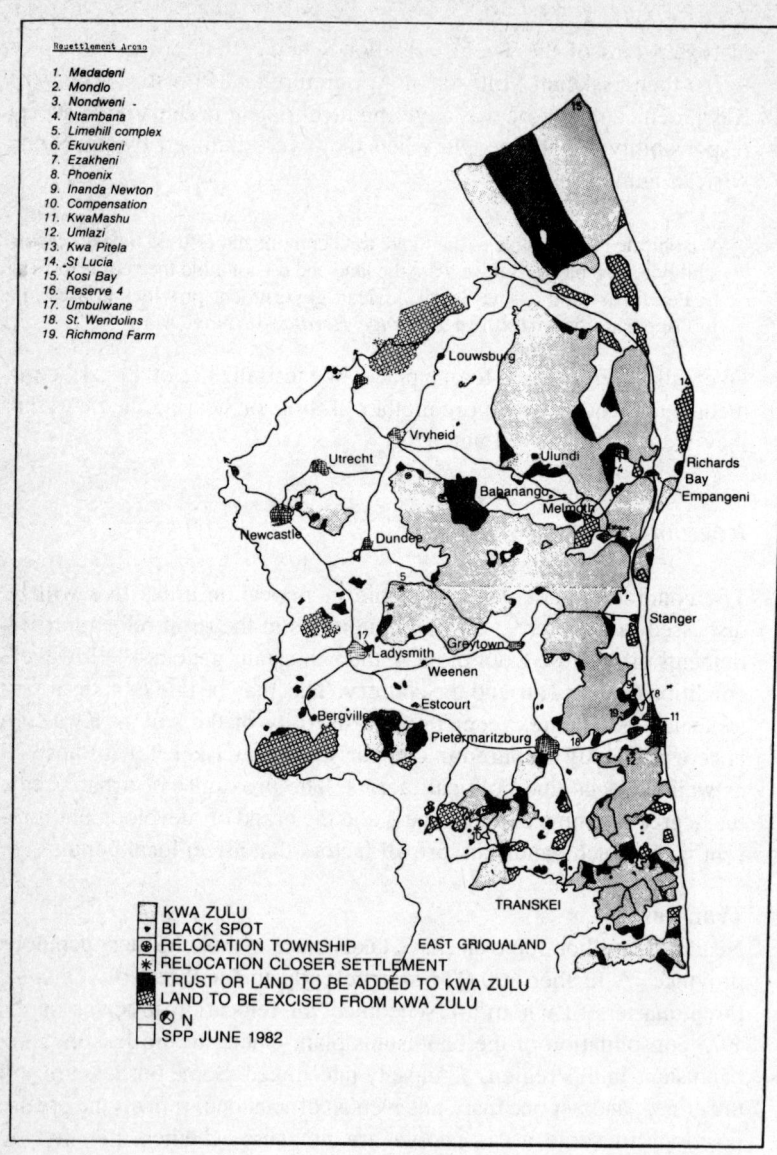

Map 6: Natal

River and its Kangwane township of Kabokweni. Strict labour recruitment measures and control on housing over the years have served to restrict access to prescribed areas. Most black spots have already been moved but in the few that remain in the Western and Eastern Transvaal there is active resistance.

In the Transvaal more than in any other province, ethnicity has been used to divide people and reorganise them into bantustans. Ethnic conflict is growing in the Northern and Eastern Transvaal as a result. For example, people who have lived peacefully together in Tshikota, the township of Louis Trichardt, are divided into Vendas, Pedis and Tsongas. Some wish to resist the move, others feel they are too weak. This frustration is reflected in comments such as 'We Pedis will never move. It's all the stupid Venda's fault — they took independence.'

Following the abolition of labour tenancy and the growth of mechanisation of agriculture in the Transvaal, rural removals began far earlier than in Natal.

The next bantustan to take independence is in the Transvaal. It is KwaNdebele, 75 kilometres east of Pretoria. It is one of the driest, dustiest, smallest and most overcrowded of the bantustans.

Natal

Natal differs in some significant respects from the other regions. Only one bantustan is involved. From the viewpoint of Pretoria, KwaZulu is the critical test for the bantustan policy. It has the largest population and is the most fragmented. Many parts of KwaZulu abut white urban areas. This has encouraged the proliferation of informal settlements. Access to jobs is a little easier, and commuting is possible on a much wider scale.

Farm evictions and group areas removals have been very extensive but overall the relocation programme is no more than half way to completion. Nearly 750 000 have to be moved but a further 622 000 are estimated to be under threat, mainly in terms of consolidation. The consolidation of KwaZulu is a particularly sensitive issue for the government. White Natal farmers are reluctant to give up their land and Zulus are 'unwilling to move', according to Dr Koornhof. Consolidation removals have barely begun and there are still some 189 black spots to be moved. Resistance from some of them has been quite fierce. Pretoria has also had to contend with strong opposition from organised agriculture to its land purchase and consolidation programmes.

Strategic removals in Natal have been significant. The establishment of the missile range at St Lucia, the clearing of the northern coastline of African residents, and the removal of people away from the Mozambique border have all been carried out for military purposes.

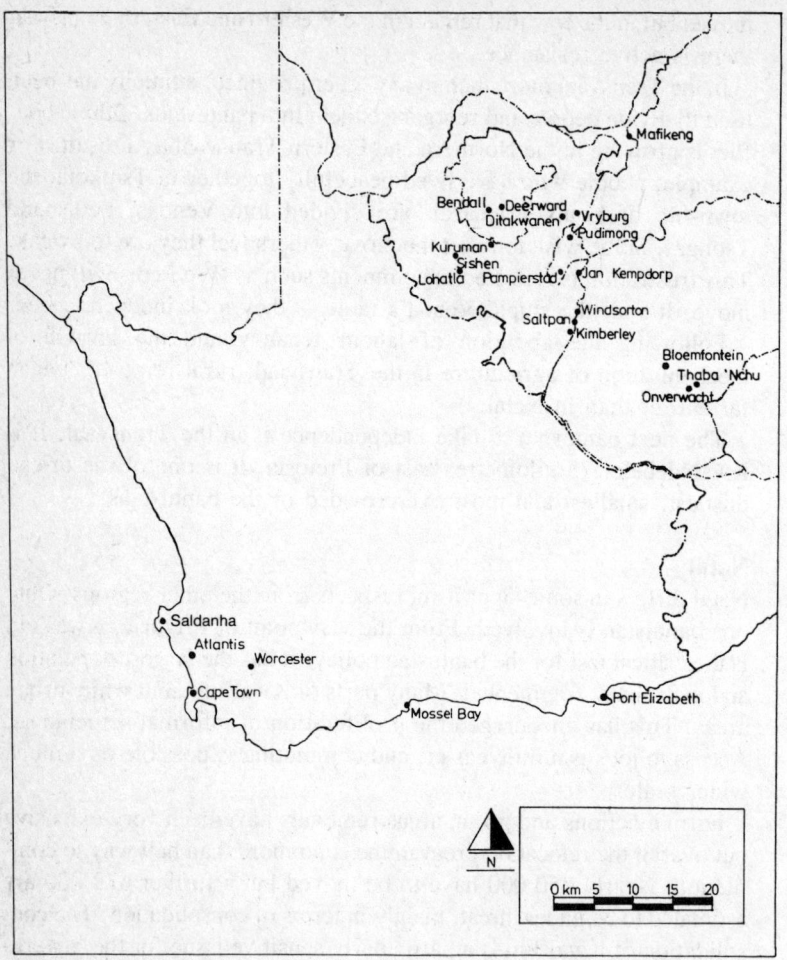

Map 7: Orange Free State, Northern Cape and Western Cape

Orange Free State
In the OFS over half a million people have been moved to Bophuthatswana and Qwaqwa, mainly off white-owned farms, but also from towns and villages. People evicted from farms where they have lived for generations have no option but to take themselves to desperately overcrowded Qwaqwa, or to the southernmost enclave of Bophuthatswana around Thaba 'Nchu, depending on whether they are Sotho- or Tswana-speaking.

Once Bophuthatswana took independence in 1977 the Sotho-speaking people of Thaba 'Nchu were harassed and fled to a Trust farm, Onverwacht. Here a closer settlement to be given to Qwaqwa was established in 1980. It is said to hold 200 000 people. Most of them live in shacks with the most rudimentary facilities although township-style housing is being built for those who can afford it and those being moved from Bloemfontein and OFS towns. This is the largest single relocation area in the country, accommodating more people than the city of Bloemfontein.

Northern Cape

The Northern Cape bore the brunt of removals in the early 1970s. Thousands of people were moved from reserves, both scheduled and released, to one of the two segments of Bophuthatswana (Taung and the Tlhaping-Tlharo/Ganyesa area north of Kuruman).

Some of the most depressed areas in the country are found north of Kuruman. The Wyks, Bendall, Deerward and the Batlharos areas are poverty-stricken, dry, dusty, isolated and forgotten by the rest of the country. Obtaining water is an all-consuming struggle. The more recently established relocation area of Vaalboschhoek, near Jan Kempdorp, where people were moved after they had fought their relocation in the first place, is little better. Vegetation is slightly more evident. The people of Vaalboschhoek are under threat of removal again — by Bophuthatswana officials this time.

While resistance was strong in some parts of the Northen Cape, in most cases it was quickly and easily quelled.

Except for some isolated people actively resisting urban relocation from the white towns of Vryburg and Jan Kempdorp, most of the relocation planned for this area has been completed. As in other parts of the country, people are still having to leave the white-owned farms and head for Bophuthatswana. Although the population density is relatively low — 30 people per square kilometre (the lowest in the bantustans) — gleaning a living from the semi-desert is almost impossible.

Eastern Cape

Conditions in the Eastern Cape are the worst in the country. The average unemployment rate is 30% and the overcrowded, desolate Ciskei accommodates thousands of people who have been moved from the cities and towns of the Western and Eastern Cape into closer settlements and townships in the Ciskei since the early 1960s. Early relocation areas

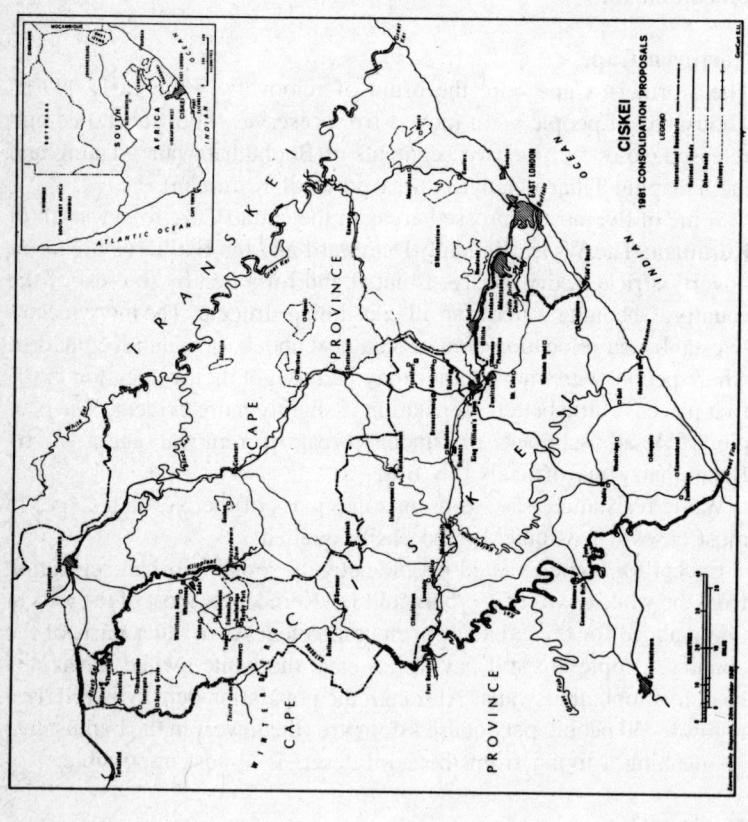

Map 8: Eastern Cape

such as Sada, Ilinge and Dimbaza were the subject of international exposure in the 1960s. They are still amongst the worst in South Africa despite international protest and South African government investment in factories at Dimbaza.

By far the most important movement of people has been from the white rural areas — off the white-owned farms — into the Ciskei. However, other forms of relocation were evident too. When the Transkei took 'independence' in 1976 thousands of people fled from the Herschel and Glen Grey districts to the promised land of the Ciskei, where they still wait at Thornhill, Zweledinga and Oxton for land and facilities. In 1981 the Ciskei took 'independence' stripping two million people of their South African citizenship.

Seven black spots in the corridor between Ciskei and Transkei are due to be moved shortly as part of the consolidation of Ciskei. Already some people have been moved to Frankfort. Others are trying to resist the move in the face of the highly repressive Ciskei authorities.

Over the past twenty years the government has established that it has moved 80 000 people out of Duncan Village, an African area in East London, to Mdantsane. In June 1983 a partial reprieve for Duncan Village was announced; now approximately 40 000 people will be able to stay in Zipunzana but more than 10 000 will be moved from the 'squatter area' of Ndende Street.

Western Cape

The Western Cape is a very distinct region in terms of relocation since there is no adjacent bantustan. The major categories of removal have been those of group areas and influx control.

Thousands of African people are endorsed out of the Western Cape every year in an attempt to implement the Coloured Labour Preference Area policy. This policy aims to give preference to whites and coloureds in employment. Where a prospective employer can prove that there is no 'suitable' white or coloured labour available, she/he may obtain a permit to employ an African. The policy also ensures that provision and allocation of housing for Africans is strictly controlled.

Informal settlements built up over the years have been destroyed, the Africans sent to the Ciskei and Transkei and the coloureds moved into housing many cannot afford. These people are then forced to move in with other families in tiny houses, or to squat illegally on the peripheries of housing developments like Atlantis, a coloured commuter township 50 kilometres from Cape Town. Here houses stand empty as their former occupants can no longer afford the rent or repayments, particularly as so many workers in the area have been retrenched. Crossroads, the last remaining African informal settlement, has gone through a series of crises under international focus. At the time of writing it seems that many of the people will not be able to stay in Cape Town. Permits both for them and for more than 2 000 others camping in the Nyanga Bush for two years have been refused, and they have been told to move elsewhere. Pass raids have escalated dramatically. In the course of 1982 an average of over R52 000 per month was collected in fines imposed on Africans charged with being in the Cape Town area illegally.

Each year the Administration Board attempts to rid Cape Town of Africans (who may have been in the area for many years) having no formal shelter. Every means to clear them forcibly was used in 1983, including teargas, shooting (rubber bullets), dogs and baton-wielding police. In May 1983 officials even went as far as confiscating mothers' and babies' clothing, and shelter and medical supplies.

A major threat to the security of all Africans in Cape Town is the planned relocation of all four African townships (Langa, Nyanga, Guguletu and New Crossroads) to Khayelitsha, a township to be built at Driftsands east of Mitchells Plain, more than 30 kilometres southeast of Cape Town city centre. The government plans to phase out the three main townships and accommodate the 6 000 families on the waiting list for housing in a high density township on 2 500 hectares. Dr Piet Koornhof, Minister of Co-operation and Development, estimated that between 200 000 and 300 000 would live there, and that it would take 20 years to complete the scheme. (It took 20 years to move nearly 200 000 people out of Cape Town group areas to the Cape Flats.)

The position in 1983

Nearly two million people are scheduled for relocation in terms of present government policy. The largest category is that of clearance of black spots and consolidation of the bantustans (1,1 million) while more than 430 000 are threatened with removal from urban areas. Unknown numbers from farms and towns are under threat of removal in the light of the proposed Orderly Movement and Settlement of Black Persons Bill.

Both internal and external pressures on the government are making consolidation in particular, and relocation in general, a difficult task. Increasing numbers of communities refuse to be moved. There is press coverage of their plight at home and abroad. The war against SWAPO in Namibia and the ANC in and around Southern Africa escalates. Right-wing white voters accuse the government of softening apartheid with a slowdown in consolidation. Yet they are not prepared to be expropriated and compensated at present rates. The government is in a crisis.

As a result, the pace of removals has slowed. In the House of Assembly, Hennie van der Walt said that 360 000 people had moved of their own volition (since 1979):

> We do not have to force them to move. Our methods are different. The hon. member for Lichtenburg knows that we had to change our methods. Therefore it is not correct to allege now that the government is no longer prepared to remove people. (Interjections) I have just proved that we caused 360 000 people to move. We caused them to move. They moved of their own volition. If this is not an achievement, I do not know what it is. (Interjections) Times have changed. We can no longer remove people by simply leaving them in tents in the veld. Everyone who is moved will be moved for a purpose.... Removals are undertaken with a view to development. (*Hansard,* Col 8735, 6 June 83.)

While mass removals have slowed down in the 1980s, the policy has not changed. With pressures mounting from right-wing white voters, the government is preparing to consolidate bantustans more systematically, thereby increasing conflicts within and between them as people fight for scarce resources among the spoils offered for taking 'independence'.

As consolidation proceeds ethnic conflict will grow, resulting in divisions and making control easier for the central government. As one man in the Northern Transvaal area of Sekgosese, which has been reprieved, put it:

> They want to divide us so that when the liberation comes we will be like ZANU and ZAPU, only worse, and they can say — look, the blacks fight so much amongst themselves, they can never run a country.

In the longer term, forcibly removing five and a half million people is in itself an extremely dangerous policy. Resentment and deprivation can only serve to alienate the black population further, making them sympathetic to mobilisation behind popular opposition and hastening the very process towards majority rule that the government is so desperately trying to postpone.

In speaking of short-term action, Brigadier Lloyd (then in charge of civil action in the SADF, Natal) told the Urban Foundation in August 1979:

> Wherever we have a local population in our border and rural areas we will have to ensure their loyalty, goodwill and co-operation against insurgents. Where this is not feasible, we will have to move them out of the critical areas and resettle them elsewhere. It is essential that we have a white local population in the white border and rural areas.

But that very process of relocation is already seen as one of the destabilising factors preceding majority rule in South Africa.

CHAPTER THREE

Why removals? Some popular explanations

One of the questions SPP asked the people it interviewed in relocation areas was 'Why did you have to move?' The replies varied considerably, bringing out vividly how many different reasons the authorities can have for removing people, and highlighting what a complicated issue relocation is.

People who were moved off white farms said it was because a new farmer had arrived and was cutting back on his labour force, or because the farmer had been told by the magistrate to get rid of some of the people living on his land. Some people said they were moved because the government or private businesses had wished to plant forests on their land or establish new industries there, or because a dam had been planned for that area. Others said they were moved because their land fell outside a bantustan, or because it had been declared a white or a coloured or an Indian group area, or a slum, or because they did not have papers to be in town — they were 'illegals'. Many people did not know why they had been moved. Many people knew only that the government had wanted their land and had the power to take it.

> The police said there is land for us and no questions were expected. Those who asked were taken to prison. We tried by all means to find the real reason. But we were pointed with guns and no answer — (A resident of the Mfengu reserve, removed in 1977, who was interviewed by SPP at the relocation camp of Elukhanyweni, in the Ciskei.)

The perspective of most people who have been moved is inevitably local, particular, and very personal. They know what they have suffered and they know how their lives and the lives of their community have been changed. Usually, they know what happened to their land or houses after they were removed, and who is benefiting from its use. However, most are not aware of the national dimensions of the crisis that has come upon them, or of the way in which the different categories of removal overlap and interlock within the overall system of white domination in South Africa. Most urban blacks are all too familiar with the bitter hardship and insecurity caused by influx control and the Group Areas Act, but few are informed about the massive relocation programmes that have been enforced in the countryside. Even fewer rural people know about developments beyond their district. Rumours and vague stories from other areas may drift through to them, but factors such as distance, poor communications, authoritarian local government and widespread illiteracy lock them into their own separate experiences of being removed.

WHY DID YOU HAVE TO MOVE?

The following answers to this question are drawn from the many hundreds of interviews carried out by SPP in relocation areas around the country. They represent a cross-section of the most common types of response.

- The farmer did not want us.
- It was said that we should move out of the area because it was for coloureds.
- They said that that was not the place for blacks; our place is Transkei.
- They told me that we are going to be moved from this farm (black-owned) because it is in the white area.
- I don't know.
- We were told that we are old and not working. Therefore we are not entitled to a house at Middelburg.
- Our land was wanted by industry.
- The police said we had to leave because we had no right to live there. When our shacks were destroyed we rebuilt them. For several times we were fined. When we heard that there is a place that we can settle on, we came here.
- Some Ciskeian Cabinet Ministers told us to leave. They said that we have our own place in the Ciskei, land of plenty.
- The soldiers who pointed us with rifles told us to leave. There was no reason but we were drove out like animals. We and the others tried to ask why they did so, but the answer was to be taken to prison at once.
- We should go to our 'own land'.
- The government has given orders.

> — We were not on good terms with the farmer.
> — Because my father was a pensioner, the farmer said it would be better at Pampierstad.
> — The police said that the government was in need of the place.
> — The new farmer said he had bought the land and we should move.
> — We were too close to town.
> — We were told our location was too overcrowded.

Yet most of those who have been removed or are threatened with removal recognise, in a very immediate and direct way, the issues of power and of dispossession that are involved.

Similarly, many of the whites who push for the removal of communities in their district have personal and concrete reasons to offer. They are not necessarily concerned with the larger policy. Rather: they don't like having blacks as neighbours, they want their land, they can't afford to keep so many workers on their farms any more, it's good land going to waste. At times they present their case with a directness and a lack of sophistication that is almost unbelievable, as in the article 'Roosboom must go' reproduced below.

Roosboom Must Go —Ladysmith Farmers Association

ROOSBOOM, the "Black Spot" just south of Ladysmith, should be given top priority in the Government re-settlement programme, says Mr. B. J. de Lange, Vice-President of the Ladysmith and District Farmers' Association. Mr. de Lange and Mr. Thys Wessels were the Association's delegates at a recent meeting of an ad hoc committee formed by Mr. V. A. Volker, M.P. for Klip River, so that farmers and representatives from commerce and industry could discuss the clearing of Black Spots, African housing, and other matters with top government officials.

> At this meeting representatives from six farmers' associations in the Klip River and Bergville districts voted that Roosboom should head the priority list.
>
> **REASONS**
>
> The Ladysmith Association believes that:—
>
> ● "Over and above the ordinary 'border farmer' problems such as fences, stray cattle, dogs, hunting, theft of grazing, minor thefts, soil erosion, stock theft, veld-fires, vindictiveness, stock poisoning, Roosboom is unique in having certain outstanding problems.
> (a) It is the only "Black Spot" through which the Durban-Johannesburg National Road passes, with a very heavy recurrence of road accidents, which is a constant source of possible racial friction;
> (b) it causes harmful injury to the image of Ladysmith-Colenso border industrial potential;
> (c) it causes harmful injury to the image of South Africa in the eyes of overseas tourists;
> (d) it provides a golden opportunity to hostile overseas journalists and photographers.
>
> ● In event of terrorism, this Black Spot lies on both sides of the Durban-Johannesburg national road, and is within easy reach of the main Durban railway line. (Nelson Mandela addressed several meetings there in 1963, during the eleven months before his imprisonment).
>
> ● Notwithstanding any political grounds, Roosboom in its present state, will have to be moved when the Ladysmith-Colenso area is to be planned, because:—
> (a) It is a permanent source of danger to health in Ladysmith;
> (b) more than 50 known cases of crippling to stock have occurred on adjoining farms.
>
> ● The inhabitants have no ties to any tribe, and need not be resettled in one area.
>
> ● The properties are not situated systematically for the possible development of a township in its present form.
>
> ● Nearly all the labour is employed in Ladysmith, which, in event of re-settlement, would cause the minimum of dislocation.
>
> ● To a large extent the soil consists of the very erodible Estcourt type soil which causes silt problems in dams. The only solution would be the immediate withdrawal from uncontrolled intensive human occupation.
>
> ● Owing to the continual influx of squatters the re-settlement becomes more difficult by the day.
>
> **EZAKHENI**
>
> The association emphasises that the highest priority should be given to the provision of water and housing at Ezakheni, and other site-and-service areas for re-settlement, and we feel that the Department owes a debt of honour to the farming community of Ladysmith, considering the record of continued and full co-operation with the Department.

Source: Natal Agricultural Union, 15 Feb. 74.

By contrast, those looking at removals from the outside tend to adopt a perspective that may be broader but is also far more abstract and generalised. Their understanding may be impersonally simplistic as a result.

The response of some observers is shock and outrage that such things can be happening. To them, removals make no sense. In their opinion, only crazy racists, relics of another time, could think up schemes that deliberately destroy housing, move people away from the centres of work, prevent families from living together and destroy long-established communities. Others seek the explanation in single, all-embracing theories of apartheid, the state, the nature of capitalism in South Africa. The sweep and coherence of these theories is often impressive. However, their usefulness in explaining the different types and phases of removal and in accounting for all the numerous exceptions and inconsistencies that exist in practice is less satisfactory. A sense of the people who are affected is often lost, and an indequate account is given of the complexities and contradictions of the processes involved.

One popular explanation of this type has been the dumping-ground theory — that the government has used relocation as a way of getting rid of all the black people not needed by industry or agriculture, all the economically redundant or surplus: old people, sick and disabled people, women and children, the unemployed. This has certainly been one very important aspect of relocation. The General Circular sent out by the Department of Bantu Administration and Development in 1967 made this brutally clear:

> It is accepted Government policy that the Bantu are only temporarily resident in the European areas of the Republic for as long as they offer their labour there. As soon as they become, for one reason or another, no longer fit to work or superfluous in the labour market, they are expected to return to their country of origin or the territory of the national unit where they fit ethnically if they were not born and bred in the homeland. (General Circular 25, 1967)

These attitudes were repeated — though not quite as crudely — in the revised and updated circular sent out by the Department of Co-operation and Development in 1982.

However, the dumping-ground theory does not explain the large number of workers who have been removed, notably from black spots and from urban townships. Nor does it account for the development of commuter townships in the bantustans in the late 1960s and 1970s.

Another fairly popular explanation has been that of labour allocation — that the government is using relocation to move people from places where they are not needed by the economy to places where they are. The removal of black spots has been sometimes explained in this way — that by moving these people off their land, into the bantustans, the government is making a pool of labour available to border farmers.

It is also pointed out that many relocation areas have been established to serve border industries or the more recent decentralisation points that the government is promoting.

However, this explanation conflicts with the dumping-ground theory, if either is to be regarded as the only explanation. Also, it cannot explain why reasonably settled labour forces have been uprooted and moved from one area to another, with no intention on the government's part that they should no longer work at their previous jobs. The location of the labour force inside a bantustan, not its allocation to another industrial area or branch of industry, is generally the main motive behind such removals. The removal of the black spot of Roosboom in 1976 — two years after the *NAUNLU* article was published — illustrates this. Roosboom was situated about 10 kilometres from Ladysmith, among white farms. The relocation township of Ezakheni, to which its people were taken, has been built about 25 kilometres from Ladysmith, inside KwaZulu. The removal did not disrupt the labour supply of Ladysmith noticeably, or direct it elsewhere. Those Roosboom people who had jobs in Ladysmith continued to hold them, although this has meant travelling longer distances to work each morning. What has changed, however, is that now the whole community is no longer regarded as being the responsibility of the white magistrate and local government of Ladysmith (the place where they work and spend their money). They have become the responsibility of the Kwazulu authorities instead.

Another common explanation of removals is a political one: that the government is moving people out of what it has decided is white South Africa into the different bantustans, as a way of dividing black people, controlling their political organisations and preventing them from trying to claim rights in a common South Africa. This argument has become stronger in recent years. As pointed out in the previous chapter, many of the actual and threatened removals of the present time relate to the government's attempts to consolidate the bantustans and, in the Transvaal especially, divide people along ethnic lines. Yet this cannot account satisfactorily for other categories of removals, for instance farm evictions and those caused by the building of dams.

From this brief outline of each of these arguments it can be seen that they all have validity, but that none of them can account, by themselves, for every aspect of relocation over the past thirty years.

Relocation is a very general term. It covers not only a number of different categories of removal, but different historical phases as well.

The government has used relocation at different times against different groups of people. In the 1950s and 1960s most of the people who were removed were the victims of the Group Areas Act, of betterment planning in the bantustans, and of the elimination of black spots and labour tenancy in the white rural areas. The removal of whole townships (urban relocation) only began on a large scale in the late 1960s. The consolidation of the bantustans did not become a serious issue until even later, in the mid-1970s.

Relocation/forced removal is thus too broad an issue to be explained by single-causal theories: it reaches into virtually all areas of life in apartheid South Africa. Yet at the same time the mass of population removals that have scarred the country over the last three decades have not been simply random and unconnected events. They have not been merely examples of how inhuman and irrational the Nationalist government can be. The massive scale of the removals and the suffering that has been imposed on millions of people have not been incidental or accidental to the system of white domination that operates in South Africa. They have been essential to it — essential to the system of control over the black population that has been entrenched under apartheid.

Without the relocation of people the policy of influx control, which states that Africans have no rights to the urban areas, would break down. There could be no separate racial group areas, no ethnically divided bantustans. Connie Mulder could not have boasted quite as easily as he did that 'soon' there would be no more black South Africans. And, just as the apartheid system has been forced to change and adapt over the years since 1948, so the programme of relocation has had to be changed and adapted in relation to new political and economic challenges. Government planners have created new categories of removal, have refined and given different emphases to old ones, in order to deal with the changing demands. The original goals of white domination and control have not been abandoned, but the strategies by which they are to be achieved have become more sophisticated instead. It is true that some of the categories of relocation discussed in this book are not unique to apartheid. The mass, often involuntary, movement of small-scale peasant producers and redundant farmworkers off the land has been a feature of the capitalisation of agriculture around the world. Similarly, governments everywhere have moved people to make way for the construction of dams, airports and military bases. Yet even these more global categories of removal have, in South Africa, taken place in a context and a manner that has been shaped by apartheid.

The more than one million black people evicted off white farms in the last few decades have not, as with displaced peasants elsewhere, been free to move towards the cities where their only prospects for work are. They have been shunted into remote relocation areas inside the bantustans and only the lucky few have qualified for the papers that will allow them to travel as migrant workers to the urban areas. Those moved to make way for dams and roads have mainly been black and cannot vote for the central government as a result. They therefore have no direct access to, or political leverage on, the people who make the decisions about where schemes are to be sited and how they are to be developed; they seldom benefit from the schemes that become established on what used to be their land. Futhermore, dams and game reserves are sited, roads built and industrial areas located in such a way as to promote the aims of apartheid: to segregate areas, to inject some regional development into impoverished bantustans, to seal off strategically sensitive areas. Military bases are built to defend apartheid against the guerillas of the ANC, while rural black people whose loyalty to the state cannot be assured are moved out of what Brigadier Lloyd of the Natal Command has called 'critical areas'.

Thus in order to answer the question 'Why removals?' in a way that takes into account both the local and the national dimensions of this process, one needs to see how the various categories and phases of removals have been fitted together historically in the creation of modern South Africa. This is what the following two chapters set out to do: to look at relocation in the context of the origin and the development of the apartheid society, and to show how central its role has been.

Chapter 4 looks at the historical roots of apartheid in the 'native policies' of the 19th and early 20th centuries. Chapter 5, which considers the shaping of the 'Separate Development policy' (as the Nationalists like to call apartheid), starts by tracing the increasingly sophisticated elaboration of the Group Areas and (especially) the bantustan programme after 1948. It ends with a section on those developments within commercial farming which led to the massive evictions and removals of surplus farmworkers and their families from the late 1950s onwards. Although the relocation of these farm people fitted in with the bantustan policy, its causes lay in the long-term changes in the nature of farming itself. It therefore needs to be discussed separately.

Chapter 5 stops at about 1975. After 1975 — more accurately, after the Soweto riots and national upheavals of 1976 — apartheid entered a new era of reconstruction from which South Africa has not yet emerged. The reasons for this and its effects on the relocation programme — the slowdown in removals, the stress on voluntary relocation by the authorities, the reformulation of the consolidation programme — are picked up in other chapters of the book and looked at in more detail in the conclusion.

CHAPTER FOUR

'Land divided by history' — native policies before 1948

> You can't say there is an unfair division of land, because land was divided by history ... we've pegged it down and that's final.
> — the Deputy Minister of Bantu Adminstration and Development, speaking in 1975. (*Rand Daily Mail*, 7 Nov. 75)

AN EARLY 'VOLUNTARY REMOVAL'?

'[At dawn] the Governor leaves on his return journey, the wagons having preceded him three hours previously. On the way, at the 'Eerste Rivier' he was met by the Hottentot Captain, Cuijper, whom yesterday we had informed of our return journey; and as he had pitched his Kraals on the spot where we were about to mow hay, and had with his cattle done considerable injury to the Company, and further, as we shall be much in need of hay during the dry Monsoon for food for our cattle, he was told by the Governor, that for the reasons stated, he was to remove from the spot with his Kraals. This was, as far as we could observe, accepted by him without dissatisfaction, after he had been treated with a little arrack,* with which he departed well satisfied.'
— extract from the Journal of the Dutch Governor of the Cape, written in 1676, quoted in Davenport and Hunt 1974 p11.

* arrack — a type of strong liquor.

Population removals did not begin with the coming to power of the Nationalist government in 1948. In many ways the removals of the past thirty years form but one phase in a long history of dispossession and displacement of blacks by whites. One of the first things that Jan van Riebeeck did after he arrived at the Cape in 1652 to establish a base for the Dutch East India Company was to drive out the local Khoi (Hottentot) cattle from their grazing land below Table Mountain. When their leader, known as Harry, protested, he was told:

> that his claim to ownership of this Cape could not be entertained as the Honourable Company had fortified it so as to retain it in her possession. (Journal of Jan van Riebeeck, entry dated 13 May 1656.)

Two years later Van Riebeeck formalised the displacement of the Khoi from their lands in the Cape Peninsula by means of an agreement which stated:

> The Kaapmans shall permanently dwell on the eastern side of the Salt River and the fresh river Liesbeck, as the pastures on this side are not even sufficient for our own needs. (Journal of Jan van Riebeeck, entry dated 5 July 1658)

Only those Khoi who were prepared to work for the Company or the first white settlers were allowed to remain on their former grazing lands. Then, as now, the removal of all blacks not working for them was one of the ways by which the white settlers set about controlling access to land and to wealth.

Clearly South Africa in the second half of the 20th century is a very different and far more complicated society than it was in the second half of the 17th century. One cannot understand the most recent phase of removals in exactly the same way as one understands those that started three hundred years ago. The removals of the present are on a far larger scale. Their style is very different. The issues at stake — issues of control and of dominance still — are more complex now than they were in the past. Nevertheless, there is also a relationship between what is happening now and what happened before. The roots of the programme of population relocation developed by the Nationalists stretch back into the past.

The late 19th and early 20th centuries were especially important in this regard. The 'native policies' that were developed by the white ruling group during this time helped shape the society that the Nationalists came to rule in 1948. Without the creation of African reserves in the 19th century, the bantustan policy of the Nationalists could not have developed, at least not in the form that it has taken today. The systems of land ownership and occupation that developed during this time among those Africans living outside the reserves were also carried over into the apartheid period. They too have affected the implementation of the bantustan policy and shaped the relationship between white and black, employer and employee, ruler and ruled in modern South Africa.

In order to understand the policies of the present, one has to go back in time.

Native policies in the 19th century

In the three centuries that followed Van Riebeeck's arrival at the Cape, the process of displacement and relocation of blacks that he had started became increasingly far-reaching. During the 18th and 19th centuries, first the Khoi and the San (the Bushmen), later the far more numerous and powerful African chiefdoms to the north and the east of the Cape, lost most of their land to the white settlers who were moving into the interior in search of grazing, minerals and markets. Blacks were displaced into ever smaller and poorer patches of land.

By the late 19th century, whites had succeeded in asserting control over most of present-day South Africa. The land was divided between the two Boer republics of the Transvaal and the Orange Free State, and the two British colonies of the Cape and Natal. The African chiefdoms retained only a fraction of their former lands, and this land, known as reserves, had been incorporated within the overall systems of government that had developed in each of the settler territories. The spoils had not been divided without fierce resistance on the part of many of the indigenous African people. It was precisely because of this resistance that the whites did not succeed in taking all the land for themselves, but were obliged to recognise certain areas as reserves.

Although whites everywhere agreed on the supremacy of white rule, each settler government had adopted somewhat different policies towards the African areas under its control. The impact of these differences can still be seen today in some of the important regional variations that exist in the country's African areas — variations of size, of geographical unity, of some aspects of local government. These differences were the result of the interaction of a number of different factors. These included: the different histories of resistance and conquest of the African chiefdoms in each territory; the different responses among Africans to their incorporation into colonial society and to a wider, market-orientated economy; the different labour needs among the white settlers; and the different ideologies of the missionaries, merchants, frontier farmers and colonial administrators in each of the territories.

The Transvaal and the Orange Free State

Thus, in the Transvaal and the Orange Free State very little land was set aside as African reserves in the 19th century. (This development would later mean that when the Nationalists wanted to set up their system of bantustans in the 1960s and 1970s, there was very little land already available for their scheme in these two provinces.) Until after the discovery of gold on the Witwatersrand in 1886, land was the only major economic resource available to the impoverished Boer republics. The white farmers in these territories were strongly opposed to the proclamation of reserves as a result. Reserves threatened both their supply of land and their supply of labour. The Boers regarded a farm as part of the birthright of each of their sons, and feared that if Africans had land of their own they would not need to work for their white overlords.

In the Transvaal the early movement of whites in to the area was not marked by extensive conflict with the local African population. The major centres of white settlement in the Eastern and Northern Transvaal were established with the permission of the chiefs, the Boer farms being marked out on the edges of the chiefs' domains. Many of these farms were allocated along with the African people already living on that land. As most Boers were not farming their land intensively — most of them were hunters and cattle farmers — they often encouraged other Africans to settle on their land and work it as tenants as well. Their rent could be paid either in labour (3 months a year) or produce (a certain proportion of the crops produced by the African tenants): the beginnings of the labour tenant and sharecropper systems.

However, following the British occupation of the Transvaal (1877 — 1881), the Transvaal launched on a series of wars of conquest against the independent chiefdoms on its still poorly defined borders. The Boers brought large new tracts under white ownership, and their original occupants under white domination as well. Because of the militant resistance of some chiefs and their people, the Boers were unable to assert control over all the land. In 1876 they were obliged to legislate for the first of a number of small African reserves that were dotted across various parts of the territory. By 1905, however, only a tiny fraction of the total amount of land in the Transvaal had been officially proclaimed as reserves — 2 120 square miles. (Davenport and Hunt 1974 p9).

In the Orange Free State the advancing Boers succeeded in taking away even more land from the local chiefdoms. Only two tiny reserves were created in the 19th century, amounting to a mere 128 square miles in 1905 (Davenport and Hunt 1974 p9). The first consisted of little more than several farms at Witzieshoek, on the northern flank of the Drakensberg. This land the Free State government recognised in 1857 as the land of the Sotho chief Mopeli and his followers — the nucleus of present-day Qwaqwa. The second was in the Thaba 'Nchu area which had been settled by the Barolong people under Chief Moroka in 1833.

In 1884 the Boers annexed this territory. Subsequently they recognised two tiny African locations and 95 farms belonging to individual Barolong landowners, and took over the rest — the bulk of the territory — for themselves. In the years that followed, many of the Barolong landowners lost their land to the whites by taking out mortgages which they could not pay back. By 1900 only 54 of their original 95 farms remained intact. Moroka's territory, annexed as a single piece in 1884, was in shreds.

Thus by the late 19th century the greatest concentration of African settlements in the Boer republics was on land controlled directly by whites. However, although many Africans had been forced to enter into labour tenant agreements with private white landowners, many others had managed to retain a large measure of economic independence. In the Transvaal a very large number of Africans were living on state land — land belonging directly to the government and not to individual landowners — which they farmed for themselves. In addition, many of the Africans living on private white land in both the Transvaal and the Orange Free State were sharecroppers or straight cash tenants who worked the land for themselves and not directly for their white landlords. Much of this was on land that had been bought up on speculation by mining and land companies who were pleased, in the short term, to rent it out to Africans. Some of the land was church-owned.

In addition, a very small number of Africans had title to their land. In neither of the republics were Africans able to buy land freely and thus the amount was very small. In the Orange Free State freehold title among Africans was confined to the few Barolong farms that were not bought out by whites. In the Transvaal Africans could only acquire individual title to land under a complicted and restricting system of trusteeship — the land had to be held in trust for them, by the Commissioner for Native Affairs. After 1905 this limitation was lifted as a result of a legal judgement by the Transvaal Supreme Court. However, very few African people were in an economic position to take advantage of the Supreme Court ruling in the short time that elapsed between then and the passage of the 1913 Land Act.

One group that did was the Native Farmers' Association. This was a company formed under the leadership of Pixley ka Isaka Seme, a founding member of the ANC. It had the specific purpose of acquiring land by purchase, lease, amalgamation or otherwise for sale to Africans. This company was responsible for buying the three farms of Driefontein, Daggakraal and Driepan in the Wakkerstroom district of the Transvaal in 1912, just before the passage of the Land Act put an end to its activities on the open market.

The Cape and Natal

Developments in the Cape and Natal followed somewhat different lines. In both territories the military strength of the various Nguni chiefdoms — Xhosa, Mpondo, Zulu etc — ensured that relatively large areas remained under African occupation during the 18th and the 19th centuries. Over time, the British adminstrators came to see the value of reserves, at first as a means of providing cheap administration of the African population, later as a means of maintaining a supply of labour.

Throughout most of the 19th century the Cape's economy was more vigorous, its settler population larger and more firmly established, and the liberalising influence of missionaries and merchants sturdier than in other parts of Southern Africa. All this influenced the development of its 'native policy'. Compared to the three settler territories to the north, the Cape policy was based on more liberal principles.

In the Cape, the Eastern Frontier was the site of a series of wars between settlers and the African chiefdoms which saw most of the land to the west of the Kei River opened up to white settlement by the 1880s. Several small reserves were proclaimed here, interspersed among the white farms, for those Africans who had supported the white settlers in these frontier wars. Out of these fragments of land the Ciskei would later be created. These reserves could not possibly accommodate all the African people living west of the Kei, however. As in other parts of the country, by the end of the 19th century most of the African population of the Eastern Cape were living on white-owned land. Unlike the northern territories, however, labour tenancy was never that widespread in this region. Most of the Africans living on white farms were full-time servants. Some were cash tenants or sharecroppers on what came to be known as 'private locations' — white-owned land given over entirely by its owner to African tenants. A small number had individual title to their land.

This was in keeping with the general principles of 'native policy' that were developed by Sir George Grey, Governor of the Cape from 1854 to 1861. He believed in 'civilising' the indigenous African population, to create 'an enduring and peacable master-servant relationship in a civilised context'. His land policies in the reserves favoured individual tenure over the traditional system of communal tenure under which every household had access to land. Grey wanted to limit the power and influence of what he called 'the haughty, hereditary chiefs', and encourage the growth of a limited class of African smallholders — small-scale landowners, food producers, with a stake in colonial society. He hoped that in this way the rest of the population, who would no longer be assured of land, would be obliged to go and work for the white settlers.

Both the chiefs and the people who saw their share in the land threatened resisted Grey's plans; his land policies were only partially successful. Nevertheless, the African population of the Eastern Cape was integrated into the settler society — in a servant or client relationship — far earlier and far more extensively than elsewhere in Southern Africa. After 1853, any African who was able to qualify in terms of property ownership and educational status was given the vote on a common roll with the whites. While the number of black voters was always kept small — and it was never the intention that black voters would ever outnumber white — this was in marked contrast to the situation in the three northern territories. Here the principle of 'No equality in church or state' was supreme.

The colonial administration of the Cape had neither the military might nor the inclination to open up the land to the east of the Kei for white settlement. Britain was, however, anxious to maintain its sphere of influence along the coast. For this reason, from the 1870s, these territories were annexed and brought under British rule as African reserves — first the Transkeian territories, later Pondoland to the north. By 1905 a relatively large area of land — some 21 000 square miles — had been set aside as African reserve land in the Cape (Davenport and Hunt 1974 p9). Although the African chiefdoms of the Eastern Cape lost a far greater proportion of their land than those in Natal, the amount of land set aside as reserves in the Cape was far larger overall and territorially more unified than anywhere else in the future Union of South Africa.

In Natal the British administrators found themselves in a far weaker position than their counterparts in the Cape when they took the area over in the 1840s. They faced a complicated range of conflicting interests which had to be balanced against each other:
— a very large group of 'refugee' Africans, people who had been driven off their land by the Shakan wars of the early 19th century and were now returning to resettle it;
— a numerically very small group of white settlers who were claiming those same lands for themselves;

Land Divided by History

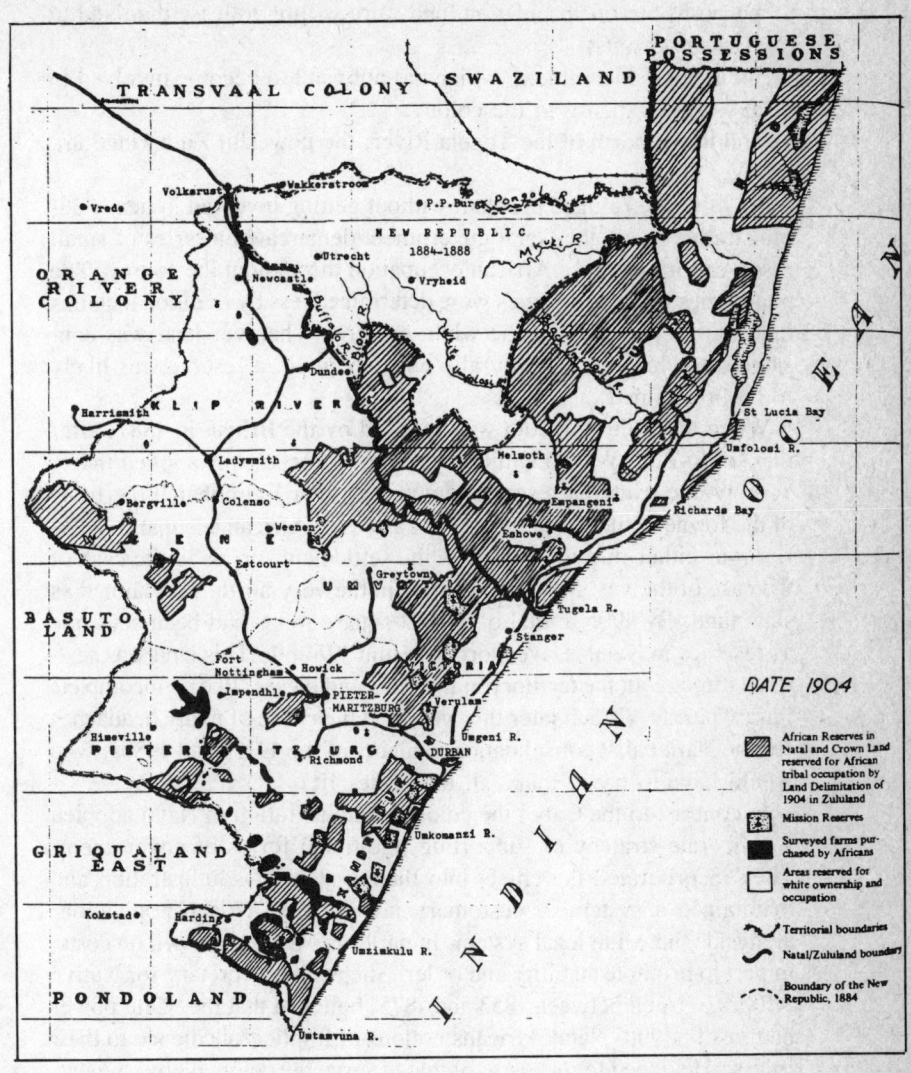

Map 9: Natal Colony

— large land companies who were buying up land not for agricultural purposes but on speculation, and were willing to lease that land to African tenants;
— the British government, which did not want to become involved in any extra expense in the colony;
— and to the north of the Tugela River, the powerful Zulu kingdom.

To solve the refugee problem without getting involved in heavy adminstrative costs, the Natal government demarcated a series of small reserves for exclusive African occupation throughout the colony. The boundaries of these reserves were determined less by traditional claims than by the priorities of the white settlers. Wherever land was considered too hilly or agricuturally not very good, a reserve was likely to be proclaimed.

When the Zulu kingdom was annexed by the British in 1887, after the Anglo-Zulu War, a similar system of reserves was applied there. Twenty-one scattered reserves, amounting to no more than three-fifths of the former Zulu domain, were set aside for African occupation. The rest was either thrown open to white settlement, or, as in the case of the case of the vast Makhathini Flats in the very north, proclaimed as state land. By 1905 a total of 13 892 square miles had been set aside as reserves in Natal (Davenport and Hunt 1974 p9). This land was scattered throughout the territory in little bits and pieces, like an incomplete jigsaw puzzle. (Much later this would be the cause of many headaches for the Nationalist consolidation planners of the 1970s and 1980s, who would have to try to make all the pieces fit.)

In contrast to the Cape, the colonial adminstration in Natal adopted a deliberate strategy of supporting traditional forms of government. They incorporated the chiefs into their system of adminstration and maintained a system of customary law for the African population, alongside the white legal system. In part this was to cut down on costs, in part to promote stability and order. Shepstone, Secretary for Native Affairs in Natal between 1853 and 1875, believed that the 'Zulu power had instilled into Natal Africans notions of implicit obedience to their rulers'. He hoped to make use of that to serve the colonial government. These principles of African administration that were developed in Natal can be seen as a very early form of 'separate development'.

Yet in Natal too, a small class of African landowners and market farmers — peasants — emerged during the second half of the 19th century. For a short time it was these African peasants rather than the white farmers who supplied the small towns of the colony with much of their food.

> In sum, much that was decried in African agriculture was a rational deployment of prevailing techniques in a relatively inclement climate and soil; much described as inefficient was the provision of subsistence in circumstances of low yield; much that was seen as ignorance was actually based upon experience and an awareness of needs and capabilities. (Bundy 1979 p25).

At first many white farmers abandoned the difficult task of farming under uncertain conditions and moved to town, leaving the produce market open to enterprising Africans. In response to these opportunities and under pressure to find cash to pay taxes and buy consumer goods, an increasing number of African households began producing an agriculture surplus for sale. Most of the small-scale producers were living on white-owned land — mission land, land leased from the land companies, and crown (state) land. However, by the 1860s some African people had begun to buy land as well. Often they formed themselves into groups and syndicates to buy farms more cheaply. Many of the early purchases were made with missionary backing.

By 1910 Africans owned almost 160 000 hectares of land in Natal. Their farms were distributed throughout the former colony, outside of Zululand (Christopher, A J, 'Natal: A Study in Colonial and Land Settlements', Thesis, University of Natal, 1969). This was the origin of the major category of black spots in that province fifty years later. Matiwane's Kop, Roosboom, Steincoalspruit, Acton Homes, Free State, Jubilee, Hlatikhulu, Meran, Thembalihle, Hopewell, Prospect Farm and Besterspruit — these and all the other freehold farms later termed 'black spots' by the Nationalists were bought during this time by means of a titledeed that assured the new owners that the land would be theirs 'in perpetuity'.

'A proper thing — a Freehold Titledeed', Eliot Mngadi, a landowner removed from the black spot of Roosboom in 1976 has commented ironically:

> And when our fathers bought the land, they were given these documents which gave them the right to own the place for ever and ever, amen. (Mngadi 1981 p5)

Gold and cheap labour

The mineral discoveries of the late 19th century, and the development of the gold-mining industry in the Transvaal from the 1880s in particular, brought about major economic changes in Southern Africa. These changes led to the political restructuring of this area.

Tensions between the Transvaal Boers and the British-dominated mining and industrial companies over who was to control and direct the wealth of the Witwatersrand led to the outbreak of the Anglo-Boer War in 1899. The eventual military victory of the British and the subsequent incorporation of the Transvaal and the Orange Free State under their rule, paved the way for the establishment of a political union between the four British colonies south of the Limpopo River, in 1910.

The impact of these developments on native policy was immediate and far-reaching. Gold and cheap black labour to mine it have been the two major commodities used in building modern South Africa. The rapid growth of an urban population and thus new markets for farmers encouraged the development of white commercial farming. Land was in demand and white farmers everywhere used their political strength to bring stronger pressure to bear against the independent African smallholders and peasants. They wanted to limit their access to land and to force them into working for them on their own farms. White farmers were especially hostile to the reserve system and to cash and sharecropping tenancies. They regarded these practices as tying up land and labour which, they felt, belonged to them.

Thus in 1885 the Orange Free State government passed an anti-squatting measure designed to limit the number of rent-paying or sharecropping African families allowed on each white-owned farm to five. In the Transvaal rents from Africans living on state land were demanded for the first time in 1903. Anti-squatting legislation was reactivated there in 1908. In Natal individual tenure was forbiddden in the mission reserves in the 1890s, and the Lands Department was instructed in 1903 to refuse all African bids at public sales of state land.

The mining industry was also anxious for laws that would force Africans into wage employment. Unlike the farmers, however, the mining industry favoured the reserve system and lobbied for it to be preserved. What they liked about this was that it guaranteed them a super-cheap, super-exploitable labour force. If their workers did not move permanently to town but became migrant workers, with a base in the reserves where their families stayed, then wages and general labour costs could be kept very low. The mine owners could justify paying their workers as if they were single men on the grounds that their families were able to make a living off the land in the reserves. They would also not be responsible for providing family housing or other services such as schools in the towns, because the bulk of the population would be living permanently somewhere else.

At the same time, the migrant labour system also made it more difficult for workers to organise and demand higher wages and better working conditions. The constant turnover of workers would make it difficult for strong unions to develop. Those workers who took the lead in organising strikes or voicing grievances could easily be fired and sent back to the reserves, out of the way.

At this stage, however, the migrant labour system was not a completely one-sided arrangement. It held certain attractions for many of the workers as well. This made it easier to entrench as the dominant form of industrial labour. Many rural people were still reluctant to break entirely from the security of their land and their way of life in the reserves. They preferred to leave these areas only for as long as it was necessary to earn what was required to pay taxes and to meet the needs of their families, and then to return to their homes.

In the Cape the interests of the mining industry were given expression in the Glen Grey Act which was passed in 1894. This Act, the work of the mining magnate Cecil Rhodes (who was then Prime Minister), extended the principles of African administration and land tenure that Sir George Grey had developed earlier. It introduced individual land tenure — small garden plots — and a limited system of self-government, weighted in favour of those who held land, into the Glen Grey district. Commenting on the Act, RW Rose-Innes, a leading politician of the time, said:

> The principles of the Act necessarily involve the creation of purely Native reserves or areas from which Europeans are excluded by purchase or otherwise .... We shall be compelled to create more of such areas as 'reservoirs of labour' .... These should grow into great Native States or colonies under the direction of British officials but with large powers of self-government and with representation in due time in a Federal Parliament of the Confederated States of South Africa. (Rose-Innes, RW, *The Glen Grey Act and the Native Question*, Lovedale 1903 pp33-35, quoted in Lacey 1981 pp16-17)

Opposition from the masses of rural people, who saw their own access to land threatened if communal tenure was abandoned, limited the application of this Act to only a few areas. The principles of the Act were very important, however. Segregated African reserves to supply the towns with a migrant labour force, with limited forms of local government within them, would be the policy goals of the extremely powerful mining and industrial sectors of the South Africa economy in the first half of the 20th century.

STRATEGIC RELOCATION DURING THE ANGLO-BOER WAR

During the Anglo-Boer War an early and relatively unknown instance of relocation for strategic reasons took place in the Orange Free State. During 1901 the British general, Kitchener, adopted a 'scorched-earth' policy in the Boer territories in an attempt to destroy the Boer guerillas' food supplies — Boer farms were burnt and the civilian population rounded up into concentration camps so that it could not support the guerillas. The white concentration camps that were established as a result have become notorious and have featured prominently in Afrikaner histories of the war. The black concentration camps that were set up at the same time have usually been ignored entirely by historians, although conditions in them were still worse. Thirty-one concentration camps were established for blacks uprooted from white-owned land. Conditions in them were appalling, the death rate reaching 436 per thousand in December 1901. After the war the larger camps were quickly broken up and most of the occupants distributed to white farms throughout the province. However, many people were stranded in the smaller camps, in desperate poverty, for several years after the war was over.

The Land Acts of 1913 and 1936

The establishment of Union in 1910 did not mean that political agreement among all the various white interest groups had been reached. The first three decades of the 20th century were marked by intense struggles within the white ruling group over the precise nature of the uniform native policy that they all agreed was necessary. Some of their differences were inherited — the result of the different systems of African adminstration that had been developed in each of the four provinces before 1910. Some of their differences were more recent — the result of the ongoing economic transformation of the country from a pastoral backwater into an increasingly industrialised and urbanised society. White farmers did not like the principle of African reserves; the mining companies did. White workers did not have the same interests as their bosses in the mines and in the factories, either.

The turmoil within white politics was further complicated by the emergence of new political groupings within the dominated population. The mining and industrial revolution within Southern Africa encouraged the development of new ideas about African political organisation and identity. In 1912 the African National Congress (the ANC) was formed. Its founders were western-educated and non-traditionalist, members of a tiny African middle class. They preached the ideal of a broad, non-tribal African nationalism and sought inclusion for themselves in the institutions of white society.

The South African Party of Generals Botha and Smuts, which formed the first government of the Union in 1910, was first and foremost the party of the mining and industrial interest groups. The main thrust of its native policy was to promote a stable labour supply for industry, and to check the growth of the small but politically dangerous African middle class. At the same time, the Botha government was not unaware of the political weight of the farmers, the large maize farmers in particular. It was prepared to support their efforts to smash the independent African peasantry in the countryside. The legislation which gave expression to these considerations was the Natives Land Act of 1913.

The Natives Land Act of 1913

This Act was one of the most important pieces of legislation of the first Union government. It has shaped land policies in this country ever since.

What it did was to take the different African reserve systems in each province and make them the basis of the Union's subsequent native policy. It made the reserves the only areas where Africans could lawfully acquire land. After the Land Act of 1913 had been passed, Africans were no longer allowed to buy land outside the proclaimed boundaries of the reserves. Nor were they to be allowed to rent such land in the future.* Those Africans who were already renting white-owned land — as cash tenants or sharecroppers — were to be phased out over time. In future Africans would only be allowed to live on white-owned land if they were labour tenants or full-time wage workers. Otherwise their place was in the reserves.

The Natives Land Act thus had something in it for both the mining industry and the farmers. By restricting the area of land for lawful African occupation, and by stripping African cash tenants and sharecroppers of their land, the Act ensured that henceforth most African people would have to go out and work for others if they were to live. The reserves were far too small to maintain them all through farming. The life of relative independence that many of them had built up as small-scale farmers and peasant producers on rented land was wiped out. To that extent the white farmers had their way.

At the same time, by preserving the reserves and not throwing all African land open to the land-hungry whites, the Land Act ensured that the African population would not become a totally landless group. Theoretically at least, the reserves could still provide them with a subsistence base and a permanent home. There was too little land in the reserves for commercial farming — few people would be able to make a full-time living there — but there was enough to sustain the migrant labour system with all the advantages to industry that have already been described. To spread this subsistence base among as many people as possible, the Natal practice of encouraging traditional forms of land tenure was adopted in most areas. The Cape practice of individual garden plots was discouraged. In these ways the Land Act of 1913 boosted the system of migrant labour on which the industrial power of white South Africa was being built.

The areas reserved in 1913

The areas reserved for African occupation in 1913 were basically those areas that had already been reserved as tribal land in each of the provinces before 1910. Most of this land was thus concentrated in the Cape and Natal. Altogether it amounted to about 9 million hectares — about 7% of all the land in South Africa. Extensive areas of African freehold land and of unsurveyed state land which has long been regarded as

---

*This restriction did not apply in the Cape until after 1936. The reason for this was that it would have conflicted with the voting rights of the Cape Africans which were still protected under the constitution.

African areas were left out of the schedule. (The schedule listed the land that had been set aside as reserves; this land thus became known as the *scheduled areas*.) In 1916 it was estimated that over one and a half million hectares of African land was excluded in this way, not counting the far larger area of rented white land that was also lost. (See below.) The Botha government accepted that the land scheduled in 1913 was totally inadequate for all the people who were being tied to it. It accepted that some other land would have to be added to the reserves if they were to function as intended — as the permanent home of most of the African population. In 1913, however, it left the tricky question of *which* land for later.

Table 10: Areas under African Occupation in 1916

TYPES OF LAND	HECTARES
Scheduled reserves	9 601 456
Mission lands and reserves	462 975
African freehold farms	861 754
Unsurveyed state land	810 361
Unoccupied white land occupied by Africans	3 574 443

Source: The Beaumont Commission (U.G. 19-16)

The Natives Land Act thus turned into law the process of dispossessing Africans of their land that had been going on for the past 200 years. Law, not war, was the final means of conquest.

> Awakening on Friday morning, June 20, the South African native found himself not actually a slave but a pariah in the land of his birth.

That was how Sol Plaatje, a leading member of the ANC, described the impact of the Act on his people. Soon after the Act had become law he set out to document its effects in the Orange Free State. In the Orange Free State the white farmers had taken advantage of the Act to demand that their sharecroppers either start working for them, or leave their farms. Plaatje wrote a book to describe the misery and outrage of what he saw: *Native Life in South Africa*. It describes one of the first mass removals of 20th century South Africa. It was mass removal to nowhere. The thousands of sharecroppers and their families being driven from their land were not given any alternative place to settle. They had to find their own way, either to the reserves or to the towns or perhaps to another white farm. The following is one of the cases that Plaatje records.

> Proceeding on our journey we next came upon a native trek and heard the same old story of prosperity on a Dutch farm: they had raised an average of 800 bags of grain each season, which, with the increase of stock and sale of wool, gave a steady income of about £150 per year after the farmer had taken his share.... All had gone well till the previous week when the Baas came to the native tenants with the story that a new law had been passed under which "all my oxen and cows must belong to him, and my family to work for £2 a month, failing which he gave me four days to leave the farm".

ANOTHER FARM EVICTION, IN THE ORANGE FREE STATE, 1913

'Among the squatters on the same farm as Kgabale was a widow named Maria. Her husband in his lifetime had lived as a tenant on the farm, ploughing in shares until his death. After his death Maria kept on the contract and made a fair living. Her son and daughter, aged fourteen and sixteen respectively, took turns at herding her cattle and assisting the mother in other ways. During the ploughing season, they hired assistance to till the fields, but they themselves tended and reaped the harvest and delivered 50 per cent of the produce to the landowner. Such were the conditions on which she was allowed to live on the farm. Maria, being a widow, and her son being but a youth, it was hoped that the landlord would propose reasonable terms for her (in terms of the Land Act); but instead, his proposal was that she should dispose of her stock and indenture her children to him. This sinister proposal makes it evident that farmers not only expect Natives to render them free labour, but they actually wish the natives to breed slaves for them. Maria found it difficult to comply with her landlord's demand, and as she had no husband, from whom labour could be exacted, the Dutchman ordered her to "clear out, and", he added with an oath, "you must get another man before you reach your next place of abode, as the law will not permit you to stay there till you have a man to work for the Baas." Having given this counsel the landlord is said to have

> set fire to Maria's thatched cottage, and as the chilly south-easter blew the smoke of her burning home towards the north-west, Maria with her bedclothes on her head, and on the heads of her son and daughter, and carrying her three-year-old boy tied to her back, walked off from the farm, driving her cows before her. In parting from the endeared associations of their late home, for one blank and unknown, the children were weeping bitterly. Nor has any news of the fate of this family been received since they were forced out on this perilous adventure.'
> — Sol Plaatje, *Native Life in South Africa*, 1916, p 80.

Attempts to add more land to the reserves

In order to meet its commitment to increase the area of the reserves, the Botha government appointed the Beaumont Commission to recommend which additional land should be added to the core that had been scheduled in 1913. This commission reported in 1916. It proposed an additional 7 million hectares of land for the reserves. Immediately there was an outcry from the farmers. In a manner reminiscent of the current squabbling over land for consolidation, the farmers supported the principle of segregation but did not want to allow any more land to go to the reserves in order to make it work. As a result, the government felt it prudent to shelve the Beaumont recommendations. It appointed five Local Committees to review its proposals instead.

These committees scaled down the Beaumont recommendations from 7 million hectares to under six and a half million. The Orange Free State Local Committee was the meanest of all. It approved of less than half the Beaumont recommendations for that province — a mere 67 000 hectares, based on the remnants of the Barolong freehold farms at Thaba 'Nchu. First published in 1918, these revised proposals were accepted in principle by the government. No legislation was passed to write the proposals into law until 1936 because parliament could not agree on all aspects of a uniform native policy before then. However, in practice, where both the Beaumont Commission and the Local Committees had agreed that an area should be reserved, then the authorities regarded that area as a reserve, even though it was not yet written into the law.

In 1924 General Hertzog's Pact government, representing the farmers and white workers, came to power. Hertzog argued for 'a difference in treatment of Natives and Europeans'. He believed in a more far-reaching system of segregation at the political and administrative levels but was not in favour of the policy of land segregation that had been pursued by the previous government. In keeping with the demands of his rural supporters, he would have liked to reduce rather than increase the amount of land set aside as African reserves. He also wanted to remove Africans from the common voters' roll in the Cape, seeing in its mere survival a continual threat to white domination.

In the 1920s he could not get a large enough parliamentary majority to turn these ambitions into law. He did, however, manage to introduce important changes into the administration of African affairs. By 1933 he had set up a completely parallel system of administration for the African population, many principles of which are still in operation today.

The Natives Administration Act of 1927 was a key piece of legislation in this regard. It was the first step towards uniformity in African administration throughout the Union — a step in the direction of the greater segregation practised in the northern provinces, and away from the limited form of integration that had been tolerated in the Cape. This Act empowered the Governor-General (in other words, the Prime Minister and his ministers) to rule by proclamation in all African areas. The far-reaching powers centred on the ruling party by means of this Act are made with special reference to removals. Section 5 of the Act provided that the Governor-General

> may ... whenever he deems it expedient in the general public interest, order the removal of any tribe or portion thereof or any Native from any place to any other place within the Union upon such conditions as he may determine.

The Act limited the powers of the regular courts to intervene in African affairs. It also deliberately boosted the authority of the traditional chiefs and headmen in local African administration. This was a conscious attempt to undermine the influence of non-tribal organisations such as the ANC, with their scandalous notions of equality, among rural people.

The Natives Administration Act, with its emphasis on centralised power and traditionalism in local government, was another fundamental Act in the making of modern South Africa. Yet although many of its principles would be carried over into the bantustan era, there are some important points of difference between the native policy of Hertzog and the Bantu policy of Verwoerd and Vorster in the 1950s and later. For Hertzog the issues were straightforward. There were the 'Europeans' and there were the 'Natives'. While there was already some vague talk of 'the national aspirations of the Native', which were to be met in 'his own area', this meant nothing like what it has become to mean today. 'Own area' was not defined ethnically. 'National aspirations' did not stretch much beyond the very limited form of local government that had already emerged. 'The Native' was still an undifferentiated unit, not yet split into Xhosa, Swazi, Tsonga etc fragments. If anything, his proper place was on the white farms rather than in the reserves.

The Development Trust and Land Act of 1936

The conflict over native policy within the white ruling group was finally resolved in 1936 by a process of compromise, made possible by the establishment of a coalition government under Hertzog in 1933. It was a compromise that involved whites only. It traded the voting rights of the Africans in the Cape for the allocation of extra land to the reserves — but the land had already been promised in 1913, and thus there was no gain to the African population at all.

By means of the Representation of Natives Act, Africans were finally stripped of their voting rights in the Cape. In its place they received a very limited form of parliamentary representation, through special, white Native Representatives. A Natives Representatives Council, with purely advisory powers, was also created. The Development Trust and Land Act of that same year completed the package deal. It formally authorised that another 6,2 million hectares of land (to be called *released land*) should be added to the reserves that had been scheduled in 1913. It also established the South African Native Trust (later the Bantu Trust, still later the Development Trust). This Trust was empowered to see that all the released land was acquired and to administer that land. It became the registered owner of almost all the reserves — title was not to be vested in the people who lived there, except in a few exceptional cases. The 1936 Act also tightened up the controls that already existed to govern the terms on which Africans were to be allowed to live and work in the white rural areas.

According to the Minister of Native Affairs the land to be released corresponded 'susbstantially' to what had been proposed by the Local Land Committees of 1918. In fact, it was less. Since 1916 white pressure groups had successfully seen to it that the land to be added to the reserves had been constantly reduced — from a little over 7 million hectares in 1916 (Beaumont Commission) to about six and a half million hectares in 1918 (Local Land Committees) to 6,2 million hectares in 1936.

In this way some of the African land that was overlooked in 1913 was finally incorporated into the reserves. Not all of that land was approved, however. Large numbers of isolated African-owned farms as well as extensive stretches of state-owned land settled by Africans were excluded. The Beaumont Commission had recommended that 'isolated Native areas' be:

> protected in their existing rights so that no expropriation of that area or removal of its occupants be carried out except with the consent of Parliament conveyed by an Act. (U.G. 19—16, p6)

This limited protection for those hard-won freehold rights was not adopted in 1936. In this way many African freehold farms were turned into 'black spots' in the white area — isolated fragments whose continued existence ran counter to the reserve policy. In the same way, those Africans who were living on state land became classified as illegal squatters, even though many had lived on that land for generations.

CREATION OF BLACK SPOTS, 1936

In 1961 a government circular put the number of African freehold farms that were turned into black spots in 1936 as follows:

Natal	'approximately'	210 farms	(41 615 hectares)
Transvaal	'approximately'	55 farms	(47 300)
Cape	'approximately'	63 farms	(53 339)
OFS		4 farms	(5 739)

Source: Department of Bantu Adminstration and Development circular.

'THE RAPE OF TONGALAND':
FROM INDEPENDENT CHIEFDOM TO SQUATTERS

One of the areas long settled by Africans but not approved as a reserve in either 1913 or 1936 was the Makhathini Flats in North-Eastern Natal. This land stretches along the Pongola River, from the Mozambique border in the north to the Mkuze game reserve in the south.

In an article in the *Natal Mercury* (18 May 82) a former Chief Commissioner of Natal recalls the day he had to tell the Tonga people who lived on this land that it did not belong to them but to the government:

'Some four years before World War II I was asked by my government to tell the Tongas of Tongaland ... that that portion of the Ingwavuma district ... was Crown land destined for occupation by Whites, and that they would have to pay rent.

'These happy, docile, hard-working Tongas were in great distress, no less than my own because I knew by what treachery they had been deprived of their own land, together with their only lifeline, the Pongola River.

'They said they had never been told of the loss of their land, and asked when it had happened. I said in 1904 at the hands of a government commission.

'They asked why they had not been told of this. I had no answer, as I knew that they had never been told until I, on that disastrous day, had come to tell them.'

Turton then goes on to describe how the Tongas had never been part of the Zulu kingdom and had not, therefore, been defeated in the Anglo-Zulu War of 1879. They had asked Britian for protection and had been incorporated into Natal in 1897:

'Then came the disaster of 1904 when the *Zululand* Delimination Commission was appointed to take certain areas from the conquered Zulus for white occupation.

'They went further. They moved into Tongaland and declared a huge area on both sides of the Pongola River to be Crown land reserved for Whites.

'All that was left to the Tongas was the semi-desert area well east of the river ... The Tongas did not complain. They could

> not be expected to, as they were never told of the shocking theft....
> When the Land Act of 1913 confirmed that the land was Crown land for eventual occupation by whites, there was again no complaint from the Tongas as they were not told of the loss of their land.'

Not all the land to be released was specified in 1936. The continued objection of farmers to the reserve policy made it politically difficult to meet the full quota of 6,2 million hectares that had been laid down. To solve this problem, the Trust was given the task of buying up the outstanding amount of land over time. The land still to be acquired by the Trust was divided between the four provinces on a quota basis — hence the terms 'quota land' and 'Trust land' for land bought up for addition to the reserves after 1936. The total allocation of released land for each province, including both the land that was proclaimed in 1936 and the land to be acquired thereafter, is set out below.

Table 11: The Quota of Released Land for Each Province

Province	Quota
Transvaal	4 324 080 hectares
Cape	1 389 760
Natal	452 360
OFS	68 800
Total	6 235 000

When added to the area scheduled in 1913, the 1936 quota brought the total amount of land reserved for Africans to some 13% of the total area of the country: 13% of the land for 73% of the people. And even this meagre amount was not to be forthcoming for many years. Until the 1960s white farmers continued to put every obstacle that they could in the way of the purchase of more land by the Trust. By 1974 it was estimated that 20% of the area released in 1936 had not yet been bought.

The sluggishness of the land-purchasing programme of the Trust would have important repercussions on the pace of removals after the Nationalists came to power in 1948. Until there was Trust land available where they could relocate the people that they wished to uproot from the white areas, it was not possible for them to embark on removals on a large scale.

Conditions in the reserves

Thus by the outbreak of the Second World War in 1939, the outline of the land on which the subsequent bantustan policy of the Nationalists would be developed had already been established. The areas that had been set aside as reserves were the creation of a process of conquest and colonisation. They had been established to serve white interests. They amounted to a fraction of what had once been 'traditional' African land. They were in no way the sum total of those traditional lands, as apologists for the bantustans would later try to claim.

By this time, too, the adverse effects of trying to force more and more people to live in these scraps of land were becoming frighteningly apparent. Areas of relative agricultural wealth — many had been grain and cattle exporting regions in the 19th century — had become places of 'frequent scarcities and famine' (Report of the Native Affairs Department, 1944, describing conditions in the 'Native reserves of the Northen Areas'). The 1932 Native Economic Commission described it as a 'race against time' to prevent 'the destruction of large grazing areas, the erosion and denudation of the soils and the drying up of springs'.

The declining yields and the growing landlessness of people in the reserves threatened both the political stability of these areas and the basis of the migrant labour system itself. People who were no longer able to make any living at all from the land were driven to move permanently to the urban areas, where the factories and the jobs were. Government planners were growing alarmed. But instead of allowing people to move freely off the land or vastly increasing the amount of land available to them — both of which would have amounted to a major restructuring of policy — they tried to stretch the already inadequate and exhausted reserves to accommodate ever more people.

Their solution was betterment planning, the first aspects of which were introduced in the 1930s and 1940s: cattle-culling, the fencing off of fields and grazing land from residential areas, the moving of people into villages set away from the farming land. They hoped that by controlling land-use more tightly, they could squeeze more life out of the soil. It was like trying to bandage a serious wound with a single piece of elastoplast, and as effective. The fundamental problem of overpopulation was not solved. As the years went by it became more and more pressing. Soil erosion, deforestation and declining yields were not halted. People resisted the new controls fiercely. Those who could, continued to trek to the towns to escape the biting poverty and the spreading landlessness of those who were trapped behind.

CHAPTER FIVE

'Pegging it down' — separate development after 1948

In 1948 the National Party of Dr D F Malan came to power as a result of an upset electoral victory over the Smuts government. With that, the era of apartheid began.

When they took office, the apartheid manifesto of the Nationalists consisted of little more than a broad set of principles: white supremacy, racial segregation, a Christian National state. Already, however, party strategists had identified certain key elements of the plan by which these principles were to be enforced:
— the classification of the population into distinct racial categories (white, coloured, Indian and African);
— strict racial segregation in the towns;
— restricted African urbanisation;
— a more tightly controlled and expanded system of migrant labour;
— an even stronger emphasis on tribalism and traditionalism in African administration than in the past;
— a drastic strengthening of security legislation and control.

In the following decades these elements were fitted together and refined, as much by the pressure of external developments as their own internal logic. Out of this process emerged the full-blown bantustan policy of the 1960s and 1970s and, with that, the era of mass removals.

The situation in 1948

The Nationalist programme did not spring from nowhere. The options of strategy available to the National Party in 1948 were limited by constraints from the past and the demands of the postwar period. They inherited the system of reserves that had already been established, including the commitment of 1936 to add more land to these areas. They also inherited the problems that were confronting the Smuts government in the early 1940s: problems of a massive housing crisis, of labour unrest, of angry white farmers and rising black expectations.

It was a time of great ferment. The years during and after the

Second World War had been ones of especially rapid industrialisation and urbanisation in South Africa. Influx control measures were not yet systematically applied and shanty towns and squatter camps grew wildly on the edges of the major cities — Cato Manor in Durban, Blouvlei and Windermere in Cape Town, Shantytown in Johannesburg. Though many of the newcomers to town found work, many others settled there simply in the hopes of doing so. They added to the restless population of the urban unemployed.

The political consequences of these developments were dramatic. The 1940s saw an upsurge in the political consciousness of blacks. The ANC grew stronger. It became more radical, establishing contact with other black and white radical groups. Worker organisations among blacks grew rapidly as well. Resistance burst into the open on several fronts at once. There were industrial strikes, urban and rural riots, bus boycotts and the beginning of mass campaigns of passive resistance against discriminatory legislation. Political rights and an end to economic discrimination were emerging as the two basic demands of the black majority.

At the same time, the old tensions within the white ruling group had burst to the fore. The war had been a time of bitter political divisions between the supporters of the war effort and its opponents. Now that there was peace, there was still conflict between the various economic interest groups, all of whom made different demands on the government.

On the one hand there was the industrial sector. It was revising some of its demands in the light of rapid industrial growth. The fast-growing branches of manufacturing industry were now keen to promote the growth of a more stable and highly skilled African workforce. They were prepared to raise wages since this would create greater spending power within the black community and thus expand their own markets. All this pointed in the direction of recognising a degree of permanent African urbanisation, at least for the industrial workforce. This, however, was not to the liking of the mining industry and many small manufacturing concerns. Their profits still rested on cheap labour, and they were unwilling to abandon the migrant labour system as a result. A permanent African population in the towns also raised political and security problems. How were urban Africans to be accommodated politically? How were their increasingly militant demands for rights to be contained, so as not to upset the dominance of the whites?

Standing in opposition to industry were the white workers and the farmers. Most white workers regarded the influx of black workseekers to town with fear. Generally these newcomers were prepared to work for much lower wages than the whites; they threatened their jobs. The main advantage that white workers had over their black counterparts was the vote. They had used it to help put the Nationalists in power, and now they looked to the new government to protect their privileges.

For white farmers the dominant issue at this time was a chronic shortage of labour. They blamed their problem on unfair competition from the towns, where wages were higher, and on the 'soft' policy of the previous government on African urbanisation and the reserves. While mining and secondary industry had both enjoyed good years during the late 1930s and the 1940s, agriculture had passed through a difficult phase. Even had farmers wanted to, they would have struggled to increase their wages to a level that competed with industry. As a result, many farmworkers and labour tenants — the sons of older tenants in particular — were abandoning the hard life of the farms and heading for the better prospects of the towns. The growth of the urban population that was taking place at this time was fed by this steady exodus of people from the white rural areas.

After the war economic conditions improved for the farmers but their labour problems continued. Farmers were beginning to mechanise — introducing machinery such as tractors and harvesters onto their land. In the long term these machines would replace many workers and thus reduce the labour requirements of agriculture. In the short term, however, they only made the labour shortage worse. At first they replaced animals rather than men — tractors in the place of oxen, etc. This made it possible for the farmers to plough more land and produce better yields per hectare than in the past. It thus increased their demand for labour, especially at harvesting time. Most farmers still refused to push up wages to make farm work more attractive. Instead their organisations lobbied for stricter influx control laws, to prevent the movement of Africans from the countryside and to trap a labour force on their farms.

The OFS Agricultural Union 1944 congress discussed the farm labour issue for several hours and

> delegates from all parts of the province complained that it was impossible to maintain adequate labour forces on their farms, no matter how well they paid their labourers. The drift to the towns would have to be stopped in some way. *(Farmers Weekly,* 23 Aug. 44.)

In the same year

> About 50 delegates attended a meeting at Pietersburg . . . to discuss the shortage of farm labour. Referring to the acuteness of the position delegates complained that the Northern Transvaal had for a considerable time been a source of recruitment of Natives for mines. It was resolved to draw the Government's attention to the seriousness of the position and ask it to take immediate steps to stop the flow of Natives to the towns and return surplus Natives to the farms. *(Farmers Weekly,* 3 June 44.)

From all sides, then, the new government faced pressures for change and restructuring. There were opportunities for a loosening of segregation in the unsettled days of the postwar period. The Nationalists, however, representative of the most conservative elements in white society, chose to strengthen segregation drastically instead. Their manifesto was apartheid: separate development. They wanted to increase the divide between whites on the one hand and blacks — 'non-whites' — on the other. They wanted to impose more rigid divisions within the dominated black population, to separate off coloureds and Indians and Africans from each other, and then to divide the African population along even finer, ethnic lines. They wanted to keep Africans out of the urban areas as much as possible. Above all, they wanted to crush the movement towards majority rule represented by the ANC and its allies.

The National Party of the 1940s was the party of the white worker and the white farmer. It was predominantly Afrikaans-speaking, suspicious of big business and foreigners. Its tradition was the old Boer tradition of 'No equality in church and state'; it rejected flatly any proposal that hinted at political accommodation and integration of blacks into white society. At the same time, the powers and privileges of government put it in a strong position to nurture the small Afrikaans middle class that had now emerged: small business men, teachers and lawyers, civil servants etc. Over the years this group would come to dominate more and more in the development of policy — segregation would be made to work in their interests.

For, while many of the speeches made by party politicians at political rallies looked back to the Boer past as to a golden age, their programme was concerned with the issues of the 20th, not the 19th, century. The task of the policy of separate development was to maintain white supremacy at a time of mounting black opposition and expanded economic growth. It was to chain that growth to the interests of the white and specifically Afrikaner group: to preserve, strengthen and modernise the system of racial domination already in existence so as to make that possible.

To achieve this, the government required enormously increased controls over all aspects of society — over land, over labour, over whom one may marry and what one may think. In the years that followed its election, the government set about constructing those controls with a singleminded and ruthless intent. The removal of several million people who did not fit in with its requirements was one consequence of that control.

The Group Areas Act of 1950

This was the earliest segregation measure of the Nationalist government. It did not develop any new principle. As far back as 1923 separate residential areas had already been established for Africans in the urban areas. There already was a fair amount of residential segregation between whites and coloureds and Indians as well. Some of this was informal. 'As soon as Coloureds gain a foothold in a street, Europeans evacuate in the mass', noted one observer about Salt River, a suburb of Cape Town (Western 1981 p52). Some of it was the result of local legislation — Indian people had been prevented by law from living in the Orange Free State and in parts of Northern Natal for many years. What the Group Areas Act did was to turn this fairly limited and unsystematic form of segregation into a rigid system that applied throughout the country.

Racial segregation became the basis of town-planning in South Africa. The Act made it compulsory for people to live only in specific areas that had been proclaimed for people of their race classification (their race classification, too, having been determined by the government). Once group areas had been proclaimed in a particular town, then all the residents who were disqualified from living in a certain area, because they were of the wrong race group, would have to move out of their homes to those places that had been set aside for them.

Massive removals in terms of the Group Areas Act got under way from the mid-1950s. These were the first large-scale removals to be caused by apartheid. By the end of 1970 a total of 111 580 families had been 'disqualified' in terms of the Act. A little over half of those disqualified had been moved. 59% of them were coloured, 39% were

Indian and only 2% were white (Horrell 1971 p35).

These and other official figures refer to the non-African people affected only. Most people think of the Group Areas Act simply in these terms. In fact, it has been used to destroy many African settlements in the urban areas as well. It has acted as another form of influx control. In 1961 it was estimated that 80 000 African people had been forced out of the central city area by group areas proclamations in Durban alone (Motala 1961 p4). Most of them were tenants living on Indian-owned land that was then proclaimed white. African freehold settlements in the urban areas have been destroyed by this Act as well: Sophiatown on the edge of Johannesburg (proclaimed white and forcibly cleared between 1955 and 1963), Lennoxton and Fairleigh in Newcastle, Natal (proclaimed Indian and coloured respectively in 1962), parts of Fingo Village in Grahamstown in the Eastern Cape (proclaimed for coloured and Indians in 1970),* and many more. In recent times, as urban Africans are being relocated into townships in the bantustans, their former houses in the urban areas are being upgraded and those parts turned into coloured or Indian group areas. SPP frequently came across people who said they had been moved because:

> They said the area is for coloureds [or Indians] so we had to move.

For most of those moved by the Group Areas Act it has been a costly, traumatic and deeply alienating experience. For the Nationalists it is a source of satisfaction:

> We make no apologies for the Group Areas Act, and for its application. And if 600 000 Indians and Coloureds are affected by the implementation of that Act, we do not apologise for that either. I think the world must simply accept it. The Nationalist Party came to power in 1948 and it said it would implement residential segregation in South Africa . . . We put that Act on the Statute Book and as a result we have in South Africa, out of the chaos which prevailed when we came to power, created order and established decent, separate residential areas for our people. (Senator P Z van Vuuren, speaking in parliament in 1977, quoted in Western 1981 p85.)

By segregating not simply white from black, but coloured from Indian and both coloured and Indian from African, the Group Areas Act

---

*The proclamations in Fingo Village were later reversed. However, they had already led to a decrease in the amount of African freehold land in the area.

represented the first deliberate manipulation of the principle of ethnicity by the Nationalists. People's perceptions are shaped by where they live and with whom the live — 'us' on this side of the railway line/highway/fence, 'them' living 'over there'.

By forcing hundreds of thousands of black people to move into segregated townships, the Act was entrenching divisions and suspicions against each other among the urban working class. It was also upholding cohesion among the whites, who were separated from blacks but not from each other — no English or Afrikaner or Greek or Portuguese group areas there.

The Act tried to encourage black people to think of themselves as 'coloured' and 'Indian' and African', rather than as blacks or workers or oppressed people who had many problems in common. Those African people who saw their land taken away and turned into townships for coloureds or for Indians were understandably bitter — but many turned their anger not against the government that had made the laws but against the people who had been directed into their former houses. In this way the Group Areas Act worked against organisations such as the ANC, which were trying to unite blacks to stand together against the onslaught of apartheid.

At the same time, the new townships were planned and sited in such a way that they were very easy to control. They were laid out with wide streets that cross each other in straight lines — convenient for police and army vehicles to patrol. They were placed on the edges of the metropolitan areas, far from the strategically sensitive business centres. Most of them have only a couple of entrances, which can easily be sealed off by the police in the event of political unrest. In 1977 Jimmy Kruger, then Minister of Justice, explained why he did not think that an organised campaign of urban guerilla warfare could get off the ground in South Africa by referring to the group areas system:

> One of the big advantages of South Africa was that the residential areas were segregated. Overseas, urban terrorism was largely sparked off by a mixture of mutually antagonistic groups within a limited geographical area and this was often accentuated by overcrowding. "We have fortunately managed to avoid this here", said Mr Kruger. (Western 1981 p75.)

What he was saying is that the Group Areas Act has been a successful instrument of political control. An African woman who was driven out of the informal settlement of Cato Manor in Durban, when that was proclaimed a white group area, described life in the new township of KwaMashu on the edge of the city in this way:

There were so many laws to deal with, now, in a somebody's four-roomed. Then, in Cato Manor, we were not even paying for this water. And you see, the life changed totally, became too expensive a life . . . There were some policemen harrassing us in this township. People couldn't do what they were doing in Cato Manor and couldn't brew all those things which I've mentioned. So life changed completely for some people. They said "Ugh, life here! Because there is somebody who is on our shoulders. It shows that this is not your land, this is not your house, you never paid a thing over it, you just pay the rent." (Interview in *Staffrider*, Feb. 80.)

The Group Areas Act also served as an instrument of economic control. Not only were the new townships placed far from the white city centres and residential areas. They were often placed near industrial areas, to provide a conveniently located pool of workers. The two group areas townships studied in some depth by SPP, Atlantis outside Cape Town and Phoenix in Durban, were both sited in this way.

Furthermore, the Act also attacked the black (predominantly Indian) trading class. The Group Areas Act disqualified hundreds of established Indian and coloured traders from their business premises in the town and city centres. They were pushed out to segregated shopping centres in their own group areas — the grandly named 'Oriental Plazas' of the big centres and the 'coolie shops' of the small towns. Many white shopkeepers used the Act to put themselves in business at the expense of their black competitors.

Whites have also made huge profits out of property deals as a result of the Act. Over the years property speculators have made fortunes out of the forced sales of houses belonging to coloured and Indian people who no longer qualify to live in them. Often the speculators have had close connections with the inner circles of the National Party. They have known in advance where and when the next proclamation is to fall. Having bought up black houses for very little, they then renovate them and sell them to white buyers as charming cottages at enormously inflated prices. In his book *Outcast Cape Town*, John Western describes this process at work in the Cape Town suburb of Mowbray in the middle and late 1960s. In one of his examples, a house bought for R2 400 from its displaced coloured owner was resold on the same day for R4 000 (Western 1981 p191).

In the 1950s black opposition groups identified these economic motives as the major ones behind the Group Areas Act:

> The sole purpose of the Group Areas Act is to deprive [Africans] of the free occupation and ownership of land, so as to ensure that they will be Government tenants at all times, and hence a source of cheap labour.

and

> The Act is nothing but the redistribution of wealth and resources in favour of Europeans . . . The main target is the Indian population. (Both quoted in Kuper, Watts and Davies 1958 p161).

However, at the time that the Act was passed, political and ideological considerations rather than economic ones were uppermost in the minds of the Nationalist planners. In introducing the Bill in parliament in June 1950 the then Minister of the Interior described the purpose of the Act as: to 'eliminate friction', to 'reduce the number of points of contact [between the races] to a minimum' and to enable each race 'to give expression to their full cultural and soul life' (Western 1981 pp85/86). The economic spin-offs, which have been considerable, have been more the calculated consequences than the immediate causes of the Act. They have been added advantages, to be manipulated by the planners and directed, as far as possible, to the benefit of the supporters of the National Party.

Restricted African urbanisation: influx control and the pass laws

The Group Areas Act largely took care of the numerically insignificant coloured and Indian population for the Nationalists. Far more urgent and difficult a problem was that of the fast-growing African population in the towns.

In 1948 it was already very clear to the National Party that large settlements of Africans living permanently in the urban areas meant political and economic conflict. Since it was determined to maintain white domination — to destroy the majority rule movement that was strongest in the towns — it was more or less inevitable that restricted African urbanisation would be a central requirement of its policy from the start. During the 1950s the ANC and its allies launched upon a series of political campaigns against minority rule: the Defiance Campaign, anti-pass campaigns, consumer boycotts and general strikes. As urban unrest reached crisis proportions, the Nationalists became even more convinced that in order to preserve their position, they would have to reduce the numbers of Africans allowed to stay permanently in the urban areas and to control strictly those who would have to remain.

This conviction has remained fundamental to their thinking ever since. Much of the increasingly elaborate structures of government that were set up under the bantustan system and many of the subsequent removals of African people have had this as their ultimate goal.

The Nationalists' first target was the spreading squatter camps that had been allowed to take root in the metropolitan areas. The Prevention of Illegal Squatting Act of 1951 was the opening shot in what has been an ongoing and increasingly vicious battle to root out the people living 'illegally' in town and to destroy their precarious hold on an urban livelihood. The Act gave magistrates powers to order squatters to leave the urban areas and to demolish their buildings. It meshed in with the Group Areas Act which, as already described, was also turned against African squatters in the urban areas.

Next, the existing system of influx control and pass laws was overhauled. It was turned into a far more radical and extensive method of limiting African urbanisation. Before the Nationalists came to power there were laws restricting the entry of African people to town, but these were not applicable in all the urban areas and were not consistently and effectively enforced. In 1952 two central pieces of legislation were passed to put an end to what was described as 'this unsatisfactory state of affairs'. The first made it compulsory for all African people over the age of 16, men and women, to carry passes at all times — to carry their 'badge of slavery', as the ANC described it, with them wherever they went. The second laid down the new terms on which African people were now to be allowed to enter and stay in the towns.

After 1952 no African person was to be allowed to stay for longer than 72 hours in an urban area unless he or she had special permission to be there. This permission would be stamped in their passes for any policeman to inspect at any time, day or night. Those who did not have the correct stamps would be arrested. They could be imprisoned and fined. They could also, in the offical phrase, be 'endorsed out of town' — told, quite simply and brutally, to leave, go somewhere else, go back to 'where they belonged'. The fundamental right of freedom of movement was thus denied to three-quarters of the population. So was the right to look for work freely. After 1952 the urban areas, the centres of power and wealth, were by right for all but Africans.

WHO WOULD QUALIFY TO LIVE IN TOWN AFTER 1952

Section 10 of the Urban Areas Act, as amended in 1952, laid down four conditions for urban residence. People who met these conditions did not qualify for residence in any urban area. Their qualification was for a specific area only and no other.

The four categories of legal urban residents created in this way were:
   (a) People who had been born in the urban area and lived there continuously ever since;
   (b) People who had worked continuously for 10 years for one employer in the same urban area, or who had lived lawfully and continuously in the urban area for at least 15 years;
   (c) The wives, unmarried daughters and the sons under 18 years of age of anybody who qualified in terms of (a) or (b);
   (d) Those who had been given special permission to be in the urban area by the authorities, generally because they were migrant workers on contract to work there.

Those people who qualified in terms of (a) or (b) would be able to live permanently in the urban area, unless they were found to be 'idle and undesirable', in which case they could be endorsed out. Those who qualified in terms of (c) could stay only as long as their status did not change. If, for instance, a wife became widowed or a daughter got married or a son became of age, then they would have to leave the area *unless* they already qualified in their own right, in terms of (a) or (b).

Those who qualified in terms of (d) would be able to stay only as long as their permission was valid. As soon as the time stipulated on their pass ended, then they would not longer qualify to be there and would have to leave.

In 1972 the Secretary for Bantu Administration and Development put it thus:

> Bantu who have left their homeland have not done so because they have a right to enter the white areas, but because they were admitted there under

the laws governing influx control and admission enacted by the white government.

He then went on to spell out what the terms under which Africans would be admitted to the urban areas were:

> They are staying there because the whites need their labour on the one hand, and because they need employment from the whites on the other.

This was the key point. Neither in 1952 nor later did the Nationalists intend to drive the African population out of the urban areas altogether. They did not put political control over economic sound sense. They tried to harmonise the two. The purpose of the new controls was to reduce the number of Africans living permanently in the towns as much as possible, so as to reduce the political threat that they posed. It was also to erect barriers: to ensure that out of the masses who would be excluded from permanent residence rights, only selected people, those needed by the economy, would be allowed back in again, and then only on a temporary basis. The rest would be permanently excluded.

At the same time, these controls could also be applied in such a way as to benefit the white farmers who had helped put the Nationalists in power. After 1952 it becamse more and more difficult for Africans living in the white rural areas to move to the towns. The new laws were also used to provide the farmers with the labour of those who were being arrested under the pass laws in town. During 1954, for instance, the Native Commissioner of Johannesburg developed a scheme that was designed to channel 'the large numbers of Africans who were charged under the pass laws' into 'rural employment'.

> Farmers, especially in the Transvaal, were invited to apply for such labour. Unemployed Africans arrested on suspicion of having committed minor technical offences were not forced to work on the farms; but if they did not do so they were returned to the police and might have to face prosecution. Thereafter they were liable to re-arrest unless they were accepted for urban employment or left the area. (Horrell 1971 p3.)

In this way the acute labour shortage of which farmers had so long complained was eased.

Although we have been unable to count exactly how many people have been removed in terms of these laws, it is clear that they have devastated the lives of millions. Since 1952 countless unauthorised shelters have been destroyed, hundreds of thousands of people have been arrested and imprisoned and endorsed out of town each year, in order to try and preserve the urban areas as the centre of white power. Over the years the old laws have been amended and new ones passed to erect still higher barriers around the white towns and cities. While the methods of enforcement have changed, the principle itself, that Africans must be kept out of the urban areas as far as possible, has remained.

SPP has caught glimpses of the suffering that this principle has caused:

> We tried to ignore the endorsement but the following month the house was locked and my clothes and furniture were locked outside.
>
> My husband and myself were given a couple of days to pack and leave Bethulie. We decided to defy the day because we thought about the hardship we will experience at Lady Frere where we originally came from. That resulted in the arrest of my husband twice.
>
> My husband was told that since he was not born at Middelburg, he was not entitled to a house of local resident right.
>
> People were continually arrested and their houses demolished and that troubled our lives for some time. We were maltreated for some time and I was also arrested . . . we spent sleepless nights, would see some torches in the early hours of the morning and we knew that they were arresting: kubomvu [to raid]. ('The Struggle for Crossroads', p20.)

Overhauling the migrant labour system

A further and necessary consequence of the policy of restricted African urbanisation was the entrenchment of the migrant labour system after 1948.

Many analyses of apartheid are based on the assumption that the migrant labour system benefited all sectors of the economy equally, and that industrialists and business men were overwhelmingly in favour of it. In fact, this was not so. As already pointed out, some sectors of manufacturing industry — mainly the larger and most profitable concerns — were beginning to support the idea of a settled, permanently urbanised labour force from the early 1940s. During the 1950s and later, they continued to argue against the migrant labour system. They wanted to promote the creation of a more highly skilled and stable workforce. They also resented the bureaucracy and red tape that surrounded the recruitment of migrant workers.

In general, however, the maintenance of the migrant labour system was broadly acceptable to the white ruling group as a whole. Certain important sectors of the economy still drew substantial benefits from it — the mining and construction industries, for instance, who drew on large numbers of unskilled workers. Many of the smaller manufacturing concerns — where a growing class of Afrikaner capitalists was developing — also relied on the migrant labour system to keep their labour costs down and to stay in business. Cheaper workers meant larger profits. Furthermore, most whites were in general agreement on the political advantages of limiting the African presence in the urban areas as much as possible. These were seen to outweigh many of the inconveniences of the system. They wanted African workers. They didn't want their families or their medical problems or their political leaders.

Under the Nationalists the migrant labour system was reworked into an increasingly sophisticated and all-embracing method of labour allocation and control. A network of labour bureaux was established. Its function was to control the numbers of people allowed to enter the urban areas for job purposes and to direct labour to those areas and sectors most in need of it: to select, allocate and then eject workers once their jobs were over. Labour bureaux officials has awesome powers over the workseekers who were channelled through their dreary offices. With one stamp they could determine where one could work, for how long one could work there, even what kind of work one could do. Once a rural person got a 'farmworker only' stamp in his pass, it was virtually impossible for him ever to break from that category legally.

At first only rural workseekers had to go through the labour bureaux to get their jobs approved. The bureaux were located in the towns, so they could travel there to look for work first. In 1964 the powers of the labour bureaux were extended to cover the employment of all African workers in the urban areas, whether permanent residents or migrants. From 1968 their control became even more far-reaching. Labour bureaux were set up in the bantustans. Thereafter rural workseekers could no longer travel to town, they had to go through their local bureau and wait to be allocated to a job by them. Control over who was to leave the rural areas to go to town was thus to be exercised at the point of supply. At the same time, it became compulsory for migrant workers who had jobs to return to their 'place of origin' at least once a year, to ensure that their ties to the bantustans, both legal and personal, would not be broken. To minimise the inconveniences to industry, a system of call-in cards was developed. This allowed migrant workers to be sent back to the same job year after year, if their employers wanted them.

The creation of the bantustans

Restructuring the reserves

Keeping pace with the new government's policies in the urban areas went a major process of political restructuring in the reserves. This was the other side of influx control. The government's answer to the drive for majority rule in the towns was to push ahead with the development of the bantustan policy.

The bantustan policy of the Nationalist government was not fully formulated when the party came to power in 1948. As already described, the party had a long history of hostility to the idea of setting land aside for exclusive African occupation. This attitude lingered on among many of its supporters after 1948, especially in the white countryside. In 1954 the chairman of the Elandslaagte Farmers' Association in Northern Natal expressed the view of hundreds of thousands of farmers when he said at a meeting called to protest against land purchases by the Trust:

> The Native is not a farmer and never will be a farmer. He would ruin every bit of land that was placed at his disposal, and it was the height of folly and irresponsibility to hand over the district to Natives. (*NAUNLU*, 5 Nov. 54)

During the 1950s, however, those in the higher levels of the party began to revise their thinking. They looked at the reserves not in terms of their farming potential but in terms of their political potential. They could see in these forgotten rural areas the solution to many of their problems in the towns.

Their interest in the reserves was twofold. Firstly, if Africans were to be kept out of the towns as far as possible, then they would have to be accommodated somewhere else. They would have to be accommodated not simply in the sense of being given some space to live, but also in the sense of being maintained. The government needed to ensure that the African population was educated, housed, fed and administered at least well enough to provide a continuous supply of workers for the towns, and prevent social and political unrest among the blacks from boiling over and swamping white society. The problem was not simply where to send those endorsed out of town, either.

There were those who would never be allowed into the towns - the 'superfluous' and the 'non-productive', as the 1967 Government Circular described them.

In the 1950s the labour needs of the farmers made it posssible to direct some of the 'superfluous appendages' to them. However, the farmers could not absorb the entire surplus population. Furthermore, as the decade wore on, it became less desirable that they should. The introduction of more and better machinery onto the farms was creating a situation where a group of surplus and unwanted people was now developing on the farms as well — redundant workers, ex-labour tenants and their families. In time these people would themselves have to be relocated in the interests of white profits and white security.

Secondly, it was also becoming very clear to the party strategists that white domination could not be maintained indefinitely by force and coercion alone. New political alternatives were needed for the black population. Force would always remain the bottom line of defence for the Nationalists. Their treatment of the political campaigns of the 1950s made that very clear. During this time the government launched upon a campaign of brutal repression, to break the ANC and stamp out political dissent. This process culminated in the banning of both the ANC and the Pan-African Congress (the PAC) in 1960.

By itself, however, force failed to guarantee long-term security and stability. It provided no answer to the subversive doctrines of non-racialism, pan-africanism and majority rule. It also gave the country a bad name internationally, while continual political unrest frightened off foreign investment.

The reserves provided an obvious, partly developed answer to these problems. They were like a pre-packaged kit which the government could assemble according to its requirements. In 1950 these areas already accommodated 40% of the African population. They had long subsidised the migrant labour system. Their function as home for the discarded and the dispossessed was written into their history. Furthermore they already had some elements of local government, based on the safer conservative prinicples of tribalism and traditionalism.

During the 1950s the government took these elements and started constructing from them a further line of defence for minority rule. Along with the ruthless repression of the political struggles of that time went a parallel process of building up the reserves as the true homes of the African population. From now on this was to be where they should look for political rights. This was where the bulk of the workforce would be maintained, together with the surplus population. Out of the overcrowded, poverty-stricken native reserves of Shepstone, Rhodes and Smuts, first bantustans, then homelands, then ten national states were born.

The first step in this direction was the Bantu Authorities Act of 1951. This made provision for the establishment of Tribal, Regional and Territorial Authorities in the reserves. In the following years Tribal Authorities, with limited powers of local government, were set up. The traditional elite of chiefs and headmen became more firmly embedded in the overall structures of domination in the reserves than before. Their powers were increased. They became salaried officials with a vested interest in the apartheid system, local agents of control for the central government. Their cooperation with the government assured them of more than their salaries. It also gave them power over the allocation of such precious resources as land, welfare and pension system, and any development money that might filter down to their district. The final transformation of their role in the rural areas had been achieved — from one-time leaders of the resistance to colonisation to (with some notable exceptions) representatives of the white government, lowly officials of state.

During this time the government also paid some attention to the increasingly serious economic decline of the reserves. It realised that if these areas were to function as intended — the home of the bulk of the African population — then it was necessary to try and prop up the remains of the reserves' economy. Their ragged resources of land would have to be stretched still further, to accommodate still more people. A degree of economic development was also necessary to make the new system of reserve government more acceptable to the people, and to offer those who would be permanently excluded from the towns some means of livelihood. Security legislation and reinforced structures of local political control could maintain a certain degree of submission among the rural African population. As in the towns, however, force could not ensure long-term stability. Recurring outbreaks of rural unrest throughout the 1950s made that very clear. Nor could force ensure the long-term viability of the migrant labour system which was still based on the assumption that the families of the migrants would each have a patch of land on which to eke out a living.

The Nationalists therefore took over the system of betterment planning. In the face of the often bitter opposition of the rural population, they introduced harsher penalties for failure to comply with the planning regulations and deposed uncooperative chiefs. They also appointed the Tomlinson Commission in 1954 to investigate and plan the future of the South African reserves.

Most of Tomlinson's recommendations the government rejected as too radical and too expensive. At that stage they did not want development that might offer the reserve population as a whole a real alternative to work in the white towns and on the white farms. Thus they rejected one of Tomlinson's proposals, that industry be encouraged to invest inside the 'Bantu areas'. They did, however, accept a further recommendation, that steps be taken to establish border industries near the reserves. In doing so the government made it absolutely clear that the primary resource to be developed in the reserves was its labour:

> The government regards the development of industries owned by Europeans but requiring a great deal of Native labour, in suitable European areas near Bantu areas, as of paramount importance for the sound socio-economic development of the Bantu areas and intends to take the necessary steps from time to time to make such areas as attractive as possible. (U.G. 14-59)

The establishment of bantustans

The next major step in the political reconstruction of the reserves came in 1959. In that year the government passed the Promotion of Bantu Self-Government Act. With this Act the policy of separate development was fully launched. The political transformation of the reserves into bantustans was established.

The Act sketched out the shape of contemporary South Africa — a large white core and a cluster of client black states dotted along its borders. It was now that the principle of ethnicity came fully into its own. The introduction to the Act stated categorically:

> The Bantu people of the Union of South Africa do not constitute a homogeneous people but form separate national units on the basis of language and culture.

With this as its justification, the Act then proceeded to remove the last traces of parliamentary representation that Africans had been left in 1936 (the Native Representatives). It offered in its place 'the gradual development of self-governing Bantu National Units'. The system of tribal and territorial authorities established in 1951 was to be extended. Considerable executive powers were to be decentralised to the Territorial Authorities of each 'national unit'; they would have the prospect, eventually, of self-government and even independence (though this was only a vague theoretical possibility in 1959).

At that stage only eight 'national units' were identified — North-Sotho, South-Sotho, Tswana, Zulu, Swazi, Xhosa, Tsonga and Venda. The system was not as refined as it would later become. Later, the Xhosa would be split into two — the Transkeian and the Ciskeian variety. Still later, in the mid-1970s, the Ndebele 'national unit' would be discovered and added to the list.

What the Group Areas Act did in a local and regional context, the Promotion of Bantu Self-Government Act did on a national scale. It took the concept of ethnic identity already present within the Group Areas Act and elaborated and expanded it into an even more radical principle of division and control. Under the bantustan system blacks are no longer divided simply along broadly defined racial lines — coloured, Indian and African. Now they are grouped along far narrower ethnic lines: coloured and Indian, as before, and thereafter the proliferation of isolated 'tribes' as determined by the government for each bantustan.

The bantustan policy outlined in 1959 was very simple. Old divisions dating from a pre-conquest past were to be redefined to make 'nations' where before there had often been only loose groupings of chiefdoms and clans. These nations were then to be tied to the bits and pieces of reserve land that had survived the process of conquest of those former chiefdoms and clans during the 19th century. That land — divided by history and pegged down by the Nationalists, as the Deputy Minster put it so aptly in 1975 — was to become the political home of the African people of South Africa. In these areas a new class of black allies of the government would be created — bantustan legislators and civil servants, whose considerable powers would be conditional on their administering their territories to the satisfaction of the central government. Power was thus diffused and fragmented to local agents of control in each bantustan.

Under the bantustan system, traditional culture was co-opted to lend credibility to the new structures of political control. Group rivalries and tensions between the different ethnic groups were institutionalised and encouraged, to counter the political message of African nationalism and of a democratic society in a common South Africa. Instead of a mass of millions of Africans clamouring for political rights, there would henceforth be only a series of dispersed and numerically less threatening ethnic groups — a 'plurality of minorities' as it was once explained. Their exclusion from the centres of wealth and of power could now be justified. Ethnicity provided the key to that ideal state where blacks would feature as 'international units of labour' only (Dr Verwoerd, quoted in Horrell 1973 p42).

> 'The Government does not view all Bantu as one single people, but the Bantu are in fact divided by language, culture and tradition into several peoples or nations, namely, the Xhosas of the Transkei and the Ciskei, the Zulus of Zululand and Natal, the Swazis of Swaziland and Bantu areas contiguous or near to Swaziland, the Bapedi of Sekhukhuneland and neighbourhood, the Venda of the Zoutpansberg, the Shangaans of the Transvaal Lowveld, the Tswanas of Botswana and Bantu areas of the Republic contiguous or near thereto occupied by Republican Tswana tribes, the South Sotho of Lesotho and Witzieshoek. Fortunately for each of these people or nations, history left to them within the borders of the present Republic large tracts of land which serve as their homelands. The Government's policy is, therefore, not a racial policy based on the colour of the skin of the inhabitants of the Republic, but a policy based on the reality and the fact that within the borders of the Republic there are found the White nation and several Bantu nations. The Government's policy is, therefore, not a policy of discrimination on the ground of race or colour, but a policy of differentiation on the ground of nationhood of different nations, granting to each self-determination within the borders of their homelands — hence this policy of separate development.'
> — Chairman of the Bantu Affairs Commission, speaking in Cape Town in May 1968.

Removals begin

> I said emphatically numbers definitely matter if they indicate the extent of integration, and that superfluous Bantu ought to be removed because their presence in the white homeland has promoted integration.
> — GF Froneman, Deputy Minister of Justice, Mines and Planning (*Rand Daily Mail*, 28 March 69)

Along with the creation of national states — the afterbirth of their delivery — went the need to define more tightly than before both the boundaries of their territories and the extent of their peoples. The 1960s and 1970s were years of convulsive upheaval for hundreds of thousands of rural people who were forced to move to try and make nations out of reserves.

Because of the bantustan policy, the removal of black spots became a priority. Although black spots were the creation of an earlier period of native policy, their removal had not been a major issue before the 1950s. Now the continued existence of these African-owned farms cut right through the argument that the bantustans were the only true and traditional homelands of the African population. In 1965 a circular from the Department of Bantu Administration and Development described the removal of black spots in this way:

> With the words 'clearance of black spots' is understood the suspension of *property rights* vested in Bantu in land situated in white areas, that is part of the larger policy of the creation of Bantu homelands that has to be *speeded up*. ('Removal of Black Spots' quoted and translated from the original Afrikaans in Maré 1980 p2. Emphasis in the original.)

Although political factors played a dominant role in generating the black spot removals programme, the choice of where to start in so massive a programme was determined largely by economic considerations. As with the Group Areas Act, there could be large profits in the forced sales and the expropriation for some. This was demonstrated most graphically in the way black spot removals were managed in Natal. The areas to be cleared first and most systematically were the coal-rich districts of Dannhauser, Dundee, Helpmekaar, Newcastle, Utrecht and Vryheid. Of the 38 African farms removed in these districts by 1973, 22 had significant coal deposits. In 1982, 12 of these properties were being mined and 4 had been mined in the past.

Consolidation of the bantustans also became an issue during this time. The officials who had drawn the boundaries of the first reserves, in the late 19th and early 20th centuries, had not had any grand political future for these areas in mind. They left to the Nationalist planners an untidy rag-bag of bits and pieces of land with little geographical and scant political coherence. Tomlinson first raised the problems of the geographical fragmentation of the reserves in the 1950s:

> Save for a few blocks like the Transkei and Vendaland, the Bantu areas

are so scattered that they form no foundation for community growth ... this fragmentation can result in nothing else than a supplementary growth attached to the European community. The fragmentary pattern also results in scattering and consequent incoherence between historically and ethnically related Bantus, and this means that cohesive forces in the social and psychological spheres are paralysed. (U.G. 61-55 pp180—1)

The government accepted consolidation as a long-term project from the early 1960s. One of the biggest problems, however, was to persuade the farmers of the overall political and economic advantages to flow to white South Africa from the major land swops of black and white land that consolidation would require. In 1961 the Department of Bantu Administration and Development sent out a memorandum pleading with Farmers' Associations to cooperate with the land purchasing programme of the Trust. ' "Black spots" cannot be cleared up if compensatory land is not offered', it pointed out. It also went on to describe how 'some smaller Bantu reserves or scheduled areas ... which are some distance away from the larger Bantu areas' could also be regarded as black spots:

The aim is to clear up these smaller reserves or scheduled Native areas and to move their Bantu inhabitants to the larger Bantu areas. This should, however, be regarded as a long-term policy. It is obvious that one should think particularly of the Bantu areas when considering the interests of the Bantu community. It is here in their own areas that they are free to develop. ('Acquisition of land by the South African Native Trust and abolition of Bantu property rights in land in European areas' 1961 p6.)

During the 1960s, as their labour problems eased, white farmers began to abandon their longstanding opposition towards the existence of separate African areas. They continued to defend their local interests vigorously and to watch the land-purchasing activities of the South African Development Trust suspiciously, but their objections to the bantustan policy as such receded. As a result, the Trust could finally begin buying up land in terms of the 1936 quota on a large scale. With this land available the government now had somewhere to dump all those it wanted to move out of the white area. Its black spot removal programme could begin in earnest.

In the early 1960s the first and most notorious of apartheid's relocation camps began to appear on remote stretches of Trust land: Mondlo, Morsgat, Stinkwater, Sada, Dimbaza. By 1969 the government had cleared a total of 119 black spots and removed over 80 000 people out of the white rural area as a result (*Hansard*, Cols 324-326, 7 Feb. 69).

As the bantustan policy was elaborated more fully, influx control became more sophisticated too. By the 1960s manufacturing industry generally had become less labour-intensive, more highly mechanised. The demand of the industrialists for skilled workers was now widespread, their need for a very large pool of unskilled workers on the decline. This meant that the government could raise the barriers that had been erected round the cities in the early 1950s still higher, without causing harm to industry. In the early 1960s it became more difficult for foreign workers from Malawi, Mozambique, Lesotho etc to get jobs in South Africa. At about this time regulations were introduced limiting the presence of Africans in the Western Cape as much as possible. More stringent controls were also placed on the presence of African women in the urban areas. Because of the position of women as the focus of family life, officials regarded them as a key index of how stable and permanent the urban African population was becoming. For this reason, they were anxious to limit their numbers in the urban areas and confine them to the bantustans as much as possible.

AFRICAN WIDOWS AND DIVORCEES IN URBAN AREAS

'During September 1967 the Department of Bantu Administration and Development distributed an official circular reaffirming policy that in some respects had been in force since the previous year.

'No African women were to be placed on the waiting list for family housing in an urban area. Those needing accommodation who qualified to be in the area must seek it as lodgers with registered households.

'If a woman became widowed while she was occupying a house with her husband and family, she could continue to occupy the house only if she qualified in her own right to remain in the area, and she was able to pay rent. If she did not qualify to remain, she must return to her "homeland" with her children, unless special exemption was granted.

'A divorced woman might stay on in her home only if she was not the guilty party and had been granted custody of her children; if she qualified in her own right to remain in the town; if she

> could pay the rent; and if her former husband agreed to vacate the house and transfer the tenancy to her."
> — Horrell, M, *Legislation and Race Relations*, 1971, p42.

From the late 1960s influx control was extended with the beginnings of the urban relocation programme, slotting into the border industry programme which had already been put into practice. The policy of relocating African townships across bantustan boundaries, and transforming their workers into commuters, constituted a major attack on the privileges of that small minority of Africans who qualified for permanent urban residence. The estimated 670 000 people removed in this way between 1968 and 1980 — into Mdantsane, Garankuwa, Kabokweni, Pampierstad, Mphophomeni and the numerous other 'bantu towns' being developed at this time to receive them — all lost their qualifications for permanent urban residence in the white urban aeas. With that, they lost the privilege of being able to look for and choose work relatively freely in these areas. They were more firmly locked into the labour bureau network. Said a woman relocated out of the East London township of Duncan Village into Mdantsane 20 kilometres away in the Ciskei:

> Nowadays I am sent to a madam by the labour office and when I get there she will say she has engaged somebody else already. I am left to pay the return fare for nothing. (Quoted in Mayer 1971 p297)

At the same time, all these people became the direct responsibility of their respective bantustan administrations. It was to them that they now had to look for the schools, hospitals, pensions and other services that are in such short supply in most black areas. 'I don't know who can help us', said one person interviewed by SPP in the relocation township of Ezakheni in Natal, 'KwaZulu government is supposed to help us, but they can't.'

Controls in the countryside

Keeping pace with the unfolding of the separate development policy, intervening in its development at several points, were important changes in the white rural areas. The process of economic growth and modernisation in the white agricultural sector that had started after the Second World War continued during the 1950s and 1960s. Backward, uneconomic methods of farming were being pushed aside in favour of a more aggressive, profit-orientated approach. Farming was becoming a big business. There were more tractors and harvesters and combines on the farms. The area under cultivation was expanding. At the same time, the size of individual farms was on the increase and the number of farmers on the land on the decline.

Table 12: Indices of Agricultural Change, 1960-1975

	REAL ANNUAL CAPITAL FORMATION (FIXED IMPROVEMENTS AND MACHINERY)		REAL ANNUAL EXPENDITURE ON INTERMEDIATE GOODS (FUEL, FERTILIZER, PESTICIDE)		FARMING UNITS (in 1000s)
	INDEX	ANNUAL GROWTH RATE (%)	INDEX	ANNUAL GROWTH RATE (%)	
1960	100		100		106
1	91		101		
2	99	0,6	102	1,9	
3	106		98		
4	111		111		101
1965	103		110		95
6	104		116		
7	126	8,5	127	5,8	93
8	138		137		93
9	148		134		91
1970	155		146		
1	170		151		90
2	167	6,9	156	2,1	86
3	174		159		82
4	175		158		80
1975	216		162		78

Source: Derived from Abstracts of Agricultural Statistics, 1981

With this, the labour requirements of the farmers began to change as well. Farmers were now wanting to develop a smaller but more highly skilled workforce to manage the new machines. In the farming industry as a whole, the labour shortages of the 1930s and 1940s and 1950s were now becoming labour surplusses; the once loud complaint of the farmers that they did not have enough labour was becoming less common. The large numbers of people that they had succesfully chained to the rural areas were becoming a further category of the superfluous and nonproductive. Only in isolated districts, where the changeover to modern methods of farming lagged behind, were farmers still anxious to keep a large African population on their land to assure themselves of a pool of labour.

Already in the 1950s many farmers were abandoning the labour tenant system of farm labour in favour of a system of full-time wage labour. Those tenants who would not agree to the change, or whose labour was no longer needed, were being evicted. Excluded from the towns, no longer needed on the farms, these were the truly surplus people. In 1962 the Chief Bantu Affairs Commissioner for Natal urged farmers who were intending to evict farmworkers to contact his Department first: the 'flood' of Africans who were being driven off white farms without having any alternative accommodation were causing the Department problems (*NAUNLU*, 27 April 62).

Along with these economic changes went changes in the structure of the rural population as well. The white rural population had been declining steadily since the 1920s, when a large exodus of white rural poor towards the towns first became noticeable. In the 1950s this process speeded up. Those farmers who could not keep pace with the new economic developments went under. They sold their farms and headed for the towns. At the same time, the black population was continuing to grow, dammed up behind the walls that had been built around the white rural areas by influx control. In many districts the population of the supposedly 'white' rural areas was almost entirely black:

> Witnesses stated that many farms occupied by Whites were now managed by Non-white foremen. The homesteads of the White farmers, managers and share-croppers are now either uninhabited, abandoned and neglected, or else are occupied by the Non-white and his family. Evidence of this development is particularly strong in the southern and south-eastern parts of the Free State and certain parts of Natal. (The Du Toit Commission, quoted in Davenport and Hunt 1974 p60.)

This was the finding of a government commission appointed especially to investigate the problem of what was being termed *die beswarting van die platteland* - the blackening of the countryside. This commission used a map that illustrated this trend with great threatening blobs of black scattered across the page. (What the commission failed to print out was that many of the Natal farms that it identified as 'occupied' by blacks on the map, were in fact owned by blacks.) What it was describing was a process of reoccupation of the land by those who had been pushed so firmly out of the way by the first white settlers. Now

Separate Development after 1948

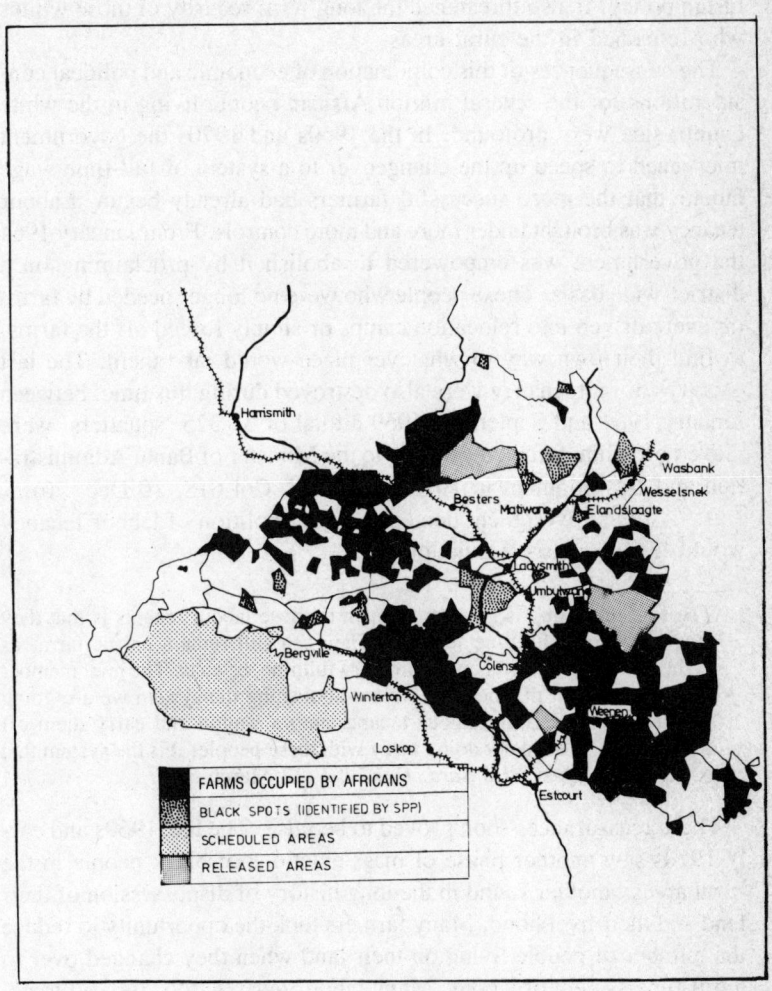

Map 10: 'Die Beswarting van die Platteland' — Natal, 1960

that farm labour was no longer in short supply, it was a development that the government could no longer tolerate. It undermined the bantustan policy. It also threatened the long-term security of those whites who remained in the rural areas.

The consequences of this combination of economic and political considerations for the several million African people living in the white countryside were profound. In the 1960s and 1970s the government intervened to speed up the changeover to a system of full-time wage labour that the more successful farmers had already begun. Labour tenancy was brought under more and more controls. From January 1964 the government was empowered to abolish it by proclaiming on a district-wide basis. Those people who were no longer needed by farming were driven into relocation camps or simply forced off the farms, to find their own way to whatever place would take them. The last enclaves of rent tenancy were also destroyed during this time: between January 1964 and September 1969 a total of 34 325 'squatters' were moved off white farms, according to the Minister of Bantu Administration and Development in 1970. (*Hansard*, Col 618, 10 Dec. 70).

At first the government denied that the abolition of labour tenancy would lead to massive evictions:

> The first thing that is going to happen to those labour tenants is that they may all become fulltime servants. They can still remain on the farms as in the past but they will now be ordinary fulltime servants. The hon. member must not suggest that because we are abolishing the system we are going to load all the existing labour tenants onto a wagon and carry them off somewhere. We are not doing away with these people; it is the system that is being abolished. (*Hansard*, Col 2957, 12 March 64)

These reassurances soon proved to be false. The late 1960s and early 1970s saw another phase of mass evictions of black people in the rural areas: another round in the long history of dispossession of their land and their livelihood. Many farmers took the opportunity to reduce the number of people living on their land when they changed over to a full-time system of labour. Many labour tenants, too, refused to accept the loss of independence and economic status that was involved:

> We then heard that the six-month system had been abolished and we had to work for the farmer all year round in order to continue living on our land. We were quite agreeable to this but said that our children would starve if we had to live on the low wages that we were getting on the farm for the whole 12 months. If the farmer would pay us more, we would gladly

stay on the farm where we were happy. The farmer refused.

The Bantu Administration Department told us if we were unwilling to work for the whole 12 months we would have to go to the location... They used GG lorries to cart some of the people and their belongings to this place. But as soon as we refused to work for the farmer at the wages he was paying us he ordered us off the land and threatened us with jail if we did not move at once. (From *'Dombi Khumalo's Story'*, SPP Vol 4 p325)

By January 1969 labour tenancy had been abolished throughout the Orange Free State and the Transvaal. The government announced that it intended to have the system phased out everywhere by 1970. In Natal, however, many of the Farmers' Associations put up a strong rearguard fight against too rapid a phasing out of the system.

'The tenant system is still in operation because it is the only one many farmers can afford', said the president of the Natal Agricultural Union, in 1966 (*Natal Witness*, 16 Sept. 66). In 1970 the Union identified the strong resistance of many labour tenants as a major reason for delaying the abolition of the system:

So until full-time farm employment is desired by employees, or movement of dissidents controlled, many farmers cannot abolish labour tenants. To decree from Pretoria that they should, is to ignore the facts. (*NAUNLU*, 9 Jan. 70.)

The Natal farmers eventually succeeded in persuading the government to slow its programme down. After 1 August 1970 no new labour contracts would be allowed, but those that were already registered with the authorities could remain. This ruling remained in force until the final abolition of the system was gazetted in August 1980.

The ultimate dispossession

As the years progressed, the function of the bantustans as enlarged relocation camps became more and more pronounced. As each new category of surplus people emerged or was called into being — labour tenants, unwanted farmworkers, the growing numbers of the urban unemployed — the dumping-ground function became progressively more important.

As more and more people were crowded on to the land, subsistence farming declined still further. From areas that had once subsidised the migrant labour system, the bantustans had been turned into areas that were almost totally dependent on income coming from the outside areas for their continued existence — on money sent back by migrant or commuter workers, on pensions, on emergency relief, and on grants from Pretoria.

At the same time as their economic decline became more severe, their political transformation became more advanced. During the 1960s South Africa was driven further and further down the path of political fragmentation that had been mapped out in 1959. In 1963 a Legislative Assembly was established in the Transkei, historically the largest and politically most developed of all the one-time reserves. In 1968 the Transkei Assembly made a formal request for independence as soon as possible. At that stage the Minister of Bantu Administration and Development described the road to independence as a 'long and difficult' one (Horrell 1973 p42). By 1970, however, with the passage of the Bantu Homelands Citizenship Act, the journey had been considerably shortened.

This Act was influx control at its most radical. Now even those African people who had permanent urban residence rights were in danger of having those rights swept away. Explained Minister Connie Mulder in 1976:

> The identification of the black man with his own nation will put the socalled privilege of Section Ten ... in the shade. Section 10 ... will possibly not need to be repealed because the nations concept will overshadow it ... No black person will eventually qualify in terms of Section 10 because they will all be aliens and, as such, will only be able to occupy the houses bequeathed to them by their fathers [in the urban areas] by special permission of the Minister. (Quoted in Maré 1980 p17)

Having ensured that the constitutional developments in the bantustans would affect the entire African population, Prime Minister Vorster then announced that the government was open to independence negotiations with the bantustans. The major stumbling-block of their economic backwardness and poverty was pushed aside nonchalantly. While greater economic viability was desirable, it was not essential for independence negotiations to begin, Vorster said.

The following year the Bantu Homelands Constitution Act was passed. This made provision for the establishment of Transkei-type Legislative Assemblies in all the other bantustans. During 1971 and 1972 these were duly proclaimed. It was now that consolidation moved to the fore as a major issue. In 1975 the Minister of Bantu Administration and Development spelt out the dimensions of the consolidation programme thus:

> It is an historic day today, since today we have come to the last round of the Parliamentary work in connection with what is called the consolidation of the Bantu areas.... There are actually four aspects in connection with this work: In the first place, the definition of the areas within which released areas for the Bantu people may be declared; in the second place, the clearing of Bantu freehold land; in the third place, the excision of poorly situated Bantu reserves, or parts thereof; and in the fourth place, the attempt to consolidate the scattered areas of the Bantu homelands, by the aforementioned three actions, into single units.... Here we have proof of the will of the Government and the National Party to carry out this task of honour actively and to meet the difficult challenge. (*Hansard*, Cols 5925/6, 14 May 75.)

At that stage government sources estimated that a million people would have to be removed to make their plans work (*Black Development in South Africa*, BENBO 1976 p23).

The final phase in this process of exclusion was reached in 1976 when the Transkei became the first bantustan to accept Pretoria-style independence. From pariahs in the land of their birth in Sol Plaatje's day in 1913, African South Africans were being turned into foreigners in the land of their birth. It was the ultimate dispossession.

THE CREATION OF GAZANKULU: ETHNIC ENGINEERING

Gazankulu is one of the ten bantustans. It comprises three pieces — two on the western border of the Kruger National Park and a third near Tzaneen in the North-Eastern Transvaal. The northern segment is normally green, with rolling hills, while the southern part of Mhala is far more densely populated, drier and dustier. The drought has taken a heavy toll.

For most South Africans, Gazankulu is barely known. For nearly one million Tsonga-speaking people, it is the bantustan they are tied to by apartheid policies. Only half of them actually live there. The rest are citizens of Gazankulu whether they like it or not, have ever been there or not, know anyone there or not.

In 1970, 41% of Tsonga-speakers lived in Gazankulu while

the rest lived in other bantustans (namely Venda, Lebowa, Bophuthatswana and Kangwane) or in 'white' South Africa. Following constant removals in the 1970s, the government has managed to shift Tsongas into Gazankulu and 'foreigners' into neighbouring bantustans, bringing the percentage of Tsonga-speakers living in Gazankulu to 43%.

The process by which this self-governing bantustan was created illustrates an issue raised in the last chapter: ethnicity is not necessarily based on traditional structures but may be a manipulation of ethnic issues such as common history, similar language or diet, to redefine a group of people. Rather than adding to the rich diversity of cultures it is used to divide and redirect people.

Tsonga people came across the Lebombo mountains from Portuguese East Africa at various times during the 19th century. They settled under many different chiefs throughout the North-Eastern and Eastern Transvaal. Although they spoke linguistically linked dialects, they did not speak quite the same language or have a common culture. Most of them had come from Gaza province, having been pushed north by various Nguni groups fleeing from the Zulu in the 1820s. (Hence the name Gazankulu — 'large Gaza'.) Once in the Transvaal they became subjects of Sotho and Venda chiefs and 'usually failed to muster sufficient strength to form tribes of any importance', according to NJ van Warmelo, the government ethnologist (quoted in Harries 1983 p6).

As urbanisation increased and Africans made political and economic demands on the government, there was a need to control the trend. As the Minister of Native Affairs said in 1950:

> It is generally acknowledged that the urban Native who no longer feels himself bound by his tribal control becomes a social danger, because there is nothing else to replace that form of control. It will definitely be worth one's while to consider whether this type of Native cannot again become part of a progressively orientated tribal relationship to the advantage of all concerned. (Quoted in Harries 1983 p28.)

Soon afterwards, the Bantu Authorities Act (1951) was passed. This Act dealt with tribal organisations and chiefs. It was not until 1959, when the Promotion of Bantu Self-Government Act was passed, that separate geographic areas were outlined. The Tomlinson Commission report had recommended a 'Tsonga-

Venda heartland' in the North-Eastern Transvaal to encourage economic and political development in certain areas. At that stage there was no thought of a separate 'Tsongastan'. But in several areas Tsonga-speakers felt they were discriminated against by Venda and North Sotho chiefs. As a result of complaints from Tsonga chiefs, intellectuals and leaders of the Tsonga Presbyterian Church, Van Warmelo and the Department of Bantu Affairs and Development drew an ethnic border between Tsonga and Venda in 1963. Over 50 000 Tsongas then fell on the wrong side of the border and were under threat of removal.

With the Bantu Homelands Citizenship Act of 1970, as outlined in Chapter 2, *all* Africans became citizens of one or other bantustan whether they liked it or not. In 1973 Gazankulu was declared a self-governing territory, with Giyani as its capital. Its Legislative Assembly comprised 68 members — 42 appointed and 26 elected. The Chief Minister, Prof Hudson Ntsanwisi, head of the Tsonga Presbyterian Church, was an appointed member who was elected to his post unopposed. Unlike Venda and Bophuthatswana, the Chief Minister here need not be a chief.

To date the Gazankulu Legislative Assembly has refused to take 'independence' while it is economically dependent on the rest of South Africa.

Meanwhile ethnic conflict grows. In furtherance of government policy people who have been living together for a hundred years find themselves on land scheduled for Lebowa or Gazankulu or Venda or Kangwane. Families are torn apart as one side is claimed by one bantustan, the other by another. Thousands of people are moved to 'clear' areas, making them ethnically pure. Reports of harassment of North Sothos by Gazankulu, of Tsongas by Venda etc are similar to the pressures sending thousands of non-Tswanas from Winterveld to settle in KwaNdebele.

Ethnic conflict makes government policy look prophetically correct, whereas it is the cause of the trouble. There are ethnic loyalties but, particularly in the case of Gazankulu, these divisions are manipulated to keep blacks competing for local limited resources such as small business development grants or jobs in the civil service. The very imposition of ethnic structures from above has resulted in ethnic conflict from below.

CHAPTER SIX

'Getting them away' — GG at work

In 1969, when the clearance of black spots and labour tenants was at its height, MC Botha, then Minister of Bantu Administration and Development, said:

> We get their cooperation in all cases voluntarily. As a matter of fact, sometimes it is necessary to do quite a lot of persuasion, but we do get them away. (Interview on SABC, 20 Nov. 69)

'Cooperation', 'voluntary removals', 'persuasion': these have been the constant themes in official accounts of removals. However, most of the people who are 'persuaded' to move describe their experience in very different terms from those used by government officials and Cabinet Ministers. Here are three examples of the massive gap that exists between what officials say is happening and what people experience as happening to them:

The removal of the Tsitsikama reserves to Elukhanyweni in the Ciskei 1977/78
What one of the women who was moved said when interviewed by SPP:

> This thing came so sudden upon us that I cannot tell you what happened, this thing came so sudden upon us, yes. We did not know that we are coming here, we did not know where we are going to...Yes, they did tell us but it took so long before they came to us. When they came to us, they stalked us. They stalked us because they did not say to us which day or which day. When they came to us, they came with guns and police and with all sorts of things they came to us. And then we see that we are here. Then we had no choice, the guns were behind us. They did not say anything, they just threw our belongings in and they broke off as they went. There is nothing to say or the gun is through your head. If I just talk, the gun is through my head. Soldiers and everything were there. What can we say now, we are not used to these things. Then we have to get in, what can we do. They shoot us dead, then we have to get in, what can we do. No they did not say anything, they just said get in, so that we are here today. We did not know, we still do not know this place... And when we came here, they dumped our things, just dumped our things so that we are still here. What can we do now, we can do nothing. We can do nothing. What can we do?

What Dr Koornhof said in parliament:

> Initially 82 families were voluntarily resettled... However, the remaining approximately 426 families refused to move... It then became necessary to obtain a State President's order, in terms of Section 5 of Act No. 38 of 1927, to bring about the resettlement. That was five years ago... (*Hansard*, Col 9491, 11 June 82.)

The removal of the black spot 'The Swamp' to Compensation on Trust land in 1978
What the former landowner of this black spot said:

> It was in September when the Europeans from Pretoria came to our farm The Swamp. They said they are the GG company. They told me that we are going to be moved from this farm because it is in the white area. We were told that they need no cattle, no sheep and no goats at Mpendle, where we are at present, and that there is not sufficient place for ploughing. We were given three month time notice. I did not want to move from The Swamp. I asked them to give some more months so that I can have some provision. They refused to do so. There came the magistrate from Himeville court telling me that we are left with three days. On Monday the GG lorries started their work. They finished their job within three days. (Letter, AFRA files.)

What Dr Koornhof said:

> ...the heir of the land was provided with compensatory land of equivalent agricultural or pastoral value — in size actually far bigger — and the squatters were placed in a properly laid out settlement with cash compenstion for their improvements and adequate temporary accommodation. Previously these people were illegal squatters on the owner's land but the settlement area has now been provided in addition, and adjacent to his land. In conclusion I must say that the slum conditions under which these people lived on the swamp [*sic*] created a health hazard and we had no option but to remove them. (Letter, AFRA files.)

The removal of the tenants from Klipfontein to Glenmore (destined for the Ciskei) in 1979*
What one of the people said in an affidavit:

> That the authorities came to our home on the 3rd April and that my mother informed them that we could not move because my father was in hospital. The authorities again came on Wednesday the 4th April. The officials from the Eastern Cape Administration Board then informed my mother that they

---

*Both the Tsitsikama and the Klipfontein removals are described in the following chapter.

were going to break the house down. When I returned to my house I found my mother on the truck and that all our possessions were on another lorry. My wife and children have been transferred involuntarily to Glenmore.

What the Chief Commissioner for the Eastern Cape Administration Board said:

All we used was persuasion. How 6 whites can force 1 400 people to board trucks is beyond me. If we had tried there would have been incidents and there were no incidents yesterday. (*Eastern Province Herald*, 5 April 79.)

What these starkly contrasting views on removals reveal is that in this process the government is massively powerful. It has concentrated into its hands the power of the law, the power of the police and the military and of education and of control over newspapers and the radio. In removing people it is the government that holds the initiative. It decides which communities are to be moved and when; its local representatives determine the timing and the manner in which the removal will be carried out.

By comparison, those faced with removal are largely powerless. From the start they are forced onto the defensive, confronted with a decision about their lives and the future of their community that comes from outside, from above. Almost all of those who have been moved under apartheid's laws are black and thus unable to vote for the central or provincial governments. They have no say in the law-making process that surrounds their removal; neither are the officials administering the laws accountable to them. In the majority of cases the people to be moved are poor. They cannot afford expensive lawyers' fees or trips to distant government officials or sympathetic political organisations. Most have little or no formal education — many cannot read such eviction notices as they may receive and do not know what the officials may and may not do in terms of 'the law' or 'maintaining the peace'. Most of them are rural people. They are isolated from potential sources of support in the urban areas and also from information about what other communities facing similar problems to them have tried. They are susceptible to rumour and very vulnerable to intimidation and manipulation by officials and security police; they fear the informers in their midst. Almost all of them have already experienced, in one way or another, the coercive power of the government, either personally or through family members struggling for paper, for jobs, for pensions, for houses. They know the risks that a black person runs in challenging the authorities.

> We did not like to go because we were born there. It was only that we heard that the government wanted it and we submitted to that. (*AFRA* Report 14.)

That was how one woman who was removed from a black spot called Kwapitela in Natal in July 1981 described the process — submission to an alien and anonymous government with awesome powers.*

The fact that the government is so powerful does not mean that it always gets its way. As the next two chapters show, <u>many communities have fought fiercely, sometimes successfully, against being moved</u>. It does, however, mean that the government starts the removal process with an enormous advantage — an advantage that is often overwhelming.

In the rest of the chapter, the process of removal is looked at from the side of advantage — from the official side. First we describe briefly the various stages that people faced with removal have to go through. We then look in more detail at the advantages that the government exercises over them — the advantage of the law, of the police and the military, of control over resources and information.

Here we review the shift in government tactics that has taken place in recent years, away from the direct use of force and towards a greater reliance on indirect methods of coercion to pressurise people to move voluntarily. The chapter concludes by looking at the role of the bantustan governments in enforcing removals.

The other side of the process, that of the responses from threatened communities or individuals, is considered in Chapter 8. This division of a single process into two separate chapters is, of course, artificial: in practice both sides are confronting and affecting the other from the start. Linking these two chapters, Chapter 7 shows the variety of ways in which this interaction between advantaged and disadvantaged may take place. Here we describe the struggles of six different communities against relocation.

*The stages of removal***

The precise manner in which a community is removed will depend on

---

*This removal is also described in the following chapter.
**In this and the following section discussion on the legal process involved is necessarily brief. It is a very complex issue, with different laws applying in different circumstances. Readers interested in knowing more about the legal aspects of relocation are referred to Volume 1 of the SPP reports.

several factors. These include the legal status of the land on which they are living (freehold, white-owned, townships, reserve, etc); the urgency of the removal for the government; the level of organisation within the community; and the personality of the local official or officials who are in charge of seeing the removal carried out.

There is no single experience of removal. Some communities resist. Many submit. Individuals are easier for the government to move than communities; small communities are easier to move than large ones. Sometimes the removal of a community is a long-drawn-out affair. It may drag on miserably over many years — a slow whittling away of the community, a few households at a time, until eventually it ceases to exist. At other times it is a dramatic uprooting and relocating of people in a single swoop. One week there is a community, with its own particular life and institutions. The next week it is destroyed, the people gone, the buildings in ruin, its history wiped out.

There are, however, certain common stages which can be identified in most types of removal. For most communities the threat of removal starts with vague and disturbing rumours that begin to circulate. Somebody saw a government official visiting the chief; somebody heard that the people down the road have been removed; somebody was told that their community was the next to be deproclaimed. These rumours may be sufficiently unsettling to make some members of the community move away early, by themselves, in the hope that they will find a more secure place to live somewhere else.

The next stage is the official notice. This may take several forms, depending on who is being removed. In the case of a township being deproclaimed or a group area being proclaimed, the notice appears in the Government Gazette. Thereafter the people are generally informed of what is to happen to them at a meeting called by the local officials.

The removal of a scheduled area also requires that notice be printed in the Government Gazette. However, people who live on scheduled land are entitled to refuse to obey the notice. If this happens, then the government has to get parliament to authorise the removal by means of a resolution before the people can be removed legally.

In the case of a freehold farm (a black spot), the landowners should receive a formal 'Notice of Expropriation' to inform them that the government intends taking over their property:

> Kindly take notice that the following immovable property together with all improvements thereon ... in respect of which you are the registered owner(s) are hereby expropriated ... on behalf of the Republic of South Africa ...

The tenants, not being registered owners of their land, do not qualify for a legal notice of this sort. Depending on who is in charge of the removal, they may get written notice that they are to be moved. More commonly, however, the local magistrate or administration board official will call a general meeting to tell them what is to happen. Sometimes there is no formal notification at all of the proposed removals. The tenants only hear about it from the landowners, or even from outsiders. SPP fieldworkers several times had the experience of arriving at a threatened community and finding out that nobody there had any inkling that the government intended to remove them.

During this notice stage officials may arrive to number properties. The large number painted carelessly on the front door has become one of the symbols of relocation. Often it is the first sign that a community will get that they are earmarked for removal. Whether or not officials have the right to deface properties in this way has never ben tested in court, but most people are too scared to paint out the numbers on their own. These numbers appear to serve several functions for the officials. They are a way of identifying households for compenstion purposes — house No. X, worth so much, belongs to family Y. This provides a count of how many households there are in the community. They also have a control function. Any house or building that is not numbered is easily identifiable, making it difficult for new people to enter the area or for established residents to erect new buildings.

If officialdom regards the occupants of an area as illegal — as squatters — then their position is far more precarious. They may get no warning of their impending removal at all. At the black spot of Umbulwane in Natal, the first notice that tenants got that they were to be removed, apart from numbers on their doors, was the arrival of bulldozers to demolish their houses. (This case is described in the following chapter.) Local officials may, however, issue their own notices to squatters to move or demolish their shacks. These notices range from neatly typed messages on official notepaper to hastily scrawled notes without dates or letterheads. At the informal settlement of Richmond Farm near Durban the process of notice had an especially vicious twist. Occupants had to sign an undertaking that they would move on demand from the officials — a kind of 'hanging' notice that the authorities could use as and when they wished.

Farmworkers are in the most precarious position of all. Unless they are on a special contract, they are not entitled to more than a calendar month in notice time, although individual farmers may give longer.

The farmer is also not compelled to give any reason for ordering a worker and his family to move. As in the case of Jamangile Tsotsobe, it may be simply because he dislikes the worker, or considers him to be 'cheeky'. Often the farmer does not even go through the legal motions of notice — he dismisses the worker on the spot, knowing that very few farmworkers are in a position to challenge the legality of what he is doing. The farmer also has no responsibility for finding alternative accommodation for those he has evicted. They may apply to the local commissioner for a site in a relocation area. Often they wander desperately from farm to farm searching for a new place to stay and a new job.

RICHMOND FARM UNDERTAKING

UNDERTAKING

I, - - - , N.I.N. - - -, occupier of shack No. - - - on the South African Development Trust Farm Richmond/Dalmeny do hereby acknowledge that I am occupying premises and have erected structures on the said Farm without permission and that I am, therefore, illegally in occupation. I do hereby undertake that:-

(a) I will demolish the structure erected by me and remove the Building materials and other property belonging to me and my family, and
(b) vacate the aforesaid Farm together with my family,

immediately I am advised by written notice that the structures I am occupying are in the way of developments in the area or of any planning of the area. In my absence at the time of delivery of the notice at aforesaid premises, the service of the notice on an adult inmate or the fixing of the notice to the door of said premises shall be deemed to be sufficient notice for purposes of this undertaking.

Should I not have demolished aforesaid structure occupied by me and not have removed the materials upon my departure from the place I hereby give consent to and acknowledge the right of the Commissioner Durban or his authorised representative to demolish said structures and to dispose of the materials at his discretion.

I specifically acknowledge that the State shall not be liable to pay or compensate me for any buildings, structures or improvements and for any expense, inconvenience, loss or damage of whatever nature incurred as a result of my having to vacate premises or having to remove from aforesaid area, and specifically also in respect of any building material or other property left behind upon my departure.

I undertake to take steps immediately to find alternative accommodation and, in any event, to organise now to place myself in a position to build a house of my own elsewhere should a residential site become available to me in a planned area. I acknowledge that this document does not confer on me any occupational rights or any preferential claim on alternative accommodation on state-owned land.

WITNESS
1.
2.   SIGNED

Signed before me at NTUZUMA on this the - - day of - - - 19 .

(SIGNATURE)

DESIGNATION

THE DIVISIONAL COUNCIL OF THE CAPE

P.O. Box 1073
Telephone: 41-3266

44 Wale Street,
CAPE TOWN.
8001

DATE: 5/10/77

Mr./Mrs. W. M'onyeni
Structure No. AQ21

Dear Sir/Madam,

PROPOSED DEMOLITION IN TERMS OF SECTION 3B OF THE PREVENTION OF ILLEGAL SQUATTING ACT, 1951 AS AMENDED.

Please note that within 5-Five ~~7~~ days of the date hereof my Council intends to demolish the structure which you are occupying without legal permission in contravention of Section 1(a) of the Prevention of Illegal Squatting Act No. 52 of 1951, as amended and to remove the material thereof from the land.

Yours faithfully, *[handwritten Xhosa text]*

for W.R. VIVIER
SECRETARY

I hereby certify I have served a copy of this letter on
..Mrs. Angelina M'onyeni..
Place: Crossroads
Date: 6/15/77

SIGNATURE

5-Day Eviction Notice (This was actually used as a 5-hour eviction notice at Crossroads in 1977)

> **STATEMENT BY A WOMAN EVICTED OFF A FARM AT WEENEN, NATAL, 1980**
>
> I have always lived at _____ and my father and my grandfather. I have 6 children. The eldest is about 18, the youngest about 5. My husband deserted us a long time ago. One of my children worked on the farm — a boy. He's about 16. He earns R12 a month. The farmer gave us three months' notice. We didn't get a letter. This was before Christmas but we had nowhere to go. So I was arrested with two other women. I was in jail for 6 days. I paid R35 to get out, and am still staying on the farm. We expect to be arrested again at any moment.

The length of time between notice being served and the actual removal of people varies considerably depending on the circumstances of the community. This may be a period of negotiation between the community and the officials — about the removal, about the terms on which the people are to be moved, about compensation. Often, however, it is a dead time. Sometimes years may go by between the first notice of removal and the actual event. In the case of The Swamp, the landowners were expropriated in 1970 but not moved till 1978 — eight years later, by when most people had allowed the threat of removal to slip into the back of their minds. When the removal began, it was an unexpected shock.

The actual process of removal varies as well. In the rural areas, official removals are almost always by truck — the infamous GG trucks — sometimes supplemented by buses. 'We were brought on GG trucks like cattle' is how one person described it to SPP. The government keeps fleets of trucks at removals depots located at central points in the various regions. These can then be sent wherever they are required. Another common feature of rural removals is that the workers who are used to demolish the houses and drive the trucks are often not local people. They do not speak the language of the people whom they are moving so that the possibility of communication between the workers and the removed is eliminated. Thus the removal of the Zulu-speaking people of Kwapitela, in Natal, was carried out by non-Zulu-speaking workers from the Transvaal. Similarly, the removal from the Tsitsikama reserves in the Eastern Cape was carried out by workers from Natal.

Compensation

Compensation for the value of the houses and other improvements left behind by those who are removed, is only paid out to those whom the government considers legal residents of an area — registered landowners, registered or approved tenants, established residents in a reserve area. Squatters do not qualify for compensation for their houses; neither do farmworkers. (They are, however, entitled to take whatever they can of their building material etc with them.) The level of compensation varies as well. Only registered landowners are compensated for the value of their land, for instance. Tenants and reserve communities who do not own the land on which they are living are compensated for their improvements only (houses, trees, fences etc). However, reserve communities living under a chief on land held on communal tenure are normally given some agricultural land at their relocation site.

Compensation is a particularly controversial issue. Few people who are removed are satisfied with the money they receive, yet few are prepared to challenge the officials. Most people do not know what the law says about compensation. Frequently they are scared that by making a fuss they will draw unwelcome attention to themselves and will lose the little money they have been given. For many of those battling to live on small and irregular incomes, their compensation money appears at first like an unexpected bonus. They are usually paid in cash. Although the amount is unlikely to rise above several hundred rands in most cases, this is still a very large sum for them to receive all at once. It is only when they start to rebuild that they realise how inadequate the money is — how little it covers. By that stage, much of the money is already gone, spent on household goods and other items that previously had been totally out of reach.

'Daybreak robbery' is how one person who was removed in 1976 has described the process of compensation.

> In fact, nobody was happy with the compensation they got for either their land or their houses. In my case, I had a tea-room which I built in 1964 ... you know what I was offered for that tea-room? For the shop I was offered R1 680; for the toilet R5 ... ; for the trees (we had good trees round the shop) R10; the place was fenced and for the fence I was offered R5. Gross compensation — for everything — R 1 700. That is what I was expected to take. But to build a shop elsewhere, today, you need R20 000! (Mngadi 1981 p.66.)

The advantages of power

The law

The government goes to great lengths to insist that in removing people it acts in a lawful and humane way. It is quick to justify its actions on the grounds that many of those being removed are 'illegal', with no rights to be where they are. Thus, in the letter already quoted, the landowner's tenants at The Swamp, (many of them tenants of long standing) were described as 'illegal squatters' by Koornhof. Similarly, those families being harried and arrested and endorsed out of town in informal settlements around the country are branded with the labels 'illegals', 'aliens', 'unqualified persons'; also, on occasion, 'criminals' and 'vagrants'. Their houses are described as slums, illegal structures that contravene health and town planning regulations. Where removals of clearly lawful communities are carried out, they are 'in accordance with policy' and always with 'compassion and due respect for human dignity'.

South Africa, we are told over and over again, is a Christian and democratic country. Dr Koornhof would never allow blacks to be simply dumped in the veld, said his Deputy Minister in April 1980: 'The Minister of Co-operation and Development is a Christian and he would not allow such a thing to happen'. (*Natal Mercury*, 17 April 1980). South Africa upholds Western values. In South Africa the rule of law prevails.

And so it does. People are driven from their homes, loaded onto trucks and transported to relocation sites, their properties are numbered and expropriated, their houses are demolished by bulldozers and they are prevented from entering certain areas, all in terms of the law. Legislative sanction exists for every one of these procedures; in most cases more than one law can be used as authorisation for officials. Different laws apply in the various categories. In some the law does offer greater protection than in others. Those with titledeeds are assured of better treatment than those without; scheduled land cannot be cleared quite as easily as non-scheduled land.

None of the protections that do exist can stop removals, however. In all categories relocation takes place in terms of the law. Individual officials may get carried away and go beyond the bounds of the law — evict a lawful resident from his property without giving proper notice, for instance. Yet such excesses are never really necessary; the powers granted officials in South African law are sufficiently sweeping to enable them to get rid of whoever they want lawfully.

In South Africa the law is an instrument of control. It is there to implement government policy. The rule of law is the rule of a repressive, minority government.

As already described, the government has built up its arsenal of laws systematically, since the 1950s. Successive Acts of parliament have concentrated massive discretionary powers in the hands of the Prime Minister and his Cabinet. Parliament's own power to decide policy has been whittled away, the courts' power to review legislation and to judge on the legality or otherwise of government actions has been bypassed.

Thus, the Black Administration Act (which was passed in 1927 but retained and adapted by the Nationalists) empowers the State President (i.e. the Cabinet) to define by proclamation the boundaries of the land set aside for any African tribe, to alter that from time to time, to divide tribes into two or more parts, and to order any African tribe, community or individual to move from any one place within the Republic to any other place that he may specify. Neither parliament nor the courts can intervene to prevent him exercising these powers as and when he wishes. The prevention of Illegal Squatting Act empowers officials to demolish illegal structures without having to give prior notice to the owners. The Expropriation Act allows the government to expropriate (take ownership of) any property that it considers is needed for 'public purposes'. The owner or lawful occupier of that land cannot challenge the expropriation in court. All the owner can do is go to court to contest the compensation that the government offers for the land, if he or she is not satisfied with that. The National States Constitution Act empowers the government to amend the boundaries of the bantustans merely by proclamation in the Government Gazette — to say 'This piece of land is no longer part of Lebowa, it is now part of KwaNdebele' or 'This piece of KwaZulu is now to become white land'. The only restriction on this power is that the government does have to 'consult' with the executive council of the bantustan concerned first — but it does not have to get the council's consent.

Even where it can be shown that the government may be acting illegally in the way it is removing people or demolishing housing, the victim cannot go to court for an interdict to get the government to stop whatever it is doing while the courts decide whether its actions are illegal or not. The Black Prohibition of Interdicts Act prevents this — prevents what is considered a basic right in democratic law throughout the world, and prevents it specifically for Africans. In terms of this law, the courts cannot intervene to restrain a government official from proceeding with any order, warrant, direction, notice or instruction issued under any law or purporting to be issued under any law, which orders an African person to be removed from or not to enter any particular area. In other words, an African person with legal qualifications to be in Cape Town may be arrested and incorrectly deported to the Transkei, but cannot get the courts to suspend the deportation order while his or her qualifications to be in Cape Town are proved. All that this person can do, in terms of the law, is apply for the deportation order to be set aside after it has already taken effect, i.e. from the Transkei. Similarly, a community who are removed from their land before all the legal requirements have been properly met can only challenge their removal afterwards — from their relocation site.

Further strengthening the government's lawful grip on any removals situation is the vicious security legislation it has at its disposal. 'State security' is equated with Nationalist policy and in defence of that the government has amassed far-reaching powers to suppress dissent. It may detain people suspected of being 'terrorists' indefinitely, subject to periodic reissues of their detention orders. It may banish and ban them. The local magistrate may refuse people permission to hold meetings if he is satisfied that this may endanger the public peace. All these powers have been delegated to the bantustan governments and all of them may be drawn upon to crush opposition to removals.

At Mgwali, a threatened black spot in the Eastern Cape, for instance, six prominent opponents of removal were detained under R252, a Ciskeian security measure, in August 1981.* Earlier, at a meeting called by the Ciskeian Chief Minister Lennox Sebe, any objections raised by the people of Mgwali to their proposed removal were met with the question 'Are you a terrorist?' or 'Why are you supporting terrorism?' The only place where the people are free to meet is at church. Community discussion of issues is limited to 'notices' during religious services.

Where meetings do take place, security police and informers are generally active. The network of informers reaches into every village and township in South Africa. A person interviewed by a SPP fieldworker in the relocation site of Kwaggafontein, in Kwa Ndebele,

---

*The right of Ciskei to detain people outside its borders was to be debated in court, at the time of going to press.

was speaking for millions of South Africans when she said:

> Look, I don't quite like that question. How can I be sure that you're not going to give those papers to the Chief? We who come from locations are watched suspiciously and if it is heard that I said anything bad, I am for it. So please do not feel bad if I seem not to trust you but I don't want to answer that question.

The law gives the government the power to control and suppress information as well. Publications dealing with relocation have been banned — most famous of all being Cosmas Desmond's *The Discarded People*. Newspapers need military clearance to publish anything pertaining to the South African Defence Force. This could rule out any publicity for or comment upon the relocation of people in operational areas along the Venda or Northen Natal borders, for instance. Whites and any other non-authorised persons are not allowed into all the bantustans without permits, and may not publish the results of any approved research without first submitting them to the authorities concerned. The government's control over what may be published was further extended in 1982, by means of the Laws on Co-operation and Development Amendment Act which provides for 'the preservation of secrecy' in connection with matters dealt with by the Commission for Co-operation and Development.

MAJOR LAWS DEALING WITH BLACK LAND RIGHTS
AND RELOCATION

1 The Black Land Act, No. 27, 1913
2 The Black Administration Act, No. 38, 1927, as amended
3 The Development Trust and Land Act, No. 18, 1936, as amended
4 The Black (Urban Areas) Consolidation Act, No. 25, 1945, as amended
5 The Group Areas Act, No. 41, 1950, as amended
6 The Prevention of Illegal Squatting Act, No. 52, 1951, as amended
7 The Blacks (Abolition of Passes and Coordination of Documents) Act, No. 67, 1952
8 The Blacks Resettlement Act, No. 19, 1954
9 The Black Prohibition of Interdicts Act, No. 64, 1956

10 The Trespass Act, No. 6, 1959
11 The Promotion of Black Self-Government Act, No. 46, 1959
12 The Black Laws Amendment Act, No. 76, 1963
13 The National States Citizenship Act, No. 26, 1970, as amended
14 The National States Constitution Act, No. 21, 1971, as amended
15 The Admission of Persons to the Republic Regulations Act, No. 59, 1972
16 The Expropriation Act, No. 63, 1975
17 The Slums Clearance Act, No. 76, 1979
18 The Laws on Co-operation and Development Amendment Act, No. 83, 1982

The above list is not comprehensive but includes the most important laws with a direct bearing on relocation. There are many apparently innocuous laws and local by-laws with no clear link to relocation which may be used to remove people as well, e.g. local health regulations or town planning regulations in terms of which residential areas may be zoned for industrial or other non-residential purposes. Many of the laws listed above overlap with each other, allowing the authorities a choice of which to apply in a particular case. It should also be noted that frequently the procedure to be followed in removing people is not spelt out in the legislation itself, but is set out in administrative regulations, drawn up at a departmental and not a parliamentary level and not readily available to the public.

Each new challenge to the authority of the state has been met by new laws defining new categories of political offences, new forms of control over black people's freedom of movement, new powers for Cabinet Ministers to govern by proclamation and decree. Where one law doesn't work, another one will. (See, for instance, the box on the laws governing the eviction of farmworkers.) As loopholes are discovered in existing legislation, they are closed. For instance, in 1956 the Appeal Court set aside a banishment order that had been served to a Mr JH Saliwa (to move from Glen Grey to the Pietersburg district), on the grounds that he had not been given prior notice before he was required to move. Shortly afterwards the government amended the Black Administration Act to do away with the need for prior notice and to prevent the courts from intervening. Twenty years later, in 1977, squatters at Modderdam outside Cape Town successfully challenged the legality of the demolition notices with which they had been issued. The response of the government was to amend the Prevention of Illegal Squatting Act a few months later. Thereafter officials could knock down shacks without giving the occupants prior notice and the court were powerless to issue any orders and to stop or delay them.

The stage has been reached where it is possible to challenge removals in court on technicalities only — on the failure of the relevant authorities to comply with the requirements of the law (giving insufficient notice, not serving expropriation orders on the registered owners of a property etc).

Some politically sympathetic lawyers are almost reluctant to expose technical weaknesses in the law, fearing that to do so will only lead to a further tightening up of the legislation in question. The principle of removal itself cannot be overruled by legal procedure. This point is brought out very clearly in both the Tsitsikama and the Klipfontein stories in the following chapter.

The law is a potent form of control over black people, in relocation as in other spheres. People threatened with removal are confused and intimidated by the complexity of the language, the far-reaching array of laws that confronts them. Most consider themselves peaceful and law-abiding citizens: to challenge the law or what officials tell them is the law is a radical step. The government likes to play on this by mystifying the legal process involved in relocation. It often presents relocation to threatened people not as the result of laws that it has passed and has the power to change, but as something far more abstract, beyond its control: 'decided by parliament', 'the law', 'government policy'. Thus, when the KwaZulu Minister of the Interior appealed to the Deputy Minister of Development to withdraw expropriation orders that had been served on the landowners of Matiwane's Kop, a black spot in Northern Natal, he was told that there were 'legal problems' with regard to that which meant that it could not be considered (Minutes of a meeting held at Pretoria, 27 May 1981). The people of Driefontein in the Eastern Transvaal were told by Koornhof that their 'resettlement ... was properly dealt with by the South African Parliament and reconsideration of the removal is not possible' (Letter, Koornhof to Mkhize, 13 Oct. 81, reproduced on next page). In a similar vein, the people of

Republiek van Suid-Afrika · Republic of South Africa

Ministerie van Samewerking en Ontwikkeling
Ministry of Co-operation and Development

Vermysingsnommer:
Reference Number: 5/5

Hendrik Verwoerdgebou
Hendrik Verwoerd Buildings
Kaapstad
Cape Town

1 3 -10- 1981

Mr. Saul Mkhize
P.O. Box 1172
JOHANNESBURG
2000

Dear Mr. Mkhize

RE-SETTLEMENT OF THE RESIDENTS OF DRIEFONTEIN

I refer to your letter dated the 4 June, 1981 and wish to give the assurance that the matter regarding the resettlement of the Driefontein people was properly dealt with by the South African Parliament and reconsideration of the removal is not possible. I wish to give the undertaking that the move will be dealt with in a most humanitarian way and with the least possible incon=venience and disruption to the Driefontein people.

It is therefore particularly important that the Driefontein Community give their full support to the officials of my Department who have already visited the area several times in the presence of the Magistrate of Wakkerstroom, so that the planning of the removal and of the compensatory land can be commenced with.

I also wish to draw your attention to the fact that a Community Board for the Driefontein people was duly elected and is now the official mouth piece of this community. You are therefore advised to discuss any further problems with this Board, who in turn will communicate with the Department of Co-operation and Development.

Warm regards

Yours sincerely

MINISTER OF CO-OPERATION AND DEVELOPMENT

Dr Koornhof's letter to Mkhize

FARMWORKERS AND THE LAW: LEGISLATIVE OVERKILL

The authorities have a superabundance of laws to ensure that a dismissed or former farmworker who continues to live on his land after his notice has expired, is driven from the land. Any one of the following legal procedures may be adopted to evict him:

1. Conviction and subsequent removal from the land by the authorities in terms of Section 26 of the Development Trust and Land Act;
2. Conviction under the Trespass Act for 'entering and being upon' the property without the permission of the owner;
3. Civil ejectment proceedings in terms of the common law;
4. Summary ejectment proceedings in terms of Section 37 of the Development Trust and Land Act;
5. Conviction and summary ejectment under the Prevention of Illegal Squatting Act;
6. Demolition of his house without notice
    a) by the owner of the land if it was built or occupied without his, the owner's, permission, in terms of the Prevention of Illegal Squatting Act
    b) by the authorities, in terms of the Prevention of Illegal Squatting Act or in terms of local health and building restriction regulations.

Furthermore, even if the particular method of eviction adopted is not carried out in the lawful manner — for instance, if a house is demolished without the authority of the Prevention of Illegal Squatting Act being invoked — the farmworker cannot appeal to the courts to stop or suspend the unlawful action because of the Black Prohibition of Interdicts Act. All he can do is apply for compensation for any damages wrongfully suffered by him *AFTER* the eviction or demolition has already been carried out.

Cornfields, a black spot in the Natal Midlands, were told by the commissioner in early 1983 that there was no point in discussing whether they wanted to move or not since their removal had already been decided; Dr Koornhof himself could not go against an Act of parliament.

The effect of this on threatened communities can be paralysing. It can be even more paralysing for outside support groups who work within boundaries carefully defined in terms for 'respect for the law', 'legal action' etc. Lawyers are particularly hamstrung since all they can work with and advise their clients on, is the law as it stands on the statute books at present.

The law is not a neutral arbiter between two equal parties. In South Africa it is very clearly a tool that the government has fashioned and that it controls. Nowhere is the lack of protection offered to blacks by the law more apparent than in the area of removals.

The agents of control: the police and the army

Standing alongside the legal machinery that has been constructed to remove people are the agents of control — the police and the army. They are the concrete embodiment of the government's power, holding the instruments of violence and physical force. They are there to back up the laws, to ensure that the government's master plan is not thwarted and to enforce it where it may be resisted. Sometimes their presence in the process of relocation is very low-key; sometimes they are not visible at all. When Kwapitela was moved in July 1981, for instance, there were no signs of any policemen at either Kwapitela or the place to which they were removed. Whether apparent or not, however, the presence of the police is always implicit in any dealings between people and the authorities. They are always on call — and the people know it.

From the very beginning, direct force in the form of the police and the army, with their guns, has provided the basis of the government's power to move the people. As the woman quoted at the beginning of this chapter said about the arrival of the police at Tsitsikama: 'What can we say now ... Then we have to get in.' In the early stages of its relocation programme, however, the government was far less self-conscious about the use of overt force to crush resistance than it is now.

In 1969/70 illegal labour tenants were hounded off the land in the Weenen district of Natal as if they were some kind of vermin or noxious weed to be rooted out and destroyed. The police and local farmers combined forces to demolish the huts of illegal tenants with bulldozers and fire. There were large-scale arrests and prosecutions: a press statement issued by the local Bantu Affairs commissioner in October 1969 listed convictions for '291 kraal heads (2 246 souls)' who were squatting illegally on their former land. There was some negative press publicity but no official statement of regret. In 1974 some 3 700 people were cleared off the Mayen reserve, a scheduled area in the remote Northern Cape, also under police supervision. In this case the Deputy Minister of Bantu Affairs did not try to claim that this was a voluntary removal, but he did feel that he needed to explain the presence of the police:

> It was difficult to say how many people would move voluntarily, the Deputy Minister continued. Among their ranks was a very small group of agitators who were intimidating and victimising the rest. In consequence members of the police had been in the area to maintain order. (SAIRR, 1975 p136.)

Two years later, evicted labour tenants in the Dannhauser district of Natal received similar treatment, being moved under the surveillance of 'soldiers, police and dogs' (see below). The removal of the people from the Mfengu reserve the following year saw the same heavyhanded tactics.

During this time the army was called upon to assist directly in the relocation of people on several occasions. In the early 1960s 400 families were moved off a Lutheran mission called Gertrudsburg, near Louis Trichardt, by the army. In 1968 the army was involved in the removal of some 500 people from a fragment of scheduled land called Mosita, near Vryburg. A few years later, in 1973, the army was again called in to move about 3 000 people from another small scheduled reserve in the Vryburg area, Di Takwanen. In 1974 and again in 1976 the army physically transported some 1 500 people out of the area that had been demarcated for a missile range, on the northen coast of Natal near Lake St Lucia. These removals were planned as full-scale army manoeuvres, complete with code names.

All these places were rural, away from the attention of journalists and urban activists. In 1977/78, however, the government provided a dramatic and devastating show of force on the outskirts of Cape Town, when it demolished the squatter camps of Modderdam, Unibel and Werkgenot. The *Sunday Tribune* compared the demolition of Modderdam to 'a scene from hell':

> An eye-smarting hell of teargas and snarling dogs, of laughing officials and policemen, of homeless families crouched pitifully with their meagre possessions beside the Modderdam Road. (14 Aug.77.)

14 *A landowner stands in front of his numbered door in Steincoalspruit, a black spot in the Klip River area, Natal. (See pages 79 and 279.)*

15 *'GG' trucks removing households from Kwapitela, a black spot near Himeville in Natal, to Compensation, a closer settlement near Pietermaritzburg, July 1981. (See pages 232-238 and index.)*

16 *Houses under demolition in Kwapitela following the removal (see opposite, bottom) in July 1981.*

17 *The view remains, the people have gone: after the demolition in Kwapitela.*

The following year the government demonstrated the same commitment to brute force when it launched an attack upon the still surviving camp of Crossroads. In a police raid on the camp in September 1978, over 900 people were arrested, many were brutally beaten and one man was shot dead. A *Rand Daily Mail* reporter described the scene thus:

> I saw docile squatters . . . dragged by their clothing and beaten with batons and sticks during the second raid on Crossroads . . . in less than six hours. Passes were grabbed by the police and other officials and thrown to the ground or temporarily confiscated. Ten policemen were injured when they were stoned in an earlier raid . . . . A squatter had been shot dead and soon a baby was to die on his mother's back as they were trampled by panic-stricken squatters attempting to escape yet another teargas attack . . . .   (*Rand Daily Mail*, 15 Sept. 78.)

The next year similar tactics were used to force about 650 Makgato families to move from their tribal land in the Sekgosese district near Pietersburg, in the Northern Transvaal. Most of the Makgato people had believed that the decision about whether they would move with their chief to the proposed relocation site at Kromhoek, 128 kilometres away, was an open one: that only those who agreed to be moved would have to go. They were rudely awakened to the truth at 6:30 a.m. on 1 October 1979, when about 30 trucks and 11 police vans arrived in the village. Camouflaged police patrolled the area while others started demolishing the houses, using a heavy chain attached to a truck. Those people who did not manage to flee into the bush were forced onto the trucks by the gun-toting police and driven away to their relocation site. (This removal is also described in the next chapter.)

THE REMOVAL OF FORMER LABOUR TENANTS FROM DANNHAUSER TO QUDENI, NATAL, 1976

'We were removed from a farm of whites together with tenants who were staying at Utrecht and also children. We only saw whites arriving with police alleging that boys refused to work which allegation was denied.

'Thereafter we were given letters to vacate which we took to the Commissioner's office at Dannhauser and reported the affair to Bantu Affairs Commissioner. He wanted to know our ideas. We told him that we only needed assistance because our children were no longer keen to work in farms.

'He promised to approach his senior officer at Pietermaritzburg to contact the KwaZulu government. We then awaited the outcome.

'While we were still awaiting police came to arrest us and we were kept in Dannhauser cells.

'A fine of R30 per head was fixed. We requested the Magistrate to call senior Magistrate at Pietermaritzburg and also requested help from Minister CJ Mthethwa from the KwaZulu government. The 2 officers arrived at Dannhauser on the 6th January 1976.

'Mr Dreyer and Mr Mthethwa welcomed our request and told us that there is a place at Nondweni but it is a town and no preparations had been made yet. They wanted our opinions about the suggested place. We told them that Nondweni can't be a good place for us; in particular that we have stock, and if we were interested in town life we would be going to nearer towns such as Osisweni and Madadeni. The reason why we don't go to these places is only because town life is not good for us.

'Mr Dreyer advised us not to sell our beasts and further promised to fix something for us within six months.

'During the waiting period we were summoned to come before the Commissioner's Court at Dannhauser where we were told that we are not required in the place and further were threatened that if we do not move away we shall be arrested and sentenced to imprisonment for a period of six months or pay a fine of R30. We told him that we are not refusing to move but we were still waiting for Mr Dreyer as he promised to fix something for us. Then we were told to leave till a further order.

'On the 15th July 1976 G.G. trucks arrived with soldiers, police and their dogs. They said they don't need any argument but have just come to move us to Qudeni. We

> enquired: how could we be moved to Qudeni while we were still waiting for something from Mr Dreyer?
>
> 'We were told that what was happening was his instructions. They also told us that we were already provided with 4 roomed houses which we discovered to be false.
>
> 'All our building equipment was left behind and on arrival we had to start from nothing, buying building material. In addition this place has no schools, no clinics, no grazing land for our stock and no lands for cultivating. We have got absolutely nothing and are very much surprised because Mr Dreyer made a fair promise to us and he said he won't make any mistake.' — From *Report from Mzimhlophe, Qudeni,* a memorandum prepared by the community and sent to the Department of Cooperation and Development in June 1981.

It was during this time that the shift away from such blatant use of force became a strategic consideration for the government. Its handling of the Makgato and especially the Crossroads cases received extensive, overwhelmingly critical publicity, both locally and internationally. Crossroads is situated very conveniently for hard-pressed foreign journalists with deadlines to meet — right next to Cape Town's international airport. Just as Dimbaza had become a name synonymous with racial oppression and suffering in South Africa in the early 1970s, as a result of the focus on it by Cosmas Desmond and others, so in the late 70s and early 80s Crossroads became an internationally recognised symbol of the brutality of apartheid and of popular resistance to it.

As described in Chapter 1, this was the time of reform, of the new outward policy of PW Botha and his *verlig** Cabinet. Pretoria was sensitive to the hostile publicity that tarnished its attempts to restore its international standing. 'There are other factors which have made removals difficult', admitted the Deputy

---

*Verlig — literally, 'enlightened'; a term used to describe the less right-wing element in the National Party.

Minister of Development and Land Affairs in June 1983:

> In a certain sense these problems have acquired international overtones.   (*Hansard*, Cols. 8829/30, 7 June 83.)

At the same time, Pretoria was also becoming increasingly aware of the dangers of inflaming black resistance still further after the national upheavals of 1976. For key members of Botha's government, winning 'the hearts and minds' of the people was becoming more important than direct coercion as a strategy of control.

One of the earliest but little publicised indications of the change in approach was provided in 1978/79 when the last set of people to be cleared out of the missile range at Lake St Lucia were moved. Whereas in the first two phases of relocation from this area the army had been the agent of removal, in this final phase it distanced itself as far as possible from the proceedings. Although it was party to the decision to move the approximately 2 000 people still living in the missile zone, it refused to have anything to do with the physical transportation of the people and the demolition of their houses. To be identified with that, army strategists felt, would direct the local people's hostility to being moved against the army; this would be detrimental to the long-term security of what had become a particularly vulnerable area since Mozambique gained its independence in 1974.

A more public sign of the new approach was the renaming of the former Department of Bantu Administration: first, in 1978, the Department of Plural Relations, and then, in an even more exuberant mood of public relations, the Department of Cooperation and Development in 1979. During the negotiations over a reprieve for Crossroads the new style came into its own. Cooperation and development became catchwords of the government with regard to removals, and have remained so ever since.

> As I have said in the beginning, if you assist the officials to fill in these forms in a truthful way, we can solve this problem in a humane way. You have heard me say often that I want cooperation . . . I tell you now again that I want cooperation between the officials and you. If there is cooperation then all these things will go well. I have been in this Department for 30 years and these officials have put up with a lot of difficulty which you don't know of but I know of, and I really request you to make it as easy as possible for them by cooperating. If I was preaching, my message would be simple, it would consist of two

words,'Please cooperate'. You will not be sorry. That is the way in which this problem will be solved. I wish you God's blessing.
(Dr Koornhof, at a meeting with Crossroads residents in February 1979. Transcript.)

The era of 'voluntary removals'

In this new, more image-conscious period, the public emphasis is on people moving voluntarily after due consultation and participation in the planning of their own removal. In speech after speech the theme of 'voluntary removals' is hammered out. In July 1980 Koornhof was reported in newspapers as saying that:

> he would see to it that there were no more forced removals of people from their homes . . . he said that this approach would be adhered to 'as far as is humanly possible'. (*Daily News*, 17 July 80.)

In February 1983 he reiterated, in parliament:

> I am on record as stating that the Government and I will do everything possible to abolish the forced removal of people as far as it is practicable and possible. (*Hansard*, Cols. 839/40, 11 Feb. 83.)

He went on to say that the 'resettlement programme' of the Department of Cooperation and Development would have to continue since the process of consolidation 'is in the interests of all the people of the Republic of South Africa'. However, future resettlement would be on a selective basis, would involve the 'cooperation of the bodies concerned', and would, moreover, be development-orientated. He stressed the break with the past:

> The point I am therefore making is that there is a reformist approach and also an approach involving new initiatives in respect of resettlement . . . there is a programme of reform in progress in connection with this matter . . . I therefore want to tell hon. members that when they rise to their feet here and try to make everyone believe the falsehoods which they wish to bruit abroad about hundreds of thousands of people that are going to be moved . . . when they also implied that these were 'forced removals', then they do not know what they are talking about. (*Hansard*, Cols. 841-2, 11 Feb. 83.)

Not only are people not being forced any more. According to some Nationalists, they are not being removed either. In the same debate DM Streicher, the MP for De Kuilen, enlarged on the community development theme thus:

> The word 'removal' should not be used at all. It is the hon. member for Houghton who uses the word "remove". The correct word is "resettle". If you remove a person, then you remove him. You do not see him again and you do not take any responsibility for him. But if you resettle a person, that is a completely different matter.
> (*Hansard*, Col. 867, 11 Feb. 83.)

In relation to specific communities that are threatened with removal, Ministers and officials endlessly repeat the claim of consultation and cooperation. About Reserve Four on the Natal North Coast:

> In conclusion, I may say that the people are not forced in an inhuman way to move but are moved on a negotiation basis to provide for the needs of the community. (The Deputy Minister of Development, in a letter to R Swart, MP, quoted in parliament, *Hansard*, Col. 835, 11 Feb. 83.)

About Mathopestad in the Western Transvaal:

> In the case of Mathopestad, I personally, along with the Deputy Minister H van der Walt, Mr Rex le Roux and senior officials, recently had discussions with the leaders of the community. It was thereafter decided to establish a planning committee and jointly investigate an alternative site. (Press release issued by Dr Koornhof, Cape Town, 6 June 83, translated from the original Afrikaans.)

About Driefontein in the Eastern Transvaal:

> In the case of Driefontein I also, along with the abovementioned gentlemen, had long discussions, first with the Chairman and Community Board members and thereafter with the Board of Directors that is against being resettled, and thereafter with both groups together. They were fruitful discussions where it was decided 1) that the two bodies would first consider a document of mine about an alternative site before a planning committee would be established, and 2) that a general meeting would be called at Driefontein by the Chief Commissioner and the Commissioner of the area where the two bodies and the residents of Driefontein would be present and a report back could take place. (*Ibid*)

About Umbulwane and Matiwane's Kop in the Northern Transvaal:

> ... the resettlement actions [would] as far as practical, be conducted

after consultation and in collaboration with the committees concerned as well as the Government of KwaZulu. (Koornhof quoted in the *Natal Mercury*, 27 April 82.)

In an attempt to lend greater credibility to these claims, the Department has recently developed the idea of steering or planning committees to handle each removal. These committees are to consist of representatives of the Department, the relevant bantustan and the community concerned. The planning is not a one-sided exercise, said Koornhof in February 1983, since the Department 'insists' that the community be also involved:

> and to give effect to this, the community is requested to appoint a representative group . . . to serve on the planning committee so that they may advise the department and make recommendations on matters on which they have special knowledge. (*Hansard*, Col. 846, 11 Feb. 83.)

Pretoria is trying to impress this reformist approach on departmental staff in the districts as well. The Department's General Circular of 1982 changes a number of the phrases used in the 1967 circular, which it replaces. The language is softened; the sense remains the same. This circular also emphasises the importance of 'motivational efforts' on the part of local officials to persuade the people who are to be moved that it is in their own best interests. Attached to the circular is a copy of a form that officials can use to simplify the bureaucracy that surrounds the removal of people from one administration district to another. This form is couched in the polite language of voluntary removals throughout: the person would like to move to . . . he requests government assistance for, etc.

In addition to playing down the coercive aspects of relocation, the government has also begun to stress the fact that relocation affects not only blacks but whites as well. In December 1981 the Deputy Minister of Development used this as part justification for the impending removal of the Driefontein community. In a letter to the chairman of the Driefontein Community Board he wrote smoothly:

> In conclusion I must stress that, like you, there are many whites who also had to leave land which they have owned and occupied for generations and on which members of their families were born, raised and

were subsequently buried. Everyone of us has to make sacrifices in some way or other to further peace and prosperity in this beautiful country of ours. (Letter dated 18 Dec. 81.)

In the parliamentary debate on removals in February 1983 Dr Koornhof went to considerable lengths to show that whites also 'have a share of the sacrifice'. (*Hansard*, Col. 845, 11 Feb. 83.) As pointed out in Chapter 2, this involved some dubious mathematical calculations — comparing the number of white *individuals* bought out in terms of consolidation planning with the number of black *families* moved in this category to date. In June 1983 he enlarged on this theme in his press release:

It must be accepted that the process of consolidation necessarily involves the resettlement of people, both white and black. The Government regards the process of consolidation as in the interests of all the people of South Africa in the search for evolutionary and peaceful solutions to our problems in a heterogeneous land. Consolidation brings *sacrifices* for both whites and people in black communities. Look at the process of consolidation in the Ciskei and now KwaNdebele. As a result of the abovementioned Cabinet decision the Department of Cooperation and Development has to go ahead, on a selective basis, with the cooperation of the concerned parties, with the resettlement of people — *both black and white*. (Press release, 6 June 83, translated from the Afrikaans. Emphasis in the original.)

However, neither the greater restraint in the use of armed force nor the stress on consultation, nor the increased attention to language, amounts to a fundamental reform of either the policy or the process of removal. Although particular aspects of this programme are under pressure from many sides, and the pace of removals has slowed down as a result, the government has not abandoned the principle of relocation as a solution to its problems. Koornhof's press release of 6 June 1983 is quite unambiguous about this. The National Party of PW Botha is still committed to consolidation. It is still committed to its plan to divide South Africa into a white core and ten black states on the periphery. It is still committed to removing as many blacks as it has to (and can) in order to make that possible.

The one or two well-publicised reprieves that have been announced have not involved any fundamental shift in policy. They amount merely to revisions within the policy — selected attempts to gain credibility with rightwing rebellious farmers or to defuse resistance in particular black areas. They do not amount to any revision of the policy itself. Compared to the large number of communities where no reprieves have been offered, and the even larger number of communities that have already been removed, they can only be seen as exceptional situations.

Furthermore, the consultation being offered threatened communities is a sham. The purpose of the new steering committees is not to consult but to coopt — to confuse and divide the people with the pretence of consultation into helping to plan their own removal. In not one of the five instances of 'consultation' between government and threatened communities cited by Koornhof and quoted above, is there any suggestion that these places will not be removed, despite the fact that every one of the communities referred to is on record as appealing to Koornhof to stop their pending removal. The question is not whether they will be removed but how they are to be removed. The agendas for their steering/planning committees have already been set, their removal decided by Pretoria before the first meeting even takes place.

This was brought out very clearly in September 1981 in a series of replies given by Koornhof to questions concerning the future of Reserve Four. First he described how the KwaZulu government had agreed in principle to the formation of steering committees to 'advise the two governments on particular problems and implications concerning the resettlement of each of the particular Black spots'. (*Hansard*, Private Question 3, 2 Sept. 81.) Two days later, when questioned specifically about Reserve Four, he said these steering committees would be formed 'for the necessary arrangements, consultation and identification of problems in connection with, *inter alia*, the proposed resettlement of the residents of Reserve Four.' He confirmed that the area had already been excised from KwaZulu 'because the people resident in Reserve Four are ultimately to be resettled elsewhere' and then evaded a further question about whether the people were being moved voluntarily or not. Without acknowledging any of the objections to being moved that the two chiefs and their councils from that area have lodged with his Department since 1978, he replied:

DIFFERENT LANGUAGE: SAME POLICY

Over the years, the language used by the government to describe removals has been carefully refined, to present removals in a more positive light: as development-oriented, voluntary, and part of a process of nation-building rather than dispossession. A comparison of the 1967 General Circular of the Department of Bantu Administration and Development with the 1982 General Circular of the Department of Cooperation and Development brings this out clearly. The language has been reformed, but not the policy.

From the 1967 circular		From the 1982 circular
SETTLING OF NON-PRODUCTIVE BANTU RESIDENT IN NON-EUROPEAN AREAS, IN THE HOMELANDS	becomes	SETTLEMENT OF FAMILIES AND WORKERS FROM THE WHITE AREAS OF THE REPUBLIC OF SOUTH AFRICA IN NATIONAL AND INDEPENDENT BLACK STATES
It is accepted Government policy that the Bantu are only temporarily resident in the European areas of the Republic, for as long as they offer their labour there.	becomes	In pursuance of the Government's policy of developing national states and bringing them to full independence the policy in practice is that Blacks should be able to live and work in such states to the maximum extent.
The Bantu in the European areas who are normally regarded as non-productive and as such have to be resettled in the homelands ...	becomes	For convenience, the Blacks in the White area who are normally regarded as non-productive in the White area and should as such be given the opportunity of settling in a national state ...
Bantu of European farms who become superfluous ...	becomes	Blacks on White farms who become unfit for work ...
... they must first sell their cattle, sheep and goats	becomes	It is therefore desirable that they sell their livestock ...
Persuasion must be continually exercised by the district officials in collaboration with the responsible officials of local authorities to persuade persons who qualify (for urban residence) and are not prepared to accept settlement in towns in their homelands, to be settled in towns in their homelands on ethnical grounds.	becomes	Motivational efforts must be made constantly by district officials in collaboration with administration board officials in order to persuade those qualifying in terms of section 10 (1) (a) or (b) of the Urban Areas Act to settle voluntarily in a national or independent state or in an SADT area.

That can be established after the steering committee, on which they will also be represented, has been formed. Then it will be possible to determine how the people themselves feel about the removal.
(*Hansard*, Private Question 3, 4 Sept. 81)

Earlier in the year, at a meeting of the Deputy Minister of Development and the KwaZulu Minister of the Interior in Pretoria, the representatives of 'the people' were defined quite unambiguously as those working within the structures of local government already created by Pretoria:

After some deliberation it was unanimously decided that it would be ideal to have a *small* committee for each problem area. This committee would have to include local people such as a representative from the Chief's Tribal Council, a local Member of the Legislative Assembly of KwaZulu and the local KwaZulu magistrate. (Minutes of a meeting held at Pretoria, 27 May 81.)

The degree to which officials are to dominate these committees has been spelt out absolutely clearly. At two threatened black spots in Natal (Thembalihle and Cornfields) a local planning committee was set up under official supervision. At the first meeting of this committee, the magistrate reportedly ousted both the chairman and the secretary who were from the community. These two key positions were then allocated to white officials.

These two examples illustrate exactly how limited Koornhof's 'reformist approach' is and what the thrust behind his 'new initiatives' is all about. The talk about 'voluntary removals' does not mean that people will not be moved, nor that they will not be moved against their will. It means that as far as possible people will be coerced and 'persuaded' by more sophisticated means than in the past, to get them to submit to being moved without a show of overt force becoming necessary. The police and the army are being pushed further into the background while the tactics of cooption and of implied force are brought to the fore. The era of 'voluntary removals' is no more than the era of indirect coercion.

The methods of indirect coercion

The range of indirect pressures available to a government with such immense powers over the law, over resources and informa-

CRITIQUE OF THE PLANNING COMMITTEE IN MGWALI, EASTERN CAPE

CRY BELOVED COUNTRY

Mgwali residents are being threatened with imminent removal from their most beloved homes — the peaceful & fertile Mgwali land which is in the district of Stutterheim.

PLANNING COMMITTEE

The Chief whip of it all, is the Planning Committee which consists mostly of Civil servants who have no say to the abominable behaviour of their superiors. They are the tools to do the Ciskeian Government's dirty work. The worst part of it all, is the bribery which prevails in the midst of this misdeanour.

PRIVILEGES

They have been offered big farms at Frankfort for services rendered in encouraging this removal, so that, while we roast in those God-forsaken tents with poor sanitation and the rest, they will live comfortable in glass houses. Shame on them!!

They will enjoy enormous grazing land for their stock, while we have to limit ours because of the scanty pastures — unlike the present valleys we have here, with the best grass for our cattle, sheep & goats.

We curse them unto their third and fourth generation for the fear they have caused to their community. They have no regard for God's Creation and so they will suffer consequences for their despisable actions.

We therefore appeal to all Nations to help us with prayers.

FROM: NEZISIZWE SIDIMA, BOLO CASH STORE, P.O. BOLO, STUTTERHEIM. 83. 07. 29.

tion as Pretoria enjoys, is chilling. The only real constraints are those imposed by the lack of imagination or cunning of the officials that preside over each particular removal.

Intimidation of people by the authorities and the security police is universal. At Driefontein in the Eastern Transvaal, officials told the residents that they should go to the commissioner's office 'to register'. 'If you are not against the law, just sign', the chairman of the board was told in early 1982. Nobody was sure what they were to sign for; those who did present themselves at the commissioner's office were told pointedly that they had not been called there but had gone voluntarily. At Thembalihle in Natal the members of the local residents' committee who attended a workshop on removals in Ladysmith in late 1981 were visited by the security police and questioned about the event soon afterwards. At Mgwali in the Eastern Cape there are potent rumours in circulation that householders who do not cooperate with the authorities will be stripped of all their assets: pensions, school facilities, drought relief, work papers. Everywhere community leaders and organisers face the very real threat of arrest and detention. The threat, even if never realised, is an enormously powerful deterrent to organisation. Detention, whether at the hands of the South African authorities or the bantustan authorities, is not a pleasant experience, as the numerous deaths of detainees and allegations of assault and torture against the security police testify.

In some areas intimidation has been supplemented by more concrete forms of pressure: schools and shops closed, bus services withdrawn, housing frozen so that no new houses can be built and those that are standing deteriorate to the point where they become uninhabitable (at which point they can be declared slums and demolished). These tactics are not confined to the rural areas. They have been widely used to implement both the group area and the African urban relocation programmes. Thus 66% of the people interviewed at the group area township of Atlantis, outside Cape Town, reported that they had moved there from Greater Cape Town mainly from overcrowded township houses and squatter camps. 'It's Atlantis or nothing for house-seekers', reported *The Argus* on 9 January 1981. Those interviewed by SPP agreed. 'Even unmarried mothers could get houses', commented one.

Even stronger pressures exist on African housing. Since the late 1960s, when the programme of urban relocation was launched, there has been a virtual freeze on the building of houses for Africans outside the bantustans. While recently this has been amended in certain cases, the shift has been a very limited one. In March 1983 the housing shortage for Africans in white areas was officially estimated at 160 000 units — and that figure is only for households officially qualified to live in the white areas. (*Hansard*, Private Question 39, 8 March 83.) Whereas in 1979/80 a little under 10 000 houses were erected by administration boards around the country, in 1981/82 only half that number — 4 674 — were built. (*Hansard*, Private Question 190, 8 March 83.)

Everywhere this is having the effect of squeezing African people desperate for the security of a home of their own into the bantustans. Commented one person interviewed by SPP in the relocation township of Mdantsane: 'There are many people who did not have houses there [Duncan Village, in East London] but have houses here.'

In May 1979 a spokesman for the Southern Free State Administration Board explained how this tactic was to be used to drive people out of the remaining African townships in the Orange Free State into the newly established relocation camp of Onverwacht. He

> stressed that people would not be forced to leave their homes in Bloemfontein, the surrounding smallholdings and other Free State towns, but would move of their own free will . . . . Mr Spies estimates that 30 000 people will be resettled from Bloemfontein, the smallholdings and country towns over a long term . . . . In Bloemfontein alone — where the housing backlog is currently 5 000 — he expects more than 13 000 people to qualify for resettlement. These figures are made up of 2 000 families who are mainly boarders and 717 families who must be rehoused because of poor housing. (*The Friend*, 17 May 81.)

Closely linked to the strategy of using control over housing to pressurise people out of the urban areas goes the ever more determined application of influx control to limit the numbers of African people allowed to live and work in these areas as much as possible. In July 1979 the fine imposed on employers for employing an illegal African worker — somebody not approved by the labour bureau — was increased from R100 to R500. And if the Orderly Movement and Settlement of Black Persons Bill is enacted, this fine will rise drastically to a maximum of R5 000 or 12 months' imprisonment — a penalty severe enough to make even the most sympathetic employer think twice before taking on somebody who does not have papers to be in the area. In Cape Town there are rumours in circulation that this fine is already in force.

In the meantime, while the Bill is being redrafted, the annual budget for the maintenance of influx control has almost doubled, from R3,6 million in 1981 to over R6 million in 1982. (*Rand Daily Mail*, 20 March 82.) The related aspects of 'residential control' and repatriation of foreign citizens (which category includes

---

HOUSING IN THE EASTERN CAPE, 1981/82

The following figures show how the policy of limiting housing for Africans outside the bantustans is being applied in the Eastern Cape. They show how many houses were built and how many new sites for future houses were made available in the various townships in 1981/82.

TOWNSHIP	STATUS	HOUSES BUILT	SITES MADE AVAILABLE
1 Mdantsane	Relocation township in Ciskei	1327	1400
2 Mlungisi (Queenstown)	Was threatened with removal. Future now uncertain.	0	0
3 Fingo Village (Grahamstown)	Was threatened with removal. Now reprieved, but freehold is being eroded.	0	277
4 Zwide (Port Elizabeth)	Relocation township	240	0
5 Hillside (Fort Beaufort)	Was threatened with removal. Now reprieved, but rumours of removal persist.	0	130
6 Ginsberg Township	Not under threat. (*Hansard*, Question 1046, 18 Aug. 83.)	0	0
7 Stutterheim Township	Was threatened with removal. Now landowners, employed and those with Section 10 rights reprieved, but 'squatters' to be moved.	0	0

Source: *Hansard*, Private Question 65, 22 Feb. 83.

citizens of the Transkei, Bophuthatswana, Venda and Ciskei) have also received financial boosts in this period, moving up from R1 million to R2,1 million and from R1,6 million to R2,5 million respectively.

What these figures show is that even if the Orderly Movement Bill is finally scrapped, existing legislation is to be used more ruthlessly to achieve the same ends. In September 1981 the Police

---

HOUSING IN THE EAST RAND, 1983

The PFP MP for Johannesburg presented figures in parliament in June 1983 that illustrate how housing policy is being used to force people out of townships on the East Rand:

— There are 13 townships on the East Rand, having a combined legal population of 700 000 and an estimated population of about 1 000 000.
— These townships have a total of 79 000 houses — this means that on average there are 9 people in each house.
— While the total township population grew by almost 6% in 1982, the supply of houses grew by only 1.9% — the East Rand Administration Board built only 1 508 housing units. In 6 out of the 13 townships the Administration Board has no housing schemes for development at all.
— About 1 000 shacks had recently been demolished by the Administration Board at one of these townships, Katlehong.

Koornhof's response to the point about the demolitions was as follows:

Action simply had to be taken. I wish to state clearly that they acted under my authority and that I asked them to act . . . . The Community Board then took the initiative and decided that illegal persons could not be permitted, particularly bearing in mind the additional burden on the provision of services that this would entail. To date, more than 8 000 families have been sent back to their national states from the East Rand, and the huts built there have been broken down. In my book, success has been achieved there.   (*Hansard*, 8 June 83.)

Liaison Officer for East London made this explicit when he said that the pass laws were to be enforced more strictly in his area. (SAIRR, 1982, p278.) Mass removals of communities may have slowed down, but mass removals of individuals in terms of influx control and the pass laws have not.

That the government has no intention of relaxing influx control was made absolutely clear by the way it responded to the Rikhoto case judgement. In this court case — described possibly prematurely as 'historic' by some enthusiastic observers — both the Supreme and the Appeal courts upheld the right of a contract worker, Mr M Rikhoto, to qualify for permanent residence in an urban area on the grounds that he had worked continuously for the same employer for more than ten years. The fact that he was obliged to return to the bantustans every year for an enforced holiday in terms of the regulations governing contract labour was not interpreted as constituting a break in his employment. This judgement was not to the liking of the authorities. In October 1982 Koornhof announced that the government intended to introduce legislation to counter the adverse effects of the court ruling — to try and close legal loopholes once again. (*The Star*, 7 Oct. 82.) The amendment to the Act, introduced in the 1983

SASH: RESIDENCE RIGHTS WITHHELD

The Black Sash has accused the government of 'sidestepping, evading, manipulating and ignoring' the court ruling in the Rikhoto case, which granted permanent urban residence rights to a contract labourer.

It also alleged that Administration Board officials around the country have been arbitrarily refusing to grant Section 10 (1) (b) rights to migrant workers who have applied for them in the wake of the Rikhoto judgement.

The judgement opened the way for contract workers to obtain permanent urban residence rights even if they had stayed in the homelands between contracts.

A Black Sash document quotes numerous examples of people who, it said, had 'been prevented from obtaining their rights by bureaucratic traps'.

The Chief Director of the West Cape Administration Board (WCAB), Mr J Gunter, yesterday denied all the allegations.

The Black Sash document claims that:
- People have been told that they will have to wait for the decisions on their cases to come from Pretoria — yet such decisions have to be taken by the local Labour Officer;
- People who fill in application forms early in June are now being told these forms have been cancelled and they have to fill in new ones;
- Workers are now being given complicated forms which their employers have to fill in with details of the precise dates of engagement and 'discharge' for each contract as well as all dates of paid or unpaid leave, even though records of all contracts are kept by Administration Boards and periods of leave are irrelevant;
- When employers are unable to fill in the whole form, even if it is accompanied by a certificate stating that the worker concerned has been in their employ for ten years, people are told to 'forget it' unless the form is properly filled in;
- Arbitrary, false reasons are being given for their refusal such as that contract workers cannot have 10 (1) (b) rights;
- Tswana, Venda and Xhosa people are being refused 10 (1) (b) rights and being told they are not entitled to them if they did not complete the 10-year period before the date of their respective homelands' independence;
- Some are being wrongly told they are classified as Section 13 workers and that they are therefore ineligible.

Mr Gunter said decisions on cases had never been awaited from Pretoria but WCAB had awaited 'firm directives . . . as the board, at that time, was not in possession of the full facts of the judgement'.

He denied the use of application forms at any stage.

On behalf of the WCAB, he invited 'any interested body' which had difficulties with such matters to contact the board's liaison officer, Dr G du Preez, who he said would investigate the difficulties and reply to them.

(*Cape Times*, 28 July 83.)

parliamentary session, strengthens the links between influx control and African housing policies. Qualifications for urban residence for those not born in the urban areas is dependent on their having approved accommodation, in terms of clause 4 of the Laws on Cooperation and Development Act, gazetted on 26 August 1983. This is a classic 'chicken and egg' situation. No African can obtain approved accommodation without the necessary qualification to be in the urban areas, and vice versa. Unless the family was legally resident in his house before 26 August 1983, he cannot bring them into the urban area. *No family* could have been in that position if he was 'illegal'. Black Sash offices report that in the meantime administration board officials are doing all in their power to thwart the court ruling administratively.

There are many subtle ways of breaking the morale of threatened communities to ensure submission to removal as well. One way is to let them simmer in uncertainty about their future for so long that when the trucks finally do arrive they are received almost with relief: at least people then know what has been decided. Thus at Kwapitela, a black spot in Natal, the people were warned in September 1979 that their removal was imminent and that they should not plant any crops because these would not be compensated for; yet in the end they were only moved in July 1981. By that time two planting seasons had passed without any harvest and many people were resigned to moving. If they could not grow anything any more, what was the use of clinging to their land? (This same community, when interviewed after they had been at their relocation site for a year, were extremely reluctant to criticise their new place openly. They feared that to do so might prompt the authorities to move them again — and anything was better than that.)

Another way is to exploit divisions within the community. The Department of Cooperation and Development is extremely skilled at widening the divisions that exist and creating divisions where there are none. The case studies in the next chapter give some indication of the range of divisions that can be worked upon to create tensions and rivalries within a threatened community. 'Legals' and 'non-legals', workers and non-workers, landlords and tenants, old residents and new residents, urban and rural, citizens and non-citizens, those people with Section 10 rights and those without — apartheid is based on the principle of divisions, and relocation brings them all to the fore.

On black spots the very real differences that do exist between those who own the land and those who simply rent the land from them are deftly manipulated by the authorities. Wherever possible the removal of the tenants is separated from the landowners' — separate meetings, separate timetable. Tenants may be encouraged to support removal by promises from the magistrate that at

---

11/5/2

AUTHORITY HOLDING OF A MEETING : PLOTOWNERS DRIEFONTEIN DISTRICT WAKKERSTROOM

In terms of Government Notice No. 557 dated 26th March 1982 the holding of a meeting by the Plotwoners of Driefontein district Wakkerstroom is hereby authorised.

PLACE OF MEETING: Cabangani Primary School, Driefontein.
DATE OF MEETING: Sunday 26th December 1982 at 9 a.m.
PURPOSE OF MEETING: (a) To discusse the proposed resettlement.
(b) To elect representatives to negotiate with the Department of Co-Operation and Development.

CONDITIONS TO THIS AUTHORITY:

(i) Only Landowners in Driefontein will attend the meeting.

(ii) The representatives to be elected to consist of landowners only.

MAGISTRATE, WAKKERSTROOM

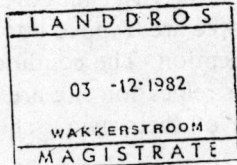
LANDDROS
03 -12-1982
WAKKERSTROOM
MAGISTRATE

their new place they will no longer be paying rent to their present landlords. Absentee landowners may be encouraged to sell the land from under their tenants by the lure of cash compensation. At Jonono's Kop in Natal the local magistrate managed to turn a dispute over rent between one landowner and his tenants into a rift that threatened the unity of the whole community when he told the tenants that nobody was under an obligation to pay rent any more since the land had already been expropriated.

Linked to the process of division is the process of cooption. Steering committees are just one of the methods of cooption available to an enterprising official. Some methods work on the greed of selected members of the community — the promise of a decent house or a trading licence or a position of authority at the other end, if they cooperate. Others work on weaknesses or fears. In rural areas the chiefs, who already depend on the government for their positions and their salaries, are often (though not always) the weak point in community struggles against being moved. Examples abound of how chiefs may be convinced that removal is in their, if not in their people's, interests. At Mathopestad in the Western Transvaal the chief was offered a house with running water — an unheard of luxury for most rural people — at their proposed relocation site near Onderstepoort. (This same community was also offered the prospect of being relocated next to the casino/resort complex of Sun City as a reason for moving.) At Reserve Six, once a scheduled reserve on the land where the boom town of Richards Bay, Natal now stands, the chief was offered the use of the empty farmhouses that stood on the Trust farms to which he and his people were moved in 1976. In the Ciskei, one of the chiefs who moved from the Herschel district when that was handed over to the Transkei became a Cabinet Minister within the Ciskeian government very soon afterwards.

Finally, people are trapped into agreeing to move by false promises and deception. The conditions and opportunities awaiting people at their relocation site are described in glowing terms: no rent, a house of their own, schools, clinics, security . . . even freedom.

> We were made to expect a paradise of a homeland in the urbanised form.
> We were given to believe that it was to be a wonderful model township

for our freedom. (Two comments made by people who had been persuaded to move to Mdantsane, the Ciskeian township outside East London, quoted in Mayer, 1971, p278.)

At Makgokgwane in the Western Transvaal, landowners were promised R10 000 compensation but only received R2 500. At Klipfontein in the Eastern Cape some of the people earmarked for removal were taken by officials to see their proposed relocation site — and shown not Glenmore but land at Tyefu, the Ciskeian irrigation scheme next door. At Matiwane's Kop in Natal the community were told that their removal had actually been requested by their former chief. After they had pointed out that the chief in question had died two years before he was alleged to have made that request, they were told that Chief Buthelezi had requested their removal so that all 'his' people would be living together in KwaZulu (another allegation that was subsequently disproved). ('Proposed Removal of the Matiwane's Kop Tribe', memorandum, 1979, and fieldwork.)

At Inanda Newtown, the site-and-service scheme outside Durban, many people applied for a site in the belief that they would be given Section 10 status once they were there. Others expected to find formal township housing. 'We haven't got any of the things we were promised initially', said one of the people interviewed by SPP.

Methods of indirect coercion and pressure are not new to removals. M C Botha was clearly familiar with them when he spoke of 'persuasion' in 1969. In the Koornhof era, however, these tactics have been given a much greater prominence than before. Disorganisation and deception are the chosen methods of weakening resistance, to reduce the role of direct force in removing people.

Yet even while the methods of indirect pressure have moved to the fore, the government's power to remove people still rests on direct force. In a less guarded moment, Koornhof declared in June 1983:

> I said . . . that as far as it was practical and physically and humanly possible — something which is now being omitted for the sake of convenience — there would not be forced removals. I did not say that there would be no forced removals . . . it is not humanly possible when majorities and large numbers of people are prepared to

cooperate with the government in this process, to allow other people who are absolutely stubborn and recalcitrant, to simply continue doing what they are doing. If it is impossible to carry out a development process in a normal way, as a result of the actions of these people, we shall have no choice but to find methods to encourage those people to join other members of such a community who are prepared to move. (*Hansard*, Col. 8783, 7 June 83.)

The killing of community leader Saul Mkhize on 2 April 1983 at Driefontein in the Eastern Transvaal provided a grim reminder that the potential for violence in the removals process is always strongly present. Mkhize was spearheading the Driefontein community's fight against being moved. According to the official police statement, he was shot dead by one of two police constables (aged 21 and 23 years respectively) who had been sent to investigate a complaint that an illegal meeting was being held at the Driefontein school. The crowd 'became riotous', forcing the two policemen to fire teargas and retreat:

> Once Constable Nienaber managed to get to the vehicle, he took the shotgun that was left in the vehicle when he first went to address Mr Mkhize, and fired a shot into the air over the heads of the riotous crowd. This had no effect on the crowd's behaviour. As the riotous crowd kept advancing towards the two constables and the vehicle in a threatening manner, Constable Nienaber fired a shot into the crowd. Mr Mkhize was fatally wounded and the crowd dispersed immediately. (Quoted by the Minister of Cooperation and Development in parliament. *Hansard*, Col. 987, 15 April 83.)

According to Opposition MP Helen Suzman, speaking in parliament on the same day and quoting eyewitness reports, the policeman was standing on the other side of a 1,8 metre high fence when he fired a shot, and the crowd had already dispersed.

> It is my firm belief that the constable either lost his head or that he had decided that Mkhize was just a black troublemaker with whom he could deal in any way that he saw fit. (*Hansard*, Col. 4796, 7 April 83.)

In the case of Mkhize's death, senior members of government were embarrassed by so blatant a contradiction of its claim to have moved away from forced removals. Thirteen days after Mkhize died, Koornhof announced stiffly that it was 'regrettable

Republiek van Suid-Afrika · Republic of South Africa

Ministerie van Samewerking en Ontwikkeling
Ministry of Co-operation and Development

Verwysingsnommer: 5/5
Reference Number:

Hendrik Verwoerdgebou
Hendrik Verwoerd Buildings
Kaapstad
Cape Town

The Chairman
Driefontein Community Board
Private Bag X101
ISWEPE
2380

1 8 -12- 1981

Dear Mr Msibi,

RESETTLEMENT : DRIEFONTEIN 388 I.T. : WAKKERSTROOM

Further to your letter dated 10 August 1981, I would, in the first instance, like to point out that the removal and relocation of so-called "Black spots", or poorly situated areas, is carried out in accordance with a policy which has as its goal the improvement of the standard of life of all people of South Africa. You will therefore appreciate that it sometimes becomes necessary for people to be encouraged to move for their own ultimate good.

In regard to your reference to forced resettlements I must emphasize that it is certainly not part of declared policy that people should be forced to move and be resettled elsewhere without due consideration of their residential and other rights, nor that they should be exposed to hardship. In your particular case the reason for your resettlement has been discussed with you and your Board on various occasions. It was pointed out to you that the Department of Water Affairs is building a dam which is of national importance, on the Assegaai River and which will on completion towards the end of 1982, inundate some of your properties.

In conclusion I must stress that, like you, there are many Whites who also had to leave land which they have owned and occupied for generations and on which members of their families were born, raised and were subsequently buried. Everyone of us has to make sacrifices in some way or other to further peace and prosperity in this beautiful country of ours. Although the Government therefore appreciates and respects your feelings the relocation and resettlement of your people will have to be carried out in the interest of all concerned.

Yours faithfully,

J.J.G. WENTZEL M.P.
DEPUTY MINISTER OF
DEVELOPMENT AND LAND AFFAIRS

ST WENDOLINS: THE TACTICS OF 'VOLUNTARY REMOVALS'

St Wendolins lies on the edge of the Durban/Pinetown complex, an African community of some 21 000 that grew up on land owned by the Roman Catholic Diocese of Mariannhill and individual African landowners. The first threat to this longstanding community came in 1966 when the Group Areas Board moved in and divided the area into separate white, coloured and Indian group areas; an industrial zone was also demarcated. The removal of people did not get under way until the late 1970s, however, once the relocation townships of KwaNdengezi and KwaDabeka had been established. The first to arrive were the tenant households. In early 1979 officials issued notices to all tenants in the St Wendolins Ridge and Savannah Park sections of the community, instructing them to vacate their premises within a year. Nobody responded to the notices and in January 1980 the Port Natal Administration Board (PNAB) began to demolish houses. After representations from lawyers the removals at St Wendolins came to a stop, but those at Savannah Park continued. By 1981 the PNAB claimed that a total of 68 families had moved from Savannah Park voluntarily.

The following were some of the tactics used to bring about this 'voluntary removal':

1. Some residents were interviewed by officials who, after asking them questions about their families and houses, got them to sign documents stating that the information they had given was correct. Only after they had signed did the people discover that the documents were forms requesting that they be settled in KwaZulu.

2 Eviction notices were served on wives, children, pensioners and lodgers during the day, when the head of the household was away at work. When he returned home at night he was presented with a closed situation.

3 The PNAB 'invited' certain people to their offices and offered them alternative accommodation, making it appear to the rest of the community that these people had gone to them of their own accord.

4 Many residents who moved agreed to do so because their neighbours had already been moved, leaving them feeling insecure and isolated.

A letter issued by the PNAB to a household at St Wendolins stated very clearly the bleak options open to this person should he refuse to move:

> Should you, however, elect not to take up residence in KwaNdengezi, you are hereby notified to vacate the house you are at present occupying and take up residence in a black homeland and to vacate and demolish the house you are at present occupying.
> Should you fail to accept the alternative accommodation offered and should you fail to vacate your present house and demolish same before this date, your house will be demolished and you may be prosecuted. (Quoted in the *Sunday Tribune*, 6 Sept. 81.)

In a press interview, the PNAB official responsible for clearing St Wendolins insisted that the people were moving voluntarily but later admitted that those who had been instructed to move, 'must go':

> I have been given a task and I am doing it until I get instructions to stop. (*Sunday Tribune*, 6 Sept. 81.)

PENSIONS IN WINTERVELD: RESPONSIBILITY ABANDONED

A clear example of South Africa abandoning social responsibility is the plight of the old people of Winterveld. Having been moved to Winterveld more than 20 years ago from group areas such as Lady Selborne in Pretoria, having lived and worked in South Africa all their lives, they find that no one will pay their old age pensions. Since 'independence' in 1977, Bophuthatswana will only pay pensions to its citizens.

According to a 1981 Black Sash survey of old people in Winterveld, nearly all were non-Tswana, well over 65 years old, and had lived in Winterveld over 17 years. While more than 62% had worked in South Africa, 93% had never received a pension. Only 40% had applied for pensions because they knew non-Tswana were not eligible. (None had any other form of income.)

The Pension Act No. 18 of 1978 states that:

> Subject to the provisions of this Act, any person shall be entitled to the appropriate social pension if he satisfies the Secretary —
> a) that he is an aged, blind or disabled person or a war veteran; and
> b) that he is resident in Bophuthatswana at the time of his application for a social pension; and
> c) (i) that he is a citizen of Bophuthatswana; or
>   (ii) that he has lawfully resided in the Republic of Bophuthatswana for the period of five years immediately preceding the date of such application.

In other words, the conditions are the same as for citizenship.

Of the 534 cases documented by the Pretoria Advice Office, an examination of a random sample of 45 cases shows that:

> 75,6% are females
> 24,4% are males
> 97,8% are non-Tswanas
> 13,3% have applied for citizenship
> 100,0% have no income whatsoever
> 93,3% have never received a pension
> 40,0% have appplied for pensions
> 60,0% have not applied for pensions*
> 62,2% have worked in the RSA
> 24,4% were forcibly removed to Winterveld
> 66,7% have the Winterveld Community Authority stamp in their reference books
> 15,6% applied for disability grants.
>
> The average age is 68,6 years and the average time lived in the Winterveld area is 17,4 years.
>
> *The usual reasons given for not applying for pensions are:
> — not knowing where to go
> — friends, relatives and neighbours have been shunted from pillar to post and have received nothing
> — to apply is regarded as hopeless in any case and some don't know that a pension is due to them by right
> — non-Tswanas know that their applications will not be accepted
>
> (from Report of the Pretoria Advice Office to Black Sash National Conference, 1982.)

that it was at all necessary for an incident like this to occur'. (*Hansard*, Private Question 14, 15 April 83.) The Nationalist MP for Pretoria West was more concerned about the international consequences. 'That completely internationalised the matter, perhaps giving it more publicity than the Biko case', he said. (*Hansard*, Col. 8813, 7 June 83.)

In other cases, however, the government is clearly not at all embarrassed by the use of force. Its handling of the recurring squatter crisis in the metropolitan areas has made it very clear that influx control is one area where consultation plays no part. Here policy continues to be enforced as brutally as ever. Police raids at KTC (Cape Town), Inanda (Durban), Rockville (Soweto), Blue Rock (East London), Soweto (Port Elizabeth) and elsewhere; daily demolitions of the shelters of homeless people, teargas and spotlights — these have been the chosen methods for dealing with those who challenge this fundamental structure in the apartheid system. The police and the soldiers have not been withdrawn. They are still on call to handle situations where resistance is fierce and where the government is convinced that to yield will weaken rather than strengthen its overall position of dominance.

Ultimately the distinction between direct and indirect force becomes blurred, irrelevant. It draws attention away from the massive imbalance of power that exists between those who remove and those who are removed. In the final analysis, all mass removals of blacks under apartheid are forced. Whether people resist or whether they submit, whether the government methods of compelling obedience to its plans are direct or indirect, force is built into the process from the start. In a situation in which blacks do not possess political rights or freedom of movement, there can be no question of their exercising a real and free choice about being removed.

The role of the bantustans

The overall programme of relocation originates with the central government in Pretoria. It is the central government that called the bantustans into being and initiated the programme of consolidation. It controls the finances and determines the priorities, whether removal or reprieve. It defines the boundaries of what is to be the white and what the black areas in South Africa. Through the Trust it controls much of the land on which the relocation sites are established — many of these have not yet been incorporated into the bantustans.

Most of the bantustans leaders like to distance themselves as far as possible from removals — to play on their powerlessness in relation to Pretoria in this regard. They claim that they themselves try to have nothing to do with removals, but that they are powerless to stop it, if Pretoria insists. The larger bantustans, notably KwaZulu, Bophuthatswana and the Transkei, have managed to achieve a degree of autonomy in relation to Pretoria in certain respects. They have used that to oppose certain removals and to embarrass the central government on occasion. Chief Buthelezi of KwaZulu is particularly outspoken:

> We have said before that we are not prepared to cooperate with the removal of people. We don't want to be a party to the misery of our people. (*Natal Mercury*, 30 April 73.)

The leaders of the smaller and weaker bantustans are not in a position to be as publicly critical of Pretoria as he is. Simon Skosana, Chief Minister of the handful of scrubby farms that make up KwaNdebele, is probably in the most dependent position of all. He can hardly afford to antagonise Pretoria while the consolidation of KwaNdebele is being negotiated. Nor can he denounce the removals that have supplied him with most of his subjects. (According to official figures, at least 6% of all the inhabitants live in relocation areas that have been established since 1975. (*Hansard*, Private Question 22, 27 April 83.)

However, none of the bantustans want to be seen as Pretoria's stooges in so politically sensitive an issue as removals. They need to protect their own credibility. They are also acutely aware of the very real threat presented to their own political future by the hordes of landless, often jobless people that are being thrust upon them in the relocation areas. They know that their territories are already hopelessly overloaded with people. Their ability to meet the demands of all those already looking to them to supply schools, houses, hospitals, pensions etc. is dangerously inadequate. Commented Chief Mabuza of Kangwane in 1980:

> As far as we are concerned resettlement is a political bomb . . . some resettlement areas have no amenities whatsoever, no running water, no sewerage system, no schools and no clinics. Many of the people have no jobs. Some people have to drink dirty water. They think we are responsible. There is no message that we can get across to them until their problems have been attended to. (*Rand Daily Mail*, 29 July 80.)

While the bantustans want the land that is still controlled by the

KWANDEBELE: UHURU NEXT

Seventy-five kilometres from Pretoria lies the next bantustan due to take independence — KwaNdebele. In April 1982 its legislative assembly passed a motion which read:

> Whereas the Ndebele nation is desirous of obtaining complete self-determination for itself, this Legislative Assembly and the Government of KwaNdebele should consider the advisability of committing themselves to attain independence for KwaNdebele and consequently requests the Government of the RSA to assist them to obtain this ideal. (*Sunday Tribune*, 30 May 82.)

According to Chief Minister Skosana it is simply the next step in a process of establishing KwaNdebele:

> We got our territorial authority in 1977, legislative in 1979, self-rule in 1980, and now we're going for independence.

And with amazing candour he admits that he does not know what independence will bring:

> I don't know. How can my people know what independence is all about when I don't even know myself? But we're learning. (*Sunday Tribune*, 30 May 82.)

The KwaNdebele legislative assembly was never elected. No pretence of democracy such as elections has been tried as in the case of other bantustans. In arguing for more land to be given to KwaNdebele, the Deputy Minister of Development and of Land Affairs said:

> We hope that they will ask for independence shortly and that then we shall be in a position to deal with both their independence and their borders consecutively.
> (*Hansard*, Col. 13364, 6 Sept 83.)

KwaNdebele is a collection of Trust farms and parts of other bantustans situated between Groblersdal and Marble Hall in the Eastern Transvaal. The creation of the bantustan for the South Ndebele people is interesting in itself. It was not part of the original Nationalist plan for ethnic 'homelands'. The first mention of an Ndebele bantustan was only made in the late 1960s. Plans have changed according to various consolidation proposals but people only began to realise the effects in the late 1970s.

In terms of the 1975 consolidation proposals the most eastern section of Bophuthatswana, the district of Moretele 2, was to be excised and handed to KwaNdebele. The Moutse area of Lebowa was excised in 1980 to be given to KwaNdebele. According to the 1983 proposals KwaNdebele is to be extended south towards the development axis of Pretoria-Bronkhorstspruit rather than into adjacent Bophuthatswana. (Compare 1975 and 1983 maps, pp 180, 181.) White farmers in the area are being bought out and their farms will become part of KwaNdebele. Negotiation has been delicate and it seems that the consolidation of KwaNdebele has caused bitterness and opposition on all sides — Lebowa, Bophuthatswana and local white farmers.

The vast majority of people have come 'voluntarily' after harassment in Bophuthatswana or have been squeezed off the white-owned farms because wages and working conditions are so bad. Others have been moved from deproclaimed townships throughout the Eastern Transvaal. Through a process of being pushed out of other bantustans, white rural and urban areas, Ndebeles (and others) have landed in KwaNdebele with no other place to live. They had no choice but to go to KwaNdebele.

The establishment of KwaNdebele symbolises the new approach to the government's policy of relocation. Thus *Die Vaderland* reported:

> According to Mr van der Walt the great flow of black people to KwaNdebele is the best example of how the new approach is bearing fruit in practice. After plots had been marked out, and adequate water and services provided, 45 000 people moved to

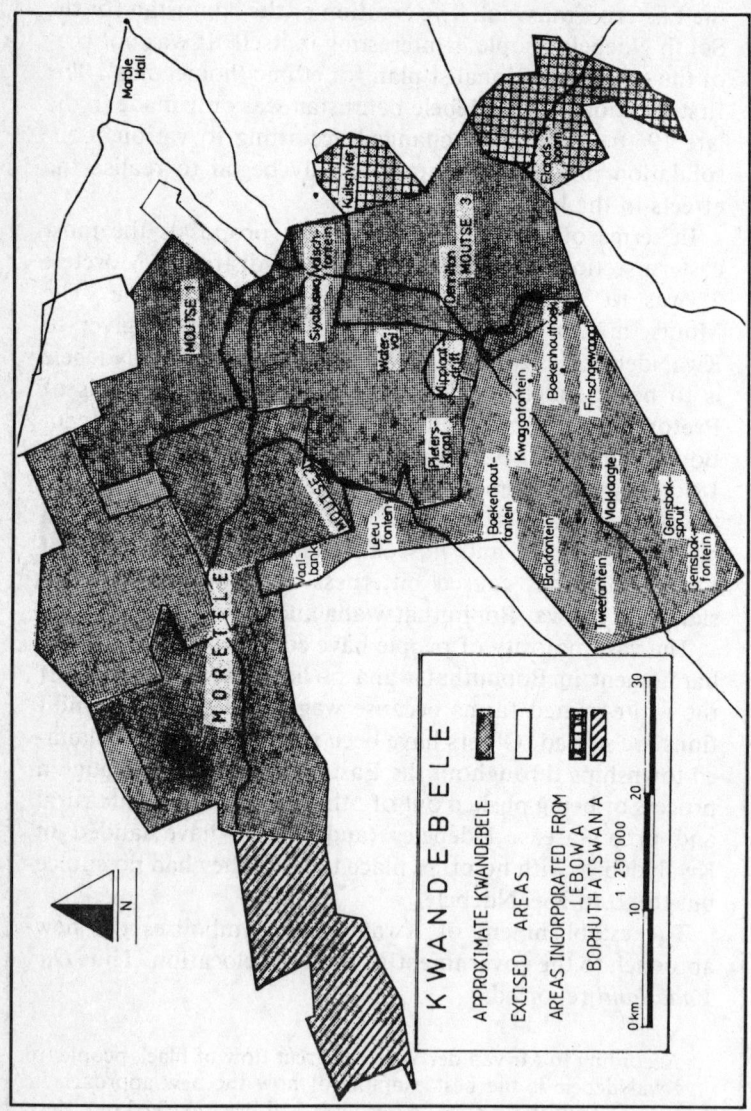

Map 11: KwaNdebele — 1975 Consolidation Proposals

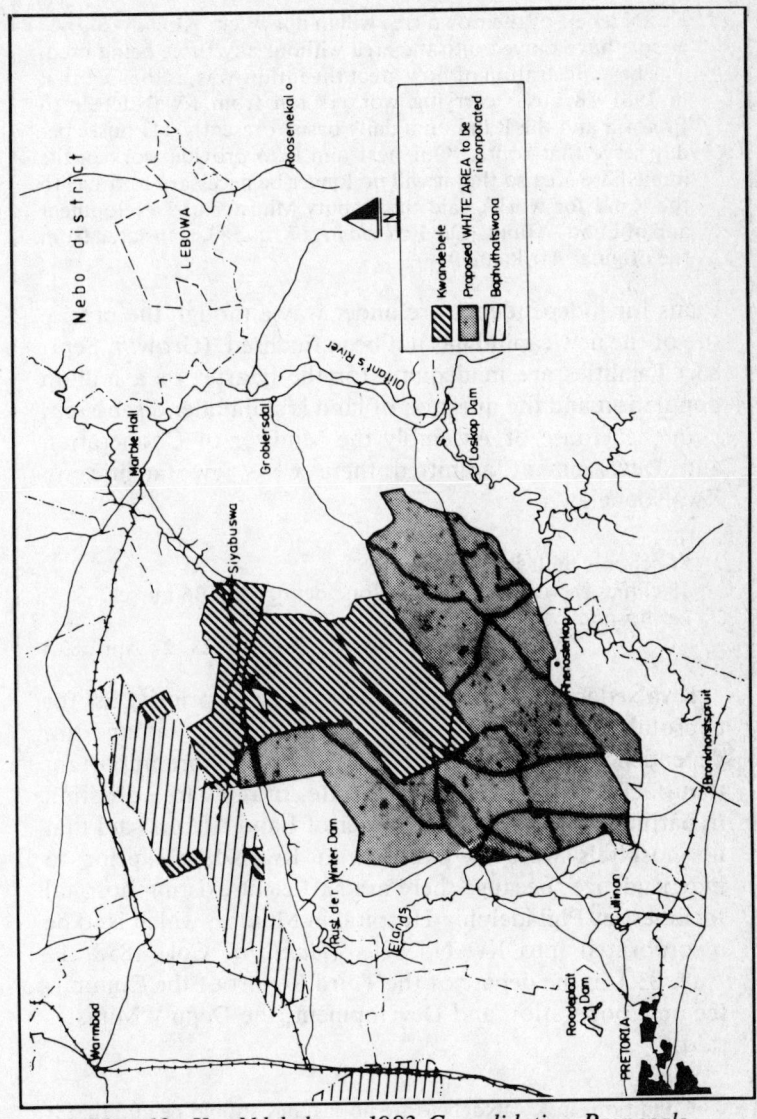

Map 12: KwaNdebele — 1983 Consolidation Proposals

KwaNdebele of their own free will in one week. Already 200 000 people have moved into the area without any force being used. The best illustration of how great the inflow was, is the fact that in 1981 38 buses carrying workers ran from KwaNdebele to Pretoria and the Rand on a daily basis. Presently 243 buses per day serve that route. 'Our next aim is to provide work in the immediate area so that it will no longer be necessary to travel to the Rand for work', said the Deputy Minister of Development and of Land Affairs. (*Die Vaderland*, 17 June 83, translated from the original Afrikaans.)

Plans for independence are under way although the precise site of the new capital has not been finalised. (*Growth*, Sept. 83.) Facilities are inadequate for the quarter of a million population and the question of land is still under discussion.

In the House of Assembly the Minister of Cooperation and Development admitted there were few facilities in KwaNdebele:

51 schools built in 1981 and 1982.
18 clinics served by 8 doctors, one dentist and 36 nurses.
No hospital.
(*Hansard*, Question 23, 27 April 83.)

KwaNedebele is high on the government's priority list for consolidation because it is amenable to taking 'independence'. The government sees land as more important than facilities for the emerging state. In reply to a question in parliament the Deputy Minister of Land Affairs said that no hospitals were to be built in KwaNdebele prior to independence 'because there are sufficient existing hospital facilities' at Philadelphia Hospital in Moutse, which is to be incorporated into KwaNdebele. (*Hansard*, Col. 1858, 17 Aug. 83.) In the debate of the Third Report of the Committee on Cooperation and Development, the Deputy Minister said:

Conditions in KwaNdebele are not as they should be and that is why it is in any case, irrespective of independence, essential for

> us to make more land available for the establishment of a residential area, to mention only one reason. That is why it has become essential to make more land available for KwaNdebele.
> At present KwaNdebele consists of only 72 000 hectares. When one thinks of development and the establishment of a new State and that half a million* people are already settled there and that people are moving there in their thousands, it is surely impossible to expect that more land shall not be made available. It is correct to accept that the Government is proceeding from the standpoint that we are working with KwaNdebele with a view to independence and that we are obtaining more land for them for that purpose. (Deputy Minister of Development and of Land Affairs, *Hansard*, Col. 13363, 6 Sept. 83.)
>
> * population is 255 000 according to *Growth*, Sept. 83.

Trust — and more — they do not want to receive it swarming with destitute people.

Where the bantustans are seen to be cooperating with Pretoria in removals they present it as acting out of humanitarian concern for the welfare of those dumped so heartlessly upon them. Thus Chief Lennox Sebe of the Ciskei in 1979:

> We do not support resettlement, but if resettlement is to take place then the Republican government is responsible to see that its policy is carried out, but once these people are settled in the Ciskei, they are not slaves, they are people, and for humanitarian reasons, we have to give assistance to them, not that as some say we encourage resettlement.
> (*Ciskei Legislative Assembly Debates*, Vol. II (1979), p62.)

Yet despite their attempts to shake off any responsibility for relocation, all the bantustan governments are deeply implicated in the process of removals. Their opposition is largely verbal, not actual. They are implicated firstly by virtue of their status. They are the creations of Pretoria, on whom they all depend for most of their revenue and much of their technical and senior administrative staff. Their very existence provides relocation not simply with a place where all those not wanted by Pretoria can be dumped, but also with a justification for the dumping: removals as a process of nation-building, of restoring people to their land.

That is one of the main reasons why the bantustans were set up by Pretoria in the first place.

Now that some of them have become independent, the justifications have grown even more sophisticated. Those endorsed out of urban areas and sent to the Transkei, Venda, Bophuthatswana or Ciskei are not South Africans; they are foreigners being repatriated. Questions about conditions in relocation areas in or even near the independent bantustans are fobbed off: that is said to be the concern of foreign states, and Pretoria never meddles in the affairs of its neighbours. Referring to Mgwali and the other black spots in the white corridor in the Eastern Cape, the Deputy Minister of Development and Land Affairs rebuked a PFP MP for raising the issue of their removal.

> The hon. member must not interfere in Ciskeian affairs. I do not want this side of the House to interfere in Ciskeian affairs either.
> (*Hansard*, Col. 887, 11 Feb. 83.)

All the bantustan governments are party to this process of nationbuilding, regardless of their public postures on removals. They have to be. It has provided them with their position and their power. They depend for their continued existence not only on handouts from Pretoria but also on the promotion of a strong ethnic identification among the people under their control. Without that they have no legitimacy, no basis for support. Even Buthelezi, who claims to favour a broad-based black rather than Zulu nationalism, played very successfully on Zulu 'national' pride in his handling of the Ingwavuma affair. Much of his grassroots support came from people who were outraged that a piece of KwaZulu should be offered to the 'Swazi dogs'. In Ingwavuma people of pro-Swazi sympathies were harassed by the local KwaZulu authorities.

The bantustans are also implicated in relocation as agents of removal themselves. Not only do they provide Pretoria with an ethnic justification and a location for its removal programme. Most of them have been directly responsible for removing people on a large scale as well, in the name of ethnic purity and ethnic identity. Much of the growing ethnic conflict that has accompanied the creation of the bantustans has been sparked off by the bantustan authorities playing their allotted role of ethnic policemen. Large concentrations of other ethnic groups in their territories are an embarrassment to them, undermining their claims to represent the national aspirations of a particular group of people who belong to a particular piece of land. These 'aliens' also act as a drain on their very limited resources. For these reasons they have tried either to squeeze out those who do not qualify ethnically to live in their territories or to exclude them from participation in bantustan institutions.

Their methods have been those ones already tried and tested by Pretoria. At Winterveld, the huge informal settlement outside Pretoria, the Bophuthatswana authorities — the dreaded 'YB' — have combined direct force with a range of more indirect pressures to drive out the thousands of non-Tswana people living there. There have been vicious raids and arrests of those without the correct Tswana papers; Tswana is the only medium of instruction allowed in the schools; non-Tswana people are refused work permits and pensions; tensions between landowners and non-Tswana tenants are manipulated so that the tenants will be evicted. From their side the KwaNdebele authorities have capitalised on this by encouraging Ndebele-speaking people to move to their area with glowing accounts of freedom.

> Today, precisely 100 years after the Ndebele were alienated from their land, spurred on by their own nationalism, tens of thousands of South-Ndebele are returning to their own national geographical home to build canals and schools, thereby expressing their newly-found national consciousness.
> ... the National Party has created the opportunity through consolidation for the Ndebele to return from diaspora and to exchange the yoke of exile for political self-determination and their own national pride ... an NP wanting to create a place in the sun for all peoples in South Africa, thereby ensuring that only through the freedom of peoples can an orderly pattern of civilisation continue to exist here at the southern tip of Africa. (Mr A T van der Walt, MP for Bellville, *Hansard*, Col. 8705, 6 June 83.)

According to the Department of Cooperation and Development, some 10 000 people had moved to KwaNdebele from Winterveld by 1979; by 1983 this figure had risen to 27 000. (*Hansard*, Col. 8778, 7 June 83.)

A similar process of harassment from the side of the Bophuthatswana authorities and inducement from the side of the

Qwaqwa authorities led to the massive influx of Sotho-speaking people out of Thaba Nchu and into the relocation site of Onverwacht in 1979. A few years earlier, in 1976/77, between 40 000 and 65 000 people fled from the Glen Grey and Herschel districts in the Eastern Cape to the Ciskei because they feared the consequences of becoming part of Matanzima's Transkei. Initially the Ciskeian authorities led them to believe that there would be land and opportunity for them if they moved. They took several busloads of people to look at the Trust farms that had been allocated to them but failed to explain to each busload that the land that they saw was not intended simply for the people in their bus — they would be sharing it with many thousands of others as well.

Furthermore, all the bantustans have removed people in the name of bantustan development. The implementation of betterment planning is now the responsibility of the bantustan governments. To them has been delegated the extremely unpopular task of forcing people to move into rural villages in order to pack as many people onto the land as possible. In 1980 Koornhof denied any responsibility for betterment planning:

> The information required relates to matters over which the various National States have full jurisdiction and the Department of Cooperation and Development is therefore not in a position to furnish it.
> (*Hansard*, Private Question 540, 22 April 80.)

As noted in a study on social change in KwaZulu:

> Buthelezi has privately expressed his fears . . . in regard to peasant reaction to agricultural planning in KwaZulu, which must unavoidably cause discontent to many. (Schlemmer and Muil, 1975, p113.)

The bantustan governments are also assuming more and more responsibility for removing people off land required for large, capital-intensive agricultural schemes. These are prestige projects. Whatever income they may generate does not go to the people whom they have displaced off the land. It gets soaked up by the central bantustan administration and by the highly paid expert management staff who control the projects. There are examples of this sort of bantustan-sponsored and approved removal all over the black-controlled areas. Thus in Venda, tribal land has been taken over by an extensive tea production project sponsored by the Venda Development Corporation and the Corporation for Economic Development. In KwaZulu fairly properous small-scale farmers have been driven off their land in the Makhathini Flats to make way for a cotton-growing scheme that was launched by the KwaZulu Development Corporation. By 1982 about 1000 ha. had been fenced off for this project. The irony of this removal is that the people being driven off the land were themselves growing cotton. In Kangwane people were moved in 1981 to make way for a sisal project at Tonga. In the Ciskei several hundred villagers are being forced off their land and into the Elukhanyweni relocation site to make room for a dam and the ever-expanding Keiskamma irrigation scheme; and the people of Glenmore are facing a further removal in order to make way for the expansion of the Tyefu irrigation scheme. As whole communities are ousted, so the bantustan authorities try to persuade observers that these schemes really benefit the locals even though those dim-witted masses may not appreciate the fact immediately.

> [Lennox Sebe] . . . said a number of critics had said the schemes benefited only a few people and, therefore, were not to the advantage of the Ciskei nation. However, the schemes [Tyefu and Keiskammahoek] clearly satisfied international stipulations on such undertakings, he said. They generated a shift in power to the powerless and helped individuals who were, at the initial stage, powerless, to see their common interest with others . . .   (*Daily Despatch*, 7 May 80.)

Finally, all the bantustans are involved in removals by virtue of their function as the local agents of control for Pretoria. An example of this is provided by KwaZulu's response to the presence of squatters in the township areas administered by it. Despite KwaZulu's angry insistence that it will have nothing to do with removals, it has been removing people out of squatter camps on the edge of Umlazi township (near Durban) and relocating them in areas further away from Durban. In administering this area it has been forced to accept problems created by the central government's housing policy for urban Africans. It has to cope with the major shortage of housing in the Durban townships since these fall in its area. Saddled with this responsibility, lacking the funds to implement a major house-building programme of its own, and very nervous of the restless people of the Durban townships, it has chosen to deal with the problem by using methods learnt from Pretoria: to remove the squatters further out into the rural periphery.

Ultimately, no matter how outspoken particular bantustan governments may be, they are party to Pretoria's programme of relocation. At best they are powerless to stop Pretoria if it is determined to press ahead with a particular removal. In general, however, they are Pretoria's accessories. They are accessories because they are participants in Pretoria's scheme for dividing and controlling the black population. As participants they cannot escape responsibility for the effects of that scheme. Nor can they offer an adequate base from which to challenge it. Far more effective, as the following two chapters demonstrate, have been strong local organisation coupled with pressure from outside support groups.

CHAPTER SEVEN

Communities in crisis — six case studies of relocation in practice

1. The Tsitsikama reserves

In 1977/78, 400 families were moved, despite strenuous resistance, from a number of small scheduled reserves in the Lower Tsitsikama forest near Humansdorp in the Cape. They were moved in terms of the consolidation proposals for the Ciskei from land that was first granted to their forebears in 1835, and later scheduled in terms of the 1913 Land Act, into a closer settlement known as Elukhanyweni, 300 kilometres away in the Ciskei. They resisted and argued but eventually, in the face of guns, they gave in and moved.

For these people relocation has been a particularly savage process. They have emerged at the end of a brutal experience as a landless people, totally dependent on migrant labour for their survival. The sense of bitterness and frustration within the community is immense. Most people want only one thing, to return to the place where:

> We had fields.
> We had work.
> We had food.
> We had a better life.

Notice to move

On 21 April 1975 the parliamentary select committee dealing with the consolidation of the bantustans recommended

> in terms of the provisions of section 5 of the Bantu Administration Act, 1927 . . . the withdrawal of the Bantu tribes, Bantu communities, and Bantu persons residing in the . . . District of Humansdorp . . . comprising the following properties: Doriskraal Location, Fingo Location, The Gap, Palmietrivier Location, Snyklip Location, Wittekleibosch Location and Witte Els Bosch. (SC 9-75)

On 14 May 1975 these recommendations were approved by the House of Assembly.

The various communities in the Tsitsikama reserves were then informed about their impending move to Elukhanyweni. According to them, they were made lavish promises: agricultural land equivalent to what they already had, and decent housing. The Ciskeian authorities were also drawn in at these meetings:

> Two white guys asked us to move. They said that the Chief Minister had built for us permanent homes.

> A South African Government official asked us to leave. He said that the land belonged to whites and Mr S., the Ciskeian Minister, was encouraging us to move saying that land was available for us in the Ciskei.

> Mr S. and other black agriculturalists told us to move. They said that land was available to us in the Ciskei.

> The whole thing started in the 70s. There used to be meetings where people were asked by Mr S. to vote for Ciskei. We didn't. They said Ciskeian government was in need of us.

A meeting of those who were prepared to move was called and about 50 people turned up. As their reward, the *inywaki*, as they are called by the rest of the community (literally 'meerkat', i.e. collaborators), were offered agricultural land. Though most of them received dryland fields, 14 fortunate families were incorporated into a Ciskeian irrigation scheme at Keiskammahoek. They all moved before the rest of the community and although some initially lived in the relocation camp, they now all live close to their fields. In a sense these collaborators are no longer part of the Elukhanyweni community, many of whom view them with contempt.

The bulk of the Tsitsikama people, however, refused to move. On 12 September 1976, Pretoria responded. The State President issued an order for the removal, as provided for in the Bantu Administration Act of 1927. At the same time an order went out to the South African police to arrest and detain any person who refused to move.

On 5 October a magistrate and an official from the Department of Bantu Administration and Development called a meeting of residents from the various reserves. The magistrate read out the contents of the order issued by the State President. The meeting was also addressed by the official. He informed them that the date for the move was set for 15 November 1977. He also asked for their cooperation — and told the meeting that as a sign of his own commitment to cooperation, he had decided to wear a suit and drive a clean car that day. Then, in the same breath, he made it clear that anyone who refused to move would be arrested and moved regardless. Some questions from the floor were permitted, but as soon as someone questioned the removal itself the meeting was closed. The following is a transcript of some parts of the meeting, translated from Afrikaans.

Official Listen, are there any of you with any questions about the move? Right, let us just have the names . . . [First question and answer.] Right there is another question. Wait a moment, is this man a resident here, let me have a look at his book, I have never seen his face before.

Fingo 1 I am a teacher here, an old teacher.

Official But I have never seen your face before.

Fingo 1 I am an old teacher, I built this place. I wrote a letter to Mrs Ballinger and a letter came back which said that we would not be moved. I do not know what is happening here today.

Official But the point is, it does not matter to whom you wrote. The point is, this is the final order from the State President and that is what I am conveying to you. Wait a moment, are there any other questions?

Fingo 2 Yes.

Official Right, let us hear.

Fingo 2 Mr G. and the people who stand with you, we understand now why you are here today. There has already been decided about the people who are seated here, and they know nothing about it.

Official I just want to say to him that is why we are here today.

Fingo 2 We know nothing about it. Mr K. has always been around, and on the few occasions he came here, he always said he wanted people who were willing to move. We told him directly that we did not want to go, we will not go anywhere because we have been here for more than 250 years.

Official I just want to interrupt you. I am not going to permit this. We are not going to discuss this question. I am not going to allow anyone to talk about it. I am willing to answer questions about the move, but anything else would be a waste of time, there is nothing we can do about it.

Fingo 2 We are not willing to move on the 15th. You can do what you

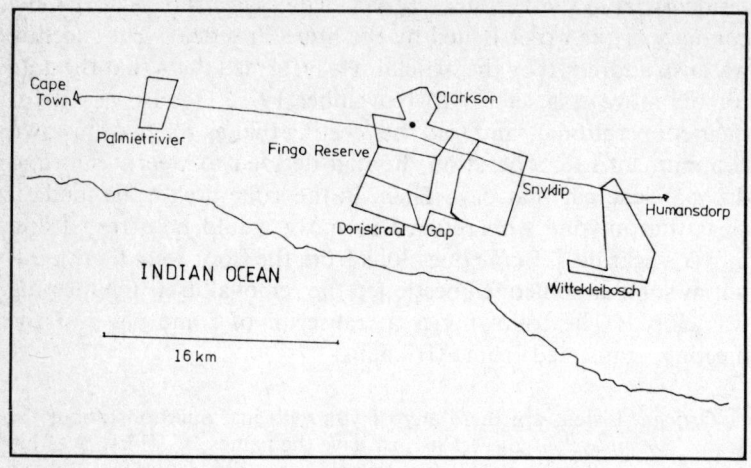

Map 13: The Tsitsikama Reserves

	like, but we are not willing to move on the 15th. We paid for this ground with our blood when we fought with these people.
Official	Is he finished, is he now finished?
Fingo 2	Peace, peace, we cannot be moved from here.
Official	Now look here, I will not allow any more questions because no-one has asked any questions about the move. Everyone is now asking questions about something about which nothing can be done. So in other words, I am going to close this meeting now. You have been informed about this, and we request your cooperation.

The people still remember this meeting:

> We argued with him and when we were defeating him he told us that we would leave under any circumstances. We later even fought court cases.

Organisation

The community started to organise against being removed straight away. Some people tried to reason:

> We formed our committee for asking the reason of our departure, but who can we ask, for there was a confusion.
>
> We tried to stay by asking why we were being moved, because prior to this the government said we would live there up to the seventh generation. All they said is we can't disobey the law.

They formed groups and held meetings:

> We tried to resist by attending some meetings about resistance to our removal.
>
> We attended meetings that were held and we pledged never to go to a place unknown to us.
>
> We organised ourselves as a community and had long talks with the authorities.

Some even tried to ignore the order:

> The magistrate in Humansdorp called a meeting and told us that we must leave in November, but we take no notice.

On 15 November the removal squads arrived for the first time. By then, it seems, the authorities were no longer willing to talk. Although Dr. Koornhof has subsequently denied that any force was used, this is not how the 82 people interviewed by SPP remember that time:

> We held meetings discussing the issue and unanimously agreed with other households not to move. But the boers got tired of what we were doing and came with guns to evict us. All households were eventually moved to this place. All resistance was in vain.
>
> We held several meetings and agreed not to leave but at gunpoint we were moved to this place. We could not resist them because they had weapons for unarmed people.
>
> Meetings were held and people unanimously agreed not to move but eventually we were moved out at gun point.
>
> We organised some of the households and met to discuss our plight, clearly refusing to move. But in 1977 we were moved at gunpoint. We had no option.
>
> We formed some groups and had long talks with the officials, but

being tired of our questions they sent police.

Despite the chaos many still tried to find an explanation:

> The soldiers who pointed us with rifles told us to leave. There was no reason, but we were driven out like animals. We and the others tried to ask why they did so, but the answer was to be taken to prison at once.

> The police and the army told us to move. The only reason was the point of a gun, no other reasons were given.

> We endeavoured to ask the cause but the answer was to be thrown in prison.

> We were not even given one reason, but brutally evicted at gun point.

> We formed a group and asked the police the cause but the answer was to be pointed with guns.

> No reason for the move was given except promise to shoot us or take us to prison.

Some claim that they did receive an explanation:

> The police who said that they were sent by the South African Government said that bastards would emerge if blacks kept on staying near whites.

> The police said we had to move because we have a special Canaan in the Ciskei.

> The boers told us through the police to leave. The reason they give is that at this side we could educate our children better.

> They said we have our land in Keiskammahoek where we could get anything.

> The government sent police to kick us out. The police said the government was in need of the place. We asked various questions and we were told that we could get houses here.

Here and there, resistance turned into acts of desperation:

> Some took big stones and put them across the street to prevent the trucks from coming to this side and some were imprisoned.

The community also sought legal means to fight the move. On 21 November the headman gave notice of an application on behalf of the community for a legal injunction against the removal. Their application was based on the grounds that the parliamentary resolution approving their removal did not meet with all the necessary conditions: although the resolution stated the places from which the community had to move, it failed to state the place to which they had to go. Judgement, however, went in favour of the state.

The headman started an appeal, but then this was withdrawn. There are conflicting stories about why the appeal was withdrawn; some people have claimed that the headman was bribed, although this has never been proved. Later, other members of the community tried to start their own appeal against the judgement but they were refused permission to do so by the courts. It was claimed that only the person in whose name the case was originally fought could take the case on appeal.

The removal
At the time of the court case, one man described his experiences:

> He had been on his way home after hearing that lorries were near his house and was stopped on the road by police.
> They had his name on a list and told him he was one of the people influencing others not to move. He denies this allegation in his affidavit.
> He accompanied the police to his house but refused to hand over the house keys, which would enable them to move him and his effects, because his children were at school and his wife was not at home.
> He alleges the door to his house was broken down by the police and his belongings damaged in the removal.
> Thereafter he was taken to the Humansdorp police station and allegedly told to sign a document without being allowed to read it and then paid R740 in compensation. He was asked whether he wished to stay in the bus or in a cell until he was moved to Keiskammahoek at 10 that night. He elected to stay on the bus which was guarded and no one was allowed to leave it. (*Eastern Province Herald,* 24 March 82.)

The Mfengu people resisted for as long as they could, but eventually they were overwhelmed. They were too few, too isolated. There was some publicity but their struggle did not become a major political issue. They were removed group by group over a period of two months.

> We stayed when others were moving. The boers came back after some weeks and forced us to move at gunpoint as well. Other households also tried to resist likewise but were also evicted and brought here later.
>
> Other households were left behind when we moved because of the shortage of transport. But they eventually joined us for nobody could resist the barrels of the guns.
>
> We could not do anything because even those who tried to resist were jailed and immediately after their release were sent straight to this place.
>
> The soldiers just said that we were leaving at that moment and pointed us with guns. Other households were still refusing and the soldiers promised to shoot them.
>
> We tried to stay. But an official commanded his messengers to demolish our houses. Then we were evicted at gunpoint.
>
> During this period the police often arrived while the people were still asleep. They would surround their houses, force them from their homes and shunt them onto buses and trucks early in the morning.
> (*Eastern Province Herald,* 24 March 82.)

Over time the pressures became too much.

> We were told to move on 5 October. We refused to go. On 16 December there arrived 14 bakkies with soldiers carrying rifles plus 22 trucks. The soldiers asked us in Afrikaans whether each person wanted to be removed or not. Many residents replied positively.

Finally, by the end of January 1978, the Mfengu reserves were empty.

> We were driven out like dogs.

Once evicted the people were transported in convoys — buses for the women and children, open trucks for the men and furniture — to Keiskammahoek:

> We were brought like animals on GG trucks.

> We were brought by trucks, some with our properties, but much were damaged.

> We were brought on overloaded buses with children and men were on GG trucks with furniture.

Their passage was supervised by the police, Eastern Cape Administration Board officials, and troops. Zulu truck drivers from Natal were specially employed for the job. The Ciskeian authorities assisted.

> We were brought by the police of South Africa . . . by the boers . . . by the boers of the Republic . . .

> GG trucks were driven by Zulus and some few clerks sent by South African government.

> The South African government reached an agreement with Ciskei.

> The South African and the Ciskeian government brought us here.

On arrival, after the slow 300 kilometre journey, they were given a tomato-box house or tent:

> The government labourers took us to these clustered houses.

> They pushed us each to his own house.

> The boers gave us tents. Later we got houses.

> The police allocated us this land and ordered us to erect tents.

> We were brought by the trucks and ordered to erect your tent.

Thus the reality of life at Elukhanyweni dawned on them. The first of a number of promises was shattered — there were no good houses.

But their greatest shock was about land. Before they were moved people had understood that they were to be given land equivalent to what they had had at Tsitsikama — in most cases about three and a half hectares of arable land plus about 25 hectares of grazing land on the common for each household. At Elukhanyweni, however, the majority ended up with house plots only.

> There we had fields, here we have none.
>
> We used to take something from the garden, but now I have to spend much money buying vegetables, which we didn't do before.
>
> I am the agriculturalist, but I have no fields to grow.
>
> We have no fields and that is why we despise this place.

Another outrage was being stripped of their livestock. They were encouraged to sell some of their animals before the move. Not being free to decide the timing, those people who did sell could not even set their price. They had to let their animals go cheaply, accepting whatever offers they got. Nobody felt satisfied with the prices. Some people lost their stock in the confusion of being moved, as well — when the removals squad arrived unexpectedly, animals disappeared into the bush and there was no time to find them.

> People who sold their stock had to give them away to the white farmers who bought them for R16 or R20 a cow. If you didn't sell, they said, well then we'll fetch them up off the road after you have gone.
>
> We sold the stock with less money because we were in a hurry.
>
> Stock were lost because we sold them cheap caused by our eviction.
>
> Stock went out of sight when GG trucks arrived here.
>
> Land were lost and stock disappeared into the bushes.

Many people did take their stock through to the Ciskei, only to lose them there. Some died in the drought. Some were sold. The rest were simply stolen:

> When we arrived with our stock there was a drought here and so some died.
>
> We had 27 goats and 20 cattle which we brought here. They all died.
>
> We sold our stock when we found there is a shortage of grazing land here.
>
> Because of problems with grazing we sold our stock — cheaply.

Our stock was stolen the second day we live here.

Many people brought stock, and have not even got one head now.

Compensation
Although everyone had had land in the Tsitsikama reserves nobody had had freehold title to it. In those reserve areas, ownership was vested in the Trust. As a result the people were not paid any compensation for losing their land. Nor were they compensated for the unreaped crops that they left behind.

About a third of the 82 households that SPP interviewed were compensated for the loss of their houses. One person who had an eight bedroomed wattle and daub house received R300. Another who owned three houses — one stone, one brick and one mud brick — was paid R500 for the lot. Most compensation ranged between R80 and R180. One man received only R70 for his mud brick house.

Everyone thought the amount was insufficient:

What can you do with that amount?   (*Eastern Province Herald,*
                                                                        24 March 82.)

At one stage the Ciskeian government attempted to deal with the question of compensation and other complaints. Officials came to Elukhanyweni and wrote everything down, but that was the last of it. They never returned. Officialdom forgot them:

They just came and dumped us here and never looked back again.

After the move
Six years later, many of the Mfengu people at Elukhanyweni want only one thing, and that is to return to their lands in the Tsitsikama forest.

I don't want any improvement. I don't know about the others. I just want to be escorted back to Humansdorp.

If only they can return me back to Humansdorp to stay there I will be like a fish in the river.

On several occasions some members of the community have

tried to reverse the removal. In 1979 they wrote a letter to Koornhof in which they mentioned some grievances and asked to be allowed to return to their former lands. All they got in reply was a blunt refusal.

In early 1982 the removal became a public issue for a short period. Community leaders approached the opposition Progressive Federal Party (PFP) to ask for help in their struggle to return to the Tsitsikama forest. At that stage their former land was about to be sold to white farmers by the government. After investigating both the legal and parliamentary background, the PFP challenged the sale in parliament. They pointed out that it broke a number of legal requirements, in particular the 1913 Land Act. Since the Tsitsikama reserves had not been taken off the schedule of reserve land, they could not be owned by whites. Only once they had been formally excised from the 1913 schedule, by a resolution of parliament, could they be sold. In addition, no compensatory land had been set aside for the schedule in place of the excised reserves.

At first the government denied that this was the case — the Minister of Agriculture and Fisheries described the press reports as 'extremely malicious'. Then, however, Koornhof announced that a select committee would be appointed to investigate the excision.

This committee duly reported in June 1982. Not surprisingly, it recommended that the land be excised from the schedule immediately. At the final sitting of the 1982 parliamentary session, in the early hours of the morning on June 12 and after a heated debate, the required resolution authorising the excision of the Tsitsikama reserves was passed. During the debate the PFP MP for Albany, Mr Moorcroft, highlighted one of the most bizarre aspects of the whole process. The resolution passed in parliament scheduled land near Queenstown in the place of the Tsitsikama reserves — land that has since been incorporated into the Transkei. In other words, not only has the government not compensated the people for the loss of their land. It has also not compensated the bantustan that received them.

Once the formality of the parliamentary resolution had been met, the sale of the Tsitsikama land could proceed. The selling price, which has been described as a gift, came to a little over one million rand. This works out at R211 a hectare — for what a representative of the Department of Agriculture has called potentially the most productive land in the country, the New Zealand of South Africa.

During this period the Mfengu community mounted a last-ditch attempt to return to the Tsitsikama. A delegation was sent to meet Dr Koornhof. He refused to grant them an interview and instead referred them to the Ciskei Department of Foreign Affairs as they were now citizens of an independent state. The response of the Ciskeian Minister of Interior was equally dismissive. He could only say that the leader of the delegation 'wasn't even a Fingo' and that the real problem with the issue was that white political parties made blacks their political footballs. The delegation was thus left with no other option but to sit and watch from the gallery as parliament put the final seal on the removal.

2. Huhudi and Valspan

> "United we stand and divided we fall"
> — motto of the Huhudi Civic Association

Two of the townships under threat of removal in the Northern Cape are trying to resist removal to Bophuthatswana. They are Huhudi (township of Vryburg) and Valspan (township of Jan Kempdorp), 100 kilometres apart. These townships are controlled by the Diamond Fields and Northern Cape Administration Boards. They have been under threat of removal since the late 1960s but recent attempts to clear the townships only became serious in the 1980s.

In terms of government policy there will be no family housing for Africans in RSA if they work within commuting distance of a bantustan. The Huhudi people are supposed to move 55 kilometres south to Pudumong (Pudimoe) and the Valspan people 30 kilometres north-west to Pampierstad — both destinations in Bophuthatswana.

The threatened removal of the townships illustrates similarities and differences in tactics, both by the authorities and the people. In the 1970s and early 1980s both communities fought the removal through the community councils; now Huhudi has an elected civic association. The administration boards used identical strategies to 'persuade' people to move in both cases. Chambers of Commerce in both Jan Kempdorp and Vryburg are concerned about the potential loss of income from the removal.

The removals
Valspan is 3 kilometres from Jan Kempdorp, across the railway line from the industrial area and adjacent to a large military camp. Already some local families have been removed on ethnic grounds. The coloured people were moved to Andalusia on the other side of Jan Kempdorp. Nearly half the Valspan African population had been moved by late 1983 — the Sotho-speaking people to Onverwacht (scheduled for incorporation into Qwaqwa), the Xhosa to Ciskei and Transkei, and the Tswana to Pampierstad.

55% of the households surveyed by SPP in Pampierstad in 1981 had come from Valspan, in two main groups — in 1972 and 1980. Since then houses costing R13 000 have been built in Pampierstad. Many stand empty waiting for people from Valspan who do not want to move. Some of those interviewed in Pampierstad felt they had left Valspan under false pretences:

> They said they had built houses for us at Pampierstad, we must go.
>
> It was a modern suburb, we were told.
>
> They said we will not pay rent after five years, but we have been here nearly one year and they have doubled the rent from R6 to R12.

Huhudi is one kilometre from Vryburg. People walk to work. As a result of group area removals, the Indian community has been placed within walking distance of Huhudi, on the edge of Vryburg. A large modern shopping centre here serves the Huhudi people, saving them from travelling to the centre of Vryburg.

Various tactics have been used to persuade people to move to Pudumong. According to the Huhudi Civic Association:

> Exorbitant rents are harshly demanded. Forced lodgers' permits are given to students. Regular midnight raids are carried out against innocent residents. Residents are threatened against participation in HUCA . . .   (*Memorandum to Black Sash,* 14 July 83.)

As with Valspan,

Physical development in Huhudi has been actively frozen since 1970. People have been prohibited from putting up new structures because according to the National Party policy the place had been earmarked for removal.

This was done without the consultation and consent of the people to be removed. Since 1970 people have been involved in an 'owner's risk' campaign. Although such development has been illegal, rent hikes have always been legal and repeatedly implemented. The idea of removals started being practical in 1980 when 60 families were moved out of Vryburg (Huhudi) to be forcibly resettled in Pudumong. This was the beginning of the sad process of alienating people of Huhudi in a place of their birth and growth. (*Memorandum to Black Sash, 14 July 83.*)

Although the Administration Boards prohibited owners from improving or even maintaining their houses over the years, they are now using the fact that the houses are dilapidated as a reason for clearing the areas. The Boards claim the townships are largely slums. The people ask who prohibited them from preventing slum conditions.

In 1980 an anonymous leaflet was handed out, entitled 'Information Leaflet for All Residents of Valspan concerning Settlement in Pampierstad'. It transpired that this attempt to persuade the people to move voluntarily was made by the Administration Board. In 1981 a very similar leaflet was handed out in Huhudi:

INFORMATION LEAFLET TO ALL RESIDENTS OF HUHUDI CONCERNING SETTLEMENT AT PUDIMOE

You are, no doubt, already aware of the fact that the idea of settlement at Pudimoe has, ever since 1970, been brought to the notice of the people resident at Huhudi. To ensure that everybody is fully conversant with the true facts as regards the envisaged settlement, the following particulars are conveyed to you:—

1. WHY SHOULD I LEAVE HUHUDI?

   1.1 Because Huhudi's planning leaves much to be desired, housing is poor and the possibilities for expansion are very limited it would be far too costly to convert Huhudi into an attractive modern residential area.

   The majority of its inhabitants will not be able to pay for the development of the town with proper streets, sewerage and water on every stand. It has been estimated for instance that a sewerage system for the entire town will cost you in the vicinity of R40 per month extra (over and above what you are paying presently towards site rentals).

   Should more dwellings be built, an additional amount ranging from R15 to R55 for the dwellings in addition to your present site rental, might have to be charged.

   An electricity scheme for the town would increase your charges by a further amount of approximately R16 per month, etc. etc.

   1.2 In Huhudi I shall never be able to own land, in other words I cannot really possess my own plot of ground.

   1.3 In Huhudi the required standard of health can only be attained with the utmost difficulty and by spending an enormous amount of money.

2. WHAT CAN I EXPECT AT PUDIMOE?

   2.1 In Pudimoe I receive a neat new dwelling consisting

of four spacious rooms plus a bathroom and indoor toilet as well as a functional sink in the kitchen. All these conveniences cost me a mere R4,89 per month plus 3 cents per kilolitre water consumed. (If a large quantity of water is consumed the combined cost of housing and water should be in the neighbourhood of only R11,39 per month).

2.2 I am also assigned an attractive fenced plot large enough to enable me to pride myself on a beautiful flower garden and to grow my own vegetables.

2.3 Pudimoe is a well-planned town whose planning makes ample provision for such amenities as, for instance, the most modern health services, sufficient schools, churches serving different denominations, business concerns, industries, etc.

2.4 In Pudimoe I am in a position to fulfil myself in the sense that, as a voter, I will have a say in the government.

2.5 By living in Pudimoe my child can further his studies at the newly founded teachers' training college right on his doorstep.

2.6 If I settle at Pudimoe I shall be able to carry on with my work in Vryburg and enjoy the comfort of my home every night.

3. HOW DO I REACH VRYBURG?

A daily bus service operates from Pudimoe to Vryburg and back at a very reasonable subsidised rate which is

> currently as follows :-
> Weekly on a 5 day basis : R 3,70
> Weekly on a 6 day basis : R 4,50
> (Once the route is incorporated into the subsidy scheme the tariff might even be reduced.)
> The total cost of accommodation and daily transport combined is thus between R29 and R33 per month.

In reply to a protest from the Community Council of Huhudi, the Director-General of the Department of Cooperation and Development wrote that
1 Family housing would be frozen, hostel accommodation would be expanded.
2 About 1 050 existing habitable houses would have upgraded services. That, according to him, implied that people who live in 'good' houses can improve and maintain them decently.
3 Superfluous (*oortollige*) people, including families lodging, must be provided for in Pudimoe (Pudumong). Blacks who qualify in terms of Section 10(1)(a) and (b) of the Urban Areas Act of 1945 would maintain their rights in terms of employment opportunities in the white area. Commuters will be handled on merit (*Sleutelwerkers sal op meriete behandel word*). Employers with single accommodation in Huhudi could provide that.
4 Those who want to be moved to Pudimoe must be provided for.
5 The ideal, in terms of government policy, is that the maximum number of people be housed on a family basis in their own national states.

He added that incentives for industrial development would only be given to those industrialists whose black labour is 'drawn on a single basis from the national state or SADT'. (Translated from a letter in Afrikaans, dated 5 Oct. 81.)

Response
Initially the community councils of both areas were the only

organisations to oppose relocation to Bophuthatswana. Individuals were worried but too frightened to organise any resistance. Fear and helplessness underline a letter written in July 1981, from a Valspan resident under threat of removal:

> ... the Jan Kempdorp removals have been steady. It has been said that people are removing voluntarily but one could see that there was something behind it.
> To my surprise a certain man is removed by force. I do not know why. It is very heartbreaking because when he tried to refuse he was immediately locked up in jail. Meanwhile they are removing his tenants as he has quite a good number of them, over ten.
> I would have phoned you but I have no phone in my house and I am afraid of public phones. I hope someone will, or has already phoned you from Kimberley.
> I really pity this man but do not know how to help him.
> Please never mention my name in such things as the Anglicans are said to be instigators and we are earmarked.
> With all good wishes.

The Community Council of Valspan is still the only local body opposed to the removal. In July 1978 the Valspan Advisory Board (the equivalent of a community council) wrote a detailed memorandum to the Department of Bantu Administration.

ENTIRE REMOVAL OF VALSPAN

Preamble: The (Bantu) Administration Board is a key administrative body of the Department of (Bantu) Administration. We have always regarded the Department of Bantu Administration as the father of the Blacks but here in Valspan it seems it is just the direct opposite and we emphasise on immediate analysis that our Diamond Fields Administration Board seem to work actively for removal of Valspan Location of Jan Kempdorp.

As the time for the preparation of this memorandum and its presentation are very limited, we crave your indulgence for the way in which this important and difficult subject of Removal of Valspan is dealt with. It has not been possible to deal at all fully with the matter nor to systematise the material into one continuous whole. It has merely been possible to advance a number of points which have seemed to us to be most relevant and to stress certain aspect of the subject.

Among the most discouraging signs for the progressive or accelerating removal of Valspan is undoubtedly the activity displayed by our Diamond Fields Administration.

Another point to which we wish to refer, is that there seems to be a growing tendency on the part of the Administration to place the Advisory Board in a state of accusation to the residents. We are not prepared to acknowledge that the Advisory Board in their position of powerlessness have any authority to consent to removal or vice versa, we as a Board can only petition the authorities for their sympathetic dispensation on behalf of the residents we represent.

History of Valspan: Two hundred years, one hundred years, fifty years ago, Black and White in South Africa were distant from and practically independent of each other. Blacks lived peacefully in Fourteen Streams and Taung and along the banks of the Harts and Orange Rivers, but the growth of industries and other material interests and concerns of life such as the establishment of the Vaalharts Irrigation Scheme have drawn them together and made them inter-dependent. Here the beginners of the Irrigation Scheme engaged themselves in temporising and compromising with the Black inhabitants around Fourteen Streams, to move to Valspan permanently and give way to the Scheme. While some Blacks who were dissatisfied with the arrangements made chose to go their own way, the majority of others came to settle in their new area, Valspan. This is how Valspan came into existence.

Duties and functions of the Advisory Board are:
(a) To act in an advisory capacity on matters concerning the Location.
(b) To receive and consider complaints, representations and suggestions from the inhabitants and, if deemed necessary to make representations thereon to the Council or to any Committee appointed by the Council to deal with the affairs of the Location.
(c) To receive and consider any report concerning the Location by the Council or any of its officials, and if necessary to make representations in regard to such report to the Council.
(d) To perform the functions assigned to it by the Natives' (Urban Areas) Consolidation Act, 1945, or any amendment thereof, and
(e) To render every assistance to the authorities in preserving law and order in the Location.

Sirs, the argument is roughly this: When scanning through these duties and functions, one would unnecessarily assume undue importance not understanding their demoralising effect especially when it comes to where one has to be told that the function of the Board is purely advisory. That the Board can advise but the Department is not bound or compelled to accept the advice as we are not part of the final decision-making machine. In view of this prolonged explanation anybody saying that the Advisory Board of Valspan have agreed and accepted removal would be talking untruth.

Surveying behind the Location: It is a well known fact among the residents that the area behind 'R' Canal in Valspan Location was surveyed and that plans were drawn and put up in the Location Superintendent's office during 1954 or thereabout for every one to see. It was then stated that some time in the future the Location would be moved back to be settled in that area. What we advance here is true, nothing but the whole truth. A few years after that this was sunk into oblivion and an entirely new and different talk cropped up.

The Advisory Board was told that all *Tswanas only* were to be moved to Pampierstad and that that was the desire of Chief Mangope of Bophuthatswana before he became President. Sirs, here this is well to remember and to be weighed that nothing whatsoever at this stage was mentioned of the area surveyed and it was dropped like a rotten potato.

President Mangope: It is not President Mangope who wants us to be at Pampierstad but the Diamond Fields Administration Board. Bophuthatswana never went to borrow money from the Bantu Trust Fund to build us a Location in Pampierstad. It is the Diamond Fields Administration which did it and we say with emphasis that by doing so they want to cast us out as we are just in their way. They have proved to us beyond all doubt that we are not only a burden to them but an unnecessary evil. The policy of Bophuthatswana is not to move settled communities from one place to the other, theirs is, that Tswanas are to stay in the Urban areas, to preserve their identity and uphold the prestige of their race. Of course it is a fact that some listeners would think that we are actuated by prejudice. We have no prejudice whatsoever against the Diamond Fields Administration Board. In actual fact we are merely trying to prove that we are leaders of people who have somewhere in them the spark of divine inspiration and that it is well to see the evil thing in this setting.

Sirs, would we not be justified to mention that all these plans and drawings could have been pulled down from the

Superintendent's office on the command of the Diamond Fields Administration when it took over the Location?

Removal of Valspan to Pampierstad: In 1967 and January 1968 rumours of removal became rife as houses in Valspan were valued. In the seventies families were moved twice to Pampierstad without the Advisory Board being properly consulted and it was later hinted that those who had been moved had volunteered to go across the river for settlement. We were sorely provoked when two members of the Advisory Board were moved much against their intentions. For them it was like the Captain leaving the sinking ship first. We are pointing all this out to prove how the Administration can act unreasonably even to the members of the Advisory Board in their enforcement of removals. Is this not adequate proof of our powerlessness?

Correspondence with Authorities: A Swazi knows his soil just as a Xhosa knows Transkei to be his soil. It became a strange thing to hear it spoken that Tswanas only were to be moved out of their soil namely Jan Kempdorp, which bears no connection with Swazis and Xhosas etc. That they and other tribal groups would be left to enjoy the facilities of this place. On hearing this the Advisory Board started a long interchange of letters with the authorities objecting strongly against this decision which objection appeared to have found reasonableness because of the audible silence on their part eventually. It would be better for the authorities to assert that this is going to be so or not while at the same time expecting that this will not be interpreted as consenting to removal by any means.

Reports and rumours again: At one time reports and rumours again flooded Valspan, this time, mainly from the neighbouring coloured community that Valspan was being moved to Pampierstad to give way to coloured settlement. Here again the Valspan Advisory Board took the matter up in the Location Superintendent's office with the Chief Commissioner of Bantu Affairs of Kimberley, who denied the knowledge of it. It is incongruous for the Commissioner now that this point, not being long ago gainsaid, should at the time of writing be heard confirmed by the radio and the public press.

Construction of hostels: It is being stated that hostels are going to be put up for all those doing key jobs. In fact as we understand that whole set-up there will still be blacks exemptionally staying permanently in Valspan. There is no reason why these hostels cannot be erected for them across the river and these workers fetched from there. How many of us are able and willing to give an impartial and unbiased opinion that this would be total removal?

Our school and plots' children: In 1976 the population statistics of National Units in Jan Kempdorp was reported as follows: Tswana 5 359, South Sotho 914, Xhosa 1 017 and Zulu 87. Now, all these people have school going children who are absorbed by our school in Valspan. If Valspan has to move these children will be without a school as it is reported that the school in question will be totally demolished. Surely, humanity is important here and it can easily happen that important human considerations are undervalued by the officials. The acceptance of these plots' children in our school, we have always viewed it in a humanitarian point of view.

Accommodation at Pampierstad: Let us take the example of something that might be thought to be unessential namely accommodation in this instance. Everything that has been said concerning the removal of Valspan so far has been based on the idea that there is no great crisis in accommodation at Pampierstad whereas there is. An acute crisis exists. A great number of people who have been removed twice to

Pampierstad still lack proper accommodation despite being there for a number of years. Some have been accommodated in smaller-roomed houses, while others live in plank houses or wooden houses. The result of all this is that it is extremely difficult for the authorities of Bophuthatswana to provide them just yet with decent houses and it does illustrate that it will take many years before any radical change follows.

There is also an enormously high list of applicants requiring houses in Pampierstad. One would pose the question, why is it that the Diamond Fields Administration did not find it essential to firstly extricate the Bophuthatswana Government out of this serious situation instead of adding hardship upon hardship? No matter what can be said, one can see the ostrich's head in the sand here.

Joint Advisory Board meeting: On 23 May 1978 at a meeting of the Joint Advisory Board of the Valspan Location in which Messrs Faber and Claasen of the Diamond Fields Administration Board were present, we learnt verbally that the Location will, within a period of two years, be removed to Pampierstad. Certain promises in connection with our settlement at Pampierstad were also verbally made to us. The Village Board, in this particular that Location Advisory Board, accordingly took the message to the residents and the following is their reaction to and the expression of their feelings.

Rejection of removal: We learn with shock and disappointment that we are to be removed to Pampierstad within the next eighteen months.

May it be known that this will be done against our wishes. Sirs, experience gained elsewhere has shown that removals of this nature have always resulted in:—

(a) People being thrown into misery and hardships through

heavy losses in both movable and immovable property.
(b) The disruption to the lifes of the people employed and to the lifes of those who of necessity become unemployed.
(c) Non-Tswanas who may not wish to be adopted by Bophuthatswana or who may not be acceptable in Bophuthatswana yet having been born and lived all their lifes in Valspan and thus having no other home but Valspan, will be frustrated and become a social problem and burden.
(d) Adding to the social problems of ill-feeling, illness and high mortality.

We believe, sirs, that:

(1) Valspan and its people are an integral part of Jan Kempdorp and its community.
(2) That our stay here has always been and always will be an asset to the economic development of this town, Jan Kempdorp.
(3) That our removal will be tragic to the many businesses which will eventually have to be closed down.

Conclusion: Lastly to conclude this memorandum, as we said in the beginning, that we as a Board never agreed to the removal of Valspan, we are leaving no doubts about this. It is the Diamond Fields Bantu Affairs Administration Board that has taken up a high-handed manner in our removal, to them alone, we humbly extend these words:—

The parts and signs of goodness are many. If a man be gracious and courteous to others, it shows he is a citizen of the world, and that his heart is no island, cut off from other lands, but a continent that joins to them. If he be compassionate towards the affliction of others, it shows that his heart is like the noble tree, that is wounded itself when it

> gives the balm.
>
> We petition the Diamond Fields Administration to let us stay across the 'R' Canal in Valspan, after all the ground has long been earmarked for the purpose. We have lived in stagnation, suspense and apathy long enough, please relieve us from this intolerable situation.
>
> **BY MEMBERS OF THE VALSPAN LOCATION ADVISORY BOARD.**
>
> *Jan Kempdorp, July 1978*

The community council was refused permission to hand out their pamphlet in reply to the 'anonymous' ones. The people are still being moved despite Dr Koornhof's reassurance: 'If they want to stay where they are, then they are welcome to do so. They will not be evicted.' (*Rand Daily Mail*, 16 July 80.)

Many of the people who were moved to Pampierstad kept strong ties with Valspan. Until 1983 some still sent their children to Valspan schools, and paid for them to board with those who had not moved. Then the authorities stopped registering children whose parents were not resident at Valspan.

Valspan people are well aware of the poor conditions which await them in Pampierstad. For some, the insecurity is overwhelming:

> Benjamin, my elder son, could not stand me, the grandmother, as I did not want to move. He was tired of the instability of the area. He said that he would like to take up a job in Welkom and see us settled somewhere. They told us that there is no place to go, other than Pampierstad. They supplied us with lorries to head to this area.
> (One member of a household of four interviewed by SPP in Pampierstad in 1981.)

The other three members left Pampierstad to find work. Such people are desperate for employment. When they cannot find work locally they have to migrate and need a home base for their old people. With Valspan under threat of removal Pampierstad is the only option, so the household is indirectly forced to move — there is no choice.

Unemployment is a major problem. Many people said there was no point in looking for work as there was none available. Others said members of their household had found work and never returned. Mothers complained:

> One of my children left in a Transvaal lorry.
>
> He left with the harvesting group.
>
> He went with a recruiting agent from Pretoria.

So the people of Valspan are fully aware of the dismal prospects in Pampierstad. Yet half the population has been forced, one way or another, to move. The Administration Board is taking its time, moving a few families each week.

Meanwhile 100 kilometres north in Huhudi, resistance to the removal to Pudumong gained new momentum early in 1983 with the establishment of Huhudi Civic Association (HUCA). Until then the community council had tried to protest but 'even if the community council is not soft, what can they say when their bosses say we must move?' (A HUCA spokesperson in an interview in August 1983.)

In terms of the constitution of this elected representative body, the aims and objectives are:

1 to combat any decision made by the local authorities that be not in the interest of the masses
2 to instil the spirit of self-dependence amongst the residents of Huhudi
3 to discourage the apparent built-in inferiority complex amongst residents
4 to make the outside world aware of whatever plight we might have in Huhudi
5 to invite outside aid either morally or financially should the situation deem it fit in matters of the residents
6 to attend fully to the cries of the members of the community either as individuals or as groups
7 to take an active part in the physical development of our township, e.g. in building libraries, creches, schools, recreation centres, etc.

8 to enquire from time to time about the financial matters of the community, i.e. rents, liquor tax, cinema/bioscope tax, etc.
9 to galvanise and harness the youth of our township and rally them around community issues
10 to guide the youth in the educating of our parents so as to build a strong alliance between youth and parents
11 We pledge ourselves to the unity and mutual collaboration of our people in Huhudi, hence therefore we repeat it that: 'United we stand and divided we fall.'

There have been tensions between the Community Council and HUCA but both have accepted that the former is not a popular body and has no power. The Community Council can only transmit information between the authorities and the residents.

Attempts at silencing HUCA officials are being made:

> On May 28 this year HUCA arranged a protest rally against forced removals. Placards were held high by angry residents. Immediately after the dispersal of chanting residents, a convoy of hippos [troop carriers] was sent into the township to intimidate people. Unfortunately for them, people had dispersed already and no crowd (as they thought) could be provoked so as to retaliate violently thus creating grounds for them to detain organisers of the meeting.
>
> On the morning of Sunday 5th June this year, spray paintings were found on the walls of selected buildings in the township. These messages on the walls were explicitly marrying HUCA to the ANC thus creating a platform for them to accuse us whenever they pounce on us. (Memorandum to Black Sash, 14 July 83.)

But HUCA has remained firm. It outlined tactics used to force people to move to Pudumong:

1 Demolition of 462 houses in the near future. Repeated calls have been made by HUCA to the local authorities to have the numbers of the victimised houses released and to keep the rents constant, but to no avail. The NCAB and Community Council have been clandestinely giving information to some of the owners of the affected houses, thus dividing them in their individual entities so as to perpetuate their struggle against the unity of the masses involved.
2 An ultimate forced resettlement in Pudumong (55 km away from our working places and our birth places).
3 Exorbitant and unserviceable rent hikes. Housing throughout the country has become top priority in the budget of any sensible community. Our 'leaders' in Huhudi, undemocratically in the lead, have opted for a water pipes system for the sportsground as a

priority for the financial year 1983/4. Do you sleep at the sportsground? Do we enjoy as human beings the individual privacy entitled to citizens of the free world at a sport stadium? Do we bring up our children (i.e. our future leaders) in a sportsground or in a house? Anyway, after they have moved all of us out, who is going to be the benefactor of all the luxuries of that uncalled for initiative?

4 Forced lodgers' permits on over-18s, students and non-students alike. As if all the above are not enough to turn a person into a churchmouse, a system of lodgers' permits has recently been introduced and enforced. Everyone, 18 years and above, whether student or non-student, whether employed or not, whether you qualify under Section 10(1) (a) or (b), are expected to carry and pay monthly such a permit. (*Memorandum to Black Sash,* 14 July 83.)

HUCA has attempted to research and compile the history of Huhudi but claimed that the authorities were unwilling to disclose information. HUCA approached the Black Sash for help with their records as they wanted to question the government on measures taken to prevent people from living in urban areas.

LETTER FROM HUHUDI CIVIC ASSOCIATION TO THE BLACK SASH

Dear Ma'am,

The above-said association has felt it necessary to invite your practical attention in its attempt to stop pending forced removals from Huhudi to Pudimong in Bophuthatswana.

Since 1970 the subject township (viz. Huhudi) has been practically and literally stopped from developing physically. Petitions have been signed in the past expressing the people's willingness to be let to stay in the township. Ad hoc committees had been appointed and reappointed to voice the seriousness and cruelty involved in the harassment of people by a 'democratic' South Africa. All the attempts were in vain.

In 1980 a reasonable number of families was moved after much psychological intimidation, another group again in 1982.

> Presently the looming danger is that 462 houses are to be demolished since they've been declared dilapidated by the Northern Cape Administration Board in collaboration with the Community Council.
>
> According to the Admin. Board it is against the government policy for us to live in decent houses.
>
> Could you please intervene and take up our serious problem as far as possible you can. Any kind of help will be highly appreciated, as it shall have crushed the monstrous intention of the Government and quenched the victimised masses' thirst for freedom of movement.
>
> Thanks in anticipation.
> Yours faithfully,
> GENERAL SECRETARY
>
> P.S. May I on behalf of the Huhudi Civic Association express our immeasurable appreciation for the memorial service to the late Mr Saul Mkhize. Your action has shown that the fighting masses are having a shoulder to cry on.
>
> Yours hopefully again,
> GENERAL SECRETARY HUHUDI CIVIC ASSOCIATION

Business interests

The Chambers of Commerce of Jan Kempdorp and Vryburg have also protested against the removal of families from their respective townships. The chairperson of the Jan Kempdorp Chamber of Commerce, Mr Phillip Botha, was reported as saying that the town's economy would suffer a heavy blow with the removal of the black community. A delegation of businessmen went to Cape Town to see senior government officials, but the government's attitude was that it was a 'closed case'. (*Argus,* 9 July 80.) Forty percent of the cash income of Jan Kempdorp is generated from Valspan business.

Similarly, the Vryburg Chamber of Commerce made representations to the government. Delegates were told that housing which met certain standards would be allowed to remain. The dilapidated stock would be demolished and the people moved to Pudumong. It seems that the Chamber has accepted this strategy.

Meanwhile the Huhudi people are angry. They say only those who defied prohibition on improvements to their homes are allowed to remain.

The Vryburg business community has already experienced one blow from relocation. When Indians were moved from the business district to the Indian group area, they took a large slice of black clientele with them.

If the people of Valspan and Huhudi are all moved into Bophuthatswana they are likely to shop there as goods would be cheaper from chain stores. Those operating in the rest of South Africa have to charge General Sales Tax, while those in Bophuthatswana have no sales tax obligation.

Schools issue

> Police used dogs and teargas to disperse about 1000 marching students in Huhudi township . . . after the arrest earlier this week of 31 of their classmates. (*Star*, 2 Aug. 83.)

Thirty-one pupils were held on charges of public violence related to unrest at Bopaganang School. Apparently the unrest followed internal dissatisfaction within the school but parents related it to the broader feeling of insecurity and anger. They accused the authorities of overreaction. Detention of pupils and three civic leaders was seen as part of an ongoing attempt to harass and repress the community.

The future?

> When one takes rounds in Huhudi, the beloved ghetto, one finds building materials neatly packed in some stands. Owners are awaiting a green light to continue the struggle against housing shortage but poor people, will they ever get it? (*Memorandum to Black Sash*, 14 July 83.)

It is indeed ironic that those who defied the authorities and improved their houses will be allowed to stay in Huhudi. Meanwhile week by week the Administration Board moves families, isolating and dividing the community struggle to remain in their townships. Increasingly people realise that theirs is not an individual plight, it is part of national policy to divide and dispossess: '. . . the people of Driefontein are not involved in a regional struggle, but a national struggle', they said in their memorandum to the Black Sash. They stressed that they wanted to realise their dream: 'A dream of political freedom and economic independence, a true non-racial democratic dream'.

3. Klipfontein

The farm Klipfontein lies across the river from the tiny holiday town of Kenton-on-Sea, on the Eastern Cape coast. It is run by four coloured men, usufructuaries with all the rights of landowners except that they hold the farm under a trust. Until it was forcibly cleared in 1979, this land housed a community of some 200 African families. They rented their sites from the usufructuaries and built their own shacks and houses. Some of the tenants had been living at Klipfontein for a long time. Many, however, had moved there more recently, most of them because they had been evicted off white farms in the district.

The Klipfontein community was reasonably cohesive. There was a school for the children. Most households had gardens in which they grew vegetables on a satisfactory scale. Some kept stock: cattle, goats, pigs and poultry. A few people worked for the municipality in nearby Kenton. Many others were seasonally employed on the local pineapple and chicory farms.

In September 1977 the community elected a Residents' Committee at a mass meeting on the farm. It had eight members, who met fairly regularly and took up various community issues. This committee was to play an important role in the subsequent fight against removal, a fight that centred on the courts.

Notification of removal
The Klipfontein community had been under pressure for some time. In 1976 there was an unsuccessful attempt by the local authorities to clear the farm of its residents, whom they labelled squatters: the Supreme Court overturned a conviction for illegal squatting in early 1977.

Then in March 1978 the usufructuaries and 173 African family heads were charged under the 1936 Development Trust and Land Act. The four coloureds were given a suspended sentence 'on condition that they assist police in controlling the squatters' (*Eastern Province Herald,* 30 June 78), but the case against the Africans, who had secured legal representation, was dropped — apparently because the Eastern Cape Administration Board (ECAB) was uncertain as to what would be done with them if they were evicted. This difficulty was resolved in June 1978, when an official from ECAB announced that the Board planned to reduce the black population of Kenton to the barest minimum to meet the labour needs of the town. The 'unemployed African squatters' of Klipfontein were to be moved to Glenmore.

By March 1979, as the move loomed closer, the officials had widened their scope to include some people who were living in the nearby Kenton emergency camp as well. This camp had been established on the edge of the white town in 1956 'for the purpose of accommodating homeless Bantu'.(*Grocott's Mail,* 3 April 79.) It had not been allowed to develop into a permanent location because it was considered a temporary solution to the housing problems of Kenton's black workers. Nevertheless, those black workers who lived there did have Section 10 rights to be in the municipal area.

On 22 March 35 households at the emergency camp were given handwritten notices informing them that their site permits were about to be cancelled and that they would be removed in 12 days' time:

> Take notice that you and your family are being moved to Glenmore district Peddie. The move takes place from April 2 1979.

That same day verbal notice was given to most of the community at Klipfontein that they too were to be removed on 2 April. They were told by a sergeant of the SAP who said that the move had been sanctioned by a judge of the Supreme Court. The people told the sergeant that they were not prepared to go until after their trial had been completed. The sergeant replied that anyone who did not leave 'would have to see the consequences with his own eyes'.

Then, on the morning of 28 March, the residents noticed three copies of a document and an attached list of names. One was posted on the door of the school on the farm, another was found in a farm road with a stone placed on top so that it would not blow away, and a third was nailed to a pole on the western boundary of the farm. The documents were in English and Afrikaans only, while the overwhelming majority of the inhabitants of the farm were Xhosa-speaking. These papers were notices to inform the people that they were creating a health hazard and that their move had been sanctioned by the magistrate at Alexandria.

The plan of the authorities was very simple. The number of households who had been given notice in the emergency camp corresponded to the number of municipal workers living at Klipfontein. Those selected for eviction at the camp were mainly the elderly and unemployed. The intention was to shift the municipal workers and their families from Klipfontein into these houses in the emergency camp and then shunt everybody else in Klipfontein to Glenmore under the Prevention of Illegal Squatting Act. An Administration Board official put it very clearly:

> It was planned to remove only the unproductive and the unemployed squatters to Glenmore. We have a responsibility to the permanent African population which is indispensable to our economy. (*Eastern Province Herald,* 3 April 79.)

The Progressive Federal Party and the Black Sash took up the plight of the emergency camp people — they pointed out that many of the people had Section 10 rights and that the required 30 days' notice had not been given. Following the outcry, their removal was temporarily halted. The officials were determined, however, to press ahead. The school was closed down and the teachers transferred to Glenmore. So were many pension payments. Said one pensioner indignantly:

> If they want to take off the roof they will do it themselves. If they force us to leave we will telephone our lawyers. (*Daily Despatch,* 2 April 79.)

A few days later six Klipfontein residents made the 200 kilometre round trip to Glenmore to collect their pensions. One 80-year-old man said that they had to hire a van at a cost of R11 each to make the trip — his pension at that stage was R45 every two months.

> I was angry at this. They shouldn't have put my money where I am not. It's hard to come out on my pension money. (*Daily Despatch,* 6 April 79.)

Other pressures were more subtle. The authorities took a group of people from Klipfontein to see their proposed new home and showed them not Glenmore but the Tyefu irrigation scheme next door.

Despite all these pressures, the Klipfontein people were adamant. They were not going to move. The response of the Administration Board was to threaten them with prosecution if they continued to resist. It also claimed that there had been consultation:

> As far as we are concerned there has been the necessary consultation over the move. We met them and so did the Ciskeian Minister of the Interior, Chief Lent Maqoma. The Klipfontein people indicated that they were in favour of the move. (*Eastern Province Herald,* 3 April 79.
> The chief subsequently denied that the people wanted to move.)

At this stage, before the removals had begun, the Chief Director of ECAB, Mr Louis Koch, stated that nobody would be forced to board trucks or be treated in an undignified way. 'There are other ways of dealing with these things', he was reported as saying. (*Eastern Province Herald,* 3 April 79).

The removals begin
On 3 April government trucks arrived at Klipfontein. According to an affidavit prepared by the chairperson of the Residents' Committee, Administration Board officials assisted by the police started packing the people's belongings into the trucks. They told the people that they were now being removed. Some dwellings were broken down and the corrugated iron and other building materials loaded onto the trucks. Eight families were moved that first day, and more the next.

One man, a father of three, said the removals squad arrived at his two-roomed house and ordered him to break it down.

> I told him I would not do it. The man in charge then told the others to take my furniture out and they broke the house down. (*Weekend Post,* 7 April 79.)

A woman who worked away from Klipfontein as a domestic worker 'returned to her home in Klipfontein for a visit . . . found it levelled and her family gone'. (*Weekend Post,* 7 April 79.) Her employer reported that she then left to try to find her aged mother and her two children. They were at Glenmore, 100 kilometres away.

At this stage both Glenmore and Klipfontein were sealed from the press. When asked about the press bans, the Chief Commissioner replied that 'there is nothing to hide', but he did not want photographs taken 'because there was too much interference at this stage'. (*Daily Despatch,* 4 April 79.) He denied the allegations that force was being used as 'not the truth'. (*Eastern Province Herald,* 5 April 79.)

Legal struggles
The Klipfontein community had great faith in lawyers. They had turned to them before, in 1976 and in 1978, and they had not been removed. Now they looked to them once again.

On 4 April 200 Klipfontein people met their attorney to discuss ways of challenging this latest and most drastic threat to the position of their community. It was decided to make an urgent application to the Supreme Court for an order to stop the Administration Board and the chief magistrate of Alexandria from removing any more families from the farm, as well as to allow those already removed to return. The application was based on a technicality — that the original order from the Alexandria magistrate authorising the removal gave the people insufficient notice and, not being made in Xhosa, could not have been understood by the majority of those to whom it was addressed. In support of the application the chairperson of the Residents' Committee lodged an affidavit which denied that the removals were voluntary. He also claimed that the families had the consent of the usufructuaries to be at Klipfontein. This was later endorsed by one of the usufructuaries in a supporting affidavit. The case was heard on 5 April. The Administration Board asked for a postponement to 12 April so that they could respond to the allegations. After they had assured the court that they would not move anybody else in the meantime, this was duly granted. At that stage 95 families had been moved to Glenmore.

Though the people of Klipfontein had won round one of the legal battle, this did not stop the removals. Between 5 and 12 April families continued to be trucked to Glenmore at a rapid rate. By the time the court case was resumed, the Administration

Board estimated that there were already 140 families at Glenmore — 45 more than there had been the previous week. (*Eastern Province Herald,* 13 April 79.) All those moved after 5 April were on the basis of a 'letter of consent'. According to 26 people who made affidavits complaining about the actions of the officials and the police, this 'consent' was forced out of the people in various ways.

> I heard about our pending removal on 2 April 79. The ECAB officials came on 3 April 79. They came again on 6 April 79. I saw Sergeant K. in the township and said that I shall not be leaving and he replied that we cannot remain in Klipfontein. K. took a piece of paper and asked me to place my thumb print thereon. I refused and further said all the people must leave. Sergeant K. took my hand and placed my thumb on his book. This was a blank piece of paper. My name was written on this paper in his presence. Sergeant K. took my thumb on the ink stamp pad and thereafter he placed my thumb print on this blank piece of paper on which he had written my name. (Affidavit made on 11 April 1979, and now lodged in Cory Library, Rhodes University, Grahamstown. See also other affidavits reproduced in box.)

VOLUNTARY REMOVALS AT KLIPFONTEIN

The following are extracts from four more of the affidavits that were made by 26 Klipfontein residents on 11 April 79, describing how they were coerced into moving.

1) That on the 5th April 1979 the officials of the Eastern Cape Administration Board came to my house and told me to move. I persist in my attitude not to move. That on the 9th April I was told by the ECAB official that 'Kaffir you must break down your house, failing which we will do it or arrest you.' On the 10th April 1979 a number of white officials came to my house, and instructed me to break my house down. There were about five officials including those from ECAB. I demolished my house and shall not move.

---

2) That on 11.4.79 I noticed that our house was demolished. I saw my sister who told me that my mother and the children were on their way to Kenton-on-Sea. I never saw my mother or the children. At the time when my house was being demolished I was waiting along the Bushmans River—Alexandria road for my attorney to consult counsel. I have no idea where I am going to stay.

3) That on the 3rd April 1979 a European sergeant asked me when I would be leaving for Glenmore. I replied saying that I would not be going anywhere. The sergeant then told me it would be wise to move to Glenmore as I would not be able to collect my pension in Klipfontein any longer but that I could only collect it in Glenmore. That on 10 April 1979 Sergeant K. came to me and asked me when I intended to leave for Glenmore. I told him that I would not leave until I had spoken to my lawyers. Sergeant K. then told me we are wasting our time as our lawyer had lost the case and that we would have to leave.

4) That on or about 21 March 1979 a Sergeant R. called a meeting and informed the residents that they will have to move on the 2nd April 1979 as the lorries were coming on that day. This European sergeant told me that he was acting on the instructions of a Judge from Grahamstown. I questioned this instruction in view of the fact that a Court case was pending during May 1979. On the 2nd April I saw these Government lorries arriving driven by black drivers. These drivers then fetched the furniture from the house and the children assisted them. I did not assist with the loading. This happened on the 9th April 1979. I was presented with a form to sign which I refused to sign. I was very worried and disturbed and I cannot say how my children or grandchildren got on the lorry. On the 11th April Sergeant R. came back and told me that they were going to break the house down. I was further told by the European sergeant that I was still going to be moved whether I like it or not.

During this time the Deputy Minister of Plural Relations also had what were described as 'fruitful talks' with the Ciskeian cabinet about the Glenmore removals. The Chief Minister of the Ciskei gave legitimacy to the removals and to the letters of consent when he stated:

> We have had enough of this phraseology about voluntary removals. Now we insist that officials have a letter of consent before squatters' possessions are removed. (*Weekend Post*, 7 April 79.)

The Administration Board's response

In preparation for the court hearing on 12 April the Administration Board filed lengthy affidavits of their own. Chief Director of ECAB, Koch, claimed in his that the Board was not responsible for moving the people; they were merely there 'as observers'

> to see that good human relations existed between the people who were being moved to Glenmore and the police.

He said that most of the people at Klipfontein were recent arrivals, who were there illegally, and that their buildings did not comply with the standard building regulations. He added that he, the Deputy Minister of Plural Relations, the Chief Minister of the Ciskei and members of the Ciskeian cabinet had visited Glenmore. The people had told them that they had not been moved there against their will and that they were happy:

> There was a jolly atmosphere and people were busy altering their homes for their needs.

Along with four such affidavits from Administration Board officials went a large number of statements collected from people at Klipfontein after the Supreme Court application had been made. On 6 April the Board handed in 17 statements, all in Afrikaans and all alike except that some of them had writing mistakes. In English they read:

> DECLARED UNDER OATH
> I am an adult black man and at present live on the farm Klipfontein in the Alexandria district.
> I choose of my own free will and without any undue influence to be removed to Glenmore.
> 1) I am satisfied with the contents of this statement and understand it.

Six Case Studies: Klipfontein

2) I have no objection against taking the prescribed oath.
3) I regard the prescribed oath as binding on my conscience.

(See box).

KLIPFONTEIN AFFIDAVIT PRODUCED BY THE ADMINISTRATION BOARD

Wilson Lamani, 55 jr. N: N/B.

Verklaar onder eed.
Ek is 'n volwasse Swart man en tans van die plaas Klipfontein in die Alexandria distrik.
Ek verkies om uit eie vrye wil en sonder dat ek enigsins daartoe beinvloed is na Glen More te verhuis.

1) Ek is vertroud met die inhoud van hierdie verklaring en begryp dit.
2) Ek het geen beswaar teen die aflê van die voorgeskrewe eed nie.
3) Ek beskou die voorgeskrewe eed as bindend vir my gewete.

Klipfontein.
14h10
1979-04-06.

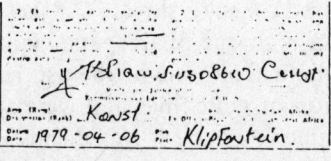

On 7 and 9 April a further 25 statements were taken. Typed three to a page, these were in English and very brief. They read:

> As it is my desire to be removed to Glenmore I request that transport be provided to take me and my effects from Klipfontein to Glenmore.

Despite these affidavits — perhaps because of them — the Administration Board clearly felt it did not have a strong case and it agreed to settle out of court. On 12 April it was announced that the parties had reached an agreement and that the eviction order would be set aside — round two to the people of Klipfontein. By then, however, most of the people had already been moved. There were only 28 families left on the farm — 17 of them still waiting to be moved into the emergency camp and the rest those who were still holding out.

The authorities now renewed their efforts to clear the farm. Speaking of the remaining families on 17 April, a police spokesman declared that 'unless the squatters changed their minds [about refusing to move] by the end of the month, they would be prosecuted'. The response of those still remaining at Klipfontein was defiant: the 17 families due to be shifted into the emergency camp now joined the others in refusing to move.

On 2 May the first of several court cases took place. A 78-year-old man was tried who claimed in court he had been living at Klipfontein for 29 years and was employed by one of the coloured usufructuaries. He was convicted not under the Prevention of Illegal Squatting Act but under the still more watertight Development Trust and Land Act — he was not a registered worker. He was sentenced to a fine of R90 or 100 days (suspended for three years) and ordered to leave Klipfontein within a month.

Another two weeks passed and then the authorities moved against the remaining families. On 19 May they were served notice that an application was to be made to the Alexandria magistrate for their eviction (under the Prevention of Illegal Squatting Act) on the grounds that they posed a health threat. On the same day police arrested ten people on a charge of trespass, claiming that they were acting on a complaint from one of the usufructuaries. Those arrested paid admission of guilt fines and were released.

When the eviction case came to court, it was dismissed on the grounds that the authorities had failed to prove that Klipfontein

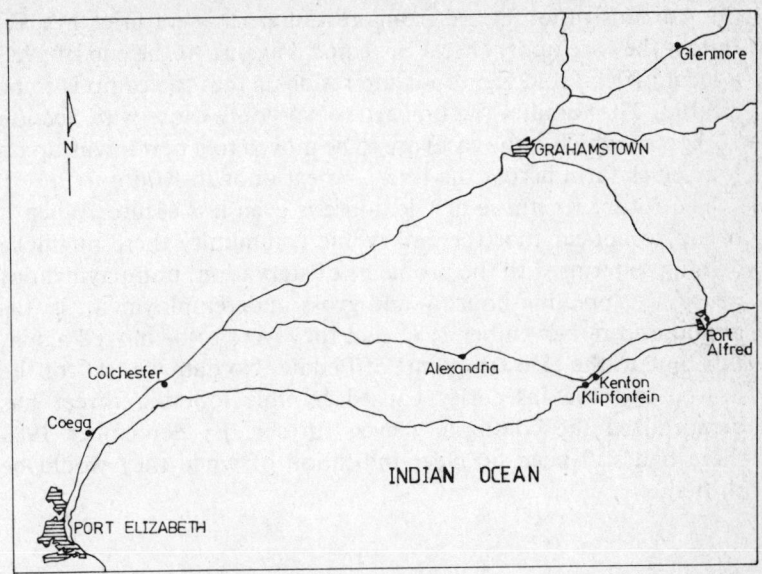

Map 14: Klipfontein

was a health hazard. Undefeated, the Administration Board then turned to the Development Trust and Land Act once more. On 6 June, 22 Klipfontein men appeared in court on various charges under this Act. One of them was convicted of not being a registered worker despite the evidence from his employer (a building contractor in Kenton-on-Sea) that he was properly registered. This man too was ordered to leave the farm within a month.

It took the Administration Board two and a half months but eventually they had worked out an effective strategy for moving the people of Klipfontein legally.

The ending
The legal proceedings against the squatters moved slowly, however, and it appears that even when the eviction orders were obtained in some cases they were not enforced because there was no more room at Glenmore. The last seven families were moved from Klipfontein in mid-1980, not to Glenmore but to the Kenton emergency camp. They don't all see the camp as an ideal solution — they have no access to grazing for stock, and they are barred by

the Administration Board from erecting permanent brick homes. In fact they are under threat of removal again. At the end of 1983 a local official told Kenton camp residents that the camp is to be cleared. The families (he omitted to say 'only those with Section 10 rights', which is the case) are to be moved to a new township on Marseilles farm across the river — next door to Klipfontein.

The future for those at Glenmore is even less secure. When it began to appear that the embryonic community there might be coming to terms with the problems of starvation, non-payment of pensions, appalling housing and gross underemployment, it was announced in November 1981 that they were to be moved again, this time to the 'growth point' of Peddie. No date was set for the move, and the insecurity caused by this looming threat has demoralized the community even further. By September 1983 there had still been no clear indication of when they would be shifted.

4. Kwapitela

Kwapitela is an African freehold farm — a black spot — situated in the foothills of the Drakensberg about 3 kilometres from the Sani Pass Hotel, near Himeville in Natal. It was bought by Pitela Hlophe, grandfather of the present owners, in 1900 at a public auction in Pietermaritzburg — 323 hectares of good quality land on the banks of the Umkomanzi River.

Over the years a small rural community developed on this farm. By 1980 there were 76 households living there: a few Hlophe landowners and their tenants. The tenants paid between R19 and R12,25 in rent each year in return for a couple of hectares of residential and arable land per household and unlimited access to grazing for their stock on the common. Most of them had been living at Kwapitela for more than 20 years. They had strong ties to the land.

It was an isolated community and a poor one, but at a subsistence level people lived fairly well. Their housing was in good repair — a mixture of cement-block and wattle-and-daub buildings scattered across the farm in several clusters, with gardens and grazing land in between. Water and firewood were in plentiful supply. There was a small stone church that doubled as a primary school during the week. Above all, there was land.

By 1980 nobody was making an independent living out of their farming. Even the landowners worked, one of them as a watchman at the nearby Sani Pass Hotel. But just about every household was drawing a supplementary income from their fields and their stock. Out of 63 households interviewed by the Association for Rural Advancement (AFRA) in 1980, only two did not produce any crops — one an old age pensioner who lived on his own and one a recent arrival in the community. People planted maize and beans and potatoes and sometimes other vegetables as well. Most people kept cattle; some had goats and pigs and horses too. Six of the households interviewed by AFRA said that from time to time they sold surplus agricultural produce outside Kwapitela while a further 24 said they sometimes sold produce within the community (*AFRA Report No 5,* October 1980).

Like other black rural communities, the people of Kwapitela depended on wage employment for the bulk of their income. However, compared to many other rural communities, the number of migrant workers in the community was small. The majority of workers at Kwapitela — 57% — had jobs in the district, mainly as farmworkers on neighbouring white farms or as waiters and domestic workers at the Sani Pass Hotel (*AFRA Report No 5,* October 1980). Wages were low but at least these workers could live at home; many could walk to work each day.

Stated an AFRA report on the community:

> Nobody can describe Kwapitela as idyllic — incomes are low, jobs hard to find, the infrastructure of transport, supermarkets, schools etc. that urban people can take for granted is lacking in this as in other rural areas. But it is a settled rural community. It has an established way of life that has been built up over many years. Because Kwapitela is black freehold land residents have greater independence and control over their own lives than they would in a township or 'closer settlement' situation. Most important of all, they have an assured access to agricultural land and have built up a lifestyle that centres around that.
> (Unpublished Report, 1980, pp 5-6.)

But neither its freehold title deed nor its modest advantages were protection against the workings of apartheid. In July almost all the tenants were removed and relocated at a closer settlement called, ironically, Compensation. This place is 70 kilometres away on Trust land intended for incorporation into KwaZulu. To date the landowners have not been moved, nor have they been expropriated, but their eventual removal is inevitable. Already they have been shown compensatory land elsewhere, and three of the four owners have accepted the government's terms. Only one of the landowners has fought against the removal; the rest of the community have submitted passively.

Notification of the move
As early as 1969 Kwapitela was destined to be removed:

> Owing to its situation, the abovementioned property is a black spot which in terms of Departmental policy will have to be eliminated in due course. (Letter from the Chief Bantu Affairs Commissioner for Natal to lawyers acting on behalf of one of the landowners.)

Nothing further happened, however, until ten years later when, in September 1979, the local commissioner and a few other government officials arrived on the farm. They told the people that the farm was to be bought by the government and all the tenants would be moved shortly as a result. They also told them not to plant any crops that scason. If they did, it would be at their own risk since they would not be compensated for them when they were moved.

Shortly afterwards workmen arrived and painted numbers on all the houses. Then there was a lull. No officials came near the place for nearly two years. There was no explanation of why they had not come back and no indication of when the people would be moved. Most people had taken what the commissioner had said about the crops seriously. They hadn't planted, and now they were without that extra food yet too insecure to defy his instructions. They became increasingly frustrated and restless.

In August 1980 a different official visited them. It was during the week and most of the adult men were away at work. He told those people who were present — mainly the women — that later that month they would be taken to see the area to which they would be moved. A number of people duly visited Compensation. According to one of the landowners, most of them were not impressed by what they had seen. He himself commented:

> But I don't like that place because there is no ploughing and no place

18-19 *Two views of Elukhanyweni, a closer settlement near Stutterheim in the Eastern Cape to which 400 families were moved from the Tsitsikama reserves, 300 kilometres away, in 1977-1978. (See pages 189-201 and index.)*

20 *Joseph Gqivana, a blind pensioner, with eviction notice in Kenton camp during the removal of Klipfontein residents to Glenmore in 1979. (See pages 221-223 and index.)*

21 *Residents of Klipfontein meet to discuss the impending removal, April 1979. (See pages 221-232 and index.)*

22 *Klipfontein residents leave the magistrate's court in Kenton at the end of the hearing under the Development Trust and Land Act that was to lead to their eviction, June 1979. (See pages 221-232 and index.)*

23 *Glenmore, the transit camp to which the Klipfontein residents were moved in 1979. It became a part of the Ciskei in December 1981. (See pages 221-232 and index.)*

24 *A community meeting in Kwapitela, the Natal black spot near Himeville, before the removal to Compensation. (See pages 232-238 and index.)*

25 *Kwapitela women after the move to Compensation, the closer settlement near Pietermaritzburg, July 1981. (See pages 232-238 and index.)*

for the cattle. I think it would be better if they can move them to the place where they can do ploughing and where their cattle can live.
(Letter in AFRA files)

This man was trying desperately to find support for his stand from church and other community organisations in Pietermaritzburg. But the tenants themselves were passive. One of the problems was that tensions were building up between landowners and tenants and among the landowners themselves over rents. Pitela Hlophe's heirs disagreed among themselves about who was and who was not entitled to collect rent from the tenants; there were allegations that some of them were demanding rent from their relatives' tenants. At least part of the reason why the landowner referred to above was so active was that he did not want to lose the income his tenants provided.

Another problem was that officials and the local security police warned the community against having any dealings with outside groups who, as one member of the community reported it, 'are likely to deceive you'.

A further problem was their isolation. There were no telephones. Very few people had cars and the main form of transport was to travel by bus or to walk. Kwapitela was completely cut off from the mainstream of political activity in urban and industrial South Africa. It had no real links with other threatened rural communities either. Few of the people could imagine challenging the government which they knew to be all-powerful and out of reach. At meetings the women whose husbands were away at work felt it would be improper for them to speak in their absence.

So they accepted the removal:

> We did not like to go away because we were born here; it was only that we heard that the government wanted it and we submitted to that.

The removal
The people of Kwapitela were finally removed in July 1981, over two and a half years after they had first been told that their removal was about to happen. It was mid-winter — the days crisp and sunny and dry, but the nights bitterly cold. The removal was spread over two days, the government employing a fleet of about 80 GG trucks and a huge crew of workers to shift the people and

their goods. The workers were not local people. They were black but they did not speak Zulu, so there was no connection between them and the people whose houses they were dismantling.

The outward appearance of those being moved was impassive. There were no signs of anger or of grief. The mood was rather one of blank resignation. They

> submitted stoically to the demolition of their houses, loading what they could salvage from the rubble and the dust onto the waiting trucks — windows, thatch, sheets of tin roofing, doors and poles and fencing. (*AFRA Report* No. 14, November 1981.)

At Compensation each family was allocated a site with a one-room tin hut and a latrine standing on it. Some of the huts were not fully assembled before their occupants arrived; none of them had floors or roofs. The very large households were given tents as well. Most households were supplied with rations: mealie meal, soup powder, powdered milk and salt, in quantities large enough to last them for about two weeks. A few that arrived at the very end found that the supplies had already run out. Fuel was also laid on, but instead of it being free — which most people had expected — it was for sale only. It was the community's first experience of paying for a basic necessity that formerly had cost them nothing except their labour, their first taste of their new life in a place where 'a person has to pay for everything'.

Compensation
According to Koornhof, a total of R35 606 was paid out in compensation for the improvements the Kwapitela tenants left behind — an average of R429,86 per household. The highest amount paid to any household was R1 457, the lowest R50. (*Hansard*, Private Question 390, 2 April 80.)

Koornhof also maintained that the tenants were informed beforehand about the amount they were to receive and had an opportunity to object if not satisfied. Those removed tell a different story. In a household survey undertaken by AFRA in August 1981, a month after the removal, 42 people said that they had not received any official notice about compensation before they were removed. One, a woman, said she did not know if her husband had been notified or not. One person's reply was not clear, and only 6 people claimed to have been prepared for what to expect in advance.

One person described the payout procedure, which took place at the time of the move, as follows:

> There was not much said. They would just shout one's name as per folio number and summon him to the temporary office. On arrival you were just given a certain amount of money and there was no further discussion.

People were paid in cash. Afterwards there were some allegations that the clerks in charge of the payout were not properly supervised and there were some irregularities — people being made to sign or make their thumbprint mark before they were given their money and then finding that they had been shortchanged. These allegations were never followed up. People were scared that by complaining they might lose the money that they had got. The dominant attitude among those who were compensated seemed to be one of gratitude that they had ben paid anything at all.

Attitudes to their new place

After their first few weeks at Compensation, most of the people interviewed by AFRA revealed much the same spirit of resignation about their new situation as they had had about the removal itself. About two-thirds of them said that they were not glad to be at Compensation, 8 people said that they were, and 11 people were non-committal:

> We have no way to like it or not.

> Because there is no alternative, we have accepted this place.

Only 2 of those interviewed reported that they had no problems, while a further 10 were unwilling to commit themselves. The remaining 42 people reported a wide range of general problems. The four major complaints were about fuel (mentioned 23 times), the lack of land for ploughing (20 times) and for stock (10 times), and the high cost of living (13 times). Yet despite their complaints and the fact that most people did not like Compensation, over half of those interviewed said it was as they expected. Explained one woman:

I expected the place not to be good for I have seen and heard of other removals. I had no hope.

5. 'The threat united us' — the reprieve of Sekgosese

In the Sekgosese district of Lebowa live the Batlokwa and the Makgato people. Altogether they number about 75 000 people — over 70 000 Batlokwa and some 4 500 Makgato. Their land lies 50 kilometres north of Pietersburg, on the strategically important road to Zimbabwe.

Their story is interesting for several reasons. Firstly there were a variety of responses from the people — ranging from the Makgato chief and a few followers who agreed to removal, to those who resisted and fought the removals with legal weapons, to those, possibly politically more astute, who used a form of passive resistance. Secondly, the history is well documented and the documentation includes a number of very clear statements from the people concerned. Thirdly, the resistance has proved successful: the majority of the people have been granted a reprieve and are not to be resettled. Lastly, there was a group who were actually removed and others who spent a period of three years under threat of removal.

Background

During the early 1970s there were three groups living in the Sekgosese district: the Batlokwa; the Makgato; and until 1977, a group of nearly 5 000 people under Chief Manthatha, at the village of Mphakane.

The land on which the Batlokwa live is their own — a combination of scheduled reserve, collectively bought farms and Trust farms.

> We were given this land on which we live by the late Honourable President Paul Kruger. Later we bought lands of our own next to the lands given to us by the Honourable President.
>
> On this our land we have entrenched ourselves with immovable properties . . . schools, expensive houses, churches, boreholes, shops and stores, garages, clinics and even post offices as well as mills and dams. (From approved agenda for meeting held on 15 Nov. 78 at Ramatjoe.)

Six Case Studies: Sekgosese

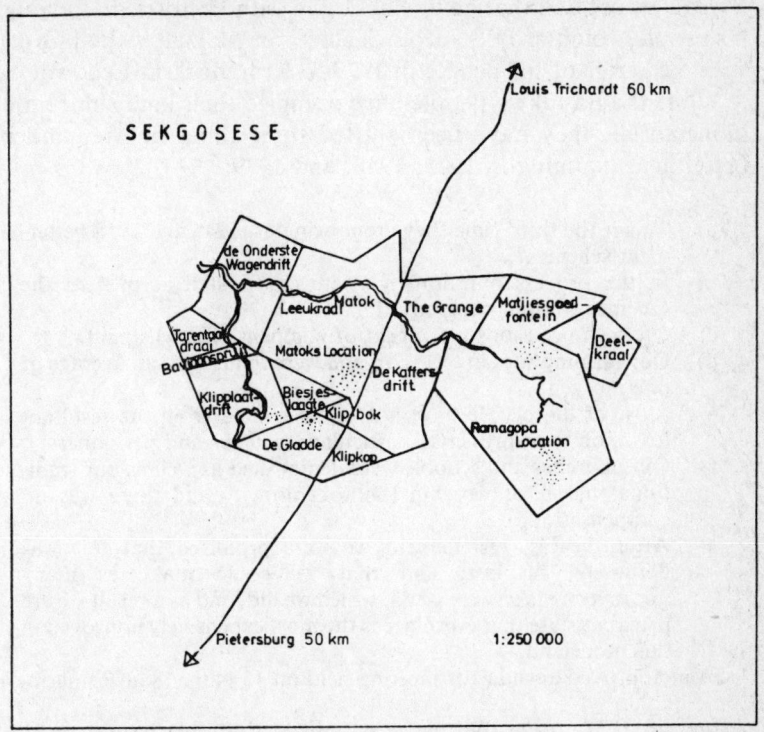

Map 15: Sekgosese

The Makgato people came from a white-owned farm at Munnik, south-west of Soekmekaar, where they had been living as tenants. In about 1962 they were moved to the Trust farm Klipplaatdrift which adjoins the Machaka tribal area, otherwise known as Matoks.

The Manthatha people had been living on Batlokwa reserve land until 1977. In that year nearly 800 families were moved 75 kilometres north-west of Pietersburg to the relocation area of Mahodi.

When the Bantu Authorities Act was passed in 1951, the officials decided to divide the Batlokwa under two, not three, chiefs: Chief Machaka and Chief Ramokgopa. Chief Manthatha objected to living under Chief Machaka and claims this was the reason for their finally moving to Mahodi. (Many believe this was a weak excuse and that he 'collaborated with Pretoria' in moving his people 'voluntarily'.) A fourth chief was Makgato who moved with a quarter of his people in 1979 to Kromhoek in Lebowa.

While the Batlokwa people have occupied their land since time immemorial, they have been shifted three times before, under betterment planning in 1945, 1958, and 1979:

a) This is the third time they are moving us [1945 and 1958 betterment schemes?].
b) In the process our donkeys were confiscated as part of the scheme, without compensation.
c) On both occasions not a cent of compensation was paid.
d) Our farming sites in terms of land were reduced to an average of one morgen.
e) Most of the people have not yet recovered from the resultant losses on their property, particularly widows and pensioners.
f) Our churches and schools were demolished as well as our traditional places of worship (Dithokgolo) . . . and there was no compensation.
g) After the last resettlement we were promised that this was definitely the last, and that we could make as many improvements as we wished, which we did, and as a result we are proud to state that our place is the most expensively improved in this homeland.

(From approved agenda for meeting held on 15 Nov. 78 at Ramatjoe.)

After the 1958 move they were promised that this would be the last one and that they could make as many improvements as they wished. This they did.

The threatened move

The Sekogesese area was excised from the jurisdiction of the legislative assembly of Lebowa in terms of Regulation R217 (Government Gazette 613, 25 Aug. 78). The area became defined as 'badly situated' within 'white South Africa'. However, the Lebowa administration remained responsible for education, for collecting taxes, stock counting etc. Thus the proclamation sought to dispossess the people of their land and South African birthright, while retaining the use of the bantustan government's services.

The reasons for the move are not entirely clear, although the strategic importance of the road to Zimbabwe has been cited. The move would also make available thousands of hectares of good farming land to white farmers. State spokespeople justified the move in terms of consolidation of the 'homelands'. In the case of the Makgato, they also claimed that they were complying with the previous Makgato chief's request by moving them to a larger area.

The Makgato were to be moved from their land at Dwars River, 50 kilometres from Pietersburg, to Kromhoek, a distance of 128 kilometres. The Batlokwa were to be moved to the Bochum/Vivo area, 62 kilometres away.

Reactions to the proclamation
On 28 August 1978 the chiefs were informed by the chief commissioner that no farms had as yet been bought in compensation. The chiefs 'agreed with him that he should not buy them' because they intended to register a protest.

On 13 September the leaders of the tribe met Lebowa's Chief Minister, Dr Cedric Phatudi, at Seshego, the Lebowa capital. Phatudi made it clear that he was totally opposed to the removal of the Batlokwa. He informed them that he had already pleaded with the then Minister and Deputy Minister, Dr C Mulder and Dr F Hartzenberg, to let the tribe remain on their ancestral land. A week later, on 20 September, the two chiefs of the area, Machaka and Ramokgopa, were summoned by the chief commissioner for the northern areas, Mr J Pieterse, and officially informed that they were to be resettled. Pieterse was curt and unfriendly. 'It is futile to discuss the matter', he told them. His attitude was 'one of master talking to his servants'.

However, officials organised a meeting for 15 November 1978. The Deputy Secretary of the Department of Plural Relations addressed the meeting which comprised mainly women. The approved agenda stated:

> the Batlokwa Tribe is convinced that the Government of the Republic of South Africa is taking advantage of our cooperation and loyalty, and that being the case, we are not interested with this removal.

The meeting was stormy. The people stated that they did not want to and would not move. The Deputy Secretary promised to forward their memorandum to Dr Koornhof who had recently been appointed Minister of Plural Relations. (On 21 November

1978 Dr Koornhof visited Crossroads, an informal settlement under threat of removal outside Cape Town. On the other side of the country he announced that there would be no more bulldozing at Crossroads, giving the people in the Northern Transvaal some hope that they would be treated likewise.)

Some months later Chief Ramokgopa was again summoned to a meeting in Pietersburg. The chief asked what was to be discussed. When this query was not answered, he refused to attend the meeting, only to be charged under the Bantu Administration Act with refusing to obey a lawful order. The charge was later withdrawn.

In the first half of 1979 the chiefs were summoned to a meeting by the chief commissioner. Ramokgopa and Machaka refused to attend because 'no agenda was provided', and possibly also because they feared they would be arrested. The meeting was, however, attended by Chief Makgato and by the Lebowa MP for the area, a shopkeeper named Kobe. It was decided that the relocation would be discussed between the Lebowa legislative assembly and Dr Koornhof at Seshego on 4 July. The Minister would outline the government plan for removals. The following memorandum was presented:

MEMORANDUM:
TO DR KOORNHOF ON 4 JULY 1979

The Batlokwa of Chiefs E.L. Machaka and G.M. Ramokgopa wish to thank you most sincerely for granting their representatives this interview.

We are aware that you have many commitments and that you have very little time for yourself and your family, but as the proverb says: Uneasy lies the head that wears the crown. At the same time we wish to state that we sincerely feel that our interview with you will definitely bring a little contribution towards the racial harmony that is so vital to this country.

This memorandum, drawn up by the Batlokwa of the two

chiefs mentioned, should serve as an eye-opener to you as Minister of Co-operation and Development in this country.

1. PROCLAMATION R217 OF 78-08-25.

    EXCISION: BATLOKWA RESIDENTIAL AREAS

    (a) NO CONSULTATION:
    In this proclamation we were not consulted, we simply read that our land was excised from the Area under the jurisdiction of the Lebowa government. This is contrary to the policy of dialogue to which the Central Government is committed.

    (b) INTENTION OF THE PROCLAMATION:
    We feel that the intention of this Proclamation is to isolate us, and to cause ill-feeling between the Batlokwa and the Lebowa Government. We crave for mutual understanding between Batlokwa, the Lebowa Government and the Central Government.

    (c) REPERCUSSIONS OF THE PROCLAMATION.
    As a result of this proclamation there is confusion on our part concerning administrative matters affecting us. e.g.

    (i) JUDICIAL MATTERS: Some matters are dealt with at Sekgosese whilst others are handled by Pietersburg.

    (ii) SOCIAL DEVELOPMENT: Building projects have come to a standstill, in this one time fast developing area.

(d) OUR STAND. We request that this proclamation R217 be withdrawn.

2. PROCESS OF INFORMATION ON REMOVAL.

   2.1 Meeting of 78-09-13 at Seshego.

   As a result of rumours pertaining to our pending removal we met the Hon. The Chief Minister Dr. Phatudi at our request on the 78-09-13. Dr. Phatudi informed us that he had persuaded the then Hon. Minister Dr. C. Mulder and the then Deputy Minister Dr. F. Hartzenberg, in vain, to let Batlokwa remain in the area in which they now reside.

   2.2. Meeting of 78-09-28.

   The Chief Commissioner, Mr Pieterse, summoned chiefs G. Ramokgopa and E. Machaka to his office on the 78-09-28. He simply instructed them that they were going to be removed and that the matter was cut and dry. We quote his exact words: 'It is futile to discuss the matter.' His attitude was not cordial; it was rather one of Master talking to his servants. The Chiefs requested Mr Pieterse to invite a Senior Official of your Department to come and address the Batlokwa on the issue. The Chiefs further pointed out that the date should suit the bulk of heads of families who are employed in urban areas. Unfortunately this request was not met.

   2.3 Meeting of 78-11-15. Venue: Mabeba School.

   The Deputy Secretary, Mr Serfontein, addressed a gathering consisting mainly of women on the Removal Issue. We presented him with a copy of the attached memorandum at his request. He was sympathetic to our case and promised that the Memorandum would reach you.

3. Reasons for our objection to Batlokwa Removal.
   We note that it is the accepted Policy of your Government to consolidate the land into various national states with the honest intention for preventing one national unit dominating another.

   We however feel that the removal of the Batlokwa from the land of their birth which they have developed to the state in which it is now, is grossly unjust, inhuman and unchristian.

   In addition to the reasons contained in the attached Memorandum we have to state the following:—

   3.1. FARMS IN THE VIVO AREA.
   (a) There is not a single flowing river. The underground water supply cannot be a guarantee to the survival of a population of approximately 80 000 and their livestock.

   (b) Research work on our part has revealed that the vegetation in the area is typical of dry-land with very scanty rainfall.

   (c) The place is unsuitable for rearing animals and it is unarable.

   (d) In contrast: we have three main flowing rivers, which flow through our bought farms. Geographically we stay in a temperate zone where the summers are neither too hot nor the winters too cold. The climate is neither too damp nor too dry. The Batlokwa area is good cattle-ranching ground with its sweet grass and the demarcation of the reserves into residential, farming and grazing areas has resulted in the area being completely reclaimed. All we need now is improved methods of farming and the installation of electricity to encourage industries.

3.2. LOSS OF LIVES
It should be placed on record that during such removals and even after settlement in such areas there is a great loss of life due to anxiety, acclimatization and associated diseases.

3.3 DAMAGE TO PROPERTY DURING TRANSPORT.
It is self-evident that loss of property in transit is inevitable.

3.4 DISTANCE FROM THE NEAREST MAJOR TOWNS.
We are at present 50 km from both Louis Trichardt and Pietersburg. Transport is relatively cheap and convenient. Many of our people employed in Pietersburg travel daily by bus on a monthly or weekly ticket. They definitely will not be able to travel daily from VIVO area. This may result in family disruption.

3.5 COST OF LIVING.
The cost of living will be much higher than in the present area.

4. SUGGESTIONS.
   4.1 The Hon. Minister is requested to consider us as people.
   4.2 We humbly request the Hon. Minister to carry out an inspection *in loco* of our area.

4.3 We further request to be restored to Sekgosese.

4.4 We hope that your coming here will be historical by restoring peace, harmony and cooperation, for the development of our beloved country.

5. CONCLUSION

On the strength of the above reasons we Batlokwa hereby humbly request you to stop this removal.

CHIEF G.M. RAMOKGOPA   CHIEF E.L. MACHAKA

Koornhof replied that he would give the matter 'his deepest thought'. The people then answered with a supplementary memorandum in which they corrected certain mistakes which Koornhof had made in his letter to them. They added several further points of complaint:

FOLLOW UP MEMORANDUM TO THAT PRESENTED TO THE HONOURABLE THE MINISTER OF COOPERATION AND DEVELOPMENT ON 1979-07-04.

- We wish to express our sincere gratitude to the Honourable the Minister of Cooperation and Develpoment for giving us a sympathetic hearing to our pleas. We further thank you for promising to give a hard look on the matter in question. We do, however, wish to supplement the Memorandum presented on 1979-07-04. There are certain points in your reply which we feel need to be rectified and clarified.

- The proposed area for resettlement is VIVO and not DENDRON as referred to in your reply.

- Bought Farms : On the 28th August, 1978 the Chief Commissioner informed us that the farms were not bought yet and we agreed with him that he should not buy them because we intended to register a protest against. If the Chief Commissioner bought the farms after the 28th August, 1978, we were not a party to it.

- In addition to paragraph 3.1(a) in the Memorandum presented on 1979-07-04 we wish to point out that it is common knowledge that all large cities, towns and villages depend on large rivers for water supply. This is not practicable in the Vivo area. Irrigation schemes are possible along the banks of the Sand and the Dwars rivers. It is our intention to exploit this aspect.

- In addition to paragraph 4.1 of the Memorandum presented to you on the 04-07-1979, we wish to point out:

    (a) that the name Department of Bantu Administration and Development has changed ultimately to the Department of Cooperation and Development. This entails the change in *attitude* and *approach*, one in which there is *consultation*.

    (b) the Chief as a symbol of authority cannot be alienated from his subjects by people who hold unauthorised private discussions with some of the officials of your Department on matters conerning the whole tribe. This malpractice by officials of your Department may ultimately lead to violence. (Bandeloosheid lei tot losbandigheid.) For instance:

    (i) Chief Ramokgopa is estranged from his blood half-brother (Motshwara-Seepe).

    (ii) Private meetings by some of your officials with the so-called S.L. Manthatha (originally headman of Chief E.L. Machaka) has caused a permanent ill-feeling and hatred between S.L. Manthatha's followers and Chief E.L. Machaka's subjects. This nearly resulted in bloodshed.

(iii) The behaviour of Mr. D.M. Kobe (M.P. Sekgosese), we are afraid, may ultimately lead to violence. He arrogantly ignores and belittles our chiefs and the tribes who have elected him.

- Inspection <u>in loco</u> : In addition to paragraph 4.2 of the Memorandum presented on 04-07-1979 the following will be apparent:
  (a) <u>Settlement in streets</u> : Money intended for the removals could be used for further improvements e.g. streets, water and electricity supply, and other facilities.
  (b) <u>Buildings</u> : The houses, school buildings, church buildings and private boreholes show that we have permanently established ourselves.

- Paragraph 4.4 of the Memorandum refers. Our removal will cause permanent hatred and mistrust for whites, and our sons will never feel obliged to fight for this land. We want to feel we are *together*.

CHIEF G.M. RAMOKGOPA   CHIEF E.L. MACHAKA
Date: 1979-07-31

Meanwhile another strategy — that of non-negotiation — was tried by some members of the Matoks group. A member of the community told the story:

MATOKS LOCATION, BANDELIERKOP:
INTERVIEW WITH A MEMBER OF THE COMMUNITY

You should know that the tribal authority members are being paid by the magistrate. So when they need to remove people they start with members of the tribal authorities. They talk to them, take them to the place where they will be moved to. They also take the chief. Show him around. Show him the house that he will live in. In many cases this is the house of a white man and he gets taken inside. Officials get promised a bonus if they persuade the people to be moved to the place.

As soon as this thing started we knew that the tribal authorities are on good terms with the magistrate and we formed an executive committee not from tribal authorities alone, but also people who were against the removal and people who could reason well, level-headed. We did not want people interested in riots; that's what we want to avoid. Then from this we built up a committee and the first thing we did was to convince the chief that we think the removals are no good. We showed him all the things: took him around; make him aware of the fact that he is the chief of all these people who will get nothing, and who are aware that he will get any car that he asks for from them. Then we invited him to a meeting. We address the meeting on his behalf and get him to say: 'What my people say, is what I endorse'. So when these people came to address us he told them: 'What the people say, is what I endorse.' He said this to the commissioner and told him how long we've been here and that we are not being paid for being put in the streets like this. And so the donkeys were taken away 'free of charge'. We were not paid. Then we said, 'Now look, we are leaving our forefathers' graves here and what we saw happening in the past we wouldn't like to see happening again. The farmers who will take this place, the first thing that they do is plough over these graves.'

The committee must always talk in front of the chief. If you hold any meeting in the absence of the chief, you are not covered. If he's there, then never mind. So in his presence we drew up a memorandum of the reasons why we think we should not go. We happened to know the place where they wanted to move us to. We went there, using our own transport and looked at the place. We saw what advantages and what disadvantages it had. Then we were able to compile a good memorandum comparing the two places. We were to be moved to Kromhoek and Eindermaak, a very dry, hot and rocky place. We travelled around all these places. We were lucky to get a map from some of the clerks at the Magistrate's office.

When we were through with the chief commissioner we asked them to call someone who is senior to him. So they called Mr Serfontein who is the secretary. He's the man who's busy with removals. So he came and we talked to him and wrote down all that was said. You see you have to choose all the speakers and have to draft what they have to say. They've got to subtract nor add nothing from their speech. We gave him a copy of all the speeches. We told him that we feel we have to take this to the Minister of Cooperation and Development. So he took the copies.

And then later we requested a meeting with him [Minister] and then we wrote to Phatudi also that he also should be present. So after six months or so he agreed and came, Koornhof with Senator Horwood. We had now a polished memorandum.

We told them we're not interested in riots. There's not a single person who's going to throw a stone at you. All we are interested in is that we retain our place. You people (the Government) said that you can solve anything by way of consultation. We said, now we are here on consultation and if you say you are not forcing anything we are saying that we are not prepared to move. We want to tell you straight away, our chiefs too, they endorse all what we've said. We drove them around, showed them all the places, showed them all what we had done and all the schools and the new school blocks just constructed.

We wouldn't like to destroy these things, because we have to remember the names of certain people.

We tell them we know that you can build good schools where you want us to go, but we feel we must stay here.

You see, if you get a lawyer you are sure to go away. Because these lawyers from SACC or Legal Resources Centre, when they come they tell you: 'Look, this is a government regulation, it's passed in parliament. It is cut and dry. There's nothing you can do to it except move.' So we said, 'Now we do away with lawyers and we handle our cases' — and we handled our cases ourselves. We paid nothing to the lawyers. So we faced the commissioner and the Ministers. We told them: 'You've got all the weapons, everything, and you could force us to go, but we will not go. We will not fight back but we will not go.' We will not go. This is the main thing.

And then again we find the most horrible man is the business man. They assure them to build a business complex so that their business will flourish. And then again they use the licences. 'We'll give you a licence for this and a licence for that.' So you must first find out who are the businessmen, who are interested in these things, in the removals, because they are going to get better sites. So as soon as we find out, nobody buys from his shop. So he'll keep open for a month or so, but ultimately he will have to close down the shop and then you have no more problems. We say, 'If you don't support us, how can we support you?'

These lawyers from Legal Resources only want us to get better compensation. So we said: 'We don't want anybody here who will get us better compensation. We don't want to go. As soon as we start discussing this question of compensation then they start numbering houses. The question of compensation must be completely cut out.'

As soon as you start mentioning 'compensation' they start numbering the houses. They suddenly arrive with buckets of paint. You confront them: 'Before you write down anything you go to the chief's kraal for permission.' They've been given instructions to avoid violence as far as possible. So they won't cause trouble if they are not allowed to paint the houses.

They also come to your house with a big iron bar and make holes in your walls and floors to see what they are made of. Then they add R5 here, R30 there and so on. Then they subtract the money you owe them for transport. And later you have to pay for the tents. So forget about compensation.

We had many meetings here. Some were just the committee and others with all the people, including school children. All the people must be given instructions not to assault any of the officials.

When the officials come and ask questions, do not answer anything. You may think it is a good answer you are giving them, but you find out that it may have other implications. Tell him: 'Give us time to think about these questions.' Discuss them. Try and find out what the implications of the questions are and then work out a reply.

Consequently there has been no violence here. At Makgato district, there wouldn't have been any violence, but the commissioners won the support of the chief. So the chief signed for the removals. There it was different. He signs on behalf of the community. So the trucks come and everybody had to move. People refused and the police came and broke windows, took out all the people's possessions and then went into the bush to search for the owners. They used dogs and trucks to find the people. There was a lot of violence, mainly because the chief had agreed to move.

A lot of people came this way seeking refuge and when they came to look for them we refused to allow them in the village. We said: 'If a man asks for cover we cannot say no. All we can do is talk to them and see how they feel about moving out.'

All the time they stayed here and now they've moved back to Makgato once they heard of the reprieve given to the area by the government. The government is now drilling new boreholes and the people are now fixing their damaged houses.

We (the committee) have been intimidated a bit. They wanted to know what we discussed. We said that all our meetings are open. We don't hide what we discuss. We were asked if any outsiders, agitators, whites were involved. We said no. We are dealing with our problems ourselves.

We found out about the talk of our removals in 1975. The magistrate sent the chief a letter asking him to a meeting with the tribal authorities. We were tipped, however, that the meeting was to talk about resettlement. So instead of the tribal authority going to the meeting, the committee went. The magistrate objected about this and we replied that it is not only the tribal authority that will be moved but the people and we represent their interests and any decisions taken by the tribal authority will not be binding.

We represented 60 000 people. We have been here since 1876. We have title deeds of the land. The land is divided into two. There is the Trust land and the 'bought' land.

People are mainly employed outside [40% in Pietermaritzburg, 20% commute and 40% on farms]. Some are involved in agriculture and employed locally here.

They promised us water in the streets, schools, business complexes, chain shops, transport and job opportunities.

I haven't seen any place where their promises have been fulfilled.

What happens with the chiefs is that they either give them a house or a car or both. Sometimes they send them overseas to make press statements about how nice the place is. Meanwhile the people here starve. Once people have moved there they start asking the chief to pay back for the car he got from the government and so the chief starts taxing his people more. A headman from this area was persuaded to go and a section of the tribe did move. When they arrived there they were not happy. They couldn't return because of

> the police. Once you are there the police guard the place so you don't return.
>
> This village got a reprieve two years after the visit by Dr Koornhof and Horwood. They said: 'We'll give you a reply in two weeks' time.'

The Makgato removals
The third chief, Chief Solomon Mathipa Makgato, of the Makgato tribe, meanwhile lent credence to the government's claims that the people had something to gain from relocation. After consulting with his tribal authority, he agreed to the move. However, none of the Makgato people were consulted. The villagers held a three-day indaba at which they tried to persuade him not to accept. When he still refused, the families petitioned the Minister of Cooperation and Development through the PFP spokesperson, Rupert Lorimer.

A Makgato woman reflected:

> The chief never organised our people. He just told them one day that he had got a letter from the commissioner that we must move from this place to an unknown place. People were surprised to hear that. That chief is the one who moved from here. He said we can't fight the government. If the government says we go, we go, whereas he had already agreed to what the government said, or what the commissioner told him. So we waited and then those people came. The commissioner sent some people to come and write numbers on our houses. They were government officials. They came back again — got identity numbers from everybody. We tried to refuse giving them those things. But we couldn't. They just wrote and then off they go. Then came the other officials to value those houses. We didn't know how much the house was going to cost. Well they went back. They just decided by themselves, secretly. They came to my house. When arriving there I greeted them and he said: 'How much did you pay for this house?' I said it was R15 000, not the present house, the previous one. They asked me: 'Is it sealed for water?' I said it is sealed, tiled, and then they asked about the furniture. I told them what I had. Well I didn't know: were they thinking of compensating me if I agreed to go? They didn't go to every house. They chose these big houses.

On 25 September the Cooperation and Development lorries and officials came to the Makgato village to take the people who had agreed to be removed. Lorimer was reported as saying:

> Dr Koornhof did not make a promise to me personally that the tribe would not be moved, but my understanding is that the Minister had said that nobody would be removed against his will.
> (*Post*, 27 Sept. 79.)

The Makgato tribe also believed this. People who were refusing to move gladly and openly assisted the group of about 50 who wanted to go with the chief.

A Makgato teacher recalled:

> One day I was in the office. There came a special branch. He threatened me, asking me, he was black. And I told him that I am not going. The last word he told me is that 'If you are not going you must not be here on Monday.' That was the following Monday but I don't know which date that was. He just told me 'You musn't be here on Monday, otherwise . . . you will go then by force.'

At 6.30 a.m. on 1 October 1979 about 30 trucks arrived again at Klipplaatdrift. They were accompanied by about 11 police vans, one of them with two police dogs. Camouflaged police patrolled the area while others started demolishing houses and huts, using a chain attached to a truck. The property in the house was then loaded into a truck. The people in the vicinity were forced into the trucks 'voor die voet', under threat from the dogs and guns. All reporters were meanwhile banned from both the Dwars River and Kromhoek areas.

A Makgato resident said:

> We don't know whether it was the chief or not, but what we heard was that it was the chief who told the commissioner that he must *bring soldiers*, dogs, to let the dogs bite the people so that they would go.
> Hey — people, really, really, my house was still standing and my husband was still there. Most people, many people were still there. Those who said 'We are not going.' Well I got up in the morning, it was the 1st. I got my sister-in-law. She told me to take everything that was in the house. My furniture, my everything, just everything. The policemen were always coming to my family — that 'Where is your husband and where is the owner of this place?' — 'Well the chief is waiting for you', that's what they always told my people, my family.
> After discovering that many people didn't like to go, or refused the

removals, they started to take them by force. Dogs were around, biting people, boys were taken to hospitals because they were just roaming about. If they get a person here, for instance the owner of the house, a man, they just get it, they get hold of that person. The truck stands here at the door of the house. They just get those chains and break the house, take everything. While holding you. So that you mustn't run away. Because most people ran away. That's why these people remained here. Because they ran away to stay with others, the Batlokwa and others.

So after holding you, other men would take all your things, your properties in the truck and then they get you into the truck too and they take you to the place. Is that not fast?

You see this place is divided into two. Some staying with the chief and some not. Those who stayed with the chief are those who went with the removal, they went with the chief. And those others who are away from the chief's kraal are those who were taken by force. That's how they removed those others who didn't want to be removed, just to take things, break everything, put it into the truck.'

Three delegates from the village arranged an urgent meeting with Dr Phatudi for 2 o'clock that afternoon to try 'to stop this barbaric and inhuman action immediately'. Phatudi felt the Lebowa government was helpless, but asked for the information in writing. The delegates abandoned this line of appeal and went to the chief commissioner's office. There they saw a Mr C Liebenberg who referred them to the proclamation and said they had had 18 months to prepare for relocation. The delegation dismissed themselves and returned to the village.

As soon as the vans and police arrived the Makgato people had begun to flee the village. Some locked the doors of their homes first, hoping that their goods would be protected. The general exodus continued for the next few days.

Using bicycles, wheelbarrows, private cars, hired tractors and vans, the inhabitants, most of them women, moved in and out of the village, taking out their belongings — corrugated iron, pots, furniture, blankets and fowls.

Women, some carrying children and bundles of clothing, were seen scampering through the bush away from the village. Eight people . . . have been arrested. Several others have been assaulted according to some fleeing tribesmen.

All day and night they streamed across the dusty road. A woman balanced a 40-gallon water drum on her head. Behind her came a young girl pushing a wheelbarrow filled with wooden struts, not far behind a young boy walking alongside his mother bore a kettle, pot,

and food in a large brown paper bag.
'We don't want to move', said a wrinkled elder tribesman, leaning on his stick, 'so we are making sure that when they come again to take us away we won't be here'.

(*Star*, 8 Oct. 79.)

The authorities were prepared to use force. They said they might 'have to detain them if they do not return to where their property is'. Besides the eight arrests, there were 14 detentions, including that of a local school principal. At least one child was bitten by a police dog. Later reports mentioned at least four deaths which could be attributed to stress caused by the removals. When 14 people who had been relocated returned to their former homes, they too were arrested. The chief commissioner, on hearing that people were returning, said this would not be allowed:

> You must expect some resistance [against the removals] but once they are settled they will be happy. (*Afrika*, 1 Nov. 80.)

Police headquarters in Pretoria confirmed 14 arrests, stating four were for assault, one for malicious injury to property, and nine for trespassing.

Seventy-eight of the total of 740 Makgato families had agreed to move. The possessions of a further 14 families were taken to Kromhoek while the families themselves fled into the bush.

> Some took their tables, in the evening when the trucks had gone to sleep. That's when they start. The people just come from the bush — take their tables, take their things. Take them on the head and run away to Batlokwa, to Matoks. When the truck is full and has gone to Kromhoek they come, collect everything, collect and run away. In the dark too, collect and run away. When you see the truck standing there in front of your house, you all run away. There was no fight. Only boys of course. They fought those dogs. At least one boy was bitten and taken to hospital. He was so much injured, very, very.
>
> Well, that's how these people managed to remain here. Well, there were many people who did not move so we all fled to the Matoks, we stood there, had to build shanties. We went to people and said: 'I'm asking to build a shanty next to your house.' They said yes. Even if they were not relatives. Our people were just scattered everywhere, Ramokgopa, and to the Batlokwas, we just asked, as in the Gospel they just asked. Because there was one of the committee, the executive committee, and he pleaded for that, that they should come and stay here while still settling the matters.
>
> (Interview with a member of the Makgato community, 1983.)

By Friday 8 October the village was absolutely deserted. Approximately 600 families had been absorbed into the surrounding countryside. The church, clinic and schools were partially demolished. It was reported that the cattle of those Makgato who had refused to move had been driven into a camp and shot by officials of the Department of Cooperation and Development, or by the police. A 'squatter camp' arose not far from the original village. It consisted of tin shacks and thatched shelters, and housed about 1 000 of the 2 000 people who had refused to move. The rest of the people had been absorbed by the neighbouring tribe, the Batlokwa, who offered this help and accommodation despite threats that their action was illegal, and despite their already fairly overcrowded conditions.

Scholar protest

Meanwhile the school children were supposed to return to classes on 2 October after a week's break. A teacher reported:

> Our children were scattered. We had no place to teach. No school to teach in. So they started arranging like this: one day the Batlokwa children said they didn't like to go to classes, not unless the Makgato children also get in classes. 'We are not going to do it.' So they marched. It was so interesting. I still remember talking to my mother. I said: 'I am going with the children.' She said: 'No, no you aren't, because you are the cause of all this.' Those children got out of their classes from *all* schools, not one school. All schools here, then they marched.
> One teacher didn't like it much. They just pushed the doors in. 'C'mon let the children *out*. We are marching to the circuit office now. What for? We are going to tell the circuit inspector that we *can't* continue when the Makgatos are at home.' So they marched, even small children. Some just went as far as the tarred road. They couldn't go further because of their age. So they passed to the circuit office at Ramokgopa — right the other side. When reaching there they drove the Ramokgopa children too to *get out*. Well, they also got out of classes. So we [teachers] were just told — we were also going to the circuit of course, to find out because we had no work — so we were told to gather those children. They had to get classes in the different schools, our children were divided in that way. Some went to the secondary, some went to the primary school at Batlokwa, and some to the lower primary school.
> And so the children wrote their final examinations of 1979. And some of our teachers were also distributed to schools and taught there.
>
> (Interview with a Makgato teacher, 1983.)

On 9 October more than 900 students from Turfloop University and Hwiti High School held a protest march in solidarity with the villagers. Then on 15 October thousands of pupils marched through the Batlokwa area in protest against the removals. The march started at the Kgarahara High School with nearly 700 students. The crowds grew bigger as they went from school to school until nearly 7 000 students, a train of over 4 kilometres, joined the march:

> Hordes of pupils went from school to school telling youngsters to join them in the demonstration. Some of our schools were completely empty in a flash.

The pupils, under the auspices of the Batlokwa African Youth Organisation, presented the inspector with their five-point petition:
— that the Department of Education and Training had shown no interest in the plight of the Makgato students;
— that the detained students should be released before Thursday;
— that a staggering 740 students were out of school due to the forced removals;
— that the Department should make arrangements for the Makgato students to write exams at the local schools;
— that crucial steps should be taken on Thursday October 10 if the authorities did not respond positively to the demands.

The inspector signed the petition, but later he denied telling the students that the schools would be opened to the 740 Makgato pupils. He said that only senior department officials could make the decision.

Just before the Std 5 exams were to be written, the Northern Transvaal Regional Council of Churches interviewed the Lebowa Department of Education. After this the Makgato pupils were accepted into the schools by Under-Secretary Kobe and Minister Marishane. 635 of the 740 who were eligible were thus able to write their exams. Their teachers were, however, prohibited from attending these schools, which made it impossible for them to carry out the preparation they had begun in Makgato. The teachers were also deprived of their salaries for a few months for having refused to move. Since then many of the teachers have been sent to areas far away from their homes and families, despite vacancies in the Batlokwa schools.

The move to Kromhoek

The Deputy Minister described the destination Kromhoek as a beautiful land and said the removals would definitely continue. He also said that all the families removed had been given free transport and compensated for their homes, and were allowed to take windows, doors and corrugated iron. Those 'few families' who were resisting the removal were acting against their tribal authority 'in an undemocratic manner'.

> . . . the area in which the tribe is being resettled offers the people more opportunity than they had in the area from which they are being removed. This is particularly true in respect of schooling, supply of water and rural resettlement of farmers.

Pieterse, the chief commissioner, said he had been to Kromhoek himself, and people relocated there had told him they were happy in their new surroundings.

Meanwhile those who returned reported that conditions were unbearable. People were not allocated arable land in time for that year's season. The compensation was totally inadequate. A good rondavel cost R700 - R800 to build. One family received R50 for an old rondavel. Another received R175 for three new rondavels. A third received R920 for two zinc rooms and four rondavels. Those forcibly removed had been separated by Chief Makgato from people who had moved voluntarily, and they feared further discrimination in matters such as land distribution.

Chief Makgato felt that the government authorities had let him down. He told reporters,

> I expected the government to protect the 78 families who wanted to be resettled with me here. But it has left most of them behind. They are now being beaten by those people who are opposed to the removal.

He was also bitter towards the other chiefs:

> These chiefs have taken away my people. Because of their attitude the 536 families who do not support the removals will not join me. They have built homes among their tribes.
>
> I am terribly disappointed but these chiefs did not support me by rejecting those of my people who don't want to follow me.
>
> I have no people now.

At his request a meeting was held on 11 October between the three Batlokwa chiefs and the chief commissioner, but it ended in stalemate. Machaka and Ramokgopa rejected Chief Makgato's accusations. The two chiefs refused to surrender the families their people were harbouring. The Batlokwa claimed the fleeing Makgato were refugees from a war which the government had declared on an unarmed and defenceless people. They compared themselves to 'Christian South Africa' which was so ready to give asylum to refugees fleeing from 'troublespots' abroad.

The Makgato chief was totally rejected by those who stayed behind and those who returned. They referred to him as 'the baas from Kromhoek'. In his place they elected a committee of four to represent their views. Each day, in the late afternoon, a hooter would sound and people would go from the homes they were rebuilding down to the river banks for their daily meeting about the relocation. After a meeting with the Pietersburg chief commissioner, Pieterse, in which he told them that they were trespassing and would have to move, eviction notices were handed out. The people gave them back saying, 'We can't read.' They were warned they faced fines of R150 or jail sentences of up to six months, and that they would still have to go to Kromhoek afterwards. They were warned they were 'making life difficult for themselves' and would end up as squatters. Pieterse issued an additional warning that those who delayed in moving might lose their compensation. Despite the warnings the community made a firm decision to resist all attempts to move them.

The aftermath

The returned families and those who had refused to move spent the next 12 months living with people who had offered them accommodation. Conditions were bad. Various organisations such as the Catholic Mission and SACC provided the people with emergency relief in the form of blankets, mealie meal, powdered milk and soup. But the donors themselves realised that this was only temporary relief:

> These people need a permanent home which we cannot offer and unless an acceptable lasting solution is found immediately real trouble with the possibility of violence lies ahead.

While friends, relatives and sympathisers continued to accommodate the people in their small dwellings, they could not be expected to share these indefinitely, and animosity was feared. Overcrowding was rife with families of 18 or more living in two rondavels.

Then, about a year after the removals, 500 of the displaced people returned to their former homes, claiming official authority to do so. In March 1980 Koornhof had replied to a question in parliament that all removals except of those agreeing to move had been delayed until the Van der Walt Commission on consolidation of the areas had reported.

On 4 August Koornhof, together with Horwood, attended an intertribal meeting in the area. Koornhof said he was not responsible for the proclamation, that it had taken place before his time, and that the Van der Walt Commission would be looking into the matter. He said he would not return to the area unless the commission decided that the people did indeed have to move. He said he did not expect to have to return. (Horwood's presence at the meeting, as Minister of Finance, was interpreted by some as an attempt to see if the government could 'pay them off'.)

When the people came back in October, the commissioner for the area would not comment on their return.

Within a few days, though, official reaction came. Three of the families were charged with 'wrongly and unlawfully [sic] occupation of SADT Klipblooddrift [Klipplaatdrift] without permission.' The summonses were delivered by white officials, travelling in three cars, and accompanied by six policemen in a van. After delivering the summonses they called the villagers together and told them to move from the area. They also told them that their former Chief Solomon Makgato was waiting for them in the new area.

The people reacted angrily. They reiterated their refusal to move and asked to be left alone. As the officials were consulting among themselves about the matter, three residents' committee members arrived and told the people to disperse. The near-300 villagers complied. A committee member complained to newsmen about the officials' actions:

> We cannot allow a situation where people just come and call our people together and address them.

He also expressed anger that only three families had been summonsed:

> If they are guilty then we are all guilty. We are all going to that court on that date. We have suffered, my sons. Look at all this rubble. We want to make a new start and rebuild our homes. What we ask from the government is to be left alone in peace.

Despite the raid by the officials, more and more families returned to the 'ghost village' to rebuild their ruins. In the absence of the action promised by Koornhof and other high authorities, the people had taken a unilateral decision to reestablish themselves. They had had enough of being handled like 'a cook turning a steak on a frying pan', as one woman put it.

> When the principal of the secondary school passed away the special branches came here saying: 'Their chief has passed away, now they'll come down to Kromhoek.' So we were called to where the stock is counted. We were told to go there with all documents concerning stock, animals . . . cows, sheep, goats and all this. We were told to get down there, only to find that trucks had come. So that if we go there they take our documents, stock, get hold of us, stock in some trucks, people in other trucks.
> So we sent one person to go there. The commissioner was there and some other assistants. So I was still standing there with the class when I heard shouts: 'Well we are going there, everybody out of your houses. Let's go up there.' Then we all fled to the place. We found the commissioner and his members doing the same thing of writing numbers on doors. Uh, oh, now what's going on? So a commissioner's staff asked another man: 'Are you the brother to Francis Makgato? Or was he your father?' He said: 'No he was not my father and what do you want here?' He said: 'You must come here and remove your possessions. Now you'll agree.' Hmph. That day I won't forget. Women got hoes, spades, forks, stones, everything. As long as somebody had something. And went there of course. Haayi, they started. They never fought, the women went to the road and drew a line down there. They just said: 'You from that side, if you enter here, you die.' Could they cross? Never. Then they sent some to go and call boys from the secondary school. That day it was a miracle. Most came *running*. The commissioner and those just got into the car and went away poo-poo-poo-poo. Then they ran away and they never came back since then.
> Well, that time women played an important part — even men joined.
> (Interview with a member of the Makgato community, 1983.)

No further official developments were reported until April

1982. Then, after a battle of almost four years, Koornhof announced that for 'practical and financial' reasons the proposed removals had been shelved. The Batlokwa and Makgato had, temporarily at least, won the right to remain on their land.

Community organisation

Throughout their struggle the Batlokwa as a whole displayed an awareness of unity that negated the government's ideology of division into tribes. A lot of bitterness was thereby avoided. Mr Alfred Masipa, a Machaka school principal and spokesman for the Batlokwa committee, put it this way:

> Adversity has drawn us very close together. On the removal issue we act as one. We have resolved to oppose any attempts by the South African government to shift us from our ancestral homes.

A lot of bitterness was felt towards the Makgato chief both for having agreed to the removals and for having conducted separate negotiations with the government. An inter-tribal committee had been set up so as to have a united strategy towards the government, and it was felt that the actions of some of the Makgato had weakened their struggle.

In 1983 members of the Makgato community discussed their group dynamics:

> We heard these rumours of the removal for years. I don't know if it was because our chief was uneducated but he thought what the government says no-one can be allowed to answer. We are not allowed to give opinions. So he just thought it is a final thing. So these people really, I can say, were helped by this one. Because when it started here they started gathering to talk about this, to talk about this and think of some years back. Because we understand that this place, Batlokwa, became ours according to old, old wars. I understand Paul Kruger was helped by the Batlokwa somehow with their fights long ago. You know about the history, long ago, and he *paid* the Batlokwas by signing for this place. That it is for the Batlokwas for the rest of time. So during this, the Batlokwa started to think and to go deep. Go to their long, long ago papers if they are not teared. And so they said: 'We know that this place was given to the Batlokwas by *Paul Kruger*.' You can imagine . . . when did Paul Kruger live? It's long ago. We never thought of being here then. *Right*?
>
> Our people were not just seated. They were going up and down — the Jo'burg ones [the migrant workers] and the ones at home. We must

organise — what to do and what not to do. Otherwise we would have fought and killed one another. We are not fighting, let them do what they do, we are not fighting. That is why no one was killed.

Other communities? Well they must first organise. If they don't accept the removal they must sit together and choose committees with executive members. And they must not fight, they must agree on one thing. That means if they say 'We are not going' they must remain saying 'We are not going'. But if one starts to say 'Ag', then they will move. But with us, the remaining ones, we said — we are not going — up till the last day. Although threatened in these manners we never said — we are going — instead we ran away — crying — carrying our things on our heads — we just said 'We are not going'. And of course, not fighting, talking together, suggesting this and that and talking to people. They didn't just sit. Imagine, they went as far as Cape Town to go and talk to that one, the big wall of course.

Here we were called Machaka, Makgato, Ramokgopa — they were one thing. Each area had its own committee and they were also combined. Since then everyone attends meetings. But before, a woman couldn't get into the kgotla and say anything. If you had something to say, you would tell somebody, a man, to go and say it. But you must tell him in such a way that he can defend himself and answer questions.

These people and others knew that unity was vital. They valued publicity because it helped to connect people of various tribes who were in the same threatened situation and to put them in touch with developments elsewhere in the country. They could then act knowing that theirs was not an isolated struggle.

It's a long story. Now we are just thinking of drinking tea with bread and saying 'This is our home. We are no longer going anywhere.' So forgetting what has happened. Gradually in one year to come, this is in 1985, maybe I shall have forgotten many stories.

6. *Umbulwane*

Umbulwane is a black freehold area falling within municipal Ladysmith in Northern Natal. By 1980 about 1000 people were living there, the residents said. Their houses, mostly small wattle-and-daub structures, are scattered across a bleak flat plain on the outskirts of town. There are 41 landowning families, most of them African, but there are some Indian and coloured landowners as well. The other residents are tenants of the landowners. Most are African but there are people classified as coloured living there too — Zulu-speaking and integrated into the community but classified as a separate group by officials.

It is one of fourteen black spots under threat of removal in the Ladysmith district. Both landowners and tenants are eventually to be moved, but at present it is the tenants who are most at risk. Together, landowners and tenants are trying to ward off the threat.

History

A memorandum drawn up by the community in December 1980 sets out the history of the place:

> Most people used to stay in town and in 1885 we moved from town to this place, Umbulwane. When we came here first life was very hard. There were no roads. We used to walk to and from work. In 1932 we first saw the roads, but there were no cars, only donkey carts and horses at that time.
>
> We started paying rates. There was no school for the children at Umbulwane. At that time the children used to go to the churches for school. In 1934 each famiy at Umbulwane paid £5 to help build a school. The school was built at Steadville which was the only location at that time and named after Mr Stead who was the superintendent. The school was opened in 1937. Children from Umbulwane still attend school there.
>
> After Steadville they built Jabavu Location, which was followed by White City Location. When they built all these locations, they used to take tenants from Umbulwane and resettle them there. When they took tenants to the locations, the landowners always used to get new tenants. The last lot of tenants they took to Ezakheni and, as usual, the landowners got new ones in 1979.

The official housing policy in Ladysmith over the past 15 years has been to force Africans out of the urban area into relocation areas in nearby KwaZulu: the township of Ezakheni (25 kilometres away) and the rudimentary settlements of Ekuvukeni and Limehill (more than 50 kilometres away). Steadville, the only official township left in Ladysmith, has been under threat of removal for years. Housebuilding there has been frozen and it is desperately overcrowded.

Despite Umbulwane's long history, officials have refused to recognise it as an African residential area. Even though the landowners are all ratepayers, the municipality has refused to provide any services: neither water nor sanitation not roads nor bus services nor refuse collection.

> As far as your request for services are concerned, I regret that it is not possible to supply services to the area, as this area is not zoned for residential purposes. (Letter from the town clerk of Ladysmith to the Umbulwane Committee, 2 Dec. 80).

Umbulwane is, instead, zoned for eventual industrial development.

Origin of the tenants

The officials have classified the tenants of Umbulwane as squatters:

> Our concern is that squatters have moved into Umbulwane. It is illegal for squatters to live there, even though the land is privately owned. In addition, in terms of the law plans must be submitted for the erection of any dwelling. No plans have been submitted by the squatters of Umbulwane. (The town clerk, in an interview with the *Sunday Times*, 14 Dec. 80.)

The Department of Cooperation and Development has adopted a similar approach:

> Those families that have settled at Umbulwane illegally and without permission, will be required to return to their places of origin or arrange for accommodation themselves with their relevant chiefs. (Letter from the administrative secretary of the Department to the Umbulwane Committee, 26 March 81.)

In fact, most residents have been living at Umbulwane for a long time. Those who have moved there in recent years have come precisely because their 'places of origin' have been destroyed by government policy or because they have been evicted off white farms and have nowhere else to go. In a letter to the *Natal Witness* (27 Nov. 80) the committee put it thus:

> To clarify the point regarding the origin of the many people at Umbulwane: it is totally incorrect to say they come from other towns. They all come from the Klip River complex and from local farms. They are all employed in Ladysmith.

In 1980-81 AFRA interviewed 13 tenant households to find out where they had come from and how long they had lived at Umbulwane. The results bore out what the committee had said:

> Four of the households had lived there for many years (between 50 and 25 years).
> One was the son of a landowner who had built his own house when he had got married shortly before.
> One, who had been living on the property of one of the Indian landowners for two years, was in the employ of his landlord. He had worked for him for years. Until about 1962 he had lived on his employer's property in Ladysmith itself. Then the municipality had said that was illegal. He had moved to another informal settlement on the edge of Ladysmith. When that was destroyed in 1979, his employer had allowed him to move to Umbulwane.
> Two of the households had moved to Umbulwane from the township of Steadville after they had got married, because there were no houses for them in the township.
> One had moved to Umbulwane to be closer to his job after getting hired by a building contractor in early 1980.
> Three of the households had come there after they had been evicted off white farms.
> One household, headed by a widow, had formerly lived on the black spot of Roosboom. When that was removed in 1976, she had moved to another black spot in the district. Then, when she had found a job in Ladysmith, she moved to Umbulwane to be closer to work.

Demolitions begin

The first warning the community had of official action against them came in June-July 1980 when officials arrived and started painting numbers on all the properties:

> In the middle of the year people came to write numbers on each and every house but they did not tell us what the numbers are for.

Then:

> On the 19th August 1980 we saw the Municipality and the Drakensberg Administration Board as well as police, all armed with guns, and a bulldozer. They started to break down houses. Most of the owners of these houses were not at home but at work or fetching wood. When they came from work they found their houses broken down. Some were left with only one small room. (Memorandum from the people of Umbulwane, Dec. 80.)

The authorities did not demolish completely. They selected only tenant houses, and knocked down only part of each family's home. Then they left, after warning that if the occupants had not moved away within a month they would return to finish off the job. Some of the warnings were verbal. Where nobody was at home, notices to demolish were attached to what was left of the house.

```
                        OFFICES OF THE BOROUGH ENGINEER
                        LADYSMITH

    .........................

    .........................
    .........................

    Dear Sir,
    REPAIRS TO HOUSE ON LOT NO..... 1514 Sub 2
                                    demolish     short
    You are hereby authorised to ~~rebuild/repair~~ your house on the
    abovementioned property.
    Yours faithfully          Within 28 days of this notice
        JA Erra
    BOROUGH ENGINEER
```

The town clerk later admitted that no notices were served in advance (*Sunday Times*, 14 Dec. 80) but also claimed that only unoccupied structures had been demolished.

> I am involved in the removal of the illegal structures and the health hazard . . . the people do not fall under my jurisdiction. I am not putting out people — just demolishing unoccupied illegal structures.
> (*Sunday Tribune*, 16 Nov. 80.)

Those who had had their houses destroyed were outraged. If that was the case, why were their houses only partly demolished, and why were further demolition notices served? Statements made by three of them, with their version of what happened, are reproduced on the following page.

DEMOLITIONS AT UMBULWANE

These statements were taken by AFRA in August 1980.

1 My six-room house was broken down on the 19th August while I was at work. My wife was out collecting firewood; there was our three-year old baby inside who was taken outside and ran away. I found my house broken down. All the doorframes and windows were broken, my tools were broken and they left me with only one room. They came back later, just to level everything. I did not receive a word of notice.

2 I was present. I was sitting in the yard with the children when they came. A white man was pointing out all the houses. They asked who the owner of the house was. They just said they were going to break them down. I tried to stop them. I explained that it was my son's house. They didn't mind — they called the bulldozer and started breaking it down. They did not give any reason. After breaking that one, they moved to the small one, where I keep all my tools and the grinding machine. They said I must take all the stuff out. I called Ndlovu to help me; we took it out and then they started to break the house.

3 They first broke the house. I was not here. I was looking after my boss's house. There was nobody at home — my wife was at work and my mother was out visiting. They took stuff out and then broke the houses with a machine. They knocked the whole house down. No furniture was damaged, but when I got back, one bed and three sheets of tin were missing. My cousin came and told me the house was broken so I came back. They came and gave me notice afterwards.

Municipal and Administration Board officials returned during the course of October, painted new numbers on some of the tenants' houses (in red, as opposed to the white paint used before) and issued several more types of notice. One dated 21 October 1980, addressed 'To Tenant Hlatshwayo' and signed on behalf of the borough engineer, read:

> You are hereby advised that the building/buildings being erected by you on Lot 1114/1 are illegal, in that plans have not been submitted to or approved by the Council of Ladysmith as provided for in Clause 26 of Section III of Chapter XI of the Council's By-laws.
>
> Under the provisions of Section 164(2) of the Local Government Ordinance No. 2 of 1942 you are hereby required to demolish the said building/buildings on or before the 21/11/80.
>
> Failure to comply with this order, within the period stipulated, will result in the immediate demolition of the building/buildings by the Council.

Landowners were also given orders to 'get the permission by form of a licence' to have tenants on their property, 'or let them vacate your property within 3 months'. These notices came from the Drakensberg Administration Board.

Community organisation

Although people were angry and bitter about the treatment they had received, most of them felt scared by the obvious power of the authorities. At first the mood in the community was one of helplessness:

> We feel at the moment that we are just like animals for which the owner decides and acts without asking their opinion.

From the start, however, some prominent landowners saw that the threat to the tenants was a threat to themselves. With encouragement from community leaders in Steadville, they organised a memorandum to be sent to the chief commissioner for Natal. This begged him 'to have the notices and breaking down of our homes and tenants' houses be stopped' and asked that 'we be consulted in time if there is anything that affects us'. Out of this activity a residents' committee emerged which came to be seen as representative of the community. Both tenants and landowners were involved in the committee from the start — the chairman was himself a tenant, although one of long standing.

Throughout this time no news of what was happening at Umbulwane had travelled beyond Steadville. Only during

October, two months after the demolitions had started, did reports begin to filter through to a few individuals connected to church and welfare groups in Ladysmith itself. Eventually, in early November, AFRA made contact with the Umbulwane committee and in this way the story of the demolitions got into the Natal and Johannesburg newspapers.

At the same time, encouraged by the interest of outside groups, the community began to rally to meet the crisis. During November the committee organised several general meetings, attended by between 50 and 150 adults. There is no community hall at Umbulwane; all the meetings took place outside under a tall, spreading gum tree. At these meetings the following decisions were taken:

1 To send a second memorandum to Koornhof, the Chief Commissioner, the Ladysmith Town Council and the local Administration Board offices;
2 To establish exactly how many people were living in Umbulwane;
3 To write to newspapers to put the community's side of the story, in answer to what the town clerk had been saying in various interviews with journalists;
4 To open a savings account in the committee's name and to collect funds from residents so as to have money available if a fresh emergency arose.

The combination of the stronger organisation within the community, the press publicity and the time of year — the Christmas holiday season was approaching — seemed to be enough to persuade the local authorities to take a softer position on Umbulwane. The demolitions stopped in October 1980. While officials continued to patrol the area regularly, they did not take any further action once the various notice periods had expired.

Memorandum from the people of Umbulwane

This memorandum was written and sent off on 1 December 1980. Th introductory parts to it have been quoted already. The second half reads:

What we want
Umbulwane is our grandfathers' place. We have been living here over

fifty years at this place. We want to stay at Umbulwane, only we beg
that our Municipality will improve the place and make it healthier.
  Most people paying rates are widows and pensioners who need the
rents paid by their tenants. Widows help educate and feed their
children with their tenants' rents. Without their tenants they cannot
live. Most people have no stock but those who have it use it to make
our living better. We use the milk to feed our children. Those who
have milk help the others with a little milk.
  What is worse is that people from Umbulwane find it hard to get
work now. They don't want to register us but we must pay rates.
Where must we work? How can we live without work?

Conclusion
This Umbulwane was bought by the white people, Indians, Coloureds
and Africans a long time ago . . .
Umbulwane has improved this town by working in this town. Up to
now and before we had locations and hostels, the workers have always
stayed at Umbulwane. Dr. Koornhof said no people must be forced to
leave their homes, in the *Daily News* on the 17th July 1980, and that is
what we want.

In February 1981 Koornhof acknowledged receiving the
memorandum, in reply to a series of questions about Umbulwane
that were asked in parliament. He said the matter was still receiving attention and that 'further negotiations will take place'. (*Hansard*, Private Question 26, 11 Feb. 81.) A few days later he denied
that the people were to be removed 'at present'.

> If the people are eventually resettled they will be removed depending
> on merit to appropriate accommodation at Ezakheni or to such
> accommodation as may be arranged by the people with the chiefs
> concerned.   (*Hansard*, Private Question 5, 13 Feb. 81.)

The people of Umbulwane only got an official reply at the end of
March, however (see box). This letter did several things:
— It tried to drive a wedge between residents who 'qualify for
  housing at Ezakheni' and those living at Umbulwane 'illegally';
— It qualified Koornhof's previous statement that there would be
  no more forced removals by stating that this 'did not imply that
  the country's legislation regarding illegal squatting' could be
  ignored;
— It excused the Deputy Minister from taking any further action.
  (The memorandum had in fact been addressed to Koornhof
  and not his Deputy.)

Republiek van Suid-Afrika · Republic of South Africa

Ministerie van Samewerking en Ontwikkeling
Ministry of Co-operation and Development

/AB

Verwysingsnommer:
Reference Number: 5/2 Natal

Hendrik Verwoerdgebou
Hendrik Verwoerd Buildings
Kaapstad
Cape Town

The Secretary
The Umbulwane Committee
Umbulwane
P O Box 327
LADYSMITH
3370

26 -03- 1981

Dear Sir

MEMORANDUM FROM THE PEOPLE OF UMBULWANE

With further reference to your memorandum dated 1 December 1980, I am directed by Dr the Honourable G de V Morrison, Deputy Minister of Co-operation to inform you that the points raised in your memorandum have been thoroughly investigated.

The so-called Umbulwane area is situated within the municipal boundaries of Ladysmith and is of necessity subject to the building and health byelaws of that local authority. It has not been set aside as an urban Black residential area and it is not the intention that it should be set aside as such. It follows therefore that my Deputy Minister is not in a position to intervene as far as the implementation of the Local Authority's byelaws is concerned.

As you are no doubt aware, the majority of the residents of Umbulwane were resettled at e'Zakheni prior to 1977. Those of the remaining standowners as well as approximately 105 squatter families that qualify for housing at e'Zakheni will all eventually be resettled there as and when sufficient development funds become available for this purpose. These families will be negotiated with prior to their resettlement either at e'Zakheni or at such other accommodation as may be arranged by themselves with their relevant Chiefs in KwaZulu.

Those families that have settled at Umbulwane illegally and without permission, will be required to return to their places of origin or arrange for accommodation themselves with their relevant Chiefs in KwaZulu.

2/....

```
                              -2-

    It should be mentioned that the Honourable the Minister's
    statement that "no people must be forced to leave their
    homes" did not imply that the Country's legislation regarding
    illegal squatting as well as other legislation could be dis=
    regarded.  Illegal squatting is an offence in terms of the
    Prevention of Illegal Squatting Act No 52 of 1951.  Likewise,
    it is an offence in terms of the same Act for an owner or
    lessee of land to erect, cause to be erected or permit the
    erection of any building or structure intended for occupation
    by persons, on his land or the leased land, as the case may
    be, and to permit the occupation of such building or structure
    unless a plan or description thereof has been approved by the
    relevant local authority.

    In the circumstances my Deputy Minister is not in a position
    to intervene in so far as the matters raised are concerned.

    Yours faithfully



    ADMINISTRATIVE SECRETARY:
    MINISTRY
```

The people of Umbulwane were not satisfied with this letter. In June 1981 they replied:

Umbulwane has not been set aside as an urban Black residential area, but it is incorrect that Umbulwane is not owned by Blacks. As we explained in our memorandum it was bought by our grandfathers more than 70 years ago. Perhaps the Government is unaware that Umbulwane has been paying rates to the local authority up to now but getting nothing from the Town Council in return. We have no services at all.

The Government states that illegal people must go back to their places of origin yet people were expelled from white farms and most of those farms were taken by the Government. Some of these people were aiming to settle in Steadville which is the urban Black settlement, but due to the fact that there was no housing, people became tenants of Umbulwane.

We do not believe that we can only live in KwaZulu. We know that we owned a lot of large pieces of land all over Natal (that do not fall in KwaZulu) and this had been occupied a hundred years or more before the Whites came to Natal and took land for themselves.

We know we can ask for rights in South Africa. We can ask for jobs, pensions, justice and more in South Africa. In other words we do not want to blame the Minister. Maybe he was not informed that we have been paying rates for so long without any services, that we have title deeds and that the Government is separating the people of Umbulwane by saying some people are illegal and that the Government cannot help them. We know they want to take this place and that is why we wrote and asked for help from the Honourable the Minister.

The Government states that those who are said to be legal will be settled at Ezakheni. It sounds as if those people will be looked after at Ezakheni. The fact that it is too far, that buses are so expensive, that there is a crime problem with violence and tribal fights that the people of Umbulwane do not now face, that rents are expensive and most are unable to pay all these things, is not being considered.

The Government said people must not be forced to leave their homes. We do not want to leave Umbulwane where there is peace. We would like to inform the Government about the local authorities who apply injustice to the people of Umbulwane who keep on paying rates but get nothing from the town council. The unhealthy situation is caused by them. We feel the Government did not answer any of our points properly. It is important that this be made clear.

The future of Umbulwane is still uncertain. For nearly two years there have been no further demolitions. The officials still patrol periodically, but their arrival is no longer regarded with the fear it once was. The community is more confident. After hesitating for a long time, most of them have restored their houses — 'stealing space' is how they describe it. Attendance at general meetings has fallen away, but the committee has been drawn into the wider network of communities resisting removal in the Ladysmith district. There has been some talk that perhaps they should take up some of the other problems facing the community — try to get water piped to some central points within it, for instance. Nothing has come of these talks so far.

Yet it is still the intention of Koornhof and his Department to remove them. In April 1982 Koornhof confirmed that Umbulwane and the other Ladysmith black spots would be moved 'after consultation and in collaboraton with the communities concerned as well as the Government of KwaZulu'. He added:

> the actual removals would only take place once the necessary housing facilities, water-reticulation, sanitation, school and clinic facilities, shops, roads and other services had been provided and made available.
> (*Natal Mercury*, 27 April 82.)

These are all services that the people at Umbulwane have been asking for for a long time. They cannot understand why they should not be given them at Umbulwane — at the place they own, which is close to their work, at which 'we all stay in peace'.

CHAPTER EIGHT

Responses:
The people wish unity

I've got three children and I'm prepared to face prosecution to stay here. At least I can find work here even if its casual. I will come back if I'm deported. I've faced hardship, it's part of my life. I just think the Administration Board can relax part of its attitude and give me the same rights as other people. (One of the KTC squatters found guilty in the Athlone magistrate's court for living in the bush in plastic shelters during a bitterly cold, wet Cape Town winter. *Cape Times,* 17 June 83.)

'Did you say anything when the chief told you to move?'
'No. People are scared to say "No". You just hang your head, like a donkey.' (Woman under threat of removal in Bophuthatswana, August 1983.)

We are not prepared to move one quarter of a millimetre. (Community member, Mathopestad, March 1981.)

The Minister has promised that people will not be moved against their will. None of the people at Jonono's or Matiwane's Kop want to move. We will not move. We intend to carry on as we always have done. They will have to bring guns to push us out or bury us here. (Spokesman for the Matiwane's Kop community, summing up their threatened position. *Natal Witness*, 22 Nov. 80)

The people who are threatened by removals unanimously resolve that they are not moving. We pray that the government calls off the removals. (Resolution unanimously adopted by representatives of the threatened communities of Steincoalspruit, Umbulwane, Ndonyane, Reserve Four, Matiwane's Kop, St Wendolins, Groutville (all Natal), Mgwali (Eastern Cape) and Driefontein (Transvaal) at a meeting in Ladysmith, 26 March 83. *Natal Witness*, 22 Nov. 80.)

Few people like being moved, but responses vary from silent resignation to violent retaliation, with many types in between. Case studies illustrate some of the responses, which vary from region to region according to local conditions.

Styles of resistance may be listed across a spectrum:

1. Silent resignation

As the removal of the tenants of Kwapitela in 1982 shows, any unorganised isolated community can be quietly relocated. Take the case of the Riemvasmaak reserve near the Augrabies Falls in the North-Western Cape in 1973. This removal was the most dramatic relocation in the last 25 years in terms of distance. 920 people were moved 1 300 kilometres north to Damaraland in Namibia and 43 families to Welcomewood in the Ciskei. Others who had declared themselves coloured were moved to Upington. Most of the people spoke Afrikaans and their choice of racial group was purely arbitrary.

The magistrate and Bantu Affairs commissioner, Mr G J J Jordaan, said: 'Some might be unhappy about the resettlement plans but my information is that the majority would be quite willing to trek.' In the same report members of the community were quoted as saying, 'Tears are flowing like water' and 'The riem that was made fast 60 years ago was now being torn loose. We are going to Riemlosmaak'. (*Cape Times*, 29 Sept. 73.)

One man was reported as saying, 'It will be hard to break down the home that you built for your family, but we will not refuse. We cannot refuse.' (*Cape Times*, 12 Oct. 73.) Today Riemvasmaak is a hot-spring tourist resort and a military area.

The Riemvasmaak case shows how a small isolated mixed group of people may be confused by ethnic divisions and threats of violence into moving thousands of kilometres apart. While one or two members of the community tried valiantly to oppose the move, most people's response was typified by the old man who said, 'We will move. We cannot refuse.'

2. Individual resistance

Most of the people evicted from farms have little chance of group resistance. Such resistance is often individual and spontaneous, reacting to the crisis as it hits. It is generally localised. In 1969 a few families evicted from farms in the Weenen district in Natal filled their bags with stones and sand, hiding their belongings in the bushes. Once they had gone through the motions of being relocated by GG truck to Madadeni in KwaZulu, they returned to collect their things and start life again in the old place.

3. Moving elsewhere in defiance and desperation
Once the shacks of about 25 000 people had been demolished at Modderdam, Unibel and Werkgenot outside Cape Town in 1977-8, a handful of people accepted free rail tickets handed out by the Department of Bantu Affairs and went to the Ciskei or Transkei. The rest disappeared into the townships and the last remaining (African) informal settlement of Cape Town, Crossroads.

4. Community consultation with lawyers
Some groups like the people of Klipfontein try fighting a legal battle. Since the 1940s the people of Machaviestad outside Potchefstroom have fought a battle similar to the Mfengu people of Elukhanyweni in the Ciskei. They were removed to Rooigrond in 1971 and have still not given up hope of returning to Machaviestad. Now they are under threat of removal by the Bophuthatswana administration which claims that Rooigrond was only a temporary site seeing they refused the land Pretoria offered in 1971.

5. Community with support group
Support groups running public campaigns are sometimes formed to help communities under threat of removal. Generally these groups are based in the major urban areas. The communities they support are usually situated close to the urban areas as well. For example, St Wendolins outside Durban is likely to be partially reprieved. On the other hand, the Valspan community under threat 3 kilometres from a town where there is little support for their stand, relies on long-distance assistance.

6. Community alone
Some groups are determined not to have any outsiders involved. As they see it, the only way to win is to be in total control of their own resistance. The people of Matoks location in the Sekgosese district felt very strongly that they wanted no outside assistance

and they have won the right to remain where they are. Few have had such an outright victory.

7. Violence

Aspects of resistance may involve violence. On the Woodstock Dam site, earth-moving equipment was burnt. The young chief of Mathopestad who did not support the people in their determination not to be moved was allegedly killed. Other incidents probably related to people under threat of being forcibly moved are the attacks on the Soekmekaar police station (close to the Sekgosese reserve which was under threat of removal at the time) and attacks on installations in and around Kangwane and Ingwavuma, when the South African government proposed to hand those areas to Swaziland.

Why some communities resist and others don't

From case studies it seems that a number of interrelated factors determine not only whether or not a community will resist, but how it will resist. Factors include people's previous experience of removals, resistance, organisation, how close they are to urban areas and support groups, and how much news coverage they have had.

There is an obvious marked difference between an isolated individual's capacity or desire to resist and that of a group of people. Individuals evicted from farms where they have little claim to land long since dispossessed, have little protection and few rights. They are usually rather desperate, poorly educated and have large extended families. Their first priority is to find a place to settle, (usually in a bantustan); then the younger men and women must move off to try to find employment through the labour bureaux. There are no farm worker organisations to take up the struggle or lobby on behalf of those evicted, moulding them into a united group. On the other hand, a community of people who have lived together, worked their own land, lived fairly self-contained lives and have seen generations grow up and continue the traditions in the same place, are unlikely simply to move at the command of some official. Such communities living on 'black spots' or 'badly situated reserve areas' have individually and collectively a lot to lose, prodding them into some sort of resistance.

Should there be a history of resistance in the area, or latent political consciousness, the people are likely to meet and talk about what could be done. Strong state action may have been taken against such resistance in the past which could inhibit new involvement. Hearing about how other people fought and won or lost may work either way: for example, the people of Mudiboon moved 'without fuss' having seen the repression of the people of Sophiatown who were viciously removed before they even had time to organise against it. On the other hand the Valspan people, hearing how Crossroads was given a reprieve, are trying to stay at Jan Kempdorp.

CROSSROADS

'The people came to Crossroads from 1975. They came because they didn't have places to stay and they wanted to stay as families.

'Life was very bad in those days. Life was bad because we had no rights to stay here. The law didn't allow us to stay. There was no peace. No rest. No happiness. We couldn't feel free. The Administration Board was always arresting us, chasing us away, warning us, trying to send us back (but we the women got off at Bellville station and came back) and telling us this place belongs to the coloureds.

'People didn't accept it, they didn't give in. The Administration Board forced us to fight back because we had no other place to go. There in the Transkei there is nothing, no jobs, just hunger and the children die.

'Then Dr Koornhof came. He heard there were people living in Crossroads. He came to separate the people, but in a decent way. Before they fought with dogs and teargas and bulldozers but he came to do it the decent way. He told the people he would give them rights, houses and permits. The rights and the houses came, but not for everybody. I hope they will get them but I don't think so. They are just waiting for this new Bill* — they are using it already.

'The law is trying to separate the Old and the New Crossroads but the people wish unity. From the beginning they wanted to be together. But they are trying to get us to have a community council. The people just chased them away. They will hold their own elections. We want to run our own projects like clinic, schools, creches . . . .

'The women are still looking to the needs of the people. Our aim is to have our own projects. It is the women who built Crossroads. They wouldn't give in, they fought all through. Even now with the lodgers of the people who are moved to new Crossroads, the women told the Board they cannot just throw them out. The lodgers are staying under plastic. We don't know what to do. They won't allow more shacks to be built and they won't give them houses.**

'People must still help us, support us. We are still struggling here in Crossroads until everyone has rights and houses.

'Other communities? They must stand together, then they will win. They mustn't allow themselves to be separated, then they won't win.' (Interview with a member of the Women's Committee, Crossroads, November 1982.)

* Orderly Movement and Settlement of Black Persons Bill

** It was only in June 1983 that the lodgers who had been registered in Crossroads were recognised and moved to Khayelitsha to live in fletcraft huts.

Past experience of relocation influences responses. The particular history of a people may therefore be either an incentive to resist or a discouragement, depending on how their initiatives have been met in the past. It was reported to SPP in field trips to the Northern Cape and Western Transvaal that the Tswana people are not particularly perturbed by relocation. They see this as yet another defeat in their history, resulting in yet another trek;

as in the past when they lost rights to water holes, they had to move on. People are angry and bitter about removals, but they do not see them as irreversible. Some communities feel particularly sore as the very land from which they were moved — the Mfengu reserves near Humansdorp, for example, or Machaviestad — were granted to them as rewards for service to whites in various wars.

Two communities, moved in the 1970s in the Northern Cape, illustrate very different attitudes to removal. The chief and people of Gatlhose reserve moved quietly, saying they would not move like slaves; they wanted to move with dignity. However, the chief at Di Takwanen, a well-watered fertile scheduled area near Vryburg settled in 1889, led the resistance to removal with all his might. He was severely punished: his house was burned and he was the first to be moved, as an example of what would happen to his people. The Gatlhose people live at Bendall, a desolate closer settlement north of Kuruman. Today they are little better off than their Di Takwanen neighbours who live in the semi-desert of Deerward a few kilometres away. The old chief is bitter and the people of Deerward are apathetic — a sad case of failed resistance.

As Chapter 6 showed, strategies used by the remover (whether the government, the farmer or a local authority) influence if and how a community will resist. If officials move in early, paint numbers on the houses, serve eviction orders, offer compensation and fulfil any other requirements within a few weeks, an unprepared community will have little choice but to move, particularly if police and military personnel accompany the removal squad. On the other hand, in recent years officials have talked of negotiations, consultation and 'no more forced removals (where practicable and possible)'. This gives the community time to think about the issue, consult and decide on action. Removal strategy varies somewhat regionally — some areas being priorities in political, economic or strategic terms. The further from concerned outsiders and press coverage, the more likely that the move will be less delicately handled. Local officials play a decisive role in timing the move and in the extent of brute force used.

Authorities — including bantustan officials — and their attitudes do partly determine whether there will be resistance.

Communities under threat of removal into the Ciskei, for example, find it far more difficult to resist than communities under threat of removal into KwaZulu where Inkatha may be approached to intervene and dissuade Pretoria from carrying out the relocation. The Ciskei security police deals more harshly with resisters than even its South African patron, as the Mgwali Residents' Association has found in its attempts to oppose relocation to Frankfort. The MRA has found it difficult to obtain permission to hold meetings. The only time members of the community hear news on the issue is during notice time at church services. Their leaders are detained, harassed and undermined. In apologising for his poor hearing, a member of the committee alleged that the Transkei security police had beaten him until blood came out of both his ears. In February 1984 a raid across the border by Ciskei security police led to allegations of gunpoint arrests and brutality. At the time of writing, the nine Mgwalians who were detained plan to sue for damages.

As described earlier, chiefs and headmen have been co-opted into the system. They are generally seen as agents of the government. Should a chief be more progressive than repressive, those under threat may use the formal channels and have some chance of making representations agains the removal. During interviews SPP was told that sympathetic chiefs and headmen are often 'processed' by their bantustan superiors. They are given the choice of cooperating with the bantustan administration or losing their status and salaries. Few continue to protest in the face of such threats.

Leadership is a major factor in directing responses. The difference between official and popular leaders was clearly indicated in SPP surveys. Respondents asked interviewers what they meant by the question 'Who are the leaders here?' Did they mean the people in charge such as superintendents, chiefs, members of the bantustan legislative assembly, or did they mean priests, nurses, business people and teachers? Replies such as 'X — we voted for him so I suppose he is a leader', 'We have none, unless you mean those chaps in Mmabatho' or 'Y — he collects our taxes' show where leadership is missing. Class differences exist in rural areas: depending on who is interviewed, different names in the same small area may be given as 'the leaders'. When outsiders hear the story of a threatened removal from teachers, priests, business people, the owner of the bottle store or the chief, they may not be hearing the story as experienced by the people.

Where resistance is shallow, where it does not stretch beyond the most articulate member of the community, or where the people are divided in their stand, there is little chance of success. Where government victimises or intimidates leaders, the community can protect them by affirming that they are representatives. And if they are removed by banning, detention or imprisonment, the community should be able to replace them with other representatives.

Frequently the elite will agree to move as they may have been offered incentives such as promotion or sole licences in the new area. These are common strategies of cooption. Where people have so little in material terms, it is hard to reject such offers.

The level of involvement of the community is partly determined by traditional leaders and partly by the community themselves from their experience of the outside world. For example, the women of Crossroads played a major role in organising the Crossroads community. Despite rival sides, the people could unite. The involvement of the whole community is important or the leaders may easily be removed or co-opted. Where leaders are away representing their communities around the country on delegations or visiting other areas under threat, they have to be careful that their local support at home is not being coopted or turned against them.

Women are playing an increasingly important role in resistance to relocation. The example of the Crossroads women has been used in other communities such as Mgwali to encourage women's involvement. In urban areas women often live 'illegally' with their husbands because the men have contract work but the women do not qualify to live with them. In such cases, as happened in Crossroads, the women may feel they have little to lose in organising against their removal. And traditional attitudes to the role of women in organisations is changing slowly in rural areas too. Although barely involved in the negotiations in Sekgosese, the women stood firm when officials tried to intimidate them in April 1982. 'We won't forget that day. The women took hoes, picks and stones. They drew a line on the dirt road. They told the officials — you step over that line and there will be big trouble', recounted one woman. The officials took one look at the crowd of women who had come from the houses and fields armed with domestic implements, and decided to head back to Pietersburg. They have not been seen in the area since.

Contacts with other communities, both those that have been moved and others under threat of removal, add to the strength of those trying to organise against removals. Communities promised land or grazing or housing years ago and still waiting may put those under threat off accepting such promises. Knowledge of government strategies to force relocation helps people prepare their resistance. At Di Takwanen the bus service was stopped and a licence for the shop was not extended, at Umbulwane half the people's houses were destroyed, at Riemvasmaak the school was closed, at Driefontein (Eastern Transvaal) a clinic nursing post was not filled, drought relief was refused to non-members of CNIP who opposed the move from Mgwali and pensioners there were told that their pensions might be suspended if they resisted the move. A community is less likely to be duped if it has been warned of such strategies.

An important determinant is the role of outside groups and individuals. Depending on how accessible the community is to urban areas, foreign visitors and press reporters, it may be spotlighted domestically and internationally. Aspects of this will be examined in more detail. Communities may feel themselves isolated even though distances are small, if outsiders ignore them. In Di Takwanen, only 24 kilometres from Vryburg, the people felt isolated, far from access to sympathetic press. In fact, they asked Cosmas Desmond to tell the lawyer representing them how beautiful Di Takwanen was, as the community was under the impression that he was not allowed to visit them. Community resistance may depend on how closely the threatened groups have been associated with outsiders. The Matoks people wanted no contact with lawyers or church people. On the other hand the late Saul Mkhize from Driefontein (Transvaal) saw the struggle to remain becoming 'really serious when the lawyers were invited in'.

A lack of rural organisers limits action in rural areas. The 1970s and 1980s have seen a dramatic resurgence in union and community organisation in urban areas, but little outside the odd rural development project has touched the countryside. Consequently it is rare for a rural community to be in touch with publications, meetings, booklets on simplified law, health care or any of the other issues fairly widely debated in most urban communities in South Africa today. Isolation from urban areas is partly overcome by the numbers of retrenched migrant workers now idle in the bantustans. Keeping migrants in touch with what is happening at home was seen as a priority, for example, by the Mgwali Residents' Association who went on a nationwide tour canvassing support for resistance to removal from Mgwali. Meetings were held in centres where migrants from Mgwali worked. The situation at Mgwali as well as that around the country was explained. Most migrants then signed the petition calling on the government to allow the people of Mgwali to remain.

Particularly in areas where people have been moved a number of times, there are low expectations. People adapt to their circumstances fatalistically. In the long term this may have some positive effect: perhaps, in that way, they arm themselves against defeat and despair.

Organisation against relocation

While resistance to relocation is important, organisation against it is only just emerging. Organisation and strategies used by African communities under threat of removal are as full of problems, if not more so, as those of any other group working for change in South Africa. There is no protection in terms of law or policy for those organising. They have no vote and few resources. Organisation for resistance takes a long time, particularly in rural areas where the pace is slower — where it may take all day to hitch a lift to the nearest town to find a lawyer to represent the community, only to find often the lawyer is out, so the whole process has to be repeated. There are few telephones. Public transport is infrequent and expensive.

The problems with organisation are not unique to people under threat of removal, but those problems are compounded by isolation, lack of knowledge, and proximity to the most conservative white communities in the country. There is some protection if organisers cannot be detained without an outcry. With high unemployment in rural areas, recruitment of informers by the authorities is relatively easy. In some areas there are official youth bands established to inform the authorities on protest and discontent. Where everyone knows everyone else, both the spies and the organisers are easily identified. When people do not know exactly how far they may organise in terms of the law, they may easily be intimidated by the threat of detention or summary removal.

While self-styled spokespeople may easily be removed by officials, it is harder to rid a community of democratically elected leadership. The people in positions of importance are then reflecting the views of the wider community and new people may just as easily be elected if some are removed. General discussion of strategies and accountability to the whole community is important. This was strongly voiced both by the chiefs and people of Sekgosese. They, among a number of groups, stressed the need to involve the traditional leadership as far as possible, to include the chief and his counsellors at all meetings, to make sure that the chief knew exactly what his people thought about the move so that there could be no confusion when he was asked by the authorities. Elected representatives as well as tribal leaders see that everyone's interests are catered for. It was also stressed that all meetings should be as open as possible, so that no-one would have the opportunity to enter deals or accuse others of subversion or incitement. At no time did the Sekgosese people give the authorities an excuse to enter the area. They kept strict local discipline. Meetings held without permission of the chief may be banned, making it essential to try to involve the chief. This is particularly the case in rural areas. In urban areas the principle remains — leadership must be accountable to the general community.

Traditional attitudes to authority prevail in many areas but, depending on how much force accompanies such authority, people may respond by ignoring or including them. In the white corridor between Transkei and Ciskei there are seven black spots under threat of removal in terms of consolidation plans for the Ciskei. Active resistance, despite severe harassment, is only evident at Mgwali. People in other areas (such as Kwelera) say they are powerless to resist in the face of the Ciskei security police. Others (at Kwelera and also at Newlands) say the resistance is in the hands of their chief and they have left it to him to negotiate a reprieve.

The small business people who stand to gain from the relocation of thousands of people to isolated areas, far from the cheaper supermarkets of white towns, move willingly. Those who own the bottle stores conspicuous throughout KwaZulu seldom oppose relocation. In particular, those who may have opposed relocation in the past may be bought off by material benefits as described in Chapter 6.

Another division amongst people under threat of removal is that between landowners and tenants as was shown in the case of Kwapitela: the tenants were removed in 1982 but the landowners are still there. Tenants on black spots may easily be persuaded by officials to move if they are promised rent-free land. Meanwhile unless landowners, let alone tenants, own more than 17 hectares, they are not entitled to more than a residential plot in a closer settlement.

In June 1983 an apparently generous compensation offer of R8 000 per household induced a group of tenants to leave the black freehold area of Mogopa, near Ventersdorp in the Western Transvaal, for Pachsdraai, an arid area near the Botswana border. The government had negotiated in secret with a headman previously deposed by the people living there. On the basis of his agreement with the government proposal it was claimed that the entire population had agreed to be moved, and demolition of schools and churches at Mogopa commenced. The majority however, remained, insistent that they would not move and would continue to resist. On 14 February 1984 the remaining residents were forcibly removed to Pachsdraai, where they immediately made plans to move as refugees to their ancestral land at Bethanie near Brits.

The people of Rooigrond refused to accept compensation. They want land, tractors, money to build the same type of houses they had had at Machaviestad, and compensation for the 12 years spent at Rooigrond without land or facilities.

Many landowners belong to an informal 'old boys' network' which involves intermarriage, common mission schooling and political participation in the ANC prior to the 1960s. They have not concentrated on grassroots community development with their tenants. They have nurtured a master/servant relationship which has hindered resistance to relocation in recent years. The reality that tenants are never given land is filtering back to black spots where tenants are still to be moved. In the longer term the attempt to form alliances with their tenants is likely to be extremely difficult for landowners.

Ethnic conflict is emerging as the most destructive element between communities under threat of removal. Often SPP fieldworkers were told that for at least the last 100 years people in various areas throughout the Transvaal and the OFS had lived peacefully, marrying each other and trading with each other. Since separate development and ethnic structures were started in the 1960s in earnest, ethnic identities have become important to people. The government has successfully set people against each other by granting resources to some rather than others. This is clearly illustrated in the case of Bophuthatswana gaining 'independence' and the South Sotho people of Thaba 'Nchu suddenly being harassed by Bophuthatswana police. (Most had been tenants of Tswana people.) Raids in the middle of the night, closure of Sotho-medium schools and the clearance of Kromdraai 'squatter' camp led to the people appealing through their Qwaqwa authorities to Pretoria for their own land. Pretoria graciously acceded to a second piece of Qwaqwa close to Thaba 'Nchu. The first group, about a quarter to a fifth of the 200 000 people now living in desperate poverty in Onverwacht, were really grateful both to Chief Mopeli and the Pretoria officials for 'saving them from the sarcasms of the YB'. Three years later a handful of jobs, a few schools, overcrowded shacks and plots and problems of crime are beginning to dampen enthusiasm for Qwaqwa and Pretoria. Thus ethnic conflict is created through establishment of divided territories and resources, and later resolved by the same system.

In some cases such as Huhudi and Valspan, people have simply not thought of working with other communities under threat of removal. They may not know of any other groups in a similar position, or they may view their own situation as special and not part of the result of national policy. This is well illustrated by people's responses about why they are to be moved, given in Chapter 3. This perception works in favour of the government as isolation precludes unity with other communities and makes activists more vulnerable.

DRIEFONTEIN (TRANSVAAL)

'We are still in some confusion about whether we are going to be moved. The landowners just refuse to be moved. We think the government is just going to force us and take us to a particular place.

'The government says this is a black spot. Secondly, they are building a dam here. They will be finished this year (1982). They say it will cover some of the land.

'The Zulus don't want to go to Kangwane. The Zulus don't want to go to KwaZulu in Natal. They want to stay in KwaZulu in the Transvaal. In the school we are teaching Zulu. There are some who speak Xhosa and Sotho. At first they wanted to remove everyone to Kangwane. That was the first decision. The second decision was that the Zulus must go to Babanango in KwaZulu. The best place they say is here in the Transvaal.

'The officials say they will send us a bus to show us the new area. But the people refused to go and say they do not want to move.

'The community board says it is not taking sides. Its position is to take the message from the Development Trust to the people and from the people to the Development Trust. Even the board is divided. Some want to go and some do not want to go. Some of the people are Swazis and some are Zulus.

'KwaNgema next to us has their own board. They also do not want to move. Daggakraal people refuse to move. They say the government must bring an agenda first before they sit down. They do not want to talk to the S A Development Trust. Here we have been issued with title deeds. In Daggakraal they refuse to move.

'There are many old people here who cannot build for themselves. They don't have sons and daughters to build for them. The people come back from Johannesburg when they are old.

'The magistrate is refusing to use the men from Driefontein [to work] on the dam because they refused to move. He also tells the people he will not get jobs for them, so they must look for themselves.

'The officials told the people to go to Wakkerstroom to sign something. They say that everyone who is not against the law of the government should go and sign. The people who did go to Wakkerstroom did sign something. Not many went. They were told by the magistrate, "You are not called here." They were told they had not been called and they had signed voluntarily.

'What can we do? We are confused as to what to do.'

(Interview with a member of the Driefontein community, September, 1982.)

Mr Saul Mkhize, secretary of the Residents' Committee, declared:

> We will never move. Our area enjoys freehold title deeds. If the whole thing comes to the worst, we will seek redress in the Supreme Court.
> At a meeting on 27 January 1982 the majority of our community rejected the resettlement moves. On the other hand our community board accepted the proposals. Only 80 residents in the area want to be resettled and most of them were tricked into this. They are now pulling off and want their names removed from the pro-resettlement affidavit engineered by the board.
> (*Golden City Press*, 31 Oct. 82.)

In contrast, the Minister of Cooperation and Development said:

> In spite of the fact that the people there elected a Community Council and in spite of the fact that many of the members of that community voluntarily signed affidavits that they would move — I have them in my possession . . . .
> (*Hansard*, Col. 8781, 7 June 83.)

> Early in November 1982 the Department of Cooperation and Development laid on three buses to ferry residents of Swazi origin for an inspection of their proposed new site near Lothair in Kangwane. About 70 residents, mainly old men and women, were escorted the 240 kilometres to Kangwane under heavy guard by policemen in camouflage dress.
> Saul Mkhize said: 'Nobody is in favour of that place. It was quite an eye-opener for those who made the trip. There is no water there or streets or houses. It's a desert. You can't live in that god-forsaken place.' But elderly Mr Johannes Ndaba saw little wrong with the trip 'because that is what the white people, our rulers, say. Man, there is nothing we can do after Pretoria has decided. Even if I was beaten up, I'd go to hospital, but still follow what the white people tell me to do.' (*Golden City Press,* 7 Nov. 82.)
> On 2 April 1983, at a meeting of the Driefontein residents, Saul Mkhize was shot dead by a young white police constable. Extracts from two accounts of the killing are given in Chapter 6. According to the latest proposal the Driefontein community is to be moved as a whole to Pongola (which is itself under threat of excision from KwaZulu according to the 1975 consolidation proposals).

Strategies used by communities under threat of removal

Strategies used to oppose threats of relocation include writing memoranda to Cabinet Ministers and officials, inspecting the new area either at the invitation of officials or independently, visiting other people under threat of removal as well as those who have been moved and learning from them, discussing promises, debating compensation, approaching outsiders for help, bringing visitors to see their present area, making statements to the press or remaining strictly silent, approaching bantustan authorities or keeping well clear of them, approaching business people, and lastly, resorting to violence.

Writing memoranda is often the first step a community takes to resist removal publicly. Having heard that Dr Koornhof had said in 1980 that there would be no more forced removals (wherever practicable and possible), a number of communities wrote to tell him that they did not want to be moved. In the case of Umbulwane the community received a reply from the Deputy Minister of Cooperation and Development saying that while the Minister had indeed made that statement, he did not mean that they should break the law. Memoranda have been written in various parts of the country. Most of them are from communities under threat in Natal. Dr Koornhof admitted in parliament that the Zulu people were proving 'unwilling to move'.

Written memoranda to the Minister of Cooperation and Development make moving reading. They mention how long people have lived where they are, how the old people have no-one to build them new homes in the new place, how people cannot be expected to leave the graves of their ancestors, how their social, economic and community life will be disrupted, how young children and the old will not survive the move, how the facilities they have built and loved over the years will have to be left (little compensation being offered), a comparison of the old and new areas, and finally, how they will lose their freedom.

Petitions signed by residents, both landowners and tenants, are another form of protest. The example of the Mgwali people who visited their migrant workers for such support was mentioned earlier.

MEMORANDUM OF LUSITANIA SYNDICATE, FEBRUARY 1982

Introduction:
Lusitania is a black-owned farm in a white district — a 'black spot' in the centre of white farmers as described by the now said government. It is some 8 km from Cundycleugh and 13 km near Collins Pass (on the border of the

Orange Free State and Natal) in the district of *Klip-River*, the magisterial district of Ladysmith, Natal.

The land is approximately 1 165 hectares in area, well watered, with the Sundays River running through one end of this property on the East, as well as a stream in the centre of our commonage which enters the Sundays River which we use for our *stock to drink*, as well as *irrigation* for our homes. It is also well grassed and relatively free from soil erosion. This property also has a lot of *water-fountains* here and there all over the land and on the mountain-side. This water we use for *our food and drinking consumption* and it is very clean water. We are a very *peaceful rural community*. There is also a big natural forest on the mountain-side with all different *indigenous* trees of many kinds; wild animals, big and small, enjoy their life here i.e. Buck, birds, snakes, snails etc.

All kinds of fruit trees grow very well at this place, e.g. orchards of oranges, lemons, nartjies, peaches, plums, pears, apricots, grapes, guavas, etc., and we use these for our family consumption and supply our nearest fruit-shops and supermarkets, as well as some farmers near us come and buy these fruits. There is a main road from Ladysmith to Newcastle on the boundary of our commonage and family freehold lands. This road goes through our place. It is easy for us to go to Ladysmith, Newcastle and Dannhauser with the value of this road.

History
The farm was bought from Mr Chcmerald Marais by 20 (twenty) landowners shortly after the Anglo-Boer War of 1899-1902, at a *Public Auction* at *Ladysmith*, Klip River District, and was surveyed amongst the twenty. It was then sub-divided into a commonage on the mountain side, and family freehold lands on the eastern side. On these freehold lands each of the twenty landowners has his own *Title Deed*. The commonage is approximately 380 hectares, and the

twenty each have equal shares in this commonage. Lusitania has its *General Title Deed* of which the landowners are the rightful heirs, with approximately 40 hectares to each holder.

The first buyers were Ndabambi, Mavuso and Mtitinyane Mahlambi. The Syndicate had a Chief Trustee and two other Trustees. Up to now this place is still under 3 Trustees and their 6 committee members.

The last of our fathers died in December 1972, Rev. Eliam Hadebe. On the death of our fathers, some willed to their sons, and a few sold their *shares*, now bringing the total number to twenty-eight landowners. We also have tenants at this place, approximately eighty households, with an additional eleven at the commonage. This brings the total to one hundred and nineteen kraals and families at this farm, who will suffer if removed.

History of resettlement:
In 1964 the Bantu Affairs Commissioner for Natal invited us to a meeting, where we were called a 'Black spot' which in terms of Departmental policy will have to be eliminated in due course. In the very same year the Government Officials visited Lusitania to inform us we were to be counted and the *Deeds of Transfer* should be made straight, to the heirs amongst everybody at Lusitania. Since then we have heard nothing from the Officials but we know the plan is to remove us, along with Matiwane's Kop etc. We discussed this and agree that we do not want to be moved.

Tenants' land:
Tenants have an average quarter hectare residential plot for growing their crops. No tenants are self-supporting on their land but their agricultural lands add to income derived from wage employment. Their standard of living is high.

Improvements:
There is a mixture of concrete block, wattle and daub huts and stone houses. There is a school building, concrete dipping tanks and domesticated wattle and gum trees as well as palm trees etc. All households have put in other improvements i.e. fencing, toilets, cattle kraals, fruit trees. As well we have subdivided our commonage for grazing. It has been fenced very well, with the graveyard on the same commonage. The value of improvements runs to many thousands of rands.

Crops:
All of us grow some products, the main crop being maize, plus kaffir-corn, potatoes, beans etc. We make a good living from our land; some of us do not have to work in town.

Livestock:
There is no limit to the number of cattle. Tenants' cattle varies from 1 to 5 head of cattle, plus goats, horses, pigs and as many poultry as he is able to keep. Total numbers of stock are as follows: cattle 278, 6 horses, 352 goats, 16 sheep, 16 pigs and approximately 800 poultry. Our stock is usually sold to Sales Camps, stock brokers and speculators at reasonable prices.

Employment:
Most people who are working are working in town while some are working outside the district. Many are farm labourers or waiters, domestic servants, commercial workers etc. Many of the women and girls work casual or seasonal employment on neighbouring farms.

Schools:
There is a school (Lower and Higher Primary) up to Standard 5 with 7 teachers and 380 to 400 children. The community is already building and has raised some funds for

another continuation (Big Building) for Standard 7, 8, and 9 as they wished. They have donated money every season to raise school funds. We have our church and want to build a clinic.

Conclusion:
We are all well to do here and the place is healthy, with daily transport from Lusitania to Ladysmith. We have lived here for almost 83 years, without tenants, without quarrels and frictions. You could hardly see a Police van coming in for cases at Lusitania. There are no shebeens and we are peacefully settled. We are friendly with the farmers surrounding us. We are their Fire Brigades, casual workers and seasonal workers. During harvesting season and in destroying unrequired wattle forests we are useful to them and they are useful to us. The owners do not stay on most of the white farms surrounding Lusitania, except for one or two. In most cases these farms are used for their stock grazing, and cultivation for crops and hays in feeding their stocks. There are rich farmers surrounding us, who do not want us to be removed from this place.

We pray we should not be removed from our Lusitania Syndicate.

Lusitania Committee
c/o Lusitania H.P. School
P.O. Box 860
Ladysmith
3370

Visiting the proposed area

Most of those unwilling to be moved want to know more about the area to which they are to be relocated. Some arrange their own transport and take members of the community to inspect the proposed area. Others are taken by officials and promised the lush green farms in the district, little knowing that they are to be moved there along with perhaps thousands of others. The people who fled to Thornhill after their district of Herschel was included in the Transkei were one such group. They now live in the desperately dry and overcrowded Ntabethemba area of Northern Ciskei. As mentioned in Chapter 6, the Machaviestad people who were moved to Rooigrond in 1971 were taken by bus to see the new area and tricked into signing a list which was later presented in court as an agreement by the leaders to move. In November 1982 officials took a group of old and intimidated people from Driefontein (Transvaal) under armed guard amid much tension to visit Lothair. The rest of the community refused to go and said that visiting the site with the officials was tantamount to agreeing to move.

In the Western Transvaal a community trying to resist removal from Motlatla refused to visit the site, not even to see for themselves. They could not believe that the government would give them anything better than they have. They live on a well-watered farm producing a surplus of grain which is sold at the nearby cooperative. When members of the community were shown photographs of the propsed new site, they were interested to see that they were right — it was flat, dry, rocky country quite unlike the fertile land they work now.

Contact with other communities

Useful ammunition for those resisting removal is knowledge of how others were treated. Promises of equal quality land and facilities have seldom been kept. Resisters are able to say that the people of Oxton or Onverwacht or Mondlo were promised land and that is why they took their farm implements which are now rusting as they still wait for land. Or they will know that where people under threat have demanded schools, clinics, streets and housing, they are expected to move when those facilities are provided. The late chief of Motlatla agreed to move on those terms. Facilities were provided; the chief died, and now the people say they never agreed to the move under any circumstances.

> What will they [we] do there? We only said yes because the government said they will move us. What about the women, the widows and the children?

The chief, they added, had not consulted them before agreeing to move. The school lies unused on overgrown land near the Botswana border. The tin shack and latrines which were laid out neatly in rows have been mysteriously removed and it is rumoured that the farm was sold to a Bophuthatswana cabinet minister. Good or bad — Motlatla or Oxton — each local story is worth sharing as widely as possible. Contact with other threatened communities may inject new strategies into the campaign. At least residents would be aware of what the government has tried elsewhere and where it has succeeded or failed.

Negotiation

> Thank you for your message but we are the eyes and ears of the people — we must report back. (Member of Nyanga Bush Committee, May 1983.)

Confidentiality must either be accepted or refused: there is no middle road when officials say they want to keep negotiations confidential.

Some people accept. They are then isolated from other communities under threat. Their representatives may not discuss proceedings with the constituents, which distances them from their own people. This inevitably leads to mistrust and cooption, as happened in Crossroads during negotiations with Dr Koornhof. In some cases the representatives become disenchanted with the lengthy proceedings. They may decide that it is in the officials' interests, not their own, to keep quiet, so they begin to talk about the issue. The press may hear, whereupon the officials may use this as a pretext to break off negotiations and continue with relocation plans.

The people negotiating in the Woodstock Dam removals finally exposed the protracted proceedings. Different officials participated in negotiations each time so that the people's minutes of meetings finally became the official ones. There seemed no point in maintaining confidentiality when the officials kept changing and little progress was evident. They moved in the end, once certain conditions were fulfilled and certain facilities provided.

Other groups refuse to be drawn into secret meetings from the beginning, saying they have nothing to hide. Officials find this hard to accept, as confidentiality gives them the initiative and stops resistance from spreading.

Engaging in negotiations, when given the opportunity, is crucial for most communities. Whether outsiders are involved or not, discussion of the proposed removal would be a priority for most communities. It gives them time which can be used to organise and broaden the base of the resistance. Because there is a shortage of manpower within most government departments and because most decisions take a long time to implement, particularly when they are challenged, people have the opportunity to organise. Some communities do not use the time but take it as a sign to revert to their normal lives, mistakenly hoping that the authorities have had a change of heart. Representatives of both Mathopestad and Mgwali were told by Pretoria officials that they should go back and develop their areas. When asked by the press, however, officials denied that the removals had been called off. The Vryburg Chamber of Commerce was told that the Huhudi people could develop their area, but removals continue. This may be a new tactic — the removal may take place suddenly when the community is off guard.

At what stage people actively begin to resist or bring in outside help may be crucial to their stopping the removal or improving the conditions of it. What was on the drawing board for years (particularly consolidation proposals) may become too expensive to implement, both in financial and security terms, and the area is reprieved. This was probably the case in Sekgosese as well as Sinthumule/Kutama in the Northern Transvaal near Louis Trichardt.

Compensation

Compensation is a difficult area. Once compensation is debated there is an underlying acceptance of the removal. Generally people do not discuss compensation if they have refused to move, but a practical danger with this tactic is that if they are forced to move they may end up with inadequate compensation. The law allows people eight months to appeal against the amount offered. After that, if they have not accepted the offer, they are not entitled to claim more.

Mobilisation on other issues

Another strategy is that of organising around something other than the relocation itself. For example, the Mgwali Residents' Association wants to start a sewing cooperative to get the women working together. They say they have seen how well the Crossroads women have organised against their removal; and if they ever do have to move, it will be useful to them. The people of Matiwane's Kop have called in private planners to draw up a development plan for their area.

Calling in outsiders

While it is not possible to analyse the role of outside groups and individuals for every community under threat of removal, some generalisations may prove useful. In some cases the local people have been only too willing to hand their problems over to someone who seems experienced and concerned. But case studies show that only where the community took a strong stand first, followed by outside support, has it been successful. How and why outsiders become involved is coloured by who invited them in, whom they relate to in the community, to whom they are accountable, whose interests they serve, whether they are wanted at all, whether the community would be in the same position without them, at what point in the struggle they entered and what resources they provide.

Raising these questions about all outsiders, black or white, religious or secular, is important for understanding the role they can play. If the community knows who brought outsiders in, there should be some indication of whose interests in the community they intend to serve. There may be factions in a community and outsiders may wish to win support by bringing in a development project, for example, not for the pure motive of employing people, but to oust potential rivals. It may be a way of boosting support for cooptable leaders or for a religious denomination. When the Ciskei was given drought relief to distribute, in 1982-83, headmen used it to win support for the Ciskei National Independence Party.

Many communities would not still be where they are, but for outside help. If intervention is sensitive and comes at a stage when the people are otherwise being hurried into something they are not quite sure of, it may serve to clarify issues.

At Umbulwane, the initial contact with community leaders in neighbouring Steadville was important in encouraging people to articulate their opposition and not simply to submit passively to the demolitions. Contact with sympathetic whites in Ladysmith was more tenuous and confined to a few individuals. Through them, however, contact was made with other groups outside Ladysmith who were opposed to removals, and this also played a part in boosting community organisation.

The contribution of outside groups was both inspirational and technical (assistance with addresses, with reproducing documents etc.). Contact helped break down the sense of isolation and opened the way for the press to visit the area. Later, it led to individuals from Umbulwane attending a number of meetings and workshops organised outside Umbulwane, where removals in general were examined and people from other threatened communities were present. In this way community leaders were exposed to new ideas about how to deal with their situation, and developed a broader perspective on what was happening. They also contributed their own experience for other communities to draw on.

The support coming from outside was limited, however. It helped foster a sense of purpose within the community and within the committee in particular. But it could not provide the leadership or the spirit necessary for ongoing organisation. Had Umbulwane been in a metropolitan area, it would probably have received far more active outside support. This in turn could have inhibited the tentative but clear growth of self-reliance among the leaders.

Outsiders may well give a community the confidence, and leaders the protection, to resist. When people are in the limelight, it is more difficult simply to remove and detain or harass them. The Umbulwane people wrote letters to the press as well as to Dr

Koornhof. Seeing them published in the press and receiving a reply from the Department of Cooperation and Development helped break down the mystique of authority. This added to their confidence in themselves as actors, not just victims of relocation.

Being accountable to an elected community group gives outsiders a responsible role. Where strategies are discussed jointly, outsiders can offer skills and opinions but they are subject to joint decision — or better, community decision. Frequently people in areas under threat are curious about anybody's motives in visiting them, let alone helping them. In the case of pure research, the interviewer leaves with all the information, never to be seen again. He or she produces a thesis which sits on the library shelves and those interviewed have no feedback, only the queasy feeling of having been investigated for purposes unknown. However, simply piling up evidence that people are suffering is not enough to change conditions, and one-sided interviews actually harm people under threat, making them feel both invaded and abandoned by the strangers who came. People need to be able to argue with facts to change their own situation, and this is where outsiders may indeed offer a resource, by teaching research methods. The community should be involved in a self-survey, thereby extending the skill of collecting the information and making sure the results of the survey are fed back to the people.

SPP fieldworkers found it interesting to compare notes about their visits. Responses varied, depending on whether they travelled together as whites, or blacks, or in mixed groups. Black fieldworkers have distinct advantages in speaking the local languages fluently and being able to merge more easily. Sometimes they would be given information completely different from that given to white members working alone. Some people would only answer questions from white as opposed to black fieldworkers, because they were used to answering whites' questions! They did not necessarily appreciate such questions being asked. Whites, on the other hand, were often told, 'We don't know', while blacks were sounded out, then confided in. In some cases it is clear outsiders are not trusted, whether black or white.

The point at which outsiders enter the struggle is important for the control people may or may not have over their issue. From the beginning in Crossroads, for example, the Black Sash helped people arrested under pass laws and anti-squatting laws. That was from 1975. It was only after the massive raid in 1978, when a Crossroads resident was killed by a policeman, that many other organisations including the Chambers of Commerce and Industry and the South African Foundation became involved.

This was the time Crossroads hit the international headlines. Anti-apartheid groups were calling on foreign investors to withdraw their financing of South African enterprises. In turn, foreign investors were worried about stability in South Africa. They wondered if another period of unrest like 1976 was about to begin. Business people in South Africa became extremely worried and lobbied to have the Crossroads problem solved through negotiation. Soon the Urban Foundation was deeply involved in the negotiations and its regional director was quoted as saying:

> The fight was actually won with the April 1979 statement of Koornhof which laid down the rules for resettlement.

He added:

> The level of tension started high but through communication this was lowered and they responded as any group under the circumstances. They were not out of the ordinary.

When a community threatens the stability of the wider society, enlightened capital is quick to recognize the threat and to respond to it by pressurising the government to change its tactics.

To judge from case studies, it seems there are a number of myths confusing outsiders who try to help communities in crisis. The more liberal helpers find it hard to accept that people may be developing their own, often slow, forms of resistance, and tend to suggest strategies that fit their understanding of how the system works. For example, they would draw up a petition to be presented to the Minister, or get church leaders to make a statement appealing to the Christian morality of those in power, or send telegrams inviting those in power to visit areas and see the situation for themselves. These tactics assume ignorance on the part of the oppressor. More seriously, they attempt to appeal to a morality which is contradicted by the very policy which is being implemented.

On the other hand, more radical concerned outsiders often view community resistance somewhat romantically. They do not see the painfully long process of organisation being hindered at every turn by illiteracy, submission to traditional authority or fear of losing what little one might have (through cattle theft, witchcraft or whatever). It all seems just a step away, the moment of deliverance when all the people will have their say and be free. When outsiders deal with the local people these misconceptions are passed on. People begin to trust in the law, in the rightness of their cause, or in the ease of organisation. While they wait for 'justice' to be handed down by the courts (which implement unjust laws) or for 'grassroots mobilisation' around an issue, the officials may move in and take them unawares.

Money is another important aspect of outside involvement — how much, who controls it, for whom is it meant and to whom does it really go? Outsiders should be careful to see that relief materials are accessible to all those in need. Power games may develop over control of such resources. Where there are limited resources to be distributed, such as a donation of blankets or milk powder, and it is clear that there will not be enough for everybody, a representative body should be given the task of investigating the most needy cases and distributing the relief items.

In 1981 during the Nyanga Bush crisis, township people came to Cape Town posing as members of the group stranded on the dunes. They collected clothing, food and tents, and later sold them to those really in need. Not only may well-meaning outsiders inadvertently encourage corruption, but they may fuel power struggles — whoever can attract the most aid usually has the best following. This has happened in the case of religious denominations competing with each other over who gives more or better relief rations. In drought-stricken relocation areas such as Elukhanyweni, a few churches give relief only to their own members. This makes some brands of Christianity more popular than others!

Who is called in?
Most communities that approach lawyers hope the law still holds some justice for them. The people of Klipfontein won two legal victories, for example, so they began to depend on the law to keep them from being moved to Glenmore. Unfortunately legal

arguments failed in the end because the law itself was against them. Areas scheduled in 1913 or released in 1936 for African occupation may be excised at any time — let alone areas where people have been living 'illegally'. All that the lawyers can do is see that the provisions have been fulfilled, that compensation is fair, and that their clients' physical needs are catered for. The Matoks people wanted nothing to do with lawyers, saying that all they could do was to help the people move.

There is a severe limitation on the role of lawyers in relocation. The law is written and administered by the policy makers, but there are cases where lawyers could try to act beyond a narrow legalistic definition of the law, where they might take test cases and perhaps improve conditions for others in future. Provided a community is aware of the severe limitations, engaging in a legal struggle may be helpful in the long run and certainly gives people a chance to organise around the issue.

In the past some communities have tried interdicts to halt or delay the removal, but the law has been tightened to such an extent that communities can no longer bring interdicts to stop removals. For expropriation or eviction from farms, at best the process may be delayed by challenging on technical details.

Section 31 of the proposed Orderly Movement and Settlement of Black Persons Bill prevents people from settling on land 'calculated to canvass support for a campaign for the repeal or amendment of any law or for the variation or limitation of the application of the law'.

The Matoks, who rejected outside help, must have had some experience on which to base this decision. Perhaps they had seen how things worked for another community. It is not for outsiders to try to find some members of the community who are willing to accept them. Supporters should understand their position and not try to interfere where a community wants to fight its own battles. It only serves to divide and undermine the group.

However, the neighbouring Batlokwa engaged legal assistance. They had significant support from the business community in Johannesburg and groups such as the Black Sash. It is not clear which of the two approaches (or a combination of both) won the battle, for both the Matoks and Batlokwa area were given reprieves in 1982.

Visitors may be useful in campaigning for a community

reprieve. Campaigns which stress a number of communities under threat should be encouraged. If visitors are taken to meet members of the community and hear people's views for themselves, they are less likely to leave with a distorted picture and try to 'save' that particular community alone. Visiting relocation areas in busloads is insensitive to the people who have already suffered many indignities, but 'seeing for oneself' may be the first step towards working against the policy. This does not apply to the policy makers and officials, of course, who certainly know about the conditions in relocation areas. Newcomers need reminding that it is not ignorance that keeps the removals going, but the implementation of apartheid. There is a naive view that the policies are enforced without the government knowing how it all happens, or what the effects are, and that 'if only they knew', a Christian government could not let it happen this way.

The church is perhaps the most important network for people in rural areas. Most black people in South Africa are Christians and expect the church to be concerned with their problems. Within the many denominations are those which advocate no community involvement. They preach that one should accept God's will and work towards entering heaven in the life hereafter. Other denominations and Christian organisations work actively towards relieving oppression on earth. Recently many denominations have concerned themselves practically with relocation. They have employed fieldworkers for research and action, particularly with those under threat of removal but also with those dumped in closer settlements. Given a clear understanding of the policy and some experience with removed communities, the church workers should be able to work with people over a long period to help them in their situation.

Church engagement varies from the remote (such as the mission opposite The Swamp in the Himeville area, Natal, where priests did not even inform their superiors that the whole local community was moved) to the integrally involved such as in the proposed removals for Woodstock Dam, also Natal. The church is a large landowner itself. Its relationship with black tenants is not always faultless. Some churches in Natal have even evicted families. In the Woodstock Dam area, while the Roman Catholic Church was supportive of people resisting the move, the Lutheran Church collected compensation handed out by the government without offering to pay any to the congregation which had been living on the land for generations.

Church involvement may be intense but somewhat misdirected. Conditions of relocation within the new areas become more important than the issue itself. For example, in a memorandum on the proposed move to Khayelitsha, a church fieldworker urged the regional council of churches to involve the churches in the development of the area. While it may be true that those homeless people of KTC and Nyanga Bush are willing to move to Khayelitsha, the majority of the Africans in Cape Town have stated quite clearly that they refuse to move. The church role could become one of dividing the people in their resistance if it involves itself in such development.

A further problem illustrated by the same memorandum is that of attitudes:

> It would appear that a whole motley crowd of people are going to be moved from different areas bringing with it a variety of problems . . . Assist . . . toward the formation of a coherent base for the development toward a stable community before the rot sets in.
> (*Quaker Peaceworker*, 6 June '83)

While the churches may intend to play a positive role in changing policy and relieving poverty, they need to examine more critically the attitudes and strategies they employ.

Government policy, embodied in recent reports such as those of the Wiehahn and Riekert Commissions and resulting legislation, encourages the rural/urban divide. Exposure to conditions in the rural areas is important if urban people are to be confronted with the other side of their privilege — rural poverty. The church is in a perfect position to do this, having both urban and rural connections throughout the country. While the government is improving the lot of blacks in urban areas, more and more people are barred from entering urban areas through influx control. Not until the unemployed are repatriated and strikers deported, is the link between the rural struggle and the urban struggle normally made.

Bantustan intervention
The role of the bantustans in relocation was outlined in Chapter 6. A closely related question is whether communities who want to resist relocation would approach the bantustan authorities for

support. As has been mentioned, the Ciskei is unlikely to favour resistance; in fact, it represses all forms of resistance. The Transkei has always opposed forced mass removals and has only one mass relocation area, Ilinge. Influx control victims and the 1981 residents of Nyanga Bush (whose removal was officially deplored by Transkei) are the main victims. Other bantustans like to claim that they oppose removals, but as has been shown, they are powerless to do so and their very existence depends on relocation. Some bantustans, KwaZulu for example, encourage resistance to be channelled through Inkatha which strengthens the organisation. While it is too early to make final judgements in this regard, no communities have yet been reprieved in Natal.

Mathopestad people tried to get Bophuthatswana to support their stand against removal. The bantustan's reply was that they should be part of Bophuthatswana as they are Tswana. The people agreed, but wanted to have their farm declared part of Bophuthatswana in that case.

Commercial interests

In the case of urban relocation, township people sometimes approach the local business community for support for their reprieve. With the blacks moved out of Louis Trichardt, for example, the white town centre is declining fast. The new Indian shopping centre was built on the outskirts, on the way to Venda. Now all the people from Venda shop at Alta Villas, the Indian area, rather than in the white town. The business community has protested about this, but it is too late. Group area removals and urban relocation have been implemented.

In opposing the removal of Walmer township in Port Elizabeth, the director of Port Elizabeth's Chamber of Commerce, Mr A H L Masters, said the removals would 'definitely have an adverse effect on Walmer's business community. Another important factor is that if we go ahead with the removals it will lead the world to look at us with jaundiced eyes. The implications of this are serious for the business community of South Africa at large.'
(*Sunday Times*, 20 Jan. 80.)

The business communities of Jan Kempdorp and Vryburg are worried about the removals of their respective African townships, Valspan and Huhudi. The people are to go to Bophuthatswana and will shop there, where there is no sales tax, making goods

10% cheaper than in the rest of South Africa. (This was an important reason for business people lobbying for Mafikeng and Thaba 'Nchu to be incorporated into Bophuthatswana, as even the white residents shopped across the 'border' in Bophuthatswana.)

Violence

The question of violence has not been explored in depth. Few communities consciously choose to repel state violence with their own. Police with teargas, dogs and guns, often accompanied by the military, were much in evidence in the 1960s and 1970s. Under the new policy of trying to persuade everyone to move voluntarily, they have not been so visible. Not that they have been absent. In April 1983, Saul Mkhize was shot dead. In May 1983 teargas, rubber bullets, and spotlights shining all night were among the means used to rid KTC of the people 'squatting' there.

Examples of violent resistance include the attack on Soekmekaar police station by members of Umkhonto we Sizwe, the army of the banned African National Congress. This is the closest police station to the Sekgosese area where over 100 families were moved by force from the Makgato village to Kromhoek in Lebowa in 1980. Officials from the Department of Cooperation and Development destroyed their village. In the Bergville area in Natal, drivers of front-end loaders who were due to destroy people's homes were threatened with violence if they went ahead. Some of the equipment was sabotaged.

At times people have died under suspicious circumstances. The Mathopestad chief was a young man who was not strong enough to overcome the temptation of promises of a better life for himself and his family at Onderstepoort, the proposed new area. In 1982, during a visit to Mathopestad by Helen Suzman MP, Sheena Duncan (Black Sash president) and others, he called the police, claiming that strange whites were in his area. The visitors had been invited by the tribal council. After some embarrassment on the part of the police, they left. Within 24 hours the chief was dead from a strange stomach complaint. It would seem that after two years of his disloyal behaviour, his presence had become too much for someone.

In the 1950s violent resistance to betterment planning was widespread.

This history is largely unwritten and forgotten and many of the issues that were involved in the earliest struggles are not clear. There are, however, indications from official reports of the reasons for resistance.

The 1949-50 report of the Department of Native Affairs states: 'Acting Chief Joel Matlala was murdered by his own people. During October 1950 a lawless section of the Matlala tribe took the law into their own hands and stoned acting Chief Joel Matlala to death. Four ring-leaders were found guilty and sentenced to death.'

(Yawitch, 1982, p82.)

Further references to the Matlala tribe near Pietersburg suggest why acting Chief Matlala was killed:

. . . Opposition to control measures, stock limitation and rehabilitation schemes is still being encountered but is more passive than in the past. (Yawitch, 1982, p74.)

Success of resistance

Is it possible to judge the effectiveness of resistance? If a community is moved, having resisted, has it lost the struggle? Has the government won? It is not easy to answer these questions, but like the continuum of types of resistance outlined above, a continuum of success to failure could be described.

Success does not always mean just winning the right to stay in a certain place. Rural conditions for those under threat are not necessarily good. On the contrary, Africans in rural areas have found themselves in a bad and deteriorating situation since the earlier part of this century. In the 1930s the reserves were already heavily overcrowded and today that is many times worse.

People who resist removal want some say over their own lives. They may not be able to make a living in their black spot. The young people may have to work in towns and send money home, but time and again the sentiment was expressed that people want to be able to go home to their farms, to be able to retire on their own land, not to have to live 'like sheep' in townships where crime rates and the cost of living are high. They wanted some control over their lives and this is what they are fighting for.

Another aspect of success or failure is that policy changes. A community that has won a reprieve may still be moved in future when plans change. Some people have been moved a number of times, despite previous reprieves; there is no security. But the longer a community can hold out, the better the chance of the government changing its mind and allowing them to stay.

A few examples of areas which have been reprieved may help to clarify the idea of a continuum, rather than a success or failure label. The most famous example of community resistance in the last five years is Crossroads, hailed as a success when the Minister of Cooperation and Development announced categories of people who would be allowed to stay in Cape Town. The people's main demands, to stay where they were and upgrade their houses, were refused. Their secondary demand, to stay in the Cape Peninsula, was fulfilled for some, it seems. Dr Koornhof announced the reprieve as a special one, for Crossroads alone. A survey was undertaken to ascertain who fell into which category. Many people missed the survey, others found themselves with six-month permits, others found that because they were lodgers they had no real claim, and so on. What happened was that the community was divided into those who would be given houses in 'New Crossroads' and those who would have to be sent to the Transkei or Ciskei. Many of those who had previously been in the forefront of the struggle became more interested in choosing new curtains and buying furniture on hire-purchase agreements. New Crossroads is a cut above many townships, better to the eye: but nevertheless a township, only for those with rights to be in urban areas. Meanwhile others fought alongside those who were not granted rights to remain. Divisions grew everywhere — between men's and women's committees, between school and creche committees, and between two rival sections of the Executive Committee. All these rivalries kept people's minds off the real issues. However, some have realised this and are trying to work together. For example, they have all (Old and New Crossroads) refused to elect a community council.

The fact that 25 000 people who fought for their rights to be in Cape Town are still there despite bulldozers, midnight pass raids, informers and divisions, is a major step forward. The Crossroads struggle did not end when Dr Koornhof made his announcement, it merely changed its form.

The effectiveness of resistance varies from place to place and according to circumstances. It depends on the local authorities and how responsive they are to representations from the people, whether people raise their issues with national authorities, how keen the farmers and business people are to see them moved, and how much disruption might be caused. For 20 years the people of Braklaagte and Leeufontein have struggled to stay on their black spots near Zeerust. Now, despite pressures like closing the post office to get them to move, they may remain in terms of the latest consolidation proposals for Bophuthatswana. Mangope comes from this area and it is thought that he has managed to persuade Pretoria to abandon the relocation.

Increasingly, security is a factor. Those whites living in rural areas are isolated and dependent on the goodwill of local blacks (they would not wish to be exposed to sabotage), so might not want to antagonise them by relocation. On the other hand, they may feel that the fewer blacks there are in the area, the safer it would be as the local population could be more easily controlled.

Limited victories
Resistance teaches people many lessons in organisation. They learn whether or not they can trust their chiefs and tribal authorities, whether they are honestly represented by their leaders, how accountable their leaders are to them (rather than to the magistrate and commissioner), and how strategies are worked on both sides. That education process is useful in the longer term, even if they are relocated. In some cases people were too easily put off their resistance: the Mfengu people who were moved from black spots near Humansdorp to Keiskammahoek in the Ciskei went to court in an attempt to halt the removal. The headman, who was the applicant, did not take the court decision on appeal. The people did not demand that, even if for some reason he had not wanted to carry on, they substitute another member or members of the tribe. He had not brought the case in his personal capacity, but for the sake of his people. Now, years later, the people are trying to find some way of returning to their land. It was descheduled according to all the correct procedures in June 1982 and there is no legal argument open to them any longer, but many have not given up. They have returned to the area and lodge with township people in Humansdorp. Others say they are content in Elukhanyweni, but would move back if they could.

Doornkop near Middelburg (Transvaal) was an example of a black spot which resisted relocation for many years. Part of the community was moved to one bantustan or another, according to their ethnic groups. The main group was moved to Lebowa in two sections. Some people went under pressure (or, some say, were coopted), to Bothashoek and were given limited access to land. The others who went to Monsterlus (Hlogotlou township) were given nothing except residential plots in a closer settlement. Today the people of Monsterlus are marginally better off than those in the surrounding closer settlements. They have a training college, better roads, a number of shops, electricity for those who can afford it. This has been attributed to the Ndebele chief who became a member of the Lebowa legislative assembly, but it is also a result of the energy of people who fought to remain where they were.

Supportive Outsiders

There are a number of guidelines for people who want to get involved with communities under threat of removal. One of the most useful resources to offer is that of information on aspects of relocation such as the law, consolidation plans according to various reports over the last decade, which other communities are under threat, and what strategies different communities have tried. The church was mentioned as one of the main networks in rural areas and it is crucial to keep members of the clergy in touch with what is happening elsewhere. Development workers, some teachers, priests and nurses usually have detailed knowledge of what is happening in their particular areas but are ignorant of similarities and differences further away.

Migrant workers, worried about what is happening at home, hear about a threatened removal and are often those who sound the alarm. They have contacts with unions, urban-based organisations and churches to which they can go for outside help. Those organisations, in turn, should be able to respond and offer resources such as access to publicity. They know who to contact in the press. They should be able to stress the necessity for focus on the wider issue of relocation, not only on one community under threat. Publicity has the effect of exposing conditions to the urban public, both black and white, as well as informing other rural areas of what is happening.

While publicity warns the authorities of the seriousness of resistance, if it is well organised it makes it more difficult for officials merely to move in and relocate people. It is more likely that they will be forced to negotiate, which gives the community a chance to organise itelf. Publicity, whether local or international, can only help if the community has stated its intention not to move and is organising against the removal. No amount of exposure of an unorganised community will save it. The official propaganda machine will soon expose ungrounded resistance. If the people are divided and unsure of their position those divisions will be used by officials to divide them further.

It helps to clarify issues when people from threatened areas come together to discuss the similarities and differences in their struggles. People learn directly from each other. They learn about government strategies (after all, the officials gather in Pretoria to discuss common strategies) and they examine strengths and weaknesses in their own attempts. Hearing what the law states, and learning the limitations of the law, all helps to dispel myths like 'the law is there for your protection'. Case studies of successes and failures and how these came about could help to inform future action.

Rural communities are isolated and keeping them in touch once they have met is important for ongoing contact. People who are very involved in their own immediate and demanding work (such as doctors, priests or community workers) need to be networked together.

While development projects cannot substitute for a national programme of rural development, they are useful means of passing on skills such as how to provide a clean water supply, health care and nutrition. Organisation around such issues prepares people for long-term developments. Care should be taken to work with representatives of the whole community and not merely the most articulate spokespeople. Control of the project should be in the hands of elected representatives and not the local elite, whose leadership would alienate others.

Support groups themselves should learn from case studies of resistance, so that in future they are less likely to direct or coopt the struggle, however unintentionally. Support groups should be particularly careful not to negotiate on behalf of communities. They invariably end up trying to persuade the community to accept a compromise and thereby form a buffer which the community may not be able to overcome. Elected representatives should be directly involved in any negotiations, rather than supporters who might find themselves justifying government strategies, and even being used as agents of relocation.

To help bridge the rural/urban gap, groups need to learn about rural issues. In some cases it may be useful for them to visit rural areas and have first-hand discussions so that rural issues can be incorporated in national demands.

A campaign to stop all future removals will not be successful until the bantustan policy is changed. In order to create, justify and maintain apartheid, the bantustans have to be built up. In order to build them, people who do not live in them have to be moved there. Relocation will not stop until consolidation is complete and all bantustans are 'independent', or apartheid crumbles. A campaign to stop removals, therefore, has to be tied to a campaign to repeal the new South African constitution, the Land Acts, the Urban Areas Act, the Abolition of Passes Act, the Citizenship Acts and the Group Areas Act in particular (as well as Bills such as the Orderly Movement and Settlement of Black Persons Bill). The call to stop relocation is part of the campaign for rights for all South Africans at every level of government, for an end to apartheid, for the right to land, for the right to subsistence, security of tenure and freedom of movement.

There are many subtleties in a community struggle which are difficult for outsiders to grasp. What is seen as a victory from outside may not be seen that way inside. Outsiders frequently pull out when they think the issue is won, leaving a community which may be quite dependent on them. When divisions begin to show as the contradictions are thrown up, the people look outside for solutions. Meanwhile the outsiders may have become involved in another issue, perhaps trying to save some other place from relocation. Disillusionment sets in and the people appeal to officials, but they too are aware that the outside supporters are absent, so they return to treating the people as they have always treated black people. All this has happened in Crossroads, for example; but the people have been negotiating for long enough and slowly they began to stand on their own feet. Today, despite divisions in the ranks, they are stronger than they ever were. They are an example to other communities, proud to tell their tale, including both triumphs and tribulations.

The value of organisation for resistance to relocation is that it involves everyone in a community. Even those who would not normally be interested in involvement are threatened with the loss of their homes. It is necessary not only to involve everyone in each community, but also to build connections between communities so as to develop stronger strategies. This helps people to understand how relocation fits into national policy.

Relocation did not begin twenty years ago: it began with dispossession of the land. In the same way resistance did not begin in the 1950s, but when the indigenous people had to fight for their land. Despite the difficulties in community organisation and despite the apparent failure of many communities, the experience of learning how to negotiate, how to accept and extend limited victories, how to turn short-term failures into longer-term victories, how to time responses and demands, is invaluable in the long run.

Republiek van Suid-Afrika · Republic of South Africa

Verwysingsnommer:
Reference Number:
5/5
3/2/1

Ministerie van Samewerking en Ontwikkeling
Ministry of Co-operation and Development

Posbus
P.O. Box } 384
Pretoria
0001

19 -10- 1982

Rt Rev J.B. Hawkridge
Moderator: Presbyterian
Church of Southern Africa
P.O. Box 72057
PARKVIEW
2122

Dear Sir

PEOPLE OF MGWALI IN THE TRANSKEI/CISKEI CORRIDOR

In pursuance of my Administrative Secretary's letter of 9 July 1982 I have to advise that the resettlement of Black people is resorted to in order to ensure their national unity, to protect their ethnic and political interests and to improve their living conditions and standard of life.

It must immediately be pointed out that as the resettlement of the people of Mgwali is a decision of Parliament I, as the Minister of Co-operation and Development must give effect to such decision.

In resettling a community every endeavour is made to ensure that work opportunities in the resettlement area are comparable with those in the area from which the resettlement is undertaken. Work opportunities arising from the development of the resettlement area are, where practicable, reserved for the people to be resettled.

Resettlement is made as attractive as possible in order to obtain the co-operation of the people concerned and to achieve this the Department of Co-operation and Development undertakes the development of residential areas prior to resettlement. This entails the supply of treated water by pipeline to central points throughout the area where water is obtainable from taps; the provision of temporary prefabricated houses for each family and in addition tents are available if required, to enable the people to complete their own dwellings in their own time; the provision of sanitary facilities, schools, a clinic and the provision of roads in the area.

Before resettlement is undertaken the improvements of the people (such as buildings, cattle kraals, fences, etc.) are valued by the Department of Co-operation and Development and the people receive fair compensation for all such improvements. In addition, they are permitted to take any serviceable materials such as doors, windows, corrugated iron, thatch grass etc., (for which they have already been compensated) with them to the resettlement area. Such materials are transported by the Department free of charge.

As far as land belonging to the people to be resettled is concerned, this is usually valued by the Department of Community Development and the land owners are paid the market value thereof. Payment for the compensatory land (which will be of at least an equivalent agricultural or pastoral value to that of their own land) is withheld from this amount. Should compensatory land (with title deeds), however, not be required, the amount offered for a person's land is paid out to such person in cash.

As <u>land owners</u> are given compensatory land (if required) they are free to take whatever livestock they have with them. However <u>non-land owners</u> are settled in closer settlements and are not allowed to take livestock with them to the resettlement area, as provision is not made for the grazing of such stock.

In regard to the Umgwali resettlement at Frankfort, the Honourable Deputy Minister of Development and Land Matters held a meeting with the Ciskeian Cabinet on 24 July 1980 and informed them of the Government's intention to start with the resettlement of the Umgwali people on their compensatory land in the Frankfort/Braunshweich area. The then Chief Minister of the Ciskei thereupon asked the South African Government to inform the Amazibula tribe of the intention to resettle them. At this meeting it was agreed that a Planning Committee be formed to handle the resettlement of the Mgwali people and that representatives of the three bodies concerned, namely the Amazibula tribe, the Ciskeian Government and the South African Government should serve on it.

A meeting was also arranged with Paramount Chieftainess Nolizwe Sandile and her followers for 25 July 1980. At this meeting the Honourable Deputy Minister of Development and Land Matters informed the Amazibula tribe of the Government's intention to resettle them in the Frankfort/Braunshweich area. The policy was explained to them in detail and they were promised that an information brochure, setting out the details of their settlement, would be made available to them for distribution amongst their people. The tribe was also asked to furnish the names of their representatives on the Planning Committee.

During February 1981 the tribe called a meeting at which Chieftainess Nolizwe Sandile announced that the tribe would move to the compensatory land and that the conditions of the move would be negotiable. Thereafter the tribe appointed eleven people to represent the Mgwali community on the Planning Committee.

At the first meeting of the Planning Committee, the tribal members stipulated sixteen conditions with which the Government of the Republic of South Africa had to comply before the tribe would agree to move to the compensatory land. Eleven of these conditions were accepted and the remaining five were, after discussion, referred to the Department for consideration. They were subsequently accepted.

Furthermore the tribe requested that a private valuator be appointed to value their improvements and although this is normally done by personnel of the Department, their request was nevertheless acceded to. The valuation of property is now reaching the final stages.

A further condition which the tribe stipulated was that a wooden type of house be supplied as temporary accommodation instead of the "Fletcraft" iron hut normally provided until the people have built their own houses. This was agreed to.

With regard to your church's historical links with Mgwali and with due respect for your feelings in this connection, I must emphasize that although a move of this nature is disruptive for a while, it is ultimately for the good of each individual involved and for the community as a whole. As is the case with other removals, the removal of Mgwali is being negotiated with the local planning committee and will be undertaken with the least possible disruption and with due respect for human dignity. Indeed, the Department of Co-operation and Development has gone out of its way to meet the wishes of the people concerned.

In conclusion I wish to emphasize that the people are well aware that the Frankfort/Braunshweich area has a higher agricultural and/or pastoral potential than the Mgwali area and they are therefore continually enquiring when the planning and development of the resettlement area will be completed, so that they can be resettled.

Warm regards,
Yours sincerely

If I can be of any further assistance, please let me know

P.G.J. KOORNHOF M.P.
MINISTER OF CO-OPERATION AND DEVELOPMENT

M.R.A
P.O. Box 380.
Stutterheim, 4930.

Paragraph PAGE 1
2. States that people who are resettled are given opportunities for work. That is the practise in Frankfurt, there are no provisions of such promises.

PAGE 3: Sub Paragraph I.
It is absutely untrue that Chieftainess Noligwe ever called a meeting in February to anounce the to Frankfurt. The first that was called by chieftainess Noligwe was in late October 1981, where she said she (Noligwe) was already in Frankfurt therefore paeple must move to Frankfurt. and said she wanted no reply nor question from any member of the Community and those who oposed the the move must not attend her meetings. furthemore it is not true to say that the planing committee was elected out that meeting.

It was in June, 1981 when President L.L. Sebe came in Sigwali and forced People to accept the principle "Ndogo" And forced the community to form a committee the so called planing committee

The community elected eleven people but subsequently that was changed later by L.L. Sebe, according to the information given by chairman Mr T. Bevu.
That committee ceased to be our committee

The first meeting that was called by the so called planing committee was in October 14-1981
Where Mr T.Bevu stated that they the planing committee did no represent the people they are there to represent the Ciskei Gov. Then the vote of no confidence was passed and accepted by the chairman and his members.
The 16 conditions stated in paragraph III not one person ever suggested not one condition.

Finally absolutely untrue to say that people of Mgwali ever chosen fabricated.
We rejected the removal in toto.

chairman
MGWALI RESIDENTS ASSOCIATION

26 *Rural scene in Wartburg, a black spot in the Eastern Cape where people are under threat of removal, 1981.*

27 *Family group in Mooiplaas, another threatened black spot in the Eastern Cape, 1981. The woman's husband works in East London during the week.*

28 *Resident addressing a community meeting in Umbulwane, a Northern Natal black spot near Ladysmith which is under threat of removal, 1981. (See pages 266-278 and index.)*

29 *Produce offered for sale at a roadside stall by a woman from Reserve Four, threatened Natal tribal land north of Richard's Bay, 1981. (See pages 153, 156, 158, and 279.)*

30 *Signpost in Daggakraal, Eastern Transvaal black spot under threat of removal. (See pages 74-75, 293, and 374.)*

31 *Elderly resident of St Wendolins, a Natal black spot near Durban which has been partly reprieved. (See pages 172-173 and 279.)*

32 *Boys in Driefontein, the threatened Eastern Transvaal black spot near Wakkerstroom. (See pages 74-75, 154-155, 293-295, and index.)*

33 Unemployed men in Thornhill, a Ciskei transit camp and closer settlement near Tarkastad, Eastern Cape. (See pages 57, 301, and 335.)

34 The face of unemployment in Nondweni, a Northern Natal closer settlement near Nqutu in KwaZulu. (See page 350.)

35 *Toilets dominate the landscape in Peddie, a Ciskei village and closer settlement near King William's Town, Eastern Cape. (See pages* xxxi *and 373.)*

36 *Fletcraft housing units in Oxton, a Ciskei transit camp and closer settlement near Queenstown in the Eastern Cape. (See pages* xxxi, 57, *and 301.)*

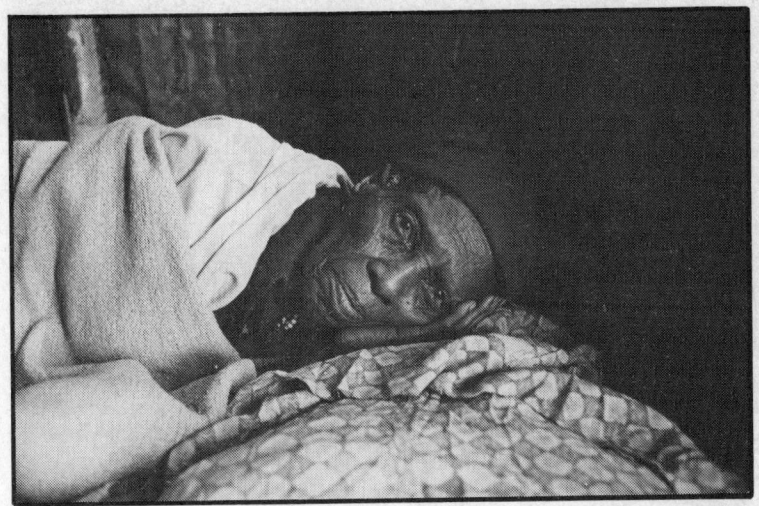

37 *Old woman in Ndevana, an informal settlement in the Ciskei, after being evicted from Zwelitsha, a township between East London and King William's Town, for non-payment of rent, December 1981.*

38 *Emadakeni, an informal relocation settlement next to Sada, a Ciskei relocation township near Whittlesea. The houses were built by people evicted from white-owned farms. (See photograph 2 between pages 35 and 36.)*

CHAPTER NINE

'Trying by all ways and means for survival': conditions in relocation areas

One of the questions critics of relocation frequently ask is: how do people who are removed manage to live?

A woman living in Sada, a sprawling relocation township of 40 000 people in the bleak north-east of the Ciskei, gave this answer: 'We are trying by all ways and means to make ends meet, only for survival. We live on bad conditions and see ourselves destroyed, bit by bit.' She came to Sada fourteen years ago, after her family had been evicted from a white farm 'because the area we were living in belongs to whites'. She is 79 years old and a widow. Her only regular source of income is an old age pension (now R80 every two months). Occasionally one of her sons, who is a migrant worker, sends her a little extra money. She struggles to feed herself, eating twice a day the same meal: mealie meal, tea, a little sugar, some bread, a bit of fat to smear on the bread.

Her situation is neither unusual nor extreme. It is repeated endlessly in relocation areas throughout South Africa. While conditions in relocation areas vary quite markedly — some are better than at Sada, some are worse — everywhere there is poverty and hardship and suffering. The lives of most relocated people are hemmed in by the daily, monotonous, oppressive struggle for jobs, for security, for adequate housing. For some people the outlook is especially grim. For them the struggle is fought on the very boundaries of life. It is about the most basic requirements for mere existence: a minimum supply of water, of food, of firewood for cooking and for warmth.

Relocation areas are not the only places in South Africa where there is suffering and hardship. In virtually every black area in the country (and even a few white), one meets people who are unemployed and malnourished and desperate. Some relocation areas may even have better facilities than areas not scheduled for relocation. However, this neither excuses nor explains the extremely low standards of life that are the norm in official relocation settlements. Poverty and suffering anywhere are to be challenged — but what makes the poor conditions in relocation areas especially unacceptable is that they are the deliberate creations of government policy. Sada did not appear of its own volition. It was planned by government experts: deliberately sited miles from any centre of employment, designed as a residential settlement only — no agricultural land attached — and then abandoned to the people who were forced to move there. When the government and its planners established the place in 1964, they knew how overpopulated and underdeveloped the Ciskei already was. They knew that the people they were sending to Sada came from among the lowest income groups in the country and had no money of their own with which to develop the place. They knew that they would depend almost entirely on work opportunities back in 'white' South Africa, from whence they had come. And yet still they sent them there. Sent them, and millions like them, to Sadas all over the country.

Despite all the information at their disposal, government spokesmen still insist that relocation is not about dispossession but about development. Just as the key words for removals are 'cooperation' and 'voluntary', so the key words for conditions in relocations areas are 'development' and 'nation-building'. Relocation is about 'nation-building, development of national states and improvement of the living conditions of the people that are resettled', stated Koornhof in June 1983. (Press release, 6 June 83, translated from the original Afrikaans.) 'It is this government . . . that is doing most in respect of the real and genuine upliftment and improvement of the standards of the broad average of the Black people', said Val Volker, the Nationalist MP, in the special debate on removals in parliament in February 1983. (*Hansard*, Col. 857, 11 Feb. 83.) Relocation involves 'giving those people an opportunity to build up a community, to live among their own people and to be able to do decent work', said Streicher, another senior Nationalist MP, in the same debate. (*Hansard*, Col. 866/67., 11 Feb. 83.)

Speaking to people in relocation areas, one realises just how cynical these glowing reassurances are.

> We can't do anything by ourselves without money. We live to die — slow death. (Another person interviewed at Sada.)

> [Before] we had fields for the future of our children. Now we don't. (Interview at Elukhanyweni, in the Ciskei.)

> We don't have money. We never did really but here we feel it more because we don't plant anything and we therefore have to buy things we never used to buy. (Interview at Mahodi, in Lebowa.)

> We don't know to whom we belong. (Interview at Ezakheni in KwaZulu)

> It's bad around at home, we just live by luck. Elvis [son] is the only one who is keeping the candles burning somehow. Otherwise the pension is a source of income. We've become popular beggars. (Interview at Pampierstad in Bophuthatswana.)

Comments like these were elicted by SPP in a series of household interviews that it undertook in 19 relocation areas around the country between 1980 and 1982. Altogether 1 671 people were interviewed. Detailed interviews — surveying a total of 198 households — were also documented in two areas threatened by removal, and extensive background fieldwork was carried out in many other areas. From this material the overall picture that emerges is very different from the one that is described by officials in Cape Town and in Pretoria. It is much uglier. It is also much more varied and difficult to describe in catchwords and slogans.

This chapter uses the material to answer some of the questions that have been asked about conditions in relocation areas. The discussion is divided into four sections:

1. The different types of relocation area;
2. Facilities (housing, services, water, sanitation etc.);
3. Economic conditions;
4. Organisation and attitudes among the people.

THE SPP HOUSEHOLD SURVEYS

In all the survey areas SPP administered both general background questionnaires (which were used in non-survey areas as well) and detailed household questionnaires. The average number of households interviewed in each relocation area surveyed was about 88; the actual numbers varied from 37 to 129, depending on the circumstances in each place. (For copies of the questionnaires plus a more detailed discussion of the surveys, see Volume 1 of the SPP report.)

Relocation areas
The 19 areas chosen were distributed across all the provinces and 7 of the 10 bantustans as follows:

Cape (8): Atlantis (near Cape Town); Mdantsane, Dimbaza, Sada, Elukhanyweni, Glenmore, Kammaskraal (all in the Ciskei); Pampierstad (Bophuthatswana).

O.F.S. (1): Onverwacht (also called Botshabelo, in Quaqwa).

Natal (6): Phoenix (Durban); Ezakheni, Inanda Newtown, Sahlumbe, Mzimhlophe, Compensation (all KwaZulu).

Transvaal (4): Kabokweni/Pienaar (Kangwane); Mahodi (Lebowa); Kwaggafontein (KwaNdebele); Rooigrond (Bophuthatswana). Before incorporation into Bophuthatswana, Rooigrond fell in the Northern Cape, but because it is more closely integrated into the Transvaal, economically and politically, it has been grouped with the other Transvaal surveys.

We cannot claim that the choice of survey areas represents a scientific sample of all relocation areas in the country. Standing in the way of that were both practical constraints (the pressure of limited funds and limited time, the problems of finding and training suitable interviewers for so wide-ranging a study) and political constraints (notably problems of access to certain areas, and harassment of both interviewers and interviewed by officials and bantustan authorities on occasion).

Nevertheless, care was taken to select as wide and representative a sample of areas as possible in each region; we are confident that the size of the total sample — covering 10 719 individuals altogether — as well as the overall quality of the interviews does allow for major trends to emerge and valid general conclusions to be drawn.

Threatened areas
Here only two areas were surveyed in depth, both freehold black spots:

Natal (1): Matiwane's Kop
Transvaal (1): Mathopestad

A total of 198 households were interviewed in the two areas, involving a total survey population of 1 275 individuals. While the sample is clearly too small for tight comparative statistical purposes, nevertheless the results of these surveys are very suggestive, particularly when read in conjunction with information and impressions gathered from extensive background fieldwork in other threatened areas in all the regions.

1. The different types of relocation area

For many concerned people the term 'relocation area' or 'resettlement camp' conjures up a picture of rural misery: of a collection of tin or wooden temporary huts (or tents), crowded together on small plots (too small even for subsistence farming) and tucked away in some remote and impoverished corner of a bantustan. In this picture, these areas can be distinguished by their extreme poverty, their very dense population (mainly women, children and old people) and their tin toilets. The tin toilet has become a symbol of forced removals. To see them in the bantustans is to know that people have been or are about to be removed there.

There are scores of such settlements scattered across South Africa — several hundred at least. Some of them have already been mentioned in this book: Glenmore, Limehill, Sahlumbe, Elukhanyweni, Mzimhlophe, Bendall, Onverwacht, Compensation, Bothashoek, Monsterlus, etc. However, although these rural settlements do capture the essence of relocation, they are not the only type, as the history of removals has shown.

Official relocation areas
General Circular 25 of 1967 distinguished between five types of relocation settlements that were to be or had already been established in terms of government policy:
1. 'Self-contained Bantu towns', to rehouse former municipal townships and provide accommodation for workers and their families in border industries;
2. Towns with 'rudimentary services', 'usually situated deeper into the homelands' than Type 1, to provide accommodation mainly for the families of migrant workers;
3. 'More densely populated residential areas', with a rudimentary layout, where people must provide their own housing, to accommodate those moved off farms and black spots; plots measure between one twentieth and one tenth of a hectare — no agricultural land is attached;
4. 'Controlled squatting' on Trust land, to absorb squatters from farms, black spots, etc. quickly; they can later be removed into other types of settlement as necessary;
5. 'Agricultural residential areas' established in terms of betterment planning in the bantustans, for 'tribal families' — similar to Types 3 and 4, but with some agricultural land attached.

The revised General Circular 2 of 1982 repeated these different categories, although in somewhat more elaborate language. In this updated version, Types 3 and 4 above are collapsed into the single category of 'closer settlement':
1. 'Full scale replacement border townships', 'planned and developed in a sophisticated way' (in the bantustans) so that

'Black workers in the nearby White areas can usually commute daily between their place of residence and place of work';
2. 'Rural townships (in the hinterland)', which 'usually lie deeper in the national and independent states' and are developed for 'families whose breadwinners are usually employed in White areas as migrant workers or for the aged, widows, women with dependent children etc.';
3. 'Closer settlements' of 600 or more plots of a hectare each, for 'squatters' from farms, black spots and mission farms;
4. 'Agricultural settlements' consisting of plots up to about one-tenth of a hectare in area, with separate common farmland, 'for people with farming rights . . . sometimes even for economic units'.

This list of relocation areas is incomplete. It refers to African areas only, and then only to those that have been established inside the bantustans. Although the government does not like to associate the group areas townships established for coloured and Indian people with either relocation or African areas, official relocation areas is what they are. A large number of African settlements outside the bantustans also need to be added to the official picture. Most of the older urban townships were themselves first set up as relocation areas. They were built as controlled locations into which all African areas had to be moved. Soweto, home to one and a quarter million people on the outskirts of Johannesburg, was built originally as a relocation township in the 1950s. One of the first groups of people to be moved into it were those who had been moved from Sophiatown, the freehold area that was destroyed in 1954.

There are also several temporary transit camps, known often as 'emergency camps', that have been established by municipal or central government officials. These are to rehouse people whom the officials do not really want to allow to settle permanently in the urban areas but who are, for various reasons, difficult to move further away. Natal has several of these emergency camps: at Dannhauser, at Winterton, and at Weenen. The Weenen camp was established in 1968 as a temporary holding-place for some of the people who were then being cleared off farms and municipal land in the district. It is still there today. Crossroads in Cape Town is another example.

In its survey and fieldwork SPP has grouped these various types

Conditions in Relocation Areas

1. Atlantis 2. Kannaskraal 3. Glenmore 4. Dimbaza 5. Mdantsane 6. Elukhanyweni 7. Sada 8. Phoenix 9. Inanda 10. Compensation 11. Ezakheni 12. Matiwane's Kop 13. Sahlumbe 14. Mzimhlope 15. Onverwacht 16. Pampierstad 17. Rooigrond 18. Mathopestad 19. Kwaggafontein 20. Kabokweni & Pienaar 21. Mahodi

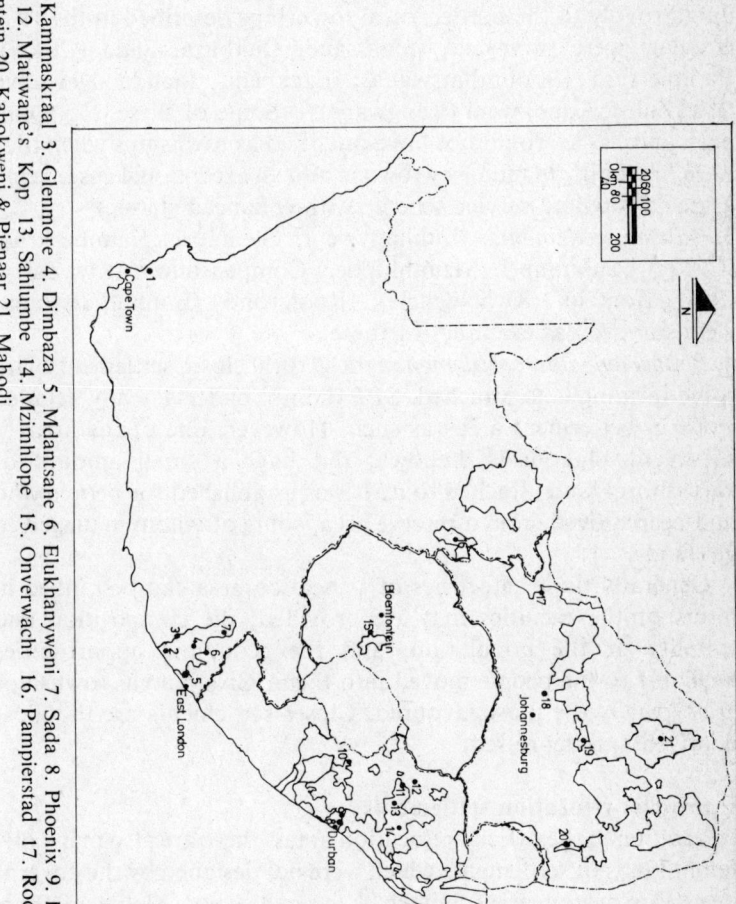

Map 16: Areas Surveyed by the Surplus People Project

of official, government-established relocation settlements into four broad categories:
1. *Group areas townships*: Atlantis (coloured) and Phoenix (Indian) were surveyed as examples of these.
2. *Relocation townships*: Only bantustan townships (corresponding broadly to the border/rural townships described in the 1982 circular) were surveyed: Mdantsane, Dimbaza, Sada (Ciskei); Pampierstad (Bophuthatswana); Ezakheni, Inanda Newtown (KwaZulu); Kabokweni (Kangwane)*. (Some of these, e.g. Dimbaza and Sada, would not have qualified as townships when they were first built. Inanda Newtown is also an exceptional case, being a special site-and-service scheme with enhanced status.)
3. *Closer settlements*: Elukhanyweni, Glenmore, Kammaskraal (Ciskei); Sahlumbe, Mzimhlophe, Compensation (KwaZulu); Kwaggafontein (KwaNdebele); Rooigrond (Bophuthatswana) were surveyed as examples of these.
4. *Betterment closer settlements*: those rural closer settlements with some farming land attached. SPP did not undertake any detailed work in betterment areas as such. However, one of the areas it surveyed, Mahodi in Lebowa, did have a small amount of agricultural land attached to it. It was established for people who had been moved from a reserve area, some of whom managed to get land.

Generally these categories of relocation area can be ranked in terms of the facilities that are provided, the composition and stability of the population, and the economic opportunities available to the people moved into them. Group areas townships are typically the most favoured. Closer settlements are the most deprived and depressed.

Unofficial relocation settlements
In addition to the official relocation areas, there are also many different kinds of settlements which were not designed by the government as relocation areas, but which in practice house large numbers of removed and evicted people. Wherever we went, we came across victims of removals living in unofficial relocation settlements.

---

* Included in the Kabokweni sample were 39 households living in the adjoining area of Pienaar. As described below, Pienaar is an informal settlement, with very poor facilities in comparison with Kabokweni.

They were there for a variety of reasons. Some did not qualify for a place at an official site, others were trying to avoid the controls and limitations of such a life, or could not afford to pay the rents that were being charged in the official townships.

The informal settlements that ring every large and many small South African towns have been mentioned already. Despite years of constant attack from the authorities these settlements have not been contained. Unserviced, unauthorised, unplanned, they continue to grow. Many of the people living in these settlements are qualified urban residents for whom there is no housing in the official townships. Many others have been moved there because they have fallen foul of influx control, farm evictions, or urban relocations. Barred from moving legally to town, they have moved there illegally. Economic necessity is the driving force. A woman who previously had been endorsed out of Cape Town but had returned to live illegally at Crossroads explained it thus:

> Well, my child, I took a ticket and went back to Thornhill [closer settlement, Ciskei]. When I get there things were tough for me because the place is dry, and there are no jobs, it is just impossible for a human being to live under those conditions. So I only stayed for two months in Thornhill, and after that I felt I couldn't take it any longer, and I forced my way back to Cape Town.

When asked if she was not worried about being arrested again, she replied:

> Well, I did think about such things, but they came secondary to my mind because the most important thing was the starvation I was experiencing and my children were in school, and time and again I would get letters that fees are being demanded by the Principal, and also they wanted some money for uniforms, and all such things . . . .So I forced my way down to Cape Town. (*The Struggle for Crossroads*, p10.)

Informal settlements are not confined to the established urban areas only. They are springing up on the edges of all the large bantustan townships as well. Many official relocation townships are themselves ringed by informal settlements. SPP undertook some household interviews in one of them — Pienaar, on the edge of the township of Kabokweni, thirteen kilometres from White River in the Eastern Transvaal.

An estimated 45 000 people live there, in a dense jumble of

shacks and mud huts, with here and there a few quite substantial houses. The settlement is squeezed out along a dirt road that runs between the dry, dusty hills. Most of the people living there have come off white farms in the district. Some are people who were formerly moved into Kabokweni but have left because they could not afford the rent. (Rent ranged up to R14,81 in Kabokweni in 1981.) Water is the main problem. In some areas people catch buses to the nearest well because it is so far away. They complain of long queues at the wells, and of dirty water. Other hardships are the lack of toilets, the shortage of firewood, schools and grazing land, and the high cost of living.

There are also numerous rural settlements that were not established for relocation purposes but have absorbed large numbers of displaced people nevertheless. One of the strongest objections that rural people have to the official relocation sites is that they do not get agricultural land there. 'We could live without work but not without fields', was how a person interviewed at the closer settlement of Kammaskraal in the Ciskei put it.

In their search for alternatives to such places as Sada, many displaced people have moved on to black spots that have not yet been cleared. There they face further removal at a later date. Nearly all black spots have experienced a considerable influx of people in the last twenty years as a result of forced removals elsewhere. This has been most marked in those places that are situated fairly close to towns with job opportunities, as at Umbulwane in Natal. At Matiwane's Kop, nearby, 31 out of the 100 households interviewed by SPP had been living there for less than fifteen years, over a third of them (11) having been evicted off white farms. (See below.)

This influx has put extra strain on land and water and fuel supplies that are already under pressure from the older residents. The overcrowding then becomes an added justification for a government removal:

> Is the Hon. member aware that under the present system of communal ownership or tribal ownership of land the vast majority of areas occupied by these Blacks are vastly overgrazed, overstocked with cattle? That land can never be re-established in the way it should be, because of the overpopulation of cattle? In the constituency which I represent there are some areas where there are well over 5 000 Blacks living on one farm, but at the same time there are four times as many

> ## WHY THEY MOVED TO MATIWANE'S KOP
>
> Twenty-four households, all of whom had moved to Matiwane's Kop within the last fifteen years, gave their reasons for moving as follows:
>
> 7 households had moved there off white farms after labour tenancy was abolished.
> 4 households had been evicted off white farms by the farmer.
> 2 households had left white farms because they were dissatisfied with the conditions.
> 3 households had moved there because they wanted farming land of their own.
> 2 households had moved there because life in an urban township was too expensive.
> 2 households had moved there after they had quarrelled with other members of their families at their previous places.
> 1 household had moved there because there was a secondary school there.
> 1 household moved there to open up a shop.
> 1 household was returning to the family home.
> 1 household had moved there after the breadwinner had been transferred to nearby Ladysmith, where he was unable to find housing in the township.

cattle as that land can carry under the most advantageous circumstances. The land is denuded; there is nothing left. (Val Volker, speaking in the parliamentary debate on removals in February 1983, *Hansard*, Cols. 860/61, 11 Feb. 83.)

Other displaced people have moved onto empty Trust land farms or onto empty white farms, and established themselves there. For instance, in 1981, an agricultural extension officer who was based at Stutterheim, in the Eastern Cape, estimated that in the Upper Kabusi Valley to the west of the town there were about 3 000 people squatting on unused white farms. (Green and Hirsch, 1983, p21.)

Displaced people have trekked into the bantustans proper and sought a piece of land from the local chief (*induna*). All the bantustans have been soaking up removed people in this way. There is probably not a single bantustan community that does not have its quota of people who have been squeezed out of wherever they were before in terms of various aspects of the government's relocation programmes. Qwaqwa, the smallest and most densely populated of the bantustans, illustrates this process most dramatically. The district of Witzieshoek is little more than one large closer settlement — a peri-urban slum in the middle of nowhere. Most of the people who have been flooding into it in the past ten years have come off white farms and small-town locations throughout the Orange Free State. They have moved there because they have nowhere else to go.

It has already been pointed out that the bantustans can themselves be seen as extended relocation camps on a large scale. Their whole history and function under apartheid makes this clear. Many rural informants to whom we spoke refused to draw a distinction between official and unofficial sites. To them all bantustan settlements were relocation sites, whether classified by the government as such or not. Although this chapter is mainly concerned with the official settlements — the direct products of policy — it is important to bear this point in mind. Though many of the people who have been displaced by apartheid are living outside the official areas, they and the places in which they live are nevertheless the government's responsibility.

2. Facilities

Different facilities in the different categories of sites
The facilities provided by the government in official relocation areas vary considerably. They are not all uniformly bad. Group area townships, relocation townships and closer settlements can be ranked in that order in terms of facilities and their general economic conditions. The government takes into account who is being relocated and what the purpose of the relocation area is

when it decides what facilities it is going to lay on in any particular site. Coloured and Indian people are favoured over African, urban people over rural people, industrial workers over agricultural workers and the employed over the unemployed. This corresponds to the divisions that it is trying to reinforce within the black population at every point.

Thus the facilities provided in group area townships are far superior to those found in most African relocation areas. The problems of the group area townships, though considerable, have to be measured on a different scale of dispossession. Popular expectations are accordingly higher.

Facilities in group area townships do not reflect an absolute lack of infrastructure and services so much as an inadequacy and shoddiness in what is available. A related problem is the very high cost of living experienced by working class families who have been pushed out to the edges of the cities and towns. In both Atlantis and Phoenix high rents, high transport costs to town and poor shopping facilities were the major complaints of the households interviewed by SPP. In Phoenix the rent issue was a focus of community organisation in 1980-1. In March 1981 2 000 households refused to pay increased rents. Their campaign was unsuccessful but it did draw attention to the intense frustration they felt about their housing situation.

Urban people, because they have higher expectations than rural people, are more critical of their poor living conditions. They want the facilities that they can see in the white parts of town. At Atlantis the list of improvements that people would like to see included supermarkets, butchers, clothing shops, chemists, banks, post offices, take-away food outlets, garages, burial companies, playgrounds, a swimming pool, discotheques and a cinema. At Phoenix, too, a cinema was high on the list of priorities. It was mentioned by 38 out of the 115 people interviewed as a desired improvement.

Although the facilities found in African areas are, overall, poorer than those found in group areas townships, here too there are marked differences between areas. One person interviewed at the closer settlement of Kwaggafontein (KwaNdebele) made the comparison forcibly:

> I think that the government should lay taps here. I don't know why

they think that you in the locations get thirstier than us here.

Best off are the townships situated just inside bantustan boundaries, as part of the urban relocation programme. These are the relocation areas for commuting urban workers and are likely to have some degree of urban infrastructure: formal, rented housing (the dreary rows of matchbox houses typical of South Africa's black townships), running water, perhaps even electricity. The closer to a major metropolitan or industrial area they are, the greater the range of community facilities there will be.

Thus Ezakheni, serving the industrial town of Ladysmith in Natal and itself an industrial development point for KwaZulu, is relatively well endowed. The 50 000 people living there have a 'modern post office and telecommunications centre' (*Natal Mercury*, 8 Feb. 78) — but few telephones — a garage, two eating-houses, three beerhalls, several general dealers, a bottlestore, two full-time clinics, one resident doctor, a community hall and several schools, both primary and high. The streets are tarred (but not lit at night). Not everyone, however, has a house. Seven years after they were first moved there, large numbers of people are still living under 'temporary' conditions in a site-and-service section where each plot has its own tap and a flush toilet.

By contrast, the Ciskeian settlement of Sada is poorly served. It too is classified as a township and its population (40 000 people) is comparable to Ezakheni's. It does not have the economic status of Ezakheni, however. It is a 'rural township' in the words of the 1982 circular. Most of the people who were moved there came from small towns in the Eastern Cape and from white farms; a small number came from the Glen Grey district. There is no local industry and no nearby border industry either — this is a community heavily dependent on migrant labour. Its facilities reflect its lower status in the eyes of the planners. Only one stretch of street is tarred. The water is piped to taps in the street — one every 100 metres or so. The toilet system is a primitive mixture of latrines and buckets (emptied once a week). There is no permanent doctor although there is a clinic. There are several general dealers and one beerhall but no post office. Residents have many complaints about their living conditions:

> Toilets should be made to prevent disease rather than encourage it.
> Streets should be tarred and electrified because of dust and violence.
> Here you have to walk a long way to the tap.

Post is one problem we face — you have to go to the factory for post. My house is built of planks. So when strong winds occur my cups get broken, because the planks are only for the reduction of wind speed.

Still more poorly serviced are closer settlements. Crude temporary shelters on arrival, pit latrines, sparse water points, perhaps if one is very lucky a mobile clinic and a temporary school — this is the most that somebody who is moved into a closer settlement can expect. Here a cinema is a luxury beyond imagining. The improvements desired most often by those interviewed by SPP were absolutely basic. They centred on water, firewood, housing and land.

> I want water. I want a decent toilet. We had similar problems at Winterveld but that does not mean I should not ask for these things here. We did not choose to be in Winterveld any more than we chose to be here. (Kwaggafontein)
> We don't have wood. We have turned, you know, into petty thieves — stealing wood. (Rooigrond)
> Here we don't do any planting, have no grazing land for our stock, no schools, no health clinic — in short, there is absolutely nothing. (Mzimhlophe)
> I am the agriculturalist but I have no fields to grow. (Elukhanyweni)
> After dumping, the houses were full of ground inside. They used to leak on rainy days. (Dimbaza)

These are the dumping-grounds for the superfluous and the non-productive. It is into these most isolated and inadequate settlements that, quite deliberately, the poorest, least skilled, least organised groups of people are moved: ex-farmworkers, tenants from black spots, squatters.

Improvement in facilities since the 1960s

Lack of basic services, isolation and struggle: this is not the image of closer settlements that the government is trying to promote. While it is prepared to admit that officials might have displayed a 'fairly rough treatment', even a 'fairly callous attitude' in certain cases in the past, it is insisting that those days are now over. (The Deputy Minister of Development and Land Affairs, *Hansard*, Cols. 8829/30, 7 June 83.) Already in 1980 Koornhof was claiming that before people are moved into them, closer settlements are

> first planned, developed and certain basic requirements such as water, sanitation, schools and clinics . . . provided without any cost to the people resettled. (*Hansard*, Col. 622, 22 April 80.)

Since then, as the debate surrounding removals has sharpened, so the claims have become even more specific, more extravagant. In the press release that he issued in June 1983 he was talking of streets, transport and even job opportunities, in addition to the more standard claims about water, schools and clinics. (See box.)

FACILITIES: KOORNHOF'S CLAIMS

The following is a slightly abridged extract from the press release issued by Dr Koornhof on 6 June 1983.

Once the preliminary planning has been finalised to everybody's satisfaction it is the function of the Department of Cooperation and Development to implement the plan and to provide the infrastructure necessary for a community. As a first priority a source of *portable water* has to be established after which the water is reticulated by pipeline to convenient points in the residential area. Provision is likewise made for livestock. Where borehole water is not available suitable purification systems are built to ensure a supply of water which is suitable for human consumption. A further high priority is the provision of *adequate and proper sanitation*. To achieve this a toilet is provided on each and every residential site. Suitable *streets* are constructed in the residential area and where the resettlement is on an agricultural basis access roads to arable lands are also constructed. During the planning stage a survey is made of *residents*, amongst other things, to determine *what school and health amenities* will be required. Once this has been established a start is made with the construction of sturdy *permanent schools* and a *clinic* where the size of the community warrants a clinic building. In cases where the construction of a building is not justified a mobile clinic service is provided. These improvements are provided entirely at the expense of the Government and nothing is recovered from the people concerned . . . .

> Families are also provided with weatherproof iron huts to house them and their belongings until such time as they have reerected permanent accommodation. Tents are also available for storage of items that are less vulnerable to the elements. During the disruptive period of the actual move each family is provided free of charge with rations which conform with the requirements of the Department of Health . . . .
>
> The fact that people are resettled does not deprive them of their rights to work in urban and other areas. Job opportunities are often available in the new area and preference is moreover given to the people involved when labour is required for the development of that area. In cases where workers are required to commute to their place of employment transport subsidies are available from the Department of Transport. That Department also has representation on the various settlement committees *inter alia* to ensure that suitable public transport is available to the community.

Up to a point these claims are true: the overall standard of basic facilities provided by the government in relocation areas has risen during the 1970s. This has been almost entirely because of political pressure.

In the 1960s, before Desmond had started his investigations, the government could afford to pay scant attention to what sort of facilities it provided — or did not provide — at relocation sites. Forced removals had not yet become a major political issue. Most of the places that were established to house the hundreds of thousands of people then being driven off white farms and black spots were far enough away from main roads and towns to keep 'agitators' and 'troublemakers' away. Often only a handful of dedicated church and health workers, those already working in these areas, were really aware of what was happening and most of them were too busy responding to the immediate crisis to take up the issue on a public platform.

In the urban areas, where there was more publicity and people were better organised, minimum standards of housing and facilities were laid down. People had a reasonable expectation of getting a permanent house. Even so, facilities were often extremely rudimentary. Thus in Durban in the 1960s, thousands of Indian people who were moved out of the central city in terms of the Group Areas Act ended up in desperately inadequate emergency camps. These had to be hastily erected because the official township of Chatsworth could not absorb the huge numbers of displaced people. At the African township of Mdantsane, established 20 kilometres from East London in 1963, the first people to be brought there found little more than the standard, four-room houses standing in the bare veld. Water was piped to taps in the streets, and each house had a bucket-system toilet (cleared weekly). By 1965, when Mdantsane had a population of about 1 200 families, the annual *Survey of Race Relations* noted that it had been started 'before necessary amenities such as police stations, streetlights, clinics and shops were available'. (*SAIRR Survey*, 1965, p199.)

In the rural areas conditions were still worse. In many instances virtually no preparations were made. At Mondlo, established 28 kilometres south of Vryheid in Northern Natal in 1963, people were provided with tents and rations for three days.

> There was no sanitation, no fuel, no building sand, no store, no school . . . water was brought in by water-cart, milk and meat were unobtainable. (Desmond, 1970, pp65-66.)

Shortly after the settlement had been established a typhoid epidemic broke out. This miserable story was repeated over and over again throughout the 1960s: at Dimbaza, established in the Eastern Cape in 1967; at Morsgat, established in the Western Transvaal in 1968; and at Sahlumbe, established on the banks of the Tugela river in Natal in 1959.

Desmond, who visited Dimbaza after it had been established (by which time conditions had reportedly improved) described it as displaying 'grinding poverty, squalor and hardship equal to the worst places I had seen.' (Desmond, 1970, p173.) A woman who was moved into Sahlumbe after she and her family had been evicted off a white farm as unwanted labour tenants remembered those early days thus:

> A BAD [Bantu Administration Dept.] man gave me a stand which had four poles at the corners and said that was where I could build my house. I was given a tent to erect on the stand. As soon as we had put a roof on the first hut, the tents were taken away for someone else.
>
> A water tanker was parked nearby so that we could get water to make the mud walls of our house. The moment the tents were taken away, the tanker was also taken elsewhere. After the tanker went, we had to carry water in 5-gallon drums from the Tugela which was a mile downhill from our place. This we still do.
>
> There were no latrines. It was horrible to have to squat in public. The stands were clear and there were many of them and everybody had to do that. There was nowhere else to go that was private. We came from homes where the nearest neighbour was half a mile away and there were thick bushes to give us privacy. Now we were all living right on top of each other. ('Dombi Khumalo's story', SPP Vol. 4, p326.)

At about this time, however, forced removals into the bantustans suddenly hit the headlines. In 1968 Desmond and various church and political organisations succeeded in exposing the fairly routine removal of several hundred black spot families into the closer settlement of Limehill (in Northern Natal). It became a national issue. Opposition newspapers carried prominent and strongly critical reports on the removals; questions were asked in parliament. Most of the attention focussed on the pathetic conditions of the people being dumped at Limehill, rather than on the fact of the removal itself. It was on these terms that the government was pushed to respond.

Much of its response was verbal. There were angry denials — in parliament, in the Afrikaans press, on the radio — that conditions were as bad as they were made out to be. The South African Broadcasting Corporation obliged by devoting several programmes to the official viewpoint — 'Current Affairs', 'Top Level', the news. Part of the response, however, was more practical. Latrines were dug at Limehill and several extra tents put up to house a temporary school.

The Limehill affair led directly to Desmond's book, *The Discarded People*. This was followed by the British TV film, *Last Grave at Dimbaza*. Together they turned the government's ongoing programme of relocation into an international scandal. Like most international scandals, relocation in South Africa did not stay long under the spotlight. The bad publicity was sufficiently unwelcome, however, to introduce a new note of

MORSGAT

900,000 Africans have been uprooted by the Government since 1959. Morsgat is only one of many resettlement camps.
'We have been thrown away.'
*More than 300 families are living there in tents and shacks. They have been moved off 'white' land to this place — part of a future Tswanastan.
*The first people were taken there in December, 1968. Nine months later and only after the *Rand Daily Mail* investigation did the Government start building houses.
*Some people have been moved from the slate quarries where they worked, others from locations in white towns.
*Some of the people were taken from poor conditions, some from good brick houses and reasonable facilities.
They lived with their families near their work.
*Most breadwinners earn R3,50 to R4 per week.
*Return bus fares to work vary between R1,10 and R1,80.
*Most men can only afford to pay these fares at weekends.
Now men can no longer live with their families.
*There is one water tank for over 1,200 people.
*There is a layer of green slime on top of the water.
*There are no latrines.
'The stink is terrible after the rains.'
*There is evidence of malnutrition. There is no clinic.
*People complain of diarrhoea and serious body sores.
*The people are allowed to build houses . . . 'They told us the bricks cost R80. We can barely afford food.'
Morsgat, Limehill, Klipgat, Stinkwater, Mondhlo, Illinge, Nxesha — all resettlement areas, closer settlements.
How many more of them are there all over South Africa?
'These Bantu live better than the whites in the stricken Boland towns.' — Dr Piet Koornhof (*Die Vaderland*.)
The earthquake in the Boland was a natural disaster, beyond man's control. *Morsgat is an act of government.* Does Dr Koornhof equate government action with a natural disaster?

(From a Black Sash pamphlet, November 1969.)

caution into government planning. Thus in the early 1970s, when the Department of Bantu Administration and the army were first discussing the removal of people out of the proposed missile range area at Lake St. Lucia, they also discussed ways of preventing a repetition of the Limehill affair. One of the suggestions was for officials to involve church people in helping out at the relocation site as the people were trucked in. It was thought that they would be kept so busy organising soup kitchens and liaising with the authorities that they would not have time to indulge in attacks on the removal itself.

The focus on Dimbaza also prompted the government to pay special attention to conditions there. In response to the international outcry — though never admitting any direct link — the government launched a major counter-propaganda drive to upgrade the settlement. Over the years it has directed most of the Ciskei's annual budget for development into Dimbaza. By February 1980 the Ciskeian National Development Corporation had spent some R30 million of its total outlay of R36 million on industrial development in that area.

Twenty-two out of the twenty-six industrial enterprises established in the Ciskei by outside investors by March 1980 were located in Dimbaza. (Green and Hirsch, 1983, p33.) Dimbaza now has a shopping centre, a market, a post office, a butchery, a clinic, and a police station for its 17 000 people. The streets are lit by electricity, although they are not tarred. There is a high school in addition to several primary and lower secondary schools. Once a dumping ground of the most desperate kind, Dimbaza has now become something of a showpiece for the government. Now foreign journalists and politicians are positively encouraged to go there. It is the government's favourite example of a relocation site.

'Dimbaza is a success', declared Streicher in parliament in February 1983:

> Not only do the people there get the opportunity to live decently; light industries have now also been established in that area. Now I want to ask the Hon. member for Houghton whether this is not the kind of situation she would rather have in South Africa . . . .
> (*Hansard,* Col. 866, 11 Feb. 83.)

Although other rural relocation sites that were established in the

1970s did not receive anything like this special attention, most of them did benefit from the outcry over Limehill and Dimbaza. More attention was paid to the provision of basic facilities such as water and sanitation. Tents were generally phased out in favour of sturdier temporary structures: single-room tin huts known as 'Fletcraft' and, mainly in the Eastern Cape, wooden-plank shelters.

However, while the overall standard of facilities provided in closer settlements on their establishment has improved, they are still a long way from the cosy settlements described by Koornhof in June 1983. In not one of the closer settlements surveyed by SPP did facilities on establishment begin to approach the levels he was proclaiming as standard.

Furthermore, in only a select few of the relocation areas surveyed by SPP has Koornhof's full range of schools, shops and clinics etc. been met at the time of writing. Even Dimbaza, favoured Dimbaza, is not the success story that it is claimed to be. Despite the factories and the township gloss, unemployment is desperately high — the unemployment rate (which measures the proportion of unemployed to employed) is 35% in the SPP sample. (In other words, for every 100 people employed, there are 35 people unemployed — a staggeringly high figure.)

Thus at Mzimhlophe, established in 1975 for ex-labour tenants, conditions were a little better than those provided at Sahlumbe six years before: the people got Fletcraft huts and latrines. The water supply was inadequate, however — and there was neither a school nor a clinic. Only now, eight years later, is piped water being installed — after repeated questions have been asked in parliament. There is also a temporary Fletcraft school. Otherwise little has changed since the settlement was started. Several hundred more sites have been staked out for a further influx of people at some as yet unspecified date.

Glenmore, established in 1979, got a full complement of temporary housing, latrines (bucket toilets) and one water tap per house. Yet though the government could thus claim that the 'basic requirements' of housing, water and sanitation had been provided, conditions in Glenmore were absolutely critical in the first weeks. Rations were provided for the first few days. When these ran out the general health of the community dropped alarmingly. Eleven people died in those early weeks, nine of them children. They died from gastro-enteritis, kidney inflammation, kwashiorkor and bronchial pneumonia: all diseases of poverty, malnutrition and insanitary living conditions. Only when outside relief organisations stepped in with food and blankets did the situation improve slightly.

The more isolated the area, the less likely it is to be visited by journalists and opposition politicians, the more likely the government is to skimp on the always extremely basic facilities that it claims to supply. Thus at Kammaskraal, established in the Peddie district of the Ciskei in 1980, the first arrivals got no more than tents and latrines. The only water supply came from a few water trucks. At Mbazwana, an even more isolated relocation area on the Makhathini Flats in north-eastern Natal, refugees from the St Lucia missile range in 1978 were treated no better than those at Dimbaza ten years before. They got tents and nothing else. There was so little advance planning that even the Department of Health did not know that people were being moved there: yet the Department runs a malaria-control programme in the area that depends on their keeping a record of every house in the district so that they can spray them regularly against mosquitoes. When SPP arrived at the district hospital two years after the removals, in 1980, the superintendent was overjoyed to see us. We were the first outsiders to visit the area who showed any interest in what he described as 'the pathetic sight' of the unprepared, disoriented people who were suddenly thrust upon him and his staff. He also reported that there was still no formal water supply. People were having to travel long distances to collect domestic water from bilharzia-infected streams. Over half the malnutrition cases dealt with by the hospital come from the relocation area.

On the other side of the country, in the forgotten land around Kuruman, are Vaalboschhoek and Bendall — among the most desolate places that we visited. Vaalboschhoek was established in 1975 for the people moved from the Mayen Reserve. When we visited it in late 1982 it consisted mainly of shacks — row after row of them, on fairly large residential plots, along a remote road between Reivilo and Jan Kempdorp. We saw some Fletcraft huts and latrines, one or two better houses, one shop, pipes lying along the main track — but no taps. We also saw a huge graveyard. Bendall, established in 1977 in the sandy wastes north of Kuruman, was memorable only for the sand and the fine secondary school — financed not by the central or Bophuthatswana governments, but by the Roman Catholic Church.

Conditions in relocation areas are at their very worst in the first few months after the establishment of the area. Then people are struggling to cope with the trauma of the removal, the unfamiliarity of their surroundings, the makeshift quality of the settlement. In closer settlements people have to rebuild their houses with very little cash. Often they do not know their neighbours. Having been a close-knit community they are flung into a situation where 'all are strangers', as one person described it to us. For rural people the adjustment is an especially traumatic one. They have to get used to a life without land, in a densely settled residential settlement where the plots are very small and their neighbours live right on top of them.

Over time, conditions do improve. People adapt. For many, life has always been a struggle. So they endure, and slowly the outline of a new settlement emerges. Permanent houses are built. Fruit tress are planted; here and there vegetable gardens are started.

> We can't do anything about our problems. Initially people were even talking about getting back to Machoka, but nobody speaks like that today . . . . People get used to hardships. (Resident of Mahodi relocation area, Lebowa, 1981.)

Most of the improvement is entirely due to the efforts of the people themselves. Unless the conditions in an area become a political issue — as in the case of Dimbaza — the government can afford to overlook its responsibilities. It took a major bus boycott at Ezakheni in 1979 to persuade the government to tar the road between Ladysmith and the township. Similarly, only once the press had exposed the poor conditions in the closer settlement of Nondweni, in Natal, during the course of 1979, did the authorities start to build a clinic there. It was finally opened in 1980, five years after Nondweni had been started.

The settlements considered above are not isolated examples. Three years of extensive fieldwork have made it apparent that at this stage Koornhof's press release is no more than a high-flying public relations exercise designed to hide what is happening on the ground from public scrutiny. More important to the government than providing facilities in relocation areas is building up a positive image of relocation as a laudable process of development in the eyes of the white public. 'The government has hidden us away', observed one person interviewed at Kammaskraal in the Eastern Cape, 'so we would appreciate any help to bring our plight to the attention of the authorities.'

3. Economic conditions

In all the relocation areas that we surveyed, people complained of poverty and were engaged in a struggle for survival. However, poverty in Phoenix has a different meaning from poverty in Sahlumbe or in Glenmore. Economic conditions vary as much as facilities do, and the further away from the established urban areas one goes, the more desperate the struggle for survival becomes.

There are also noticeable income variations among the households within any one relocation area. As well as degrees of poverty there are a few instances of individual households that have done well out of relocation — the local shopkeeper or bottlestore owner, for example. These exceptional cases often owe their advantage to cooperation with the authorities before and during the removal.

Employment levels

The government does not claim to provide work for those whom it relocates. The lack of jobs in relocation areas 'is not my problem' said the Chief Commissioner for Queenstown in 1978.

> We will provide the necessary infrastructure of water and toilets in the camp. Where the people work is not my business. It is like any other area. In the rural areas there are no jobs either — the people are migrant workers. The provision of jobs has nothing to do with me.
> (Quoted in 'Relocation', Control, DSG 1979, p51.)

It would not be said so bluntly today, but the basic attitude of officials has not changed.

The struggle for jobs is one of the most urgent issues for relocated people. In the group area and relocation township samples the percentage of the total population who were unemployed was roughly the same: about 28%. For every 100 members of the community (adults and children) there were 28 people bringing in wages. This figure does not distinguish between people who are employed near to their homes and people engaging in migrant labour — a theme which will be taken up later.

EMPLOYMENT LEVELS IN 9 GROUP AREAS AND RELOCATION TOWNSHIPS (%)

	Male	Female	Total
Group areas			
Atlantis	36	21	28
Phoenix	39	15	27
Relocation townships			
Mdantsane	30	26	26
Dimbaza	30	16	24
Sada	38	17	28
Pampierstad	30	10	21
Ezakheni	38	23	29
Kabokweni/Pienaar	48	27	38
Inanda Newtown	42	18	29
Average, townships	37	20	28
National average, African	41	17	29

The average (28%) reflected in the table above compares reasonably well with the level of employment among Africans nationally. According to the economist Charles Simkins, this was 29% in 1980 — 41% for males and 17% for females. Several points, however, are worth noting.

While the level of male employment in the relocation townships is below the national average, the level of female employment is above it — most markedly in Mdantsane, Ezakheni and Kabokweni/Pienaar. All of these are townships serving 'border industrial' regions to which entrepreneurs are attracted by wage structures much lower than those prevailing in the main industrial centres. Female labour is especially cheap and in abundant supply.

Only one of the relocation townships, Kabokweni/Pienaar, ranks above the national average. It is situated in the Transvaal, relatively close to the industrial heartland of the Reef. It also keys into the economic life of White River, the town thirteen kilometres away from which its residents were removed. The very worst township in terms of employment levels is Pampierstad, in the remote Northern Cape. It is followed, revealingly enough, by Dimbaza, the economic showpiece of the Ciskei.

Employment levels in the closer settlements surveyed are significantly below the national figures. The average employment level there is 24% — 35% for males and a very low 13% for females. The figures for each of the closer settlements surveyed are set out below:

EMPLOYMENT LEVELS IN 10 CLOSER SETTLEMENTS (%)

	Male	Female	Total
Elukhanyweni	34	21	27
Glenmore	22	9	16
Kammaskraal	26	12	19
Onverwacht	46	14	29
Sahlumbe	38	4	21
Mzimhlophe	34	18	26
Compensation	30	9	19
Mahodi	40	11	26
Kwaggafontein	48	11	30
Rooigrond	35	20	28
Average, closer settlement	35	13	24

The only areas which compare favourably with the national average are Kwaggafontein, Onverwacht and Elukhanyweni.

Kwaggafontein is only 75 kilometres from Pretoria. It is therefore relatively favourably situated, on the fringes of the Johannesburg/Pretoria complex. Onverwacht serves Bloemfontein — a mere 50 kilometres away. Elukhanyweni is a somewhat exceptional case. There the workers have clung tenaciously to jobs near their former land in the Tsitsikama. They have continued to work at Humansdorp, although they have had to become migrant workers to do so.

In most of the closer settlements the level of female employment is very low. The exceptions are Rooigrond, Mzimhlophe and Elukhanyweni. There is domestic labour in nearby Mafikeng for the women of Rooigrond, agricultural labour in adjacent formium plantations for the women of Mzimhlophe. At Elukhanyweni many of the women are domestic workers in distant Humansdorp — migrants, like the men.

In the SPP sample four of the five worst areas in terms of employment levels are closer settlements. Only Pampierstad in the Northern Cape qualifies as a township in terms of facilities. This reflects the status and the function of the closer settlements, as dumping grounds for the 'surplus' and least skilled members of society. However, while there is a broad correlation between township infrastructure and economic opportunities, the link is not automatic. Whether an area is formally declared a township or not is as important as where it is located in relation to industry.

Thus the relocation areas in the depressed Eastern Cape are, as a group, worse off in terms of employment levels than those of the Transvaal. The township of Pampierstad is worse off in this respect than the closer settlement of Kwaggafontein. Although facilities are extremely poor at Kwaggafontein, it is situated within striking distance of the Reef. Workers living there have long distances to travel each day, but at least they are within reach of jobs.

Those with jobs are the privileged members of society in most relocation settlements, especially those in the rural areas. They are, however, only relatively privileged, for wages are generally very low as a Dimbaza resident explained:

> The only problem here is that, although factories are here, people are paid very low wages. We do not think that the government knows that people are less paid by the factories. If they know they should force

the factories to pay us. They must not cheat us.

At Ezakheni a woman described the impact of low wages thus:

> My husband doesn't earn enough. The bus fare, the rent, food takes the whole salary and we won't be able to build a house.

Migrant labour
The conventional image of relocation areas is that their permanent population is the very old and the very young, plus others who are not needed to service the South African economy: women with dependent children, the sick and disabled, the unemployed, etc. This is a fair description of most closer settlements. It is less true of the relocation townships and hardly applies at all in group area townships.

There were hardly any migrants in the survey populations of two group area townships: 7 migrants out of a total population of 564 at Atlantis, and none at Phoenix. There were, however, large numbers of commuters. Fifty percent of all the adults of working age at Atlantis (those people between the ages of 15 and 64 years) travelled away from Atlantis each day. Almost all of them went away to work, mostly at Cape Town, 45 kilometres off. At Phoenix, 45% of the adult population of working age and 67% of the men of this age group were commuters, travelling mainly to jobs in the Greater Durban area.

In the African areas migrancy is part of the way of life that people have been forced to develop. Most people have to leave the relocation areas if they are to find work. Border townships are relatively favoured. They have been created to supply labour to industries and towns within commuting distance, and these workers can at least sleep at home each night. Often, however, the commuting distance can be up to 60, 70 or even more kilometres each way, and workers spend most of their 'free' time travelling between work and home in overcrowded, slow buses.

An extreme example is the little town of Alicedale, in the Eastern Cape. About 700 people were forced to move from Riebeeck East (only 48 kilometres from their work) to Alicedale in 1981-2. There was absolutely no local work at Alicedale. Some men, however, managed to get jobs in the South African Railways goods yard at Port Elizabeth. They start work at 7 a.m. and finish

PERCENTAGE OF WORKERS WHO ARE MIGRANTS IN 17 AFRICAN RELOCATION AREAS

Relocation townships	%
Mdantsane	32
Dimbaza	30
Sada	67
Pampierstad	25
Ezakheni	30
Kabokweni/Pienaar	37
Inanda/Newtown	4
Average, relocation townships	37*
Closer settlements	
Elukhanyweni	67
Glenmore	76
Kammaskraal	83
Onverwacht	57
Sahlumbe	88
Mzimhlophe	63
Compensation	56
Mahodi	72
Kwaggafontein	62
Rooigrond	84
Average, closer settlements	71
Average, all areas	55

* Inanda Newtown was excluded from the calculation of this average.

at 4 p.m. Their actual day, however, is far, far longer. In order to be at work on time, the men wake at 2 a.m. each day, wash and dress, and then walk for 20 minutes in the dark to catch the 3 a.m.

train at Alicedale station. After work, they catch the train back home again, getting back to the station at about 9 p.m. They then have to walk home, eat, and go to sleep in time to start once more the next morning at 2 a.m. Some of the men have now taken to camping on the train at night during the week, rather than bothering to go home at all.

Even in those areas relatively well favoured for commuting, a large percentage of workers are forced to become migrants in order to find jobs. In the SPP sample, about one third of the workers in the relocation townships surveyed were migrant workers. The only African township where migrant labour was not a significant category was Inanda Newtown. One of the requirements of the people who were moved into this site-and-service scheme was that they were qualified residents of the Inanda district. Only those who were already locked into the economy of the Durban region were thus eligible for sites. In the case of the closer settlements over 70% of the workforce were migrants. In three cases this figure rose to over 80% — at Rooigrond, Kammaskraal and Sahlumbe.

Migrant labour distorts the structures of both the family and the general population. The burden of childcare falls heavily on those adults who remain behind. Thirty-nine percent of the total survey population of the African relocation areas were found to be children of fourteen years and under. When migrant workers were excluded from the count, however, the proportion of children in the population stood at a little over fifty percent.

Migrant labour has an even more damaging impact on the ratio of men to women in relocation areas. In the seventeen African areas surveyed there were only 78 males to every 100 females when migrant workers were excluded from the count. In the non-migrant adult population of working age (between 25 and 64 years) the proportion of men was even lower: 48 men to every 100 women. In the African townships the corresponding male figure was 62. In the closer settlements surveyed, where migrant labour is far more extensive, the average declined to 45.

The impact of the high level of migrancy on family stability is severe. Having to migrate to find work is bitterly resented:

> We are no longer a united family like we were there, because most of the members work away from here. (Elukhanyweni)

Our problem is family disunity as a result of migratory labour.
(Mdantsane)

I wish I could see my husband more. (Kwaggafontein)

We want more jobs to be created for our husbands and sons to come back and find work here. (Sada)

MASCULINITY RATES (NON-MIGRANT) IN 17 AFRICAN RELOCATION AREAS

The figures show how many men there are for every 100 women in the permanent and commuter populations (i.e. the total non-migrant populations) of the 17 areas.

	ALL AGES	25—64 YEARS
Average, townships	76	62
Average, closer settlements	78	45
Average, relocation areas	78	48

It is difficult to find strictly comparable figures for non-relocation bantustan areas. The material that is available suggests that relocation areas do not display a significantly greater degree of sexual imbalance than other bantustan communities. The Buthelezi Commission has noted that in the rural areas of KwaZulu there are about half as many men as women in the locally resident adult population. (Buthelezi Commission, Vol. 1, 1982, p70.) In the rural Ciskei the masculinity rate has been calculated at 78 for all ages and 49 for the 25-64 age group.

Unemployment

Despite the enormous social and emotional disadvantages of the migrant labour system, migrant workers are among the relatively privileged members of bantustan society. At least they have a job.

It goes without saying that unemployment is a major problem

in the relocation areas:

> Work is scarce here. (Mdantsane)
>
> We don't find work here. There ought to be a factory or something where we can at least get work. (Elukhanyweni)
>
> We were promised jobs here. I haven't been able to find work for two years. They lied to us. (Glenmore)

Unemployment* varies across the regions and across the different categories of relocation area. The two group area townships surveyed compared very favourably with the African areas. The level of male unemployment in the Atlantis and Phoenix surveys was only 5%. In the limited sample of 12 African areas in the Cape and Natal the average rate of unemployment was 24% of the 'economically active' (either working or looking for work) population. The average was 17% for males and a very high 36% for females. The sample also reveals greater unemployment in the Eastern Cape than in Natal.

It is of some interest that the rate of unemployment is lower in the closer settlements than in the relocation townships. Yet, as we have seen, this is not because there is fuller employment in the closer settlements, where the level of employment is actually lower than in the townships. What the apparent paradox reflects is, of course, that more people of working age in closer settlements have simply abandoned hope of ever finding work, and thus do not qualify for description as 'unemployed'.

This point is brought out very clearly by comparing two relocation areas in Natal, Ezakheni and Sahlumbe. On the face of it, unemployment is a far more serious problem in Ezakheni than in Sahlumbe. The true picture emerges, however, when we consider that Ezakheni is a border industry township and a 'development point' within KwaZulu, where many people still live in the expectation, or at any rate the hope, of a job. At Sahlumbe local employment opportunities are virtually

---

* SPP tried to use a very strict definition of unemployment. To qualify as unemployed a person had to be of working age, not at school, without a job and actively looking for one. People who were neither studying nor working, nor looking for work, were classified as 'Not economically active'. The distinction was not drawn clearly in the Transvaal and OFS survey areas. The results from these areas are thus not comparable with those from the other regions and have been left out of the unemployment tables.

UNEMPLOYMENT RATE IN 12 AFRICAN RELOCATION AREAS

Townships	Male	Female	Total Population
Mdantsane	24	39	32
Dimbaza	24	47	35
Sada	19	43	29
Pampierstad	12	40	23
Ezakheni	16	28	21
Inanda Newtown	16	20	18
Average (townships)	19	36	28
Closer Settlements			
Elukhanyweni	12	22	16
Glenmore	27	56	38
Kammaskraal	23	51	36
Sahlumbe	12	21	12
Compensation	11	42	20
Average (closer settlements)	14	30	22
Average (all)	17	36	24

nil. There is thus no point in ever trying to find work there.

While these unemployment levels are disturbingly high, they are no worse than those prevailing in many other bantustan areas. They are, however, worse than the figures available for the non-migrant population in the major urban areas of the country. Unemployment in this group has been estimated recently as 13% for men and 23% for women. (Simkins, 1981, p38.) The gap between these figures and the SPP percentages for relocation areas supports the argument that unemployment is being displaced out of the cities into the bantustans. In both the threatened black spots surveyed — Matiwane's Kop and Mathopestad — the figures show that while the employment level is on a par with the relocation areas, the unemployment rate is significantly lower.

```
ECONOMIC ACTIVITY IN THE BLACK SPOTS

                    % Population          Unemployment
                      Employed                Rate

                 Male Female Total    Male Female Total
Matiwane's Kop    35    15    24       11    20    13
Mathopestad       35    21    28        4    17    10
```

Relocation upsets long established and relatively stable employment patterns. People who have been moved out of an area where they have been based for a long time often lose their jobs. As influx control tightens and the competition for jobs increases, people forced to live in the bantustans are finding it more and more difficult to get contracts as migrant workers. They are becoming increasingly vulnerable to exclusion from the prospect of work altogether.

Other sources of income

The number of workers in relocation areas is not distributed evenly across all households. There is a small but nevertheless significant minority of households that have no wage earners at all. In the six relocation areas surveyed in the Eastern Cape, 15% of all the households surveyed fell into this category.

How these households survive is not always clear to the research worker. Without agricultural land they cannot keep stock. Only the most enterprising manage to grow any food on their small plots, handicapped often enough by a shortage of water. Some households eke out a living by making goods which can be sold within the community — beer, grass mats, knitted goods, etc.

Trying to make a full-time living in this way is uphill work. The bantustan authorities are not sympathetic to informal petty traders, whom they see as a potential threat to the custom of licensed shopkeepers. A number of informal traders complained to SPP that they had been warned off by the authorities. A woman at Sada:

> The fact that I sew for a living is declared undesirable by the authorities. I have already asked permission for sewing and selling to the community but that has been refused totally.

Hawkers are harassed in KwaZulu. Lebowa enforces regulations requiring hawkers to take out licences which are difficult to obtain. People who want to form cooperatives are faced with intimidation and bureaucracy. The Ciskei Marketing Act bars people from selling produce except through the marketing boards. These measures protect commercial producers who generally form the backbone of the bantustan system, and who do not relish the competition offered by the informal sector.

Even without these discouragements those investing time and money in informal economic activity operate within the constraint of a very limited market. Usually, there are few in the community who can afford to buy their produce. Vehicles for delivery of goods or agricultural produce are scarce and public transport is expensive. It follows that the highest level of informal economic activity is found in those relocation townships where there is most money in circulation.

Some households are fortunate enough to have pensioners in the family. In the SPP survey areas pensions rank as the most important cash income after formal wage employment. Their vital role in supplementing, and sometimes substituting for wage earnings is most marked in the rural closer settlements. It is not unusual to find whole families living on the pensions of elderly grandparents — and considering themselves fortunate to have this source of income. This phenomenon is not confined to relocation areas. Throughout the bantustans pensions have come to play a very important role as lifebelts for which households are desperate to qualify.

> I'm unemployed and I can hardly cope with living costs. Rent is a problem. Now and again I'm threatened with eviction. Since I'm not a healthy person I've consulted the municipality about pensions but nothing has been taken seriously. (Sada)

> There are many handicapped people at Sahlumbe who are entitled to disability grants but are not getting them. Some do not know that they are qualified. Some have applied but never got them. Old age

pensioners are not getting the pensions to which they are entitled. Some have not applied because they have to go to Ezakheni magistrate's office to apply, about 35 kilometres away. One trip by bus costs R2. These old people do not have the money to go there to apply.

(Sahlumbe)

People also appear to depend heavily on an informal network of borrowing and support within the community.

When food is finished we are helped by our neighbours. We also help them sometimes. (Sada)

Diet

One of the questions on the SPP household questionnaire concerned diet. It was a difficult question to ask in most circumstances and the replies received sketched out only the broad dimensions of daily consumption patterns on a household basis; they did not distinguish between individual members of the household or give details of the quantities of food consumed. Nevertheless, the results are still extremely revealing: at a crude aggregate level they highlight the material difference between areas in terms of household income and provide a rough indication of poverty levels.

In all survey areas the staple diet was noticeably deficient in protein foods and greens. Starch — maize in the African areas; bread, rice, potatoes and some maize in the non-African areas — formed by far the largest part of the daily diet. Tea, coffee and sugar also featured daily in most households. However, while the general standard of nutrition was poor in all 21 areas (relocation and threatened) the degree of malnutrition varied quite considerably. In some areas people lived almost entirely on mealie meal; in others there was greater variety in the diet.

As would be expected, the more money is brought back into a community, the better the average nutrition levels in that community are likely to be. Thus, in the two group area townships, the frequency and range of supplementary foodstuffs other than the starch staple was found to be greater than in any of the African relocation areas; within the African areas, the worst-off in terms of diet were the most depressed closer settlements of Sahlumbe, Kammaskraal and Glenmore and the township of Sada.

Taking meat consumption as an index of nutrition levels, SPP found that meat was eaten regularly by most households in group area townships but only sparsely in the African areas, in some hardly ever. While 50% of the Atlantis sample reported eating meat daily and 40% at Phoenix reported eating it at least twice a week, only a handful of the most privileged households ate meat regularly in the African areas, with 50% at Mdantsane, 58% at Pampierstad, 67% at Sada, 70% at Glenmore and 78% at Kammaskraal reporting that they ate it less than once a week, and fully 92% at Sahlumbe reporting that they ate it less than once a month. The consumption of eggs, milk and greens followed a similar pattern, ranging from poor to totally inadequate across the spectrum from group area townships to the most isolated and depressed closer settlements.

In terms of diet the two black spots of Matiwane's Kop and Mathopestad can be placed at the upper end of the spectrum: a finding that can be explained entirely by the access of households in these areas to agricultural land. Although, as already pointed out, agricultural activity in these areas counts only as a supplement to and not as the basis of household income, nevertheless it makes a significant contribution to the average standard of living. Daily meat consumption at Matiwane's Kop is, at 16% of all households surveyed, the highest for any of the African areas in the SPP sample — higher even than at Inanda Newtown which in many respects is one of the most favoured African areas from the point of view of economic standing. Consumption of milk, eggs and greens in these areas compares favourably with that in the relocation townships as well, as detailed case studies of these areas made clear. Nowhere is the economic significance of the agricultural land still available to black spot households shown up more clearly than in the comparative data on diet in the SPP surveys, since, in terms of employment levels and dependency on migrant labour, most black spots do not differ substantially from most closer settlements.

This is not to say that agricultural productivity is high in black spots: in most cases fields are small and yields low, while fertility and the quality of the soil are declining alarmingly. It does mean, though, that given the severe constraints on African mobility and employment opportunities under apartheid, a rural family on a black spot is likely to enjoy a higher standard of living than a rural family in a closer settlement. The tenacious attachment of rural Africans to land is not simply a psychological or sociological phenomenon; it is a matter of basic economics, an issue totally ignored by the government in its development of the 'closer settlement' as a substitute for urbanisation.

4. Organisation and attitudes

The experience of relocation confirms in many people the belief that they cannot exercise any control over their lives or the lives of their families. The dominant mood in relocation areas is often one of passivity and helplessness in the face of the enormous problems that confront the people. Organisation is generally (though not always) poor, particularly in the most isolated areas. Relocation can thus be seen as a process of disorganisation as well as dispossession.

The anger and frustration of the community is not harnessed in the struggle against often appalling conditions but turned inwards. The grievances of the household are directed against its neighbours, or against other newcomers engaged in the competition for scarce resources. 'I am only a woman', said one person interviewed at Kwaggafontein in reply to the question, 'What do you intend to do about your problems?'

> Perhaps you could ask the men what they intend to do. In any case there's little that can be done. People here simply don't care. They don't have time to think about these things. During the week they are away at work. During the weekend they are dead drunk.

Her attitude was echoed by a person at Mahodi:

> We can't do anything about it. Initially, people were even talking about getting back, but nobody talks like that today . . . . People get used to hardships.

One of the most frequent responses to an SPP question asking people who they felt would help them with their problems was, 'GG — they put us here, they must do something.' This attitude cropped up all over the country.

> We expect the government should help us because we cannot do

> anything without their intervention, for they brought us here.
> (Sada)
>
> The South African government brought us here, we are their responsibility and they should solve the problem. (Rooigrond)
>
> We expect the whites to help us because they took us to this place and dumped us like animals. (Kammaskraal)

This attitude was never expressed with any real expectation of help. Its counterpart was the equally common response of 'Nothing', 'I don't know'.

> Who could help, because we are here by force and all we said was not considered properly by GG, so who could help? I don't see any person, unless he is involved in trouble. (Ezakheni)

Here and there people are struggling to break out of the shackles of isolation and poverty. 'If the men of this place are organised like other places then our problems would be solved', observed one person who was interviewed at Sahlumbe in Natal.

Among the 'other places' is Ezakheni, in Natal, where the community organised a major bus boycott. Most of the people of Ezakheni were involved and displayed an impressive degree of solidarity and commitment over several weeks. When people are forced to live at a great distance from their work, the high cost of transport is one issue around which community organisation is readily mobilised.

The overall impression formed by SPP, however, was that community organisation was very weak, particularly in the rural areas. Progressive leadership was lacking and people appeared to be locked into local structures of control without the capacity to challenge these.

One of the consequences of this helplessness is the deeply engrained pessimism that SPP encountered in many areas surveyed. With pessimism, though, went stoicism and a remarkable ability to endure. This could be seen both as a source of strength — people do manage to cope, and to adapt — and as a source of weakness. People accept the unacceptable — they 'get used to hardships' as the person interviewed at Mahodi put it.

It should not be concluded that responses to removal are uniform. They are coloured by the experiences people bring with them from their previous situations. For those fleeing the persecution of the 'YB' in Winterveld or in Thaba Nchu, for example, the relocation area may appear as a refuge despite the poor conditions.

A woman who was interviewed at Kwaggafontein in KwaNdebele struck a qualified ethnic note:

> Here we are almost exclusively Ndebele. At Stinkwater we were tribally mixed. Although there are advantages in being mixed like that, I am happier like this.

People who have moved off white farms are sometimes relieved to have escaped oppressive conditions there. An interviewee in Dimbaza:

> This is a location under blacks and the last place is a farm under a white farmer who does not take the blacks as people but as tools to make him rich.

And someone at Sahlumbe commented:

> The only difference is that before my family was under a farmer's rule, therefore being exploited by the farmer. So it's a little better here.

Other farmworkers displayed a more ambivalent attitude towards their relocation:

> It is better here because we are not under the rule of white farmers. But the poverty then was not like it is now. Before, I had land to farm and enough livestock.

For those who have never had a house before, a site in a relocation area may represent a security previously unknown:

> We no longer stay as lodgers but pay rent for our house. We are no longer under threat of being evicted. (Sada)

5. Conclusions

The issues at stake in relocation areas are far more fundamental than, for example, the level of facilities available. The relocation of African people into the bantustans is part of a policy aimed at dispossessing people not simply of their land or their houses, but of their South African citizenship and their claim to political rights. This process of exclusion cannot be made good by any number of taps or clinics, as hundreds of thousands of people already relocated into Transkei, Ciskei, Bophuthatswana and Venda can testify.

More significant, too, than the degree of material deprivation suffered by the people moved into relocation areas are the damaging social and psychological effects inflicted on communities and individuals.

It also needs to be emphasised that conditions in relocation areas are, on average, no worse than those found in established bantustan communities. In several instances they may well be better. After several years even the worst relocation settlements begin to resemble other non-relocation bantustan communities, at least physically. At this point, the more significant divide is not whether an area is a relocation area or not, but whether it is relatively close to or relatively remote from the urban-industrial network across the bantustan borders. Relocation townships are in this respect better off than non-relocation rural villages. Closer settlements merge into the general landscape of poverty, poor facilities and hardship in the rural areas. The most important difference between closer settlements and other non-relocation rural areas is undoubtedly the lack of land. However, given the high level of landlessness in the bantustans as a whole, even this difference is not an absolute one. To focus attention only on conditions in relocation areas can obscure the widespread lack of clean and adequate water, of sanitary living conditions, of schools and clinics in the bantustans as a whole. It can mask the general landlessness, poverty and unemployment in South Africa's black rural areas.

CHAPTER TEN

Siyabuswa:
*We are controlled**

> Unlike other places where people are forced to go, Ndebeles come here voluntarily. At their own expense they start putting up their little houses. We're trying to keep up with the demand for facilities. But they are satisfied. They accept it. They could be compared with the Israelis — they just come. (P C Vercueil, Secretary for the Department of the Chief Minister, KwaNdebele, in *Sunday Tribune*, 30 May 82.)

> [It simply shows that] if we develop the heartlands, there will be a natural flow to the national states. In the past we really failed disgracefully. (Hennie van der Walt, Deputy Minister of Land Affairs, in response to release of SPP Report, *Vaderland*, 17 June 83, translated from the original Afrikaans.)

Relocation is a central support of the bantustans, and thus of the apartheid structure. By way of illustration, this concluding chapter begins by contrasting two bantustans, KwaNdebele and Bophuthatswana. They are both products of apartheid. Despite apparent differences they are closely interrelated. KwaNdebele is literally growing as a consequence of removals from Bophuthatswana. The relationship between the two bantustans shows how ethnicity is encouraged and manipulated to extend government control.

Soon another quarter of a million people will be stripped of their South African citizenship. Unlike the Chief Minister of the area, Skosana, who has confessed that he does not know what independence will bring, some Ndebele people have clearer if not very sanguine expectations:

> Water is a big problem here, but [my husband] and I have another problem. We don't know how long we shall stay here, for it seems

---

* Siyabuswa is also the name of the capital of KwaNdebele.

sooner or later KwaNdebele will opt for independence. We are thinking of building but there is no sense in it if we are going to move again.
(SPP interview, 1981, Vol.5, p268.)

The 100 000 North Sotho people who live in Moutse are angry and bitter over its proposed inclusion in KwaNdebele. Conflict is growing. The Chief Minister of Lebowa, Dr C N Phatudi, told a cheering crowd that

> 'Moutse is part of Lebowa, it is our home and nobody will rob us of our home. We don't want to move from Moutse. We will stay here as we want to remain here . . . . But now the central government wants to cause a rift between the two tribes who have been living side by side in peace for a long time.' Dr Phatudi warned the people of Moutse not to discriminate and said that everybody, irrespective of ethnic affiliations, was welcome in Lebowa. (*Lebowa Times*, 13 May 83.)

Bophuthatswana provides a useful comparison with KwaNdebele. 'Independent' since 1977, Bophuthatswana has a greater proportion of its GDP generated within its borders than any other bantustan. Of the 'independent' bantustans, Bophuthatswana is the least repressive (it has a Bill of Rights based on the West German model) and it is unwilling to accept thousands of relocated people. Nevertheless, the interdependence of KwaNdebele with Bophuthatswana, despite the latter's public adoption of a Bill of Rights, shows how apartheid South Africa is developing. One bantustan chases people out through pressure. Another welcomes the victims who are said to flock to it willingly.

Despite its rhetorical rejection Bophuthatswana has accepted bantustan policy and continues to legitimise it. At the International Housing Conference held in Cape Town in October 1979, Chief Minister Lucas Mangope said:

> Greater than ever is the promise of reaching consensus on the need of joining together to build a constellation of states, in which each independent member nation shall enjoy the same home privileges as its peers. (*Housing in South Africa*, Jan. 80.)

Bophuthatswana may have modified its enthusiasm for the constellation concept over the years, yet it still propagates the myth of independence in 'development' rhetoric. While acknowledging variation in bantustan policies from the crudely repressive to 'enlightened', many observers, including the South African correspondent of the *New York Times*, elevate Bophutatswana as an example of a 'good' bantustan. The *Cape Times* sings Bophuthatswana's praises in an editorial:

> In Bophuthatswana Chief Mangope said the principal benefit of independence was freedom from racial discrimination. He delighted in helping to evolve a non-racial society and said South Africa's continuing racism made the country a doomed anachronism. He also rejected the idea of any political cooperation with South Africa, including the Nationalist dream of a constellation of states in the region.
> (*Cape Times*, 9 Dec. 82.)

In view of Bophuthatswana's poor record in dealing with black non-Tswanas, this picture is misleading. The people who fled under 'the sarcasms of the YB' from Kromdraai to Onverwacht would question whether non-racialism in Bophuthatswana extends beyond the grounds of Sun City and a few other enclaves. The thousands of people who have had to leave Winterveld for the desolate dumping ground of KwaNdebele, and have been denied social services such as pensions and business licences because they are not Tswana, would also disagree. As a Winterveld resident said:

> When independence came, we thought Mangope would welcome us, but he kept saying we must go away. (SPP, Vol. 5, p317.)

The authorities exert pressures to persuade non-Tswanas to leave Winterveld. Non-Tswanas who cannot get work permits from the Bophuthatswana authorities are told by the Department of Cooperation and Development to go to 'their' bantustan. They do not want to take Bophuthatswana citizenship, even if they could in practice, as they do not want to lose South African citizenship and the right to work in South Africa. Education, which they value highly, constitutes another pressure. As mentioned in Chapter 6, Tswana is the only medium of instruction allowed in official schools.

But leaving the insecurity of Winterveld offers them little more. Most go to KwaNdebele where the conditions are far worse, with the added disadvantage that it is further from work. Harassed out of Bophuthatswana, many are relieved to go to another bantustan. According to the Minister of Development and of Land Affairs, '200 000 people entered KwaNdebele of their own free will.' (*Hansard*, Col. 8735, 6 June 83.) They had no choice. They left as a result of ethnic conflict which was caused by the creation of Bophuthatswana. They found refuge in another creation of bantustan policy — KwaNdebele.

The government admits that its relocation policy has been a failure in the past. But if we consider this large-scale traffic in population between two bantustans, it is clear that the age of forced removals is by no means over. Ethnic criteria become as emphatic a theme of relocation as racial criteria. It is fatuous, if not disingenuous, to point to an improvement in black-white relations in Bophuthatswana while ignoring the violation of human rights in the differential treatment of Tswana and non-Tswana inhabitants of the region.

In the preceding chapters relocation was examined in terms of numbers moved and under threat, regional variation, history and reasons for relocation, how it is done, how it is resisted, and what conditions are like. Now we aim to summarise the present situation and in the process to draw out some of the trends. We discuss changing government strategies and how the people affected are likely to respond.

The scope of relocation

Since 1960 three and a half million removals have taken place and a further two million are proposed in terms of present government policy. The establishment of KwaNdebele alone will involve more than 100 000 Sotho people being forced to move off land to make it available for another ethnic group, the Ndebele. The vast scale of removals cannot be described in terms of statistics alone. The extent of social engineering, and the disruption of families, lifestyles and means of survival, is enormous. A future majority-elected government will be faced with nationwide reconstruction. It will have to devise an entirely new urbanisation and industrial development policy in order to redress the imbalances between urban and rural and between black and white areas.

Among those who have moved in the last two decades, farm

workers make up the largest category. Some were evicted and others left poor conditions on white-owned farms. There is only one legal option for them — to go to the bantustans. Unlike farm workers in most parts of the world who migrate to urban areas when they become redundant, these people are subjected to influx control.

Group area relocation is the second largest category, involving some 860 000 removals around the country. Most of the planned group area removals are complete. However, one or two areas may still be reprieved.

Cape Town's quarter of a million African residents constitute the largest single community threatened with removal. If the implementation of this grand plan seems impossible, it should be remembered that over the last quarter of a century 200 000 people have been moved, family by family, out of Cape Town to group areas.

Relocation is a descriptive term, covering various categories and historical periods. The categories of relocation outlined in Chapter 2 are not necessarily discrete. Many people have been moved in terms of a number of interlinked categories. For instance, those moved off black spots are sent to bantustans as the government tidies bits of black-owned land into consolidated 'national states'. Many have been moved more than once as different government departments require the land, or as policy changes. Many who have already been moved by the central government are threatened with removal by the bantustan authorities. For example, the people relocated to Glenmore are under threat of removal within Ciskei to Peddie. There they will compete for water, land and jobs with the local Peddie people and those moved in 1982 from Kammaskraal. When conflict arises the official explanation will be 'faction fights': the real reason will be that too many people have been crowded into too poor an area where they are in conflict over too few resources.

Most relocation sites are far away from the cities, down dirt roads and beyond hills. The only people who are familiar with them are those who live there and the officials who control them. Not even official maps record the names, and there are few road signs. Other sites are on the edge of urban areas beyond the city limits — Soweto outside Johannesburg, Atlantis outside Cape Town and Phoenix outside Durban.

Some areas are less accessible owing to strict control. The level of repression is so harsh in the Ciskei, for instance, that it is almost impossible to undertake research there. Nevertheless, SPP proved that relocation sites in the remote bantustans are accessible to outsiders who are determined to find them. Finding one's way around can be eventful — and very educational. One day while travelling in Bophuthatswana, three SPP fieldworkers stopped a man walking along the road to ask him the name of the adjoining settlement. 'Fokfontein', he said. 'Oh, what's the Tswana name?' 'I don't know — they just call it Fokfontein', he replied.

Information was difficult to obtain for this project. Not only is it hard to find accurate official figures, but the information is deliberately obscured by changes of categories or borders. In some cases the central government no longer takes responsibility for relocation areas since they have been incorporated into the bantustans. Questions may no longer be answered in parliament because the areas are said to be part of another country, and South Africa cannot meddle in the affairs of other countries! With the new secrecy clause in the Laws on Cooperation and Development Act of 1982, information will be even more difficult to obtain.

Relocation is becoming an increasingly sensitive issue. Even the SABC, mouthpiece of the government, finds it difficult to involve officials in open debate. In a Radio Today programme on forced removals on 26 July 1983, the producers announced that the Minister of Cooperation and Development had refused to take part. (However, interestingly, they did feel that the subject was important enough to proceed without official participation. Helen Suzman MP and a member of the Daggakraal community — under threat of removal in the Eastern Transvaal — were interviewed despite the Minister's refusal to participate.)

Conditions

Dust, wind, long distances, isolation, extremes of heat and cold, environmental degradation . . . these are the overwhelming impressions of SPP fieldworkers after thousands of kilometres of travelling through bantustans. The contrast between white farming areas such as the irrigated, green Groblersdal valley with the dustbowls of neighbouring Lebowa and KwaNdebele are the most stark. Even in areas experiencing the worst drought in decades, the white-owned farms have patches of irrigated fields and subsidised cattle feed. Such relief for black farmers as exists is often allocated on the basis of political affiliations. For instance, it has been reported that in the Ciskei only members of the Ciskei National Independence Party are given drought aid.

The land
As the bantustans become little more than large relocation sites, and drought and irresponsible farming methods take their toll, parts of the South African countryside are fast turning into a desert. But environmental degradation is not evident only in bantustans. Sheet erosion is common in the OFS and Northern Cape. Where land is ploughed before the rains, much of the top soil blows away. Where season after season vast expanses are planted with one crop alone, the land is depleted. The implications of this large-scale abuse of the earth pose major problems for the future reconstruction of South Africa.

While the bantustans are generally described as 'rural areas', this is not strictly accurate. The rapid growth of South Africa's black population is being channelled from the white metropolitan areas to the bantustans. Mass population removals into the bantustans cause severe pressure on the land. The very high population density makes agricultural activity impossible for the majority of people. They have no access to land outside a residential plot in a closer settlement or rural township. Migrant workers cannot take their families to urban areas. Economically active but unemployed people cannot leave the bantustans to look for work in urban areas. These are the people who live in closer settlements and relocation townships throughout the bantustans.

The 'new cities'
Planners say that ten cities the size of Soweto will be needed to house the black population by the turn of the century. They are already being built, often by the people themselves, in the bantustans. Settlements like Onverwacht, Ezakheni, Itsoseng, Mdantsane are growing all around the country. Urbanisation is being displaced to the bantustans. The government recognises this. Rather than trying to prevent urbanisation, it directs the process

to the bantustans. Dr Koornhof was reported as saying that the number of proclaimed townships in bantustans had grown from three to 90 over the past 20 years. The population of those townships is now about two million. The decentralisation plans form an economic base for political 'self-determination for the national states'. (Editorial comment, *Radio Today*, 7 Oct. 83.)

While it is difficult to measure suffering, one can identify the worst conditions in relocation areas as those in the bantustan territories of the Cape — Bophuthatswana in the north and Ciskei in the east. Thousands of people have been settled on land which previously supported a handful of white farmers.

Water shortage is a major theme in the relocation crisis: the dams and boreholes that have dried up, the supplies trucked in (sometimes by the SADF) to many areas, the hours that women and children spend fetching water kilometres distant, the buses that people have to catch to fetch clean water in parts of Kangwane.

Repression and resistance

Levels of repression and control vary from one bantustan to another. It is widely accepted that Ciskei and Venda are the most brutally repressive — but compared with other bantustans Ciskei has more press coverage, and it may be that the extent of repression is not reported from other areas. Some bantustans are publicly quite liberal. There are also differences between formal and informal means of control. Resistance to repression varies too. In some areas there is more organised resistance and the level of awareness is greater than elsewhere. To maintain their control, therefore, some bantustan authorities need to be more directly repressive than others.

The view from the bantustans

The bantustans are powerless to oppose relocation. As with KwaNdebele and Bophuthatswana, their very existence depends on participating in removals. Despite their stated disapproval of relocation, people are evicted and moved within the bantustans. For example, Bophuthatswana officials have told a community outside Mafikeng to leave their village as a Tswana tourist village is to be built there. On the other hand, the Transkei has managed to refuse to accept removed people. In response to Administration Board attempts to endorse Crossroads residents out of the Western Cape, the Transkei Consul in Cape Town said:

> [We] wish to make it quite clear that the Transkei government and its consul in Cape Town will not, at any stage, be party to any move that will uproot people from the Western Cape. (*Cape Times*, 13 Oct. 83.)

Because there are two Xhosa-speaking bantustans, the Transkei is allowed to get away with such a stand. At times it has prevented deportation by denying that the people concerned were Transkeians. But the central government is not disturbed by their refusal to accept these people. It merely sends all Xhosa-speaking people to Ciskei, which accepts them.

Like Bophuthatswana, KwaZulu and the others, Transkei participates in the relocation process by moving people within its boundaries to other Transkeian sites in the name of betterment and squatter clearance.

Corruption and bureaucracy

Stories of corruption are not uncommon. Some pension pay-out clerks in KwaZulu are said to pocket money once they have made the pensioner sign a receipt for it. All over, those in slightly better positions are able to take advantage of the elderly, of the illiterate, of inexperienced ex-farm workers, of those desperate for employment. The vast mass of South African blacks are used to obeying officials whether black or white. They can therefore easily be manipulated by petty clerks who are given discretionary powers. Few people have the stomach to challenge the bantustan hierarchy, backed by awesome support from Pretoria.

Facilities and housing

We have seen in the last chapter that facilities vary according to how the government ranks those it relocates: coloureds and Indians get more than Africans; urban people more than rural; the employed more than the unemployed; industrial workers more than agricultural workers. As well as serving the economy, these distinctions have a 'divide and rule' function which strengthens government control.

The type and quality of housing varies across the country. While formal housing is provided in relocation townships, it is not available in rural closer settlements. In rural parts of the Ciskei 'tomato-box' wooden plank houses are the most common, in KwaZulu and other parts tin Fletcraft huts are provided. In some cases people were loaned tents on arrival or were given no shelter at all. Then they had to build their own huts, shacks and houses. In Kangwane and parts of Gazankulu few toilets were seen. People complained that they had to use the bushes as no toilets had been provided. Not surprisingly, the most serious cholera outbreaks in the country have been reported from these areas.

Generally group area relocation sites enjoy the best conditions. But most of the people living there have been moved from central urban areas: their new situation strikes them as worse than what they have left behind. They compare themselves with whites in urban areas, not Africans in bantustans.

Loss of land
Many people moved from rural areas lost the use of small plots of land which they had cultivated — or kept small stock like chickens on — in order to supplement their incomes. Reduced now to a total dependence on cash incomes, they complain of the cost of living when everything must be paid for:

> You have to pay for everything here — for fuel, for food, rent and taxes, even for a place to be buried.

Employment and unemployment
We have seen that the further relocated people are from metropolitan and white urban areas, the more employment opportunities recede. Some labour recruitment centres in the more remote parts of Gazankulu, Venda and Transkei have actually closed down. Others offer a handful of jobs per week to unemployed men and women. People who come from 'independent' rather than non-'independent' bantustans are worse off. They are regarded as foreigners and on that account have more difficulty finding work. Yet not all distant relocation sites are simply dumping grounds for the unemployed. Certain farmers in the Western Transvaal, or the owners of asbestos mines in the

Northern Cape — for example — would recruit a labour force from the distant Transkei rather than local workers who can decamp more easily if working conditions are unacceptable. Other farmers favour the practice of trucking in seasonal labour — including children — from next-door bantustans at cash wages which sink as low as R1 a day, or payment in kind. They can do this because former farm workers are the most vulnerable of relocated people.

While employment levels in the relocation townships surveyed by SPP are similar to those for Africans nationally, the level of exploitation is higher. In terms of the decentralisation proposals no minimum wages are enforced. Women especially are vulnerable to exploitation, since their inability to leave their families means that they cannot pursue the alternative of contract work.

> It is necessary for employment opportunities to be created not only for the men, but also for the Black women. Industrialists have already told me that they have found that Black women are far more reliable workers than Black men because Black women are interested in the future of their children. They stay away from work less often and fewer of them are interested in participating in strikes.
> (V A Volker, MP, *Hansard*, Col. 8679, 6 June 83.)

The absence of money

The sheer absence of cash in circulation in relocation areas inevitably lowers the standard of living. We have seen that informal economic activity has little prospect of establishing a viable base. Remittances from migrants and government grants — mainly old age pensions — are what keep people going. Whole families are often forced to live off the pensions of grandparents. Grants to disabled people, unemployment insurance payouts and workmen's compensation barely featured in the households surveyed, which indicates that some of the available cash is simply not reaching those who are entitled to it and desperately need it. When funds dry up — a migrant loses a job, an old age pensioner dies — there is nothing in reserve. Traditionally, the use of land provided a last lifeline, but this is now denied to many who had it before they were moved.

The extent of deprivation

These poor material conditions cause major social and psychological deprivation. People moved from established homes in urban and rural areas, whether they are shacks or solid houses, have had to adjust to remarkably different circumstances. In some cases the sheer distances moved disorientate them. The elderly and the children, such as Jamangile Tsotsobe's grand-daughter, are worst affected. They cannot understand what has happened, or why. People who are removed from their homes without their consent, let alone their choice, suffer a degree of abuse that is impossible to quantify. Their basic human right of control over their own lives has been denied.

Organisation around material issues — notably bus boycotts — has helped some become actors rather than simply victims in their society, but most people remain deeply apathetic and pessimistic. Their very endurance, fatalistic as it may be, is the only positive response they make to the process of disorganisation and dispossession.

How it happened

Chapters 3 and 4 detailed the background to apartheid policy and the relocation programme specifically. To keep political power and wealth in white hands, the government needed to control the flow and location of black labour. It adopted a policy of restricted urbanisation. On one hand, this curbed the growing movement for majority rule which was based in the towns. On the other, it allowed just enough workers to enter urban areas for the needs of the economy.

Land segregation was entrenched in 1913. The 1936 Land Act extended the areas Africans were entitled to occupy and made provision for the control of those areas. The history chapters detail their development from 'native reserves' to 'bantustans'. This was the change in policy whereby land which had been allocated to Africans in general was reallocated to ten ethnic groups. Later the policy of 'self-determination' evolved into a programme of 'independence' for each ethnic group. In terms of the National States Citizenship Act of 1970 all African

South Africans became citizens of one of the bantustans. Subsequently four bantustans took 'independence' and the rest are being pressurised to follow suit.

In trying to reverse the flow of blacks to urban areas, the government began by flushing out the less economically productive. This surplus population which included the old, disabled, widows, women with children and the unemployed, was to be moved from white urban areas to bantustans. They cost too much to support in white South Africa. Further, the unemployed could become a threat to urban security.

In the 1960s and the 1970s people who were moved into the bantustans were forced into migrant labour. The migrancy rate rose faster than the rate of workers entering the labour market, because people who previously lived at home and went to work daily were forced to migrate. Next, the relocation programme promoted commuting rather than migrancy. The number of commuters rose faster than the natural increase in the work force. In the Huhudi case study it was pointed out that the government intends to encourage commuting rather than migrancy, so that workers can live with their families. Workers cannot, however, expect to live in white urban areas. They are forced to live in the bantustans and commute should they wish to live with their families. Industrialists are encouraged by generous incentives to set up on the borders of bantustans.

The government was also expected to respond to farmer's interests. While increased mechanisation in some places caused a surplus of labour, in other parts farmers complained of labour shortages. Legislation prohibiting labour and cash tenancy on farms was implemented locally as the need arose. With the final abolition of labour tenancy in August 1981, many thousands of people were evicted from the white-owned farms.

Restructuring apartheid

Since the nation-wide disturbances of 1976, the South African government has embarked on a programme of restructuring apartheid. Yet despite widespread talk of reform, apartheid is far from dead. It is entrenched in the new constitution. Race classification, separate group areas and the constructs of other major laws which exclude most South Africans from participating in the affairs of their country are all being maintained. The new constitution provides for three houses of parliament — one each for whites, coloureds and Indians. The proportion of members across the various houses is four whites to two coloureds to one Indian. Africans will have no representation at all. 'Black affairs' will be controlled by the president.

These constitutional proposals, which crown the reform effort, make it clear that the government is restructuring and not changing the policy. In response to pressures from all sides, it is trying to make existing means of control more sophisticated. On one hand it is attempting to soften the worst visible aspects of apartheid. On the other it is building repressive controls in the form of more powerful laws. It lost the support of the extreme right-wing when the Conservative Party was formed by breakaway Nationalists in 1982. And at the other end of the spectrum, black resistance has gathered momentum. Blacks have organised into trade unions and civic associations.

In the decade 1973 to 1983 there has been extensive organisation among black workers. At the same time the needs of industry have changed. More skilled labour is required. So the government has had to introduce a series of labour reforms which accommodate the growth of trade unionism among blacks and streamline the recruitment and training of black labour. Influx control continued as a fundamental means of controlling the flow of blacks from rural to urban areas. While thousands of people are desperate to leave the impoverished bantustans, there is less demand for cheap, unskilled labour. Thousands of untrained people need work to support their families. There are almost no employment opportunities outside the metropolitan areas, so they are forced to go to the cities. But with tightened influx control, they find it impossible to find 'legal' jobs. In 1979 fines were increased from R100 to R500 for the employer who hired unregistered labour. In terms of the proposed Orderly Movement Bill this would be increased to R5 000.

At the same time as keeping unqualified Africans out of urban areas, the government has embarked on a strategy to stabilise the urban working class. In comparison with the thousands of unemployed, South African black workers have become something of an elite. In fact many have managed to negotiate living wages as a result of trade union organisation. (Many more who are not members of trade unions have no protection against exploitation.) Further, there are thousands of people in the bantustans with no hope of employment. Compared with them, urban black workers are privileged. And the government is determined to entrench that privilege in an attempt to stabilise the urban workforce. The Orderly Movement Bill makes a clear distinction between Permanent Urban Residents (insiders) and those who do not qualify (outsiders). Outsiders will even be partly controlled by insiders who will be fined for harbouring unqualified people. Not only is the government attempting to coopt coloureds and Indians through the new constitution — it is also trying to coopt working class urban Africans through the Koornhof Bills.

Now that the government has managed to lock 53% of the African population into bantustans, it is determined to get those bantustans to take independence. Having lost South African citizenship, Africans no longer have any claim to political participation or economic wealth in South Africa. They have no right to social security in the country in which they have worked. They may be deported to a bantustan at any time without recourse to the courts. On top of all this, they have been divided into different ethnic groups. So their fight for survival is diverted. Opposition to apartheid which has united blacks is being broken by dividing them into ethnic units.

Apartheid is a process of exclusion and dispossession for the majority in South Africa. Divisions are created wherever possible. Those who are prevented from entering urban areas are divided from the other relatively privileged group of insiders with houses and jobs. Those in rural areas are further divided into ethnic units. Women are preferred as workers to men. The implication of this restructuring of apartheid will now be examined in terms of the relocation programme.

'No more forced removals'

As part of the restructuring programme there has been a slowdown in the removal of whole communities. The new emphasis is on 'voluntary' relocation. The term describes a more sophisticated set of long-term strategies designed to pressurise people into moving themselves. The goals of white domination and control have by no means been abandoned, but new strategies of implementation are evident.

However, whether this trend will continue is debatable. In 1978, referring to the Citizenship Act, Connie Mulder said that there would be 'no more black South Africans'. But the new 'foreigners' have proved unwilling to move from white South Africa. So now Dr Koornhof has qualified his 1981 promise of 'no more forced removals' by adding 'where practicable and possible'. Furthermore, in 1983 even the special case of Crossroads came under heavy physical and verbal attacks. Dr Morrison's statement which threatened Crossroads took the issue back five years.

What can be concluded from these apparently contradictory developments is that the policy is not being implemented uniformly. While some categories of removals such as black spots are treated with more caution and less direct force, there is certainly a concerted effort to enforce influx control and eliminate informal settlements. The government is determined to prevent African urbanisation outside the bantustans, using blatant force if necessary.

Influx control

Only those who qualify may live in urban areas. In future they will stay not by right, but by permit.

If the bantustans offered a viable standard of living, many people would stay there. Influx control would not be necessary if the bantustan policy was successful. There would be no need to extend controls on movement from rural to urban areas. But as Chapter 9 showed, conditions in the bantustans are so poor that people are forced to go to urban areas to survive.

Over the past few years influx control has been tightened and there is talk of more controls. According to a newspaper report a cabinet working committee is focussing on comprehensive influx control strategies. (*Sunday Times,* 2 Oct. 83.) Apparently this has nothing to do with the 'Disorderly Bill' which is still under review. Although that particular Bill was withdrawn for redrafting, the government has made it clear that it intends increasing influx control. The Bill can be expected to reappear in one form or another.

Furthermore, even in those categories where a slowdown can be seen, there is no fundamental shift away from a determination to remove as many people as possible. As the woman from Crossroads said, '[Dr Koornhof] came to separate the people, but in a decent way.' Before 1979 people were simply moved. Now there is 'consultation' which is an attempt to coopt the leaders. The planning committees established around the country include officials and representatives from the communities. Even concerned outsiders have been conned into assisting the government in removals. The discussion is on how, not whether, they will take place. The government is 'motivating people to move voluntarily'. But if, as the Bakwena of Mogopa were told, they refuse to move voluntarily, they will be moved by GG trucks. In reply to several pleas for reprieves, government officials have stated categorically that their 'hands are tied' and 'the law was passed in Parliament and that cannot be changed'. But as Helen Suzman said in the Cooperation and Development debate in 1983: 'National Party policy does not come down from the mount. The government can change it.' (*Hansard*, Col. 854, 1 Feb. 83).

Nevertheless there has been a measurable slowing down in the pace of large-scale community removals. Contradictory pressures are forcing the government to concentrate on short-term measures of control. As more desperate people continue to flock to urban areas in search of work and facilities, the government insists that these should only be available to them in the bantustans. But at the same time as the brutal clampdown on unqualified Africans in white urban areas, there are delays in implementing bantustan plans such as consolidation.

Bantustan consolidation
> They want to force people into a homeland which people don't want. They don't even know where it is, and it will cost between R80 and R85 billion to create. (P W Botha, regaling Nationalists at a public meeting in Pretoria with the ludicrousness of CP policy to create a homeland for coloureds. *Sunday Tribune*, 18 Sept. 83.)

Meanwhile over a million people remain to be moved in terms of NP policy to create homelands. They are Africans. And policy dictates that Africans must exercise their political rights in 'homelands'. But the NP knows that the creation of bantustans is expensive and involves force in getting and moving people there. The implementation of this policy poses many problems for them. According to the Deputy Minister of Development and of Land Affairs:

> One of the principles accepted by the government some years ago was that however ideal geographic consolidation was, it was not essential for a confederation of states to succeed. So black spots would only be moved where 'practically necessary' and 'absolutely essential'. An example quoted was Driefontein (Eastern Transvaal) where a dam is being built and the whole settlement would be inundated.
> Another reason was that removals purely for geographic consolidation in the fulfilment of ideological reasons 'was as dead as a dodo', said Mr van der Walt.
> The most important aspect of the new approach was that it fits in with government plans for regional development and decentralisation of economic activity. (*Vaderland*, 17 June 83, translated from the original Afrikaans.)

As a result there has been a move away from 'land consolidation' to 'people consolidation'. Increasingly government officials see economic and political separation through citizenship control as more important than obtaining continuous pieces of black and white areas on the map. This ties in with the decentralisation plans. Africans will live in one country and work in another. In no other country would there be serious criticism of a decentralisation policy. In South Africa, however, this policy is made by representatives of a minority group with the majority having no part in that decision although they are most affected by the policy. They are the ones moved. Their choice is between starvation in the bantustans and the possibility of a poorly paid job in an industry near a relocation township.

This shift in the consolidation programme, in which economic motives supersede ideological ones, has not been smooth. Various proposals were presented in 1972, in 1973 and again in 1975. According to the 1975 proposals, consolidation accounts for the largest group of people still threatened with removal. Many removals have been completed already. The Gatlhose-Maremane reserves in the Northern Cape, Reserve 6 in Natal, and the black spots of Putfontein and Rooijantjiesfontein among others in the Western Transvaal have been cleared. However, it would seem that the 1984 proposals will differ from the 1975 proposals. There has been no recent talk of removals in some areas such as Manyeding, south of the Vryburg/Kuruman road, which were to be excised in terms of the 1975 proposals. Other areas have been reprieved, for example Sinthumule/Kutama, Sekgosese and Mokerong 1, all in the Northern Transvaal. Proposals for KwaNdebele and Ciskei were released in 1983. There has been a reformulation of land proposals which are scheduled for release in 1984.

The government is still determined to move black spots but its priorities have changed. It seems to be intent on making the 'independent' bantustans more viable, and has concentrated on Bophuthatswana and Ciskei land claims in the 1980s. The vast majority of people to be moved into Bophuthatswana were moved in the early 1970s. A handful of black spots in the Western Transvaal remain to be removed. Pretoria has allocated more land to the Ciskei at Frankfort and has begun the 'motivational' process of trying to persuade people from the seven remaining black spots in the corridor between Ciskei and Transkei to move 'voluntarily'. The third report of the Le Roux Committee dealt with KwaNdebele. This is a priority because it is willing to take 'independence'. Next, the release of the Bophuthatswana report can be expected. Reports on the non-independent bantustans are likely to take more time.

Three main reasons for the delays can be isolated: limited finance, opposition from right-wing whites, and opposition from threatened communities. A further related factor is international pressure.

Limited finance

> Today shifting people is a very expensive undertaking associated with much criticism. (Piet Koornhof, press release, 6 June 83.)

Grandiose consolidation schemes cost vast amounts to implement. An estimate of R6 000 million was made by Hennie van der Walt when he chaired the Commission on Cooperation and Development. (*Natal Mercury*, 5 Sept. 80.) An indication of how limited available funds are was given by Deputy Minister Morrison when he was asked about facilities for the Bathurst people under threat of removal:

But you know we are going to improve the whole bloody system when funds are made available.   *(Eastern Province Herald, 10 June 82.)*

The South African Defence Force is fighting a very expensive war in Namibia. Defence expenditure also has to be increased for the internal maintenance of apartheid against the onslaught of the military wing of the ANC. Not only has South Africa been fighting a regional war with incursions into Angola, Namibia, Mozambique and Lesotho, but it is also fighting South Africans in a civil war. With the economy in recession this puts further pressures on a limited budget.

As inflation increases at approximately 15% each year, it becomes more expensive for the government to buy out and compensate white farmers for consolidation. Many of these farmers have joined the Conservative Party. They no longer support the government and so demand even more money than they would have a few years ago.

Right-wing opposition
The Conservative Party's support comes mainly from rural constituencies in the Transvaal. Many of these areas include land which is scheduled for incorporation into one of the six Transvaal bantustans. On one hand CP supporters are determined to see all Africans living in bantustans. On the other hand, when their particular farms are to be incorporated, they demand high compensation. They have accused the government of trying to abolish their constituencies through its consolidation of the bantustans.

Consolidation is an important issue for agricultural unions around the country. Conflicts at central government level are often reflected in agricultural union debates. The unions support consolidation to minimise border areas with bantustans. (Industrialists have opposite interests — the more borders, the more commuters they have.) Farmers complain of stock and crop theft and degradation of the land. Yet the agricultural unions have also had to deal with members whose individual interests are threatened. They may not want to give up their farms. Some farmers' associations have lobbied behind the unions' backs to have other areas consolidated rather than their own. Clashes then arise within a provincial union where the different regions have different interests.

While local farmers' concerns do not always coincide with party policy, the government is pressurised by both the CP and the PFP:

According to the CP no removals are taking place, while the PFP lay into me because so many removals are taking place. (Minister of Cooperation and Development, *Hansard*, Col. 8785, 7 June 83)

Resistance from other whites to relocation proposals has also played a role. In the case of urban removals in the Northern Cape, white townspeople protested because they were worried about the loss of labour and of consumer spending. In other areas some whites have protested in moral support of the threatened communities.

Popular response

The third element accounting for the recent slowdown of removals for consolidation purposes is the 'unwillingness' of people to move. Although resistance is far from being widespread and militant, it is growing. There is strong determination in many communities to stay where they are. They employ various tactics which were discussed in Chapter 8. So long as the government claims that it does not force people to move, it will have to deal with this resistance. At times the new tactics of division and cooption work. It is doubtful whether this will last in the longer run as people begin to see through these strategies.

The power of the government makes its task of relocating millions of people relatively straightforward. It has laws, policemen, soldiers, informers, resources and information on its side. In contrast, the people it wants to move are largely powerless. The majority are rural, isolated and vulnerable. Many are old or unemployed and have young children to care for. They are confused and easily intimidated.

When reprieves are granted to communities under threat of removal, this often works to keep people isolated. For instance, a year after their reprieve a woman from Sekgosese asked, 'Are they really still moving people?' She thought the government had changed its policy. She did not know that Sekgosese was an exception.

The extent to which the government is forced to negotiate with people under threat of removal depends firstly on the community's level of unity and organisation. Secondly, the extent of publicity for the community's stand is important. With conservative governments in both the United Kingdom and the United States of America in the 1980s there has been less pressure on the South African government to reform such components of apartheid as forced removals. Western pressure may mean more difficulty in obtaining international loans or trade. This worries the South African business community. In turn it exerts pressure on the South African government to reform its more blatant restrictive measures. Because international attention is usually focused on one community under threat at a particular time, it is relatively easy for the government to deflect criticism by withdrawing and waiting until the limelight falls elsewhere in the world. Rarely has focus on an individual community helped its long-term plight, as policy remains unchanged. Only exceptions and delays have resulted.

Whether resistance is widespread or not, it is slowing the relocation programme. Several communities are forcing the government to change its approach. Together with financial and political pressures, public opinion is also forcing the government to reassess it tactics. Of the three factors, resistance will become the most critical for the government.

Where is the policy going?

Despite the slowdown in certain areas, policy has not been changed fundamentally. Rather it has been reformulated in response to the above factors.

> I readily admit that we made mistakes in the past. So much so that black communities had to be moved by force and often resettled in critical circumstances. Our biggest mistake was that we did not undertake these resettlement actions in cooperation with the black authorities. A lack of consultation between the government and the black people concerned led to numerous unfortunate incidents.
>
> In 1980 the then Commission for Cooperation and Development found that the resettlement of people where only a tent or zinc hut and bucket latrines were available was no longer acceptable.
>
> The days when police had to help load people onto trucks and the resistance which followed certain actions among black people are past. (Hennie van der Walt, Deputy Minister of Development and of Land Affairs, *Vaderland*, 17 June 83, translated from the original Afrikaans.)

Van der Walt made it clear in the same article that removals would not stop and that the policy remains the same. The government is only concerned with improving methods of implementation:

> Before any resettlement takes place, it is ensured that the area to which communities are to be moved has the necessary carrying capacity to accommodate the people, and that the necessary services, housing, water supply and sanitation are available. The provision of employment opportunities in the area is a high priority.
>
> Strong and clear guidelines for resettlement areas have been laid down

by the government before black communities are moved off so-called black spots. According to Mr van der Walt there must be thorough consultation between the concerned government of the national state and the formation of joint implementation committees with those communities before the removal is begun.

Resettlement committees and development committees must be established to help settle grievances and problems of residents by taking them to the authorities.

The Deputy Minister went on to say that entrepreneurs will be encouraged to establish businesses in the areas. Building material is taken free and rations for the first few days are given. Compensation for property and improvements is paid to those moved.

The days of removing black communities with force and settling them on open plains are past. The current approach taken by the government is that removals will only take place if absolutely necessary and then only if coupled with purposeful economic development in the areas where they are relocated. (*Vaderland,* 17 June 83, translated from the original Afrikaans.)

Two points which have been mentioned often in this book need to be made in relation to the above. Firstly, the main issue of relocation is not conditions or how bad they are. The main issue is that removals are part of a process of dispossession and exclusion of the majority of South Africans which is being implemented by a minority government. Furthermore, as already pointed out, the government does not see its relocation programme as applying equally to all people due to be removed. The statement quoted above refers only to areas to be consolidated, black spots and urban townships. It does not refer to victims of influx control or farm evictions or the clearing of informal settlements. Yet all of these are aspects of relocation which are ongoing and are being applied more ruthlessly than ever.

The government programme of relocation is not working smoothly. It is full of delays, inconsistencies and inefficiencies. Although Pretoria ultimately controls the programme, local authorities have some say. In effect they can delay the removal, move some of the people, make it more or less humane. There are gaps between the policy at the centre and implementation in the regions. The prime example of this is the abolition of labour tenancy which took more than two decades to implement in all areas.

The fact that drastic measures need to be introduced shows that influx control in its present form is not working. It has caused untold misery for those forced into bantustans and for those families prevented from living together. Although the proportion of Africans resident in bantustans is greater now than it was 30 years ago, the actual number of black people in urban areas has grown. Just over half the African population lives in the bantustans, but 5,6 million now live in white urban areas compared with 2,2 million thirty years ago. Natural increase alone, not to mention 'illegal' urbanisation, is causing a major crisis in South African cities. And the government is not even acknowledging the problem. It has all but ignored increasingly militant demands for housing and facilities for Africans in urban areas. For instance, in 1983 it announced that R200 million would be spent on housing for whites in the near future — the total spent on African housing over the past five years.

Because so many bantustans abut on white urban areas, informal settlements are developing rapidly on the fringes of cities. In some cases the informal settlements are part of the bantustans (as with Malukazi near Durban or Winterveld outside Pretoria). They are close to metropolitan areas, yet the bantustans are responsible for them. To date the central government has not begun to confront the problem of these expanding settlements.

Yet another category of informal settlement is emerging. Alongside relocation townships, far from metropolitan areas, thousands of people are building huts and shacks. They are mainly people who have left white-owned farms, or those who cannot afford townships rents, or those who cannot get houses in the formal townships. They are not willing to live in remote closer settlements, neither are they eligible for land elsewhere. These people build up places such as Bekumthetho next to Mondlo in KwaZulu, Pienaar surrounding Kabokweni in Kangwane, and Bodibe next to Itsoseng in Bophuthatswana. The bantustan authorities are generally as opposed to these settlements as their South African masters. Instead of the main urban areas of South Africa being surrounded by Latin American style informal settlements, these slums are presently displaced to the bantustans.

The government uses a number of indirect measures to force people out of areas proclaimed for whites. Among these controls are the supply and location of housing and of transport. These are universally recognised planning techniques, but in South Africa they are neither devised nor implemented with approval from the majority of population.

There is a worldwide shortage of housing. In South Africa, however, adequate housing is deliberately destroyed and the residents forcibly moved. In group area removals, alternative housing is built on the edges of towns and cities far from the hub of activity. In the case of deproclamation of urban townships, people are moved into housing in bantustan commuter towns. In both cases the quality of housing may sometimes, but by no means always, be better than what people occupied previously. As has been stressed before, though, the people have no part in making the decision to move. Furthermore, they are invariably moved away from places of work. On top of this, Africans lose their urban rights and South African citizenship.

Residents of informal settlements are seldom provided with alternative accommodation. They are particularly angry when the shelters they built themselves are destroyed. They used their own initiative, time and money. They may not even have demanded houses from the government.

By limiting the number of houses built for blacks and destroying informal settlements, the government regulates the flow of people to urban areas. According to the 1981 Viljoen Committee of Enquiry into private sector involvement in housing, 168 000 units needed to be built for Africans in urban areas. This would cost R1 700 million. At current rates, not considering inflation, the present backlog would take more than 40 years to cancel. And that does not take natural population growth or increased urbanisation into account.

In the Western Cape, for example, because of the official freeze on the building of houses in the early 1970s, only hostels were built to accommodate migrant workers. The government then cancelled building phases 2 and 3 for Crossroads. Those who qualify for Cape Town residence will go to Khayelitsha. This will enable the government to control the African population of Cape Town. A limited number of sites and houses will be provided and the rest of the people will be endorsed out of the area.

Location of housing is another means of control. To safeguard the physical security of the white population, black areas are built far from towns. They are planned to allow easy access for police and military vehicles. They may also be sealed off easily in times of unrest.

In an attempt to regulate urbanisation of coloureds, influx control was introduced through an amendment to the Prevention of Illegal Squatting Act in 1982. Before employers in certain areas of the Northern and Western Cape can employ coloured workers from outside those areas, they have to prove to the Department of Community Development that 'proper housing' is available. (*Cape Times*, 8 Dec. 82).

A 1983 amendment to the Laws on Cooperation and Development Act makes it clear that wives and families of contract workers who have worked for the same employer for more than ten years will not be allowed to live in the urban areas unless they were doing so 'legally' before 26 August 1983. This is a direct result of the Rikhoto judgement mentioned in Chapter 6.

> Persons will only be able to enter the prescribed area in order to reside in it if proper family housing is available for them in that area.
> (Minister of Cooperation & Development, *Hansard,* Col. 10732, 30 June 83.)

In his argument for the amendment of Clause 4 of this Act, the Minister made it clear that husbands and wives should not expect to live together:

> Having a regard to the socio-economic aspects, however, especially in view of the shortage of housing for Black persons all over the Republic, the Government has a responsibility to guard against the creation of unrealistic expectations on the part of contract workers and their wives and children in connection with residence in the prescribed areas. Squatting cannot be allowed under any circumstances, especially in view of the sociological and health problems to which it gives rise. (*Hansard*, Col. 10731, 30 June 83.)

In 1983 the government introduced strict measures to control taxis and minibuses. This efficient and flexible means of transport should indeed be properly licensed and insured. But the government intends tightening regulations for two other reasons. It wishes to control directly the movement of black people to urban areas and it wants to protect its own vast investment in bus companies.

An example of this financial and strategic control is the route between Cape Town and Ciskei/Transkei. It is proposed that only the South African Transport Services and the Blueline Bus Company will be allowed to operate on this route. If this monopoly is introduced private bus companies will be forced to close. Influx control will be easier to implement if, for instance, prospective passengers are only allowed to buy tickets for Cape Town on production of a valid pass for the area. Transport is already used in various parts of the country to control the movement of people from bantustans.

No black South African anywhere has any guarantee of security of tenure or residence as long as the apartheid system continues. The laws of apartheid make that brutally clear. The largest single group threatened with removal is the quarter million people who are to be moved from Cape Town, the 'legals' to Khayelitsha, the 'illegals' to the bantustans.

This latest planned removal was announced in mid-1983, at the height of talk of 'reform' among government spokespeople. They are paying particular attention to clearing as many Africans out of the Western Cape as possible.

In the Western Cape preference in allocation of work and housing is given to coloureds before Africans. This policy was mentioned in Chapter 2. It is flatly rejected by both coloured and African representatives in the Western Cape. However, Cape National Party MPs are determined to retain it. Therefore the enforcement of influx control and clearance of informal settlements is particularly brutal in the Western Cape.

As far as can be ascertained the only time African South Africans have been deported was in 1981 from the Western Cape. Hundreds of people were deported from Nyanga Bush outside Cape Town to the Transkei in terms of the Admission of Persons to the Republic Act (No. 59 of 1972). Instead of being arrested in terms of pass laws and tried in commissioners' courts as usual, 'squatters' were put on buses and driven to Umtata. In terms of the Act there is no recourse to the courts. This Act is normally used for deporting unwanted non-South African criminals.

There is yet another indication that influx control is being tightened. From 1980 to 1982 African women who were employed as domestic workers in the Western Cape could be registered for six month or even one year contracts with one employer. Many hundreds of women who were previously illegally employed had their positions regularised. This has now been stopped, at the same time as other measures have been taken to prevent women settling in the Western Cape. Nearly 30% of all the women arrested in 1982 for pass law offences were in the Cape Peninsula. This is the only part of the country where more women than men are arrested for these offences. There are more African men than women in Cape Town. A special assault against women is carried out in terms of government policy to prevent black family life taking root in Cape Town. (Horner 1983, p21.)

Response to relocation

> We want the government to speak to us. We have a right to stay here in the Cape. They give us no houses, but when we make our own they take them away from us. (Crossroads woman, *Argus*, 23 Sept 83.).

The vast majority of people threatened with removal would like to negotiate with the government. They say that they are prepared to talk to officials. There are many who acknowledge the fact that the government is all-powerful and can force them to move anywhere, anytime. Others, however, are determined to fight for the right to remain where they are. There is a growing tendency to confront the issue, though organisation is uneven and sporadic.

FIVE-YEAR CYCLE

23 Aug. 78
Dr Connie Mulder, Minister of Plural Relations and Development, announced at the Cape National Party Congress that Crossroads would not be tolerated, regardless of campaigns being organised locally and abroad.

14 Sept. 78
Sindile Ndlela was shot dead by police at 2am during a raid on Crossroads.

23 Nov. 78
Newly appointed Minister of Plural Relations and Development, Dr Piet Koornhoof, visited Crossroads and began discussions with committee members.

5 April 79
Dr Koornhoof announced (partial) reprieve of Crossroads on one hand and notice of plans to tighten influx control on the other.

23 Sept. 83
Teargas and rubber bullets were used by police to control Crossroads people who retaliated to the 16th raid by Administration Board officials in the first 17 working days of September.

28 Sept. 83
At the Cape National Party Congress in George, Deputy Minister of Cooperation and Development Dr G Morrison announced that Crossroads would be destroyed as a 'symbol of provocation and blackmail of the government' and 'legal blacks would be dispersed' to Khayelitsha. Stricter influx control measures would be introduced. Mention was made of road blocks, tollgates and passport controls.

2 Oct. 83
'Crossroads residents vote to resist move' - 'they can come and kill us but we are not moving.'

29 Oct. 83
Police fired shots in Crossroads and all entrances were sealed after violence flared last night — two people were killed and at least 300 left homeless. *Die Burger* commented in an editorial that people would be relieved to move to Khayelitsha.

Some churches are becoming increasingly involved in opposition to relocation. Fieldworkers are employed to work alongside priests in areas under threat and at relocation sites. Other churches continue to be implicated in removals themselves.

Women and school students play an active role: at Sekgosese women and students demanded that Administration Board officials leave their land; Crossroads and Umbulwane women are members of committees actively resisting removal; in Huhudi school children joined their parents in the refusal to move.

SPP fieldwork confirms that communities threatened with removal in major urban areas are in the strongest position to resist. They have access to other communities, lawyers, support groups and the press. The government is clearly concerned about the effect a community such as Crossroads has on others under threat of removal. The 1983 speech by the Deputy Minister of Cooperation and Development at the Cape National Party Congress made this clear.

Those in the weakest position to resist are farmworkers and other small isolated groups under threat. Where families are moved one at a time, as in the case of group area or farm evictions, it is far harder to sustain organised opposition. The government has learned that lesson too. This is why it will take 20 years to relocate all the 'legal' Africans in Cape Town's townships to Khayelitsha.

It is not enough to call a halt to removals. While conditions in threatened areas are generally better than those in relocation areas, they are certainly not adequate. Underlying the immediate issue of removals, therefore, is the fundamental and long-standing issue of land and the distribution of resources. The fact that 3 million people have already been moved, and the country fragmented in the process, is going to make the task of redistribution and reconstruction much more complicated when finally it is undertaken.

Planning should nevertheless begin now, and it should accept as a basic principle that where people are to live is not a matter which can be decided by a government elected by 16% of the population. And if the voices of the people most immediately affected by development strategies are to be heard — now and in the future — it must be accepted that democratic organisation has to be built. It will not appear overnight, even in a more propitious climate than the present. Only when the dispossessed participate in the planning of their futures will various options — job creation, education, cooperative farms, repopulation of deserted white farms by black farmers — begin to look like real solutions.

While many of those working for change believe that the working class should lead the struggle for liberation, in South Africa there is an increasing need to involve non-workers. Those with jobs form something of an elite in rural areas. Workers are desperate to protect their jobs. Thousands of unemployed people would gladly take their jobs in the mines and factories. Already many workers prefer not to return to the bantustans. They want to establish themselves in the cities. Many rarely send money 'home'. The bantustans contain thousands of people who have lost their jobs. All they do is sit in rural areas waiting to be recruited. Seldom do they discuss rural issues, let alone organise around them. Yet these unemployed people are probably the only ones in the rural community who have any experience of organisation. They are likely to have been exposed to trade unions during their urban stay. They need to be drawn into the general movement for change. Progressive leadership in rural areas is essential to counter the present imposed tribal authorities.

The rural population cannot depend on the working class to fight for them. Those who are not economically active must also be involved. Already 53% of Africans live in bantustans, where they have to fight ethnic as well as urban/rural divisions. The use of vigilantes from the rural areas to beat up Mdantsane residents during the 1983 bus boycott shows how these divisions can be manipulated. In this case the urban/rural division was stronger than the supposed ethnic bond between Xhosa-speaking men and women.

Those engaged in urban-based organisation need to pay more attention to rural struggles. People who live in the countryside do participate in change. They put forward demands and take stands. Seldom is their courage and determination reported in urban areas, let alone integrated into the national movement for change.

Halting relocation alone will not change society. But it is a necessary prerequisite. The demand to stop all removals is not only a question of toilets, fuel and bread, but of justice, rights and dignity. It is not only a call to stop demolition of shelters in the cold wet Cape Town winter, but a call to abolish influx control and to return citizenship, economic and political rights.

In the short term those who do not want to be moved can be supported. Care must be taken not to direct or divert their struggle. Support in the form of legal aid, information and publicity can be given. It has been shown that political pressure has helped to improve conditions. As a result, conditions in the closer settlements are better in the

1980s than in the 1960s. And there have been some reprieves for areas threatened with removal.

THE NATIONAL ARENA

Relocation is becoming part of the national debate on change in South Africa. At the first national conference of the United Democratic Front, with 800 delegates representing 400 organisations nationwide, the following resolution was passed unanimously:

Removals and Group Areas

The forced and cruel uprooting and removals of our people from our land and homes as evidenced at Crossroads and Khayelitsha have been the backbone of this government's apartheid scheme.

Bulldozers and trucks remove our people daily and dump them in areas far from their working places. Children are hurt, our leaders killed, families have been torn apart and communities destroyed.

We have over the years been robbed of our land, shelter and livelihood. Our protests are met with teargas, batons and bullets.

We are divided, urban from rural, community from community.

We demand the return of our land and homes. We demand the right to live where we please in the land of our birth.

Now therefore this first National Conference of the United Democratic Front held at Rocklands, Mitchells Plain, Cape Town on 20 August 1983
SALUTES all communities who struggle against the Group Areas Act and removals;
DEMANDS that the government repeals this Group Areas Act and stops inhuman removals now and returns the land to the people;
URGES communities faced with removals to organise their people to resist removals and further urges all communities to join with the affected communities to fight removals.

The Western Cape region of the UDF announced that it would concentrate on opposition to the proposed relocation of African townships in Cape Town to Khayelitsha. Nationally the UDF has agreed to focus on relocation as part of its programme of action.

Although publicity for resistance may expose communities to repressive government action, it does highlight opposition to the policy in the longer term. It also shows up official talk of reform as untrue. The government claims support for its policies among blacks and this can be shown to be false. However, while publicity may discourage direct government force, it could intensify the more subtle strategies. This could weaken opposition from within the community rather than unite it against the outside threat as direct force tends to do. Decades of official strategies to divide and control blacks have created a deeply fragmented South Africa. So all action should be examined carefully for implications which might thwart rather than help the struggle for change.

Despite the many problems, SPP fieldworkers were deeply impressed by the degree of courage and resilience they encountered in their work. More and more communities around the country are determined to fight to stay where they are. For the government to continue to make its policy work, it will need a lot more money. More and more coercion will have to be used to clear black areas and build the bantustans. The Nationalist government is battling against the majority of South Africans who are determined to survive and fight against poverty and injustice. Ultimately, it cannot win that battle. People will not rest until they have won democracy and a fair share of the country's wealth.

> We are the landowners here and we are not prepared to go anywhere. We've got titles to this land; only if they take the titles from us can they own this land, but if we are still in possession of these titles, then they won't take it, only over our dead bodies. (Mathopestad resident interviewed in 1981, SPP Vol. 5, p.291.)

> Dr Morrison will have to kill us first and then move our bodies to Khayelitsha — because that is the only way we will move there. Dr Morrison will first have to destroy the people before he can destroy Crossroads. (Crossroads Executive statement, *Cape Herald*, 8 Oct. 83.)

> The Minister has promised that people will not be moved against their will. None of the people at Jonono's Kop or Matiwane's Kop want to move. We will not move. We intend to carry on as we have always done. They will have to bring guns to push us out or bury us here.
> (*Natal Witness*, 22 Nov. 80.)

Resources on Relocation

Slides and Films

Name		Obtainable From
The Leopard's Spots	slide/tape	SACC
The Promised Land	slide/tape	SACC
Vulamehlo	slide/tape	SPP/AFRA/ GRC/Black Sash Jhb.
The Dispossessed	video	
Housing in Durban	slides	Diakonia
Pageview	video	
Magopa	slide/tape	TRAC
Kwapitela	slide/tape	AFRA/
Matiwane's Kop	video	AFRA/SACC
Reserve 4	video	SALDRU, UCT
Khayelitsha: Desert Dormitory	slide/tape	Law Directive, UCT
Khayelitsha	video (forthcoming)	SPP (Western Cape), Western Cape Council of Churches

Organisations

AFRA:
P O Box 2517,
Pietermaritzburg 3200   0331-57607

Black Sash:
Offices in Cape Town, Durban, Grahamstown, Pietermaritzburg, Port Elizabeth & Johannesburg

Grahamstown Rural Committee (GRC):
c/o Sociology Dept.,
Rhodes University,
Grahamstown 6140   0461-2663

S.A. Council of Churches and the regional councils of churches:
P O Box 31190
Braamfontein 2017
(including Inter-Church
Media Programmes —
IMP — for media)   011-2822251/8

Legal Resources Centres:
Ecumenical Centre Trust
St Andrew's St
Durban 4001   031-66195

41 Church St
Cape Town 8001   021-238285

401 Elizabeth House
cnr Pritchard & Sauer
Streets
Johannesburg 2001   011-8369831

Centre for Applied Legal Studies:
University of the
Witwatersrand
1 Jan Smuts Avenue
Braamfontein 2001   011-7163457

Community Resource & Information Centre:
3rd Floor Audward House
Amershof St
Braamfontein 2001   011-392440

Diakonia: Ecumenical Centre Trust
P O Box 1879
Durban 4000   031-66195

Durban Housing Action Committee:
116 Prince Edward St
Durban 4001

Community Research Unit:
3 A.I. Kajee Building
Victoria St
Durban 4001   031-62050

Resources

Surplus People Project (Western Cape):
P O Box 187
Cape Town 8000 021-698531
 Ext 217

Environmental & Development Agency:
P O Box 62054
Marshalltown 2107 011-8341905

S.A. Institute of Race Relations:
Offices in Cape Town,
Durban, Johannesburg,
East London and Pietermaritzburg

Board of Social Responsibility:
Church House
1 Queen Victoria St
Cape Town 8001 021-231253

Project HOPE (Natal Churches on Relocation):
c/o PACSA
(Pietermaritzburg Agency
for Christian Social
Awareness & Action)
P O Box 2338
Pietermaritzburg 3200 0331-20052

Transvaal Action Committee (TRAC):
Khotso House
De Villiers St
Johannesburg 2001 011-238405

Natal Committee Against Removals (NCAR):
Contact AFRA, GRC,
SPP (Western Cape) or
TRAC

ACTSTOP:
c/o Auden House
68 De Korte Street
Braamfontein 2001 011-7244441

Bibliography

Newspapers and Journals

The Argus
Bantu
Cape Herald
The Cape Times
Daily Despatch
Daily News
Drum
Eastern Province Herald
Fairlady (27 August 1983)
Financial Mail
The Friend
Golden City Press
Grocott's Mail
Growth (September 1983)
Housing in South Africa: Journal of the Institute of Housing Management (January 1980)
The Natal Mercury
Natal Witness
NAUNLU (journal of the Natal Agricultural Union)
Rand Daily Mail
Sash (May 1982)
The Star
The Sunday Tribune
Weekend Post

Official Publications

Ciskei, Legislative Assembly, *Debates*.
South Africa, 1916, *Report of the Native Land Commission* (Beaumont Commission), UG 19/1916.

South Africa, 1955. *Summary of the report of the Commission for the socio-economic development of the Bantu areas within the Union of South Africa* (Chairman, Tomlinson), UG 61/1955.
South Africa, Department of Bantu Administration and Development, 1961. *General Circular*, 1961.
South Africa, Department of Bantu Administration and Development, 1967. *General Circular 25 of 1967*.
South Africa, Department of Cooperation and Development, 1982. *General Circular 2 of 1982*.
South Africa, Department of Cooperation and Development, 1983. *Press Release, 6.6.83*.
South Africa, Department of Native Affairs, 1959. *Report, 1954-1957*. UG 14/1959.
South Africa, House of Assembly. *Debates*.
South Africa, House of Assembly, 1975. *First report of the Select Committee on Bantu Affairs*. SC 9/1975.
South Africa, Senate. *Debates*.

Unpublished Sources

Huhudi Civic Association, 'Memorandum to the Black Sash'.
Association for Rural Advancement, letters in files.
'Memorandum to the Western Province Council of Churches on the resettlement of KTC', by a Quaker peaceworker, 6.6.1983.
Valspan, 'Memorandum'.

Books, Articles, Dissertations and Papers

Association for Rural Advancement, *Factsheets*.
Association for Rural Advancement, *Reports*, Number 1, 1980 —.
Association for Rural Advancement, *and* Surplus People Project, *The law and forced removals: transcript of a workshop* (Pietermaritzburg and Cape Town, February 1984).
Baldwin, A. 1975. 'Mass removals and separate development', *Journal of Southern African Studies*, *1*, 2, April 1975.
BENBO. 1976. *Black Development in Southern Africa* (Perskor, Johannesburg).

Bundy, Colin. 1979. *The Rise and Fall of the South African Peasantry* (Heinemann, London).

Christopher, A.J. 1969. 'Natal: a study in colonial land settlement', unpublished Ph.D., University of Natal.

Davenport, T.R.H., and Hunt, K.S. 1974. *The Right to the Land* (David Philip, Cape Town).

Desmond, Cosmas. 1970. *The Discarded People: an account of African resettlement in South Africa* (Penguin, Harmondsworth).

Development Studies Group. 1979. *Control*, (DSG, Johannesburg).

Dugard, John. 1983. 'Denationalisation: apartheid's ultimate plan', *Africa Report*, July/August.

Duncan, Sheena. 1982. *The New Influx Control*, (Black Sash, Johannesburg).

Green, P., and Hirsch, A. 1983. 'The impact of resettlement in the Ciskei: three case studies', SALDRU working paper, No. 49 (Southern African Labour and Development Research Unit, Cape Town).

Harries, P. 1983. 'Internal colonialism and ethnicity: the case of the Tsonga speakers of South Africa'. Paper presented to the International Conference on the History of Ethnic Awareness in Southern Africa, held at Charlottesville, University of Virginia, 7-10 April 1983 (to be published).

Horner, D. 1983. 'Labour preference, influx control and squatters: Cape Town entering the 1980s', SALDRU working paper, No. 50 (Southern African Labour and Development Research Unit).

Horrell, M. 1973. *The African homelands of South Africa* (South African Institute of Race Relations, Johannesburg).

James, D. 1983. *The road from Doornkop: a case study of removals and resistance* (SAIRR, Johannesburg).

Kuper, L., Watts. H., and Davies, R. 1958. *Durban: a study in racial ecology* (Jonathan Cape, London).

'KwaMashu speaking: an interview with Mrs M. on Cato Manor to KwaMashu', *Staffrider*, 3, 1, February 1980.

Lacey, M. 1981. *Working for Boroko* (Ravan Press, Johannesburg).

MacMillan, H. 1983. 'A nation divided? The Swazi in Swaziland and the Transvaal, 1865-1982'. Paper presented to the International Conference on the History of Ethnic Awareness in

Southern Africa, held at Charlottesville, University of Virginia, 7-10 April, 1983 (to be published).

Maré, G. 1980. *African population relocation in South Africa*, (SAIRR, Johannesburg).

Meyer, P. 1971. *Townsmen or Tribesmen* (Oxford University Press, Cape Town).

Mngadi, E. 1981. 'The removal of Roosboom', AFRA Special Report, No. 2 (Association for Rural Advancement, Pietermaritzburg).

NUSAS. 1979. *We will not move: the struggle for Crossroads*, (Nusas, Cape Town).

Plaatje, S.T. 1982. *Native Life in South Africa* (Ravan Press, Johannesburg).

1982. *Report of the Buthelezi Commission: the requirements for stability and development in KwaZulu and Natal* (H and H Publications, Durban).

1980. Report of the Ciskei Commission appointed 4 August 1978 (Quail Commission) (Conference Associates, Pretoria).

Robb, R.N. 1982. *The Orderly Movement and Settlement of Black Persons Bill* (Black Sash, Mowbray).

Roux, A. 1983. 'Relocation in South Africa: the Surplus People Project', *Reality*, August 1983

Schlemmer, L., and Muil, T. 1975. 'Social and Political Change in the African areas: a case study of KwaZulu', in Butler, J., and Thompson, L. (eds), *Change in Contemporary South Africa* (University of California Press, Berkeley).

South African Institute of Race Relations. 1965, 1975, 1982. *Annual Survey*.

Simkins, C.E.W. 1981. 'The distribution of the African population of South Africa, by age, sex, and region type; 1960, 1970 and 1980', SALDRU working paper No. 32 (Southern African Labour and Development Research Unit, Cape Town).

Simkins, C.E.W. 1983. *The economic implications of the Rikhoto judgement* (Southern African Labour and Development Research Unit, Cape Town).

Surplus People Project. 1983. *Forced Removals in South Africa* (Surplus People Project, Cape Town).

Walt, E. 1982. *South Africa: a land divided* (Black Sash, Johannesburg).

Western, J. 1981. *Outcast Cape Town* (Allen & Unwin, London).

Western Cape Administration Board. 15 September 1982. 'Notice to employers of all blacks — Chief Director'.
Yawitch, J. 1982. *Betterment: the myth of homeland agriculture* (South African Institute of Race Relations, Johannesburg).

Index

Note: Extra abbreviations are used here for black spot (b/s), Bophuthatswana (Bop.), closer settlement (c/s), informal settlement (in/s), relocation area (r/area). Place names are in italics.

accountability, evaded, 15, 66, 130, 184, 186, 201; in resistance, 213, 290, 302, 306
Acton Homes, Central Natal b/s, 79
ACTS/BILLS: titles are in the latest terminology (1985). Roughly, for Native or Bantu, *see* Black, for Black Homelands *see* National States, for Native Trust *see* Development Trust.
Admission of Persons to the Republic Regulations Act 59/1972, 26, 142, 395
Aliens and Immigration Laws Amendment Act 49/1984, *xxix*
Black Administration Act 38/1927 as amended, 88-89, 139, 141, 143, 189, 190, 242
Black Authorities Act 68/1951, 111, 126, 239
Black Communities Development Act 4/1984, 25
Black Land Act 27/1913, 83-87, 74, 89-90, 91-92
Black Laws Amendment Act 76/1963, 142
Black Prohibition of Interdicts Act 64/1956, 139-140, 141, 146
Black Resettlement Act 19/1954, 141
Black (Urban Areas) Consolidation Act 25/1945 as amended, residence rights under, 19 *and see* Section 10 rights; further amendments to, *xxvii*; Bill replacing, 25; removal under, 28-29, 35-36; and influx control, 32
Blacks (Abolition of Passes and Coordination of Documents) Act 67/1952, 141, 319
Ciskei Marketing and Agricultural Promotion Act 7/1981 as amended, 362
Development Trust and Land Act 18/1936 as amended, 89-90, 92-93; removal under, 28, 29, 231; and labour tenancy, 30, *and see* Trust Expropriation Act 63/1975, 139, 142
Glen Grey Act 1894, 81-82
Group Areas Act 41/1950 as amended, *xxiii*, 99-103; removal under 35-36, 67, 99-100, 344; incomplete figures, 13; call to repeal 399
Laws on Cooperation and Development Amendment Act 83/1982, for secrecy, 14-15, 141, 374; for influx control, 166; 1983 amendment, 393-394
National States Citizenship Act 26/1970 as amended, 18-22, 124,

142, 380, 384
National States Constitution Act 21/1971 as amended, 18-22, 124, 139, 142
Orderly Movement and Settlement of Black Persons Bill 1982, for tighter control, 23, 161-162, 309, 382, 383; used prematurely, 23-24, 284; protest at, 23; withdrawn, *xxix*, 384-385; *and see* Aliens Act
Pension Act 18/1978 (Bophuthatswana), 174
Prevention of Illegal Squatting Act 52/1951 as amended, *xxxiii*, 103, 104, 135, 139, 141, 143, 146, 223, 230, 276, 393
Promotion of Black Self-Government Act 46/1959, 112-113, 126, 142
Representation of Blacks Act 12/1936, 89
Slums Clearance Act 76/1979, 142
Status of Bophuthatswana Act 89/1977, 18
Status of Ciskei Act 110/1981, 18
Status of Transkei Acts 3/1976 and 100/1976, 18
Status of Venda Act 107/1979, 18
Trespass Act 6/1959, 142
Administration Boards, *see* Development Boards
affidavits, *see* negotiation tactics (resistance), records/minutes, 'voluntary' removal
African National Congress (ANC), 74, 85; growth, 83, 96; ban on, 110; fought, 59, 68, 88, 98, 388; for majority rule, 103; and landowners, 291
agricultural schemes, 186; and removal, 3, 47, 51, 186-187, 190, 208, 224; Ciskei comment on, 187; interest in, 38

agricultural settlements, defined, 331, 332
Alicedale, E Cape r/township at, commuting, 355-357
'aliens', *see* citizenship, influx control
Alta Villas, E Tvl Indian r/township outside Louis Trichardt, removal to, 312
apartheid, pre-1913 roots, 70-79; 1913-1948, 83, 87-89, 93-94; 1948 manifesto, 98-99; restructuring, 381-383; and removal, *xx*, 310, 319, 338, 394 *and see* removal policy; based on force, 176 *and see* force/coercion; inculcated, 100-101; campaigning against, 319, 397-398; for domination, *see* division, minority rule; as 'separate development', 95-127 *and see* ethnicity; *and see* cost, group areas, land, law, state comment/texts
apartheid disguised, by language, *see* Glossary, terminology, 'voluntary' removal; as 'separate development', 16, 27, 68, 103; as 'ethnicity', 23, 36, 100-101, 125-127; as 'reform', 381-382
army, *see* military action
arrest, *see* intimidation/threat, police action, security police action
Asiatics, *see* Indians
Association for Rural Advancement (AFRA), 129, 131, 235; monitoring/support, *xxiv, xxv*, 233, 236-238, 268-269, 273
Atlantis, W Cape coloured group area township near Cape Town, 339, 373; resistance, *xxxi*; only option, 160; for commuter labour, 57, 102; employment, 352, 355, 359; diet, 364

Index

Babanango, KwaZulu r/area in N Natal, move to, 293
bantustans, defined, *x*; creation, 34-36, 95, 109-115, 123-127 *and see* reserves; political role, 16-19, 22-23, 25, 108-110, 113, 176-188, 338, 369-372, 383; as silencer, 15, 184, 201, 374; 'independence', 22-23, 57, 112, 178, 182, 370-371, 380-381; administering RSA areas, 184, 240; citizenship/weakening RSA rights, 18-22, 25-27, 108, 164-166 *and see* citizenship; population, 17, 31; urbanisation, shift to, 375-376, 392 *and see* population; population shifts between, 38, 369-372, *and see* ethnicity, removals and bantustans; land, 8, 35, 45-46, 51, 177, 182-183, 338 *and see* land, Trust land, consolidation; conditions, 8, 51-53, 93-94, 118, 123-124, 177, 182-183, 374-376; and removals, *see* removals and bantustans; employment, 65-66, 108-109, 112, 378-379 *and see* border industries; unemployment, 32, 34, 378, 382 *and see* unemployment; investment in/economy, 27, 111, 124, 162-163, 186-187, 379; corruption, 377; credibility, 177; elections, 38, 178 *and see Bophuthatswana, Ciskei, Gazankulu, Kangwane, KwaNdebele, KwaZulu, Lebowa, Qwaqwa, Transkei, Venda*, state comment/texts
Baralong people, dispossessed, 74
Basutoland, formerly British protectorate, now *Lesotho, q.v.*
Bathurst, E Cape township at, reprieved 1982, 387
Batlharos, Bop. r/area near Kuruman, N Cape, 55

Batlokwa people, resistance case study, 238-266; and lawyers, 309
Beaumont Commission (report UG 19-1916) 84-85, 87 *and see* land
Bechuanaland, formerly British protectorate, now *Botswana q.v.*
Bekumthetho, KwaZulu in/s near Vryheid, N Natal, 392 *and see Mondlo*, its township
Bendall, Bop. c/s near Kuruman, N Cape, 55, 285, 349-350
Bergville, Central Natal area under threat, 313
Besterspruit, Natal b/s near Vryheid, cleared 1963, 79
beswarting ('blackening') *see* rural population
Bethanie, W Tvl area near Brits, 291
betterment, defined, *ix*; 9, 45-46, 93-94, 111-112, 186, 334; removal 1960/83, 10; removal threatened (1983), 11; resistance, 45, 46, 111, 186, 313-314
Black Sash, comment/texts on citizenship, 18-22; Orderly Movement Bill, 25-27; 'Rikhoto' rights withheld, 164-165, 166; Winterveld pensions, 174-175; HUCA memorandum, 202-221 *passim*; HUCA letter 218-219; Morsgat, 346; support, *xxiv, xxv,* 223, 306-307, 309
black spots, defined, *xi*, 10; *xxix-xxx,* 44-45, 67-68, 115-117, 132-133, 282-283, 386-387; shifts of meaning, 15; case studies, 189-201, 232-238, 238-266, 266-278; boxes, 63-64, 90, 159, 167, 171, 172-173, 293-295, 296-300, 321-325, 337, 361; origin, 74-75, 79, 90; removal, 52-53, 1975-1982 figures with cost 14, 128, 129, case studies as above; coercion/resistance, 53, 57, 63-64,

140, 156, 158, 159, 171, 277, 279-317 *passim*, 321-325; evasion/conflicting information on, 13, 184; influx to, 268-269, 336-337; *and see* consolidation, places in index, state comment/texts
Bloemfontein, OFS township at, removal by housing, 161
Blouvlei, W Cape in/s near Cape Town cleared by 1956, 96
Blue Rock, E Cape in/s near East London cleared 1983, *xxxi*, 176
Bochum/Vivo, Lebowa r/area in N Tvl, *see Kromhoek*
Bodibe, Bop. in/s near Lichtenburg, W Tvl, 392
Bophuthatswana, bantustan independent of Tvl, N Cape and OFS since 6 Dec. 77 under Status Act 89/1977, 370-372; in maps (1982), 48-50; ethnic origins, 37-38; approved, 38 (map 40-41); consolidation, 43-44, 179, 316, 387; area, population density (1980), 17; conditions, 213, 376 *and see* places in index; ethnic trouble, 35, 55, 126, 174-175, 179, 185, 214, 279, 292, 370, 371; and removal, 46, 177, 210, 281, 312, 376, 377; removal from, 55, 126, 179, 185, 186, 369-372; removal to, *xxvi*, 33, 162-163, 174, 202, 203, 387; resisted, *see* case study 201-221; r/areas and in/ss *see* places in index; no sales tax, 220, 312-313; *and see* bantustans, removal and bantustans
border industries, 1950s, 112; after 1960, 118, 386; incentives for, 206, 352-353, 381; labour for, *see* commuters; *and see* industrial interests
Bothashoek, Lebowa agricultural r/area near Burgersfort, N Tvl, 317
Botshabelo, see Onverwacht
Botswana, 37-38
Braklaagte, W Tvl b/s near Zeerust, reprieved, 1983, 316
Brandfort, OFS c/s at, 30
bribery, *see* cooption methods
Brits, W Tvl, 44
Buthelezi, Chief Gatsha, Chief Minister of *KwaZulu q.v.*

Cape Peninsula, W Cape area incl. Cape Town, 315
Cape Province, to 1913, 75-76, 78-79, 81; private locations, 75; removal, 55-58, with influx control 33-34, group areas 35-36, consolidation 37-38 (maps 37, 40-41), betterment 46, infrastructure 50-51; conditions, 376; SPP surveys, 329; Cape vote, *see* vote; coloured labour preference, *see* coloureds; *and see Eastern Cape, Northern Cape, Western Cape, Ciskei, Transkei, Bophuthatswana*, places in index
Cape Town area, W Cape, first removals, 70-71; removals/under threat, *xxii, xxviii*, 373, 393; 394-395; transport control, 394; *and see* places in index
cash tenants (on white farms), defined *xiv*, 30; to 1913, 74, 75, 80; phased out, 83-84, 122; *and see* farm evictions
Cato Manor, Natal in/s at Durban, 101-102
censorship, *see* information problems, information control
Chatsworth, Natal Indian group area township at Durban, 344
chiefs/headmen, to 1913, 73, 75, 76; into colonial rule, 78; boosted for

Index

control (1927) 88, (1951) 111; for removal, 168, 169, 286, 321-325
churches, *see* resistance support
Ciskei, bantustan independent of E Cape since 4 Dec. 81 under Status Act 110/1981, 55, 57, map 56; land area, population density (1980), *xxiii*, 17; approved, 38 (map 40-41); origins, 75; land deal, 38; consolidation, *xxx*, 387; agricultural schemes, 169, 186, 187, 190; to one-party state, 38 *and see* CNIP; conditions, *xxiii*, 55, 301, 326-327, 378; repression/ detentions, *xxiii*, 140, 286, 312, 374, 376; publicity, 57, 376; people lured to, 38, 168, 186, 190; removals into, *xxxi*, 5-6, 38, 55, 57, 128, 162, 163, 168, 186, 189-201 case study, 202, 221-232 case study; on 'dumping' *see* state comment/texts; pressure on black spots, 57, 140, 159, 286, 287, 290, 321-325; removal within, 46, 47-48, 57, 187, 373; squatter clearance to, 34, 377; aiding RSA removal, 201, 224, 228; not compensated, 200; industrial investment, *xxvii*, 57, 347, 348; to stop questions, 15; stopping transport, 394; *and see* bantustans, removal and bantustans, places in index
Ciskei National Independence Party (CNIP), only party, 38; coercion into, 305, 375
citizenship, dispossession, 16-22, 57; 'alien' control, 162, 163; apartheid, 386 *and see* vote, minority rule; division on, 166; in Kangwane/Ingwavuma affair, 43
closer settlements, defined, *xii*, 331 332; 7-8, 330-331; facilities, 341-346, 348-350; economic conditions, 353-355, 356, 358, 360; started with betterment, *q.v.*; SPP surveys, 334; *and see* facilities/ social services, removal (action/ reaction after), places in index
coercion/resistance, to 1913 70, 71-82; RSA urban, 58, 62-63, 102, 107, 135, 147, 148, 151-152, 160, 161, 162, 163, 164-165, 168-169, 176, 202-215, 216-219, 220, 283-284, 285, 307, 312-313, 315, 396, 400; RSA rural (incl. black spots), 5-6, 47, 61, 62-63, 86-87, 91-92, 122-123, 128-130, 133, 134, 136, 140, 144, 145-146, 147, 148, 148-150, 157, 159, 160, 166, 167, 168, 169, 170, 171, 172-173, 190-196, 221-232, 234-235, 241-266, 286, 288, 289, 291, 293-295, 296-300, 300-304, 313-314, 321-325, 400; bantustans, 140 (in RSA), 174-175, 185, 186, 199-201, 292, 366, 371
'collaborators', problem with, 253; rejected, 190, 248-249, 252, 261, 265; position afterwards, 261-262, 301-302, 313
Colchester, E Cape rural village near Port Elizabeth, removal from, 3-6
coloureds, defined, *xiii*; classified, 95; in pecking order, 339, 377, 382; pressed into role, 100-101, 383; share of land, 16; homeland planned for, 385; influx control of, 393; coloured labour preference, *xxiii, xxvii*, 24, 57, 395; mixed with Africans, 5; group area removals, 36-37, 99-102, 35-36, 103, 202 *and see* group areas, places in index
commercial interests, Chambers of Commerce, 202, 219-220, 307, 312; Urban Foundation, 35, 307; white urban, 389

community boards (later community councils, now town/city/village councils), for removal/neutral, 163, 219, 293, 294; against removal, 210, 206-207; limited in resistance, 216, 217; rejected, 217, 284, 315

commuters, defined, *xiv*; discussed, 355-357; policy shift to, 34, 206, 381; in informal settlements, 34-35, 53; made by removal, 33, 34, 51-52, 118, 353, 386; r/sites for, 34, 57, 66, 102, 352-353, 355; *and see* border industries, transport

company land, 74, 78, 79

compensation, 137, 303-304; in removal, 137, 322; justifying removal, 129, 133, 136, 252, 309; right of appeal, 139, 143; signing against, 134; lure to removal, 168, 291; deception on, 169; none/inadequate, 137, 199, 261; irregularities, 236-237; bantustan failure on, 199; for suffering, 291; bantustan failure on, 199; workmen's compensation for 'aliens', 21

Compensation, Trust land now KwaZulu c/s near Pietermaritzburg, Natal, removal to, 129, 232-238 case study; employment, 353, 356; unemployment, 360

concentration camps, Anglo-Boer War removals, 82

Conservative Party (white), growth, 382, 388; on consolidation, 42, 43, 44, 388; 'coloured homeland', 385

consolidation, defined, *ix; xxii, xxiii,* 12, 37-44, 51, 53, 115-116, 124-125, case study 178-183, 385-390; proposals (1955) 37-38, (1975) 38 (map 40-41), 386,

(1982/83) 43-44; pending, 44, 387; expense of, 387-388, on whites 1975/82 14, from 1982 12, budget 1981/84 39, land/'independence' deals, 38, 57, 178-183; removal for (1960/83), 10; removal by, 34, 38, 50-51 *and see* Trust land; enabling removal, 116; 'reason' for removal, 241; under threat (1983), *xxx*, 11, 290, 386-387; bantustan responses, 38, 51, 177, 183; black resistance, 39, 43, 53, 389, 390; black support, 57; white resistance, 38, 39, 43-44, 53, 109, 179, 388-389; white acceptance/support, 42, 115, 116; borders uncertain, 51; ethnic conflict, 59; 'white sacrifice too', 14, 38, 154-155, 171; *and see* black spots, expropriation, land, state comment/texts, bantustans listed in index, Le Roux Committee

constitution, new SA, *see* vote

consultation (for removal), *see* negotiation/consultation (for removal)

contact among communities, 288, 301-302, 318; help/joint action, 253, 258-260, 262, 265-266, 277; experience shared, 213-214, 254, 283, 288, 301-302, 305; broken, 302; *and see* isolation, resistance assets, resistance strategies, unity

control, 99-125, 369-372, 380-387, 393-395, *and see* bantustans, co-option purposes, division, identity documents, influx control, information control, labour supply, land, minority rule, removal powers, strategic control

Cooperation and Development Department (Native Affairs 1910-1959, Bantu Administration

Index

and Development 1959-1978, Plural Relations 1978-1979, present title since 1979, sharing Minister with Education Department from 1984), role shift, *xxix*; encounters with, 241, 242, 247, 251, 283, 371, 396; disinvolvement by, 15, 186, 201, 274-276, 321, 374; information, 13; and Urban Foundation, 35; directives on removal, *xxi, xxvi, xxviii, xxix, xxx, xxxii, xxxiii*, 8, 28-30, 157, 331-332; created planning committees, *q.v.*; controls the Trust and Development Boards, *q.v.*; *and see* promises broken, publicity, state misinformation, state comment/texts, terminology

cooption, 156, 158, 168, 286; *and see* Black Administration Act, following items

coopted agents, bantustans, 22-23, 35, 38, 46, 51, 176-188; committees/boards, 154, 163, 168, 321-325 *and see* community boards, planning committees; civil servants (incl. chiefs/headmen), 88, 111, 113, 159 (alleged), 168, 195, 239-240, 253, 254, 255, 286; business/private individuals, 26, 35, 168, 252, 290-291, 383; informers, 130, 140, 289; *and see* 'collaborators', state comment/texts

cooption methods, 168, 286, 287; bribery, 22-23, 38, 159 (alleged), 168, 195 (alleged), 250, 252, 254, 290-291; threat, 26, 168, 221-222; authority structure, 78, 88, 113, 154, 158, 163, 176-188, 239, 250, 321-325; other vested interests, 23, 35, 111, 239-240 (alleged)

cooption purposes, control, 23, 26, 111, 113, 130, 140, 158, 221-222;

divide, 23, 35, 113; demoralise, 130, 140; look democratic, 153-154, 163; avoid trouble/exposure, 15, 46, 184; stop court action, 195 (alleged); aid removals, 26, 35, 38, 46, 154, 159 (alleged), 163, 169, 176-177, 179, 180-188, 195, 221-222, 239-240 (alleged) 250, 242, 254-255, 256-257, 290-291, 302, 321-325

Cornfields, Natal b/s near Estcourt, 143, 145, 158

cost, of bantustans, 27, 33, *and see* bantustans; of consolidation, 12, 39, 42, 387-388; of removals, 14, 39; of influx control (incl. 'aliens'), 162-163; slowing removal, 42; cost of living, *see* shops/cost of living; *and see* state comment/texts

court action, against removal, 195, 225-230, 294, 316; for removal, 221-222, 230-231; bypassed, 26, 139, 225-228; useless, *xxviii*, 195, 225-226, 230; and Section 12, 19; on bantustan action, *xxx*, 140; on door numbering, 133; on state violence, 286; on demolition notices, 143; on banishment, 142-143; against consolidation, 43; *and see* resistance support (lawyers), interdicts

Crossroads (Old Crossroads), W Cape in/s near Cape Town, 'reprieve' and after, *xxi-xxii, xxvi, xxvii*, 13, 242, 283-284, 384, 393, 396; resistance, *xxxiii*, 33, 315, 400; state violence, 58, 148, 396; strategies, 283-284, 287, 302, 315, 395, 397; moves to, 281, 283, 335; permits refused, 58; 'no more bulldozing', 242; publicity, 58, 150; support, 306-307, problems,

319, 399; 'holding place', 332; vested interest, 307; *and see* New Crossroads
crown land, *see* state land

Daggakraal, E Tvl b/s near Wakkerstroom, bought, 74-75; resistance, 293, 374
Damaraland, Namibia r/area, 280
Dannhauser, N Natal transit camp and area near, cleared, 115, by police/army, 147, 148-150; camp, 332
death/injury, police action, *xxvi*, 148, 170, 258, 396, *and see* violence (state); resistance action, 282, 313, 314 *and see* violence (resistance); from starvation, 283, 348-349 *and see* diet/starvation; figures withheld, 15; *and see* livestock in removal
decentralisation, *xxvii*, 386 *and see* border industries, commuters
deception, about site, 5, 150, 168-169, 186, 190, 194, 202, 291; bluffs, *xxviii*, 160, 165 (denied), 172, 186, 224, 226-227, 234, 235, 254, 264, 294, 301; *and see* evasion, persuasion, promises broken, state misinformation
Deerward, Bop. c/s near Kuruman, N Cape, 55, 285
De Hoop, W Cape nature reserve and missile base near Agulhas, 46-47
delay, 166, 289, 303; for removal, 132, case study 232-238; for resistance, 136, 285, 303, 314-315; *and see* removal strategies, resistance strategies
Delmas, E Tvl district, 30
demolition, authority for, 134, 135, 138, 139; law against stopping,

139-140, 146; no notice needed, 143 *and see* notice; of tenant housing, 129-130, 133, 172, 173, 224, 226-227; of informal settlements, 57-58, 107, 146-147, 176, 224, 234 *and see* informal settlements (raids); in townships, 33, 163; rural, 6; by other agencies, 151; threatened, 217, 219, 226, 227, 270; described/cited, 148, 195, 196, 236, 253, 256, 257, 259, 269-272, 291; as slum clearance, *q.v.*; *and see* state misinformation
dependants, *see* family/dependents
'deportation', for 'aliens', 21, 34, 395; evaded, 33, 283; no appeal, 140, 395; cost, 162-163
deproclamation, *see* proclamation /deproclamation
Desmond, Cosmas, *xxi, xxiii*, 7, 12, 288,·344, 345 *and see* Foreword
detention, *see* intimidation/threat, security police action
Development Boards (arm of Cooperation and Development Department, called Administration Boards until 1982) *xiv, xxix*; removal by, 5-6, 58, 129-130, 162, 163, 172-173, 197, 202, 211, 216, 224-227, 230-231, denied, 228; pressure by, *xxxii*, 129-130 (alleged), 161, 165, 201-206, 234, 269, 271, 272, 279, 283, 377; force denied, 130, 172-173, 224, 225; removal documents etc., 24, 203-206, 228-230, 272; armed force, 58, 269; court action by, 221-222, 230-231; court action against, 225-230; credited with reprieve by state, *xxxi*; *and see* Boards listed in index
Diamond Fields Administration Board, *see* Development Boards, case study 201-221

Index 417

diet/starvation, 363-365; bad, 283, 326, 328, 335, 349; better diet, 232-233, 299, 300, 364-365; rations, 236, 343, 348; *and see* family/dependants, poverty/suffering, health
Dimbaza, Trust camp now Ciskei r/township near King William's Town, E Cape, early days, 116, 341, 344; outcry at, 57, 345, 346 (as Nxesha i.e. Mngqesha, its first name), 347, 350; development, 347; employment, 352, 353, 354-355, 356; unemployment, 348, 360
Discarded People, The, see Desmond, Cosmas
disease, *see* health
disinvestment, 307, 110, 389-390
District Six, W Cape coloured/Malay area of Cape Town finally cleared 1982, 36
Di Takwanen, N Cape b/s (reserve) near Vryburg, removal pressure, 288; resistance, 147, 285
division, for political control, *xx-xxi*, 23, 66, 95, 98-99, 101, 106, 113, 124, 188, 311, 339, 377, 383, 398 *and see* apartheid, ethnicity, population; for removal, *xxvii*, 156, 166-168, 172-173, 190, 220, 234, 235, case study 266-278, 284, 290-292, 293, 304, 315, 338-339; *and see* ethnicity, gradual removal, group areas, 'illegals', landowners, resistance problems, tenants
Doornkop, N Tvl b/s near Middelburg, removal, 316-317
downgrading (for removal), 160; freeze/bar improvement, 161, 203-220 *passim*, 234, 267; facilities stopped/refused, 160, 215, 260, 267-268, 288, 292, 316; opposed, 203, 274, 277; assets transferred, 223, 260; *and see* demolition, slum clearance, removal strategies
Drakensberg Administration Board, coercion by, 269, 271, 272 *and see* Development Boards
Driefontein, E Tvl b/s near Wakkerstroom, bought, 74-75; coercion to move, 143, 144, 153, 154-155, 160, 167, 170, 175, 288, 294; resistance, *xxx*, 279, 288, 293-295, 301; *and see* black spots
Driepan, E Tvl b/s near Wakkerstroom, bought, 74-75; *and see* black spots
drought, farm labour during, 30; and recession, 35; livestock, 198; relief abused, 160, 305, 375
'dumping', 65, 341-346, 349-351; described, 6, (1960s) 116, 196-199, 328; for 'surplus', *xxii*, 28-29, 33, 34, 111, 123, 354; justified, 183-184; denied (1980), 138; 'never again', 390-391; bantustan acceptance of, 51, 183, 228; *and see* 'surplus' people, relocation sites
Duncan Village, E Cape African township in East London, removal/part reprieve, 57
Dundee, Natal area of, cleared, 115
Durban, Natal, labour sources, 34, 34-35, 355; Indian removal, 344; *and see* places near Durban in index
Du Toit Commission on *beswarting* (1960), 120, map 121
Dwars River, N Tvl b/s near Pietersburg, see Klipplaatdrift

East Cape Administration Board (ECAB), *see* case studies 189-201, 221-232; 129-130, 162

Eastern Cape, early days, 75-76; black spots, 184, 387; removals, *xxxi*, 10, 55, 57, 340; political refugees, 186; housing, 162, 348; under threat (1983), 11, 387; employment/income, *xxiii*, 354, 359, 361; conditions, *xxiii*, 376; *and see* places in index including *Ciskei, Transkei*

East London, E Cape, 57, 164

East Rand Administration Board, 163

education (African), for Cape vote, 76; state undertakings, 205, 342, 348; community action, 212, 220, 259-260, 299-300; individual efforts for, 35, 215, 335; resistance problems, *xxiv*, 130, 160, 185, 371

Eindermaak (*Indermaak*), N Tvl c/s in Lebowa near Bochum, 251 *and see Kromhoek* (same removal plan and area)

Ekangala, Tvl township near Bronkhorstspruit, *xxxi*

Ekuvukeni, KwaZulu, 'rudimentary settlement' in N Natal near Ladysmith, 267

Elukhanyweni, Ciskei, c/s near Stutterheim, E Cape, removal to (case study) 189-201; force described, 128; local removal to, 187; views on, 316; silence on, 15; no land, 341; employment, 353, 354, 356, 357, 359; unemployment, 360; *and see Humansdorp, Keiskammahoek*

employment (of blacks), 182, 351-358, 378-379; to 1913, 71, 73, 74, 75-76; to 1948, 76, 80-82, 83, 84, 86, 96-97; and residence rights, 28-30, 84, 105-106, 393-394; and housing, 166; fining for 'illegals', 24, 26, 161-162 *and see* 'illegals'; coloured labour preference, 57; self-employment, 361-362; retrenchment, 58, 116, 177, 119-120; *and see* border industries, farm labour, farming interests, industrial interests, industry, labour supply, state comment/texts, wages

endorsing out, *see* influx control

emergency camps, *see* transit camps

ethnicity, defined, *xv*; 22-23, 37-38, 88-89, 112-114, 179, 184-186; removal/harassment, 35, 36, 53, 54, 55, case study 125-127, 214, 292, 321, 370-372; conflict/disruption, *xx-xxi, xxx-xxxi*, 53, 59, 174-175; resistance problem, 280, 292; *and see* bantustans, state comment/texts

Europeans, official term, 'whites' after 1971

evasion (of responsibility for removal by state), by disengagement, 15, 184, 201, 274-276; deflecting blame, 101, 156, 158; silence/obscurity, 133, 143, 234, 236-237; bureaucracy, 165, 270; 'not my decision', 173, 191, 192, 260, 263, 321; invoking law, 276, 296; reply from lower authority, 274-275; timing visits, 173; 'letters of consent', 226; 'upgrading too costly', 204; no agendas, 242; denial, 211-212; removal by consolidation, 34, 116, 176, 177, 183 *and see* Trust land; *and see* accountability, state comment/texts

expropriation, cash delayed, 39; helpless at, 47; of black spots, 132; removal delayed, 136; Expropriation Act, 139, 142; *and see* compensation, consolidation

Ezakheni, KwaZulu r/township in N Natal near Ladysmith, created for inclusion in KwaZulu, 34; removal to, 267, 275, 277, 366, urged by whites, 64; employment, 66, 352-

353, 354, 356; unemployment, 359, 360; facilities, 340; boycott at, 350, 366; resistance to moving to, 266-278 (case study)

facilities/social services, on sites, 36, 55, 150, 177, 182, 202, 295, 321-322, 338-351, 377-378; responsibility to bantustans, 33-34, 66, 109-110; inadequacy, 118, 174-175, 177; abuse, 160, 174-175, 305, 371, 375, 377; before removal/lost by removal, 189, 202, 238, 240, 245-246, 277-278, 296-300; refused, 267-268; *and see* education, fuel, health, housing/shelter, housing (urban), pensions, promises broken, removal (before and after), shops/cost of living, state misinformation, water/sanitation

Fairleigh, African freehold area in Newcastle, N Natal, cleared, 100

family/dependants, removal policy, 26, 28-29; of migrants, 45, 216, 357-358; split by removal, 33, 130; in towns, 105, 117-118, 166, 393-394, 395; split by ethnicity, 127; in removal, 6, 47, 129-130, 136, 223-224, 227, 257-258, 271, 279

farm evictions, *xxiii*, 30-32, 67-68, 118-123, 372-373, 381; 1960-1983, 10; under threat (1983), *xxix*, 11, 391; policy/law/process, 28-30, 133-134, 136, 145-146; resistance, 280-281, 221-232 (case study); described, 4-5, 85-87, 136, 148-150; cited, 8, 46, 53, 54, 55, 57, 62-63, 146-147, 326, 336 *and see* rural removal factors, 'surplus' people

farming (African in 'white' areas), to 1913, 76, 78-79, 80, 83-84; farms rented, 31; *and see* sharecroppers

farming interests (white), in land/labour to 1913, 72-74, 75, 76, 80; in land/labour to 1948, 83-84, 85, 87, 89-90, 92, 97-98; in local labour storage, 30; seasonal labour, 32; for/against consolidation, 38, 39, 43-44, 53, 179, 388; in removal from 1960s, 63-64, 116, 119-122; in labour tenancy in 1970s, 31, 123

farm labour, to 1913, 73, 74, 75; tenancy systems, 30, 120, 122-123; shortage in 1950s, 97-98; trapped labour, *xxii*, 32, by pass law arrest 106, 108; surplus in 1960s, 116, 118-120, 122-123; *and see* farm evictions, labour tenants, rural population, rural removal factors

fear/mistrust, 130-131, 140-141; of arrest/violence, 33, 128, 140, 160, 196, 207, 237; of lost assets, 160, 237; of removal again, 166; of authorities' power, 272, 279; from rumour/uncertainty, 132, 140-141, 166, 235, in cases of 'confidentiality', 302; *and see* intimidation/threat

fines, *see* influx control, intimidation/threat

Fingo Village, E Cape African freehold township in Grahamstown, group areas in, 100; housing, 162

force/coercion, 146-148, 169-170, 175-176, 290; land claims to 1913, 70-82; in 1960s, 35, 110; to commuting/migrancy, 32, 33, 34, 111; on bantustans, 22; by bantustans, 55, 57, 127, 140, 185, 190; by housing, 161-163, 203, 217; with lodgers' permits/licences, 218, 272; denying facilities/assets, 160, 215, 223, 260; punishing resistance, 285; against voteless, 46, 130; denied, 129-130, 153, 173, 193, 224, 225; disguised by language, 8, 28-30, 128-130, 138, 151, 154, 157; *and see* demolition, intimidation/threat, raids, removal agents, removal powers, removal strategies, state comment/texts, state misinformation, violence (state)

Frankfort, Ciskei c/s near King William's Town, E Cape, removal to, 57, bribery alleged, 159; site land, 322-323, 324, 325, 387

freehold, *see* black spots, land tenure

Free State, N Natal b/s near Bulwer, 79

fuel, 236, 326, 334, 341

Garankuwa, Bop. r/township near Pretoria, Tvl, removal to, 118

Gatlhose-Maremane, N Cape reserves cleared 1977, removal, 47, 285, 386

Gazankulu, N Tvl bantustan self-governing since 1 Feb. 73 under Proclamation 15/1973, land area, population density (1980), *xxx*, 17, maps (1982) 48, 50; origins as ethnic unit, 37-38, 125-127; conditions, 8, 44, 46, 378; *and see* bantustans

Gertrudsburg, N Tvl b/s (Lutheran mission) near Louis Trichardt, army removal, 147

GG transport, action described, 6, 128, 129, 136, 196-197, 224-225, 227, 235-236, 256, 257, 365, 366; backed by force, 6, 128, 146, 149, 195, 196-197, 256-259; goods damaged in, 6, 128, 195, 197, 213-214, 240; 'foreign' crew, *xxvi*, 136, 166, 197, 236; evaded, 257-259, 280-281

Ginsberg, E Cape African township at King William's Town, housing, 162

Glen Grey, E Cape district incl. in Ciskei until 1976, then in Transkei, land/people shifts, 38, 57; refugees from, 186, 340

Glenmore, E Cape transit camp near Grahamstown on Trust land till Dec. 81, then Ciskei, removal to, 3-6, 129-130, case study 221-232; dumping accepted, 51, 228; removal again, *xxxi*, 47-51, 187, 232, 373; early days, 348-349; employment, 353, 356; unemployment, 359, 360; diet, 363, 364

gradual removal, weakest first, 129-130, 207, 223, 224-225, 227; willing first, 190; a few at a time, 58, 195-196, 207, 215-219, 224; *and see* delay, slum clearance

Grey, Sir George, British Governor of the Cape Colony 1854-1861, 'native policy', 75-76

Groblersdal, N Tvl district, 30

group areas, defined, *xii*; 35-36, 99-103; removals (1960-1983), *xx, xxii, xxiii*, 10, under threat (1983), *xxxi*, 11, 53, 58, 61, 99-100, 160, 373; townships, 334 (SPP surveys), 339, 392-393; and profiteering, 102; no prosecution figures, 13; defended, 100, 101; *and see* coloureds, Indians, removal (whites), state comment/texts, townships, transport

Groutville, Natal b/s near Stanger, resistance, 279

Guguletu, W Cape African township

near Cape Town, under threat, 58; 99-year leasehold, *xxvi*

harassment, *see* intimidation/threat
headmen, *see*, chiefs/headmen
health, disease, 340, 344, 346, 349, 378 *and see* death/injury, water/sanitation; malnutrition, *see* diet/starvation; services, 177, 182, 340, 341, 344, 349, state undertaking 342, 348; *and see* overcrowding, slum clearance
Helpmekaar, N Natal district, cleared, 115
Herschel, E Cape district incl. in Ciskei till 1976, then in Transkei, land/people shifts, 38, 57, 168; refugees from, 186, 301; apparent bribery, 168
Hertzog, General JBM, Prime Minister in Pact government 1924-1933, policy, 87-89
Hewu, N Ciskei district near Queenstown, E Cape, land added, 38
Hillside, E Cape in/s at Fort Beaufort, housing, 162
Himeville, Natal area, 310 *and see* Swamp, The
Hlatikhulu, N Natal b/s near Dundee, 79
homelands, *see* bantustans
Hopewell, Natal b/s near Pietermaritzburg, 79
householders, for influx control, 26, division on, 166
housing/shelter, range, 55, 202, 212-213, 330, 340, 341, 378; 1983 state commitment, 343; informal, 35, 284, 335-336; tents, 159, 197, 343, 344, 345, 346, 348, 349; 'tomato box', 3, 6, 197, 213, 346, 348, 349; Fletcraft (tin huts), 232, 284, 343, 348, 349; good/urban grade, 55, 204-205, 344, 349 *and see* housing (urban); hostels, 206, 212; deception on, 5, 169, 197; as bribes, 23, 159, 168, 250, 254, 313; to channel labour, 35; building after removal, 343, 346, 350, 231-232; *and see* compensation, demolition, downgrading, rentals, slum clearance
housing (urban), crisis (1940s), 95, 212-213; removal by limiting, 160-163, 201, 206, 284, 392-393, 394; as a control, 57, 166; expensive, 35, 57-58; African in RSA, 20; outlay avoided, 187-188; profiteering, 102; described, *see* housing/shelter; *and see* influx control, removal strategies, rentals, urban residence rights (African)
Huhudi, N Cape township at Vryburg officially reprieved 1985, resistance, *xxxi*, *xxxii*, *xxxvii*, *xxxviii*, case study, 201-221; isolation, 292; lulling words, 303; vested interest in, 312
Humansdorp, E Cape town near Port Elizabeth, removal, *see* Mfengu reserves case study 189-201; return to, 316; jobs at, 354

identity documents, for bantustans, 21-22; SA reference book ('pass', 'dompas'), 22, under Orderly Movement Bill, 25; stamped 'Farm work only', 32; anti-pass campaign, 32
Ilinge (*Illinge*), E Cape c/s ceded from Ciskei to Transkei in 1976, near Queenstown, 33; exposé, 57, 346
'illegals', a forced position, 335;

policy, 24-27, 61, 104, 133, 138, 146, 161-162, 164, 166-167; action against, 32-33, 34-35, 57-58, 107, 108, 129, 146-147, 176, 263; case studies involving, 201-221, 266-278; *and see* influx control, squatters, state comment/texts

imprisonment, *see* intimidation/threat

Inanda, Natal in/s in KwaZulu near Durban, commuter tenants, 35; raids, 176

Inanda Newtown, Natal r/township near Durban on Trust land and now KwaZulu, for labour, 35; employment, 352, 356, 357; unemployment, 360; diet, 364; deception, 169

'independence', *see* bantustans

Indermaak, see Eindermaak

Indians, pressed into role, 100-101, 383; in land quota, 16; group area removals, 35-36, 99-103, 202, 312; classified, *xiii*, 95; barred from OFS, N Natal, 99; in pecking order, 339, 377, 382; b/s landowners, 266, 274; *and see* Indian townships in index

industrial interests (white) excl. mining, to 1948, 80-81, 82, 83-84; from 1940s, 96, 102, 107-108; against consolidation, 39, 388; in labour pools, 35, 102; shift to skilled labour, *xxii*, 34, 96, 117; *and see* industry

industry (white) incl. mining, in 1940s boom 95-96, worker organisation 96, opposition 96-97; and group areas, 36, 102; labour needs to 1913 80-81, 1940s-1950s, 96, 107-108, 117, 382; and bantustans 206, 347, 379; *and see* border industries

influx control, defined, *ix; xx, xxvii,* *xxviii-xxix*, 9, 32-34, 57, 58, 67, 103-109, 163-166, 382, 384-385, 391-395; 1940s, 96, 97-98; 1960s, 117-118; endorsing out defined, 104; reversing the flow, 381 *and see* 'surplus' people; and bantustans, 17, 109-110, 124, 392; and informal settlements, 35, 335 *and see* informal settlements; Orderly Movement Bill, 23-27, 383; for farm labour, 97, 106; as 'aliens' control, 18-22, 124-125, 126, 162-163, 184; with group areas, 99-100; with housing, 52, 161-163, 392-394; with labour control, 108-109; with townspeople, 24, 383, 393; with transport, 394; and Rikhoto (urban rights), 164-165, 393-394; tightened, 164, 361, 382, 384-385, 391, 396; policy failures, 391-392; and resistance, 311; *and see* group areas, family/dependants, housing, labour supply, removals policy, state comment/texts, urban residence rights (African)

informal settlements, defined, *xiii*; 334-336, 337-338; removals (1960-1983), 10; under threat (1983), 11, 34-35; developing, 96 (1940s urban boom), 34-35, 53, 57, 392; raids etc., 34, 58, 104, 107, 147-148, 176, 283; bantustan removals, 35, 185, 187; tighter control, 26, 104, 391, 393, 394; *and see* influx control, squatters, places in index

information control, by delay, 43, 51; misinformation, 13-16, 120-121; incomplete records, 9, 13; press ban etc., 14-15, 141, 142, 215, 218, 225, 256, 374; access to places, 7-8, 12, 141, 225, 256, 330, 351,

Index

373-374; 'homeland affairs', 15, 184, 186, 201, 374; *and see* evasion (of responsibility for removal by state), publicity, removal strategies

informers, *see* coopted agents, intimidation/threat, unemployment

infrastructural work, and removal (1960-1983), 10, threatened (1983), 11, 46-51, 68, 171, 186-187, 293

Ingwavuma, N Natal district, not for Swaziland, 43; ethnic stress, 184; resistance, 282 *and see* Kangwane (resisting same plan), *Makhathini Flats* (same general area)

Inkatha, KwaZulu's ruling political party, for resistance, 286; vested interest, 312

insecurity, *see* intimidation/threat, removal strategies, resistance problems

interdicts, law against, 139; ineffectual, 225-226, 309; *and see* resistance support

intimidation/threat, 160; informers, 140-141; interrogation/threats, *xxiii*, 140, 149, 191, 226, 227, 254, 256, 259, 262, 270, 280, 286; arrest/imprisonment/detention, *xxiii*, 25, 26, 32-33, 136, 140, 146, 149, 194, 195, 196, 197, 207, 220, 230, 257, 258, 283, 286; pinning people down (personal data, house numbering, etc.), 133, 225, 234, 252, 255, 264, 269, 271; isolation /insecurity, 130, 173, 215, 217, 235, 280, 290 *and see* information control, resistance support; harassment, 55, 102, 127, 179, 202, 218, 220, 256, 273, 283, 286, 290; resisted, 287; *and see* fear/mistrust, force/coercion, raids, removal strategies, resistance problems, resistance (protection during), violence (state)

isolation, and sites, 55, 341, 343, 349-350; and resistance, 130, 195, 282, 288, 289, 293, 318; 'no outsiders', 252, 281-282, 309 *and see* resistance strategies; removal, case study 232-238; through reprieve, 389; *and see* information control, intimidation/threat, resistance problems

Itsoseng, Bop. c/s near Lichtenburg, W Tvl, removal to, 33; in/s nearby, 392

Jabavu Location, N Natal r/township near Ladysmith, removal to, 267

Jan Kempdorp, N Cape town, vested interest, 312 *and see* case study 201-221

Jonono's Kop, N Natal b/s near Ladysmith, dividing, 168; resistance, 279

Jubilee, N Natal b/s near Dannhauser cleared 1970, 79

Kabokweni, E Tvl r/township in Kangwane near White River, labour pool, 52; move to, 118, expensive, 336; employment, 352-353, 356; *and see Pienaar*, its in/s

Kabusi, E Cape area near Stutterheim, influx, 337-338

Kammaskraal, Ciskei transit camp 1980-1982 near Peddie, E Cape area, 349; removal, 373; employment, 354, 356, 357; unemployment, 360; diet, 363, 364; opinions, 336, 351

Kangwane, E Tvl bantustan self-governing 1 Oct. 77 under Procl. R214/1977, origins ethnic unit, 37-38, approved 38 (map 40-41); land area, pop. density (1980) 17, 1982 map 50; resisted transfer to Swaziland, 43; removal from, 126; removal to, 33; on removal, 177; employment, 51-52, 378; removal in, 187; ethnicity trouble, 293; health, 378

Kanyamazane, E Tvl r/township in Kangwane near Nelspruit, removal to, 33

Katlehong, Central Tvl township on the E Rand, demolitions, 163

Keiskammahoek, in Ciskei nr Stutterheim, E Cape, agricultural scheme, 187, 190, *and see Elukhanyweni*

Kenton emergency camp, E Cape camp estd. 1956 at Kenton near Port Alfred, removals, 222, 231; under threat, 232

Khayelitsha, W Cape African r/township near Cape Town, plan, *xxii*, 58, 393-397 *passim*; removal to, *xxvi, xxvii*, 284; and outsiders, 311; UDF resolution, 399-400

Klipfontein, E Cape farm with in/s near Kenton/Port Alfred, removal, case study 221-232, by force, 129-130; court action, 143, 281, 308-309; deception, 169

Klipplaatdrift, N Tvl Trust farm at Dwars River, 1962 removal to, 239; under threat, 241; 1979 removal, resistance, 1982 reprieve, 253-265 (Sekgosese case study)

Koornhof, Dr PGJ, Minister 1978-1984 of Cooperation and Development Department *q.v.*

Kosi Bay, KwaZulu area in N Natal, border strip, 47

Kromdraai, Bop. in/s cleared 1979, near Thaba 'Nchu, OFS,clearance, 292, 371

Kromhoek, N Tvl c/s in Lebowa near Bochum, removal to, 148, 240, 261-262; evaluated, 245-246, 248, 251, 261; *and see Eindermaak* (same plan and area) and *Klipplaatdrift* (source of removal)

KTC, W Cape in/s near Cape Town, raids etc., 176, 313; resistance, *xxxiii*, 279; support problems, 311; under threat, *xxvii*

Kuruman, N Cape area, 55, 349 *and see* neighbouring places in index

Kutama/Sinthumule, N Tvl b/ss near Louis Trichardt cleared 1979, cost factor, 303

KwaDabeka, Natal r/township in KwaZulu near Durban, removal to, 172

Kwaggafontein, Central Tvl c/s in KwaNdebele near Dennilton, conditions, 339-340, 341, 354, 365, 367; employment, 353-354, 356, 358

KwaMashu, Natal township now incl. in KwaZulu, near Durban, labour pool, 34

KwaNdebele, Central Tvl bantustan self-governing from 20 March 81 under Proclamation R60/1981, 178-179, 182-183, 369-372; origins as ethnic unit, 37, approved, 38 (map 40-41); land area, population density (1980) 17, area (1983) *xxx*, 183, maps (1975) 180, (1983) 181, (1982) 48-50; 'independence', 22, 53, 178, 182, 369-370, 387; land for, *xxxi*, 179, 182-183, 370, 387; and ethnicity, 23, 35, 179, 185; influx relocation, 35, 127, 177, 179, 182-183, 185, 369, 370, 376; conditions/policy, 53, 177,

182, 185, 375, 376; *and see* bantustans, removal and bantustans
KwaNdengezi, Natal r/township in KwaZulu near Durban, removal to, 172
KwaNgema, E Tvl b/s near Wakkerstroom, resistance, *xxviii*, 293
Kwapitela, Natal b/s near Himeville, removal, case study 232-238, submission to 131, by 'foreigners' 136, by delay, 146, 166, 280; division on, 291; resistance, *xxx*
KwaZulu, Natal bantustan self-governing from 1 Feb. 77 under Proclamation 11/1977, land area, population density (1980), 8, 17, 53, origin as ethnic unit 37, approved, 38 (map 40-41); consolidation, *xxiii*, 34, Ingwavuma 43, 184 *and see Kangwane* (also resisting plan), 39, 53, 295; removal, role/attitudes, 39, 143, 153-154, 156, 158, 176-188, 286; removal to, 66, 148-150, 168, 172, case study 232-238, 267; removal within, 187, 377; betterment, 46, 186; vested interests, 39, 290-291, 312; ethnic trouble, 184, 293; conditions/responsibility, 8, 66, 118, 362, 377, 378; *and see* bantustans, removal and bantustans
Kwelera, E Cape b/s near East London, threatened, 290

labour bureaux, *see* labour supply, influx control
labour supply, to 1913, 71-76 *passim*, 80, 81; from bantustans, 65-66, 108, 112 *and see* border industries; from pass law arrests, 106; with group areas, 102; to towns, 106, 117, 380; labour bureaux, 35, 108-109, 118; transport for, 36, 66, 182; recycling, 65-66; recruitment after 1948, 107-109, strict in Tvl, 52, stopped, 34, 378; *and see* employment (of blacks), coloureds, commuters, farm labour, 'illegals', migrant labour
labour tenants, defined, *xiii*, 30; origins, 73, 74, 75; abolition of, 30-31, 120, 122-123, 381; delayed in Natal, 31, 53, 123; eviction of, 30-31, 146-147, 148-150, 381 *and see* farm evictions
Lady Selborne, area of Pretoria, Tvl, removal under group areas, 174
Ladysmith, N Natal town and district, b/ss threatened, 277, 296-300, case study 266-278; authority upheld, 275; and support, 305; labour supply/relationships with town *see* nearby places listed in index
Lake St Lucia, N Natal state land in KwaZulu, removal, 47, 147, 151, to bad site 349
land, to 1913, 70-79; segregation, 82-83, 380; quota land, defined *xi*, 92; for population groups, 16-17; for reserves, *q.v.*, 89, 92; scheduled land, defined *x*, 85 *and see* scheduled land; released land, defined *x*, 89-90, 92; condition in reserves to 1948, 93-94; condition in bantustans, *q.v.*, 35, 45-46, 55, 374-375; congested, damage to, 17, 93-94, 123-124, 177, 336-337, 375, *and see* overcrowding; landlessness, *xx*, 197-198, 237, 240, 336, 341, 350, 367, 368, and standard of living 364-365, 378, 379; for bantustans, 177, 183 *and see* consolidation; for removals, 198, 200-201, 240; agricultural sites, 331, 332; *and see* black spots,

company land, land tenure, state land, Trust land

landowners, and state, 132, 137, 138; division on, 167-168, case study 232-238, 291; tricked, 169; and outsiders, 45

land tenure, freehold (incl. company, mission, private locations) and tribal land to 1913, 74-79; black freehold limited, 83-85, 90, 100; state (crown) land proclaimed, 78, 91-92, excluded from reserves 90; African urban leasehold, *xxvi-xxvii*, 20; *and see* Glossary for definitions

Langa, W Cape African township near Cape Town, under threat, *xxvi*, 58

law, *see* Acts/Bills, court action, expropriation, interdicts, laws, 'law and order', legal rights held/lost, removal powers, resistance support

'law and order', removal for, 26; banning for, 140; justifying police action, 147

laws, to 1913, 71-80 *passim*; on removal, *xxiii*, 138-146, 309; resistance attempts, *see* case studies 189-201, 221-232; loopholes closing, 143, 144; mystified/for evasion, 143, 276, 296; disguising apartheid, 138; *and see* Acts/Bills

lawyers, *see* resistance support

leadership/group structures, 250, 266, 286-288, 288-289, 290, 315; resistance leaders, 170, 175, 242, 285, 290; resistance committees, 193, 216, 217, 221, 254, 262, 266, 272, 286, 289, 325; 'we women', 264, 284, 287-288; students, 260; elite, 287, 318; traditional, 250-251, 290; state-claimed, 291, 322-323, 324-325 *and see* coopted

agents; attacked, 140, 160, 170, 195, 196, 211, 217, 220, 285, 290; *and see* negotiation (resistance), political parties, resistance strategies

leasehold, *see* land tenure

Lebowa, N Tvl bantustan self-governing from 20 Oct. 72 under Proclamation 225/1972, land area, population density (1980), 17; origins as ethnic unit 37, approved 38 (map 40-41), 1982 maps 48-50; and consolidation, *xxx*, 179, 240, 370; administering RSA area, 240; removals to, 239, 240, case study 238-266, congested from 46, opposing 241, 244, 257; removal from, 126; conditions etc., 245, 261, 362, 375; *and see* bantustans, removal to bantustans

Leeufontein, W Tvl b/s near Zeerust, reprieved 1983, 316

legal rights held/lost (by Africans), citizenship, 18, 21; RSA urban residence, 19, 34, 104-105; RSA urban leasehold, 20; against deportation, 21; vote, 19, 89, on farms, 31, 32, labour tenants 30-31, sharecroppers/cash tenants 84; land ownership/rental/purchase, 74, 80, 83-84, 89; in border shifts, 34; pensions 20, unemployment insurance 20-21, workmen's compensation 21; in removal, 132, 138-146; *and see* influx control, urban residence rights (Africans), vote

Lennoxton, N Natal African urban freehold area in Newcastle, destroyed, 100

Le Roux Committee, on consolidation, previously Van der Walt, reports, *xxix-xxx*, 387, 390-391

Lesotho, in Tomlinson proposals, 37-38; labour, 117; fighting, 388

Lichtenburg, W Tvl African township at, cleared, 33

Limehill, N Natal r/camp in 1968, now c/s in KwaZulu, near Ladysmith, removal to, 267; exposé and response, 345, 347

Local Land Committees 1918, *see* Beaumont Commission

livestock in removal, loss/prohibition, 6, 129, 157, 159, 198-199, 240, 259; no grazing, 150, 198, 231, 234-235, 237; overstocking, *see* land (congested)

Lohatla, military base on cleared N Cape reserves *Gatlhose-Maremane, q.v.*, 47

Lothair, E Tvl town and r/area in Kangwane, 'persuasive' visit, 295, 301

Louis Trichardt, N Tvl town, land clash, 43; ethnic clash, 53; vested interest, 312; *and see* related places in index

Lusitania, N Natal b/s near Ladysmith, resistance memo, 296-300

Machaviestad, W Tvl b/s near Potchefstroom cleared 1971, views on removal, 281, 285; tricked, 301

Madadeni, N Natal r/township in KwaZulu near Newcastle, move evaded, 281

Madikwe, Bop. r/township, *see* Morsgat

Mafikeng (Mafeking), Bop. town, W Tvl area, consolidation, 313; group under threat, 376

Mahodi N Tvl c/s in Lebowa near Pietersburg, removal to, 239-240; conditions, 334, 350, 356, 365

Makgokgwane, W Tvl b/s near Ventersdorp, deception, 169

Makgato, N Tvl people and their village area, *Klipplaatdrift q.v.*, case study 238-266; removal, 148, 150, 313; publicity, 150; and lawyers, 309

Makhathini Flats, N Natal state land orig. Tongaland, now *Ingwavuma q.v.*, Tongas dispossessed, 78, 91-92; 1980s removal, 187

Malukazi, Natal in/s in KwaZulu near Durban, 392

Mangope, Chief Lucas, President of Bophuthatswana, *q.v.*

Manyeding, N Cape Reserve in Kuruman area, consolidation unsure, 387

Maremane, N Cape reserve, *see Gatlhose-Maremane*

Mathopestad, W Tvl b/s near Boons, removal strategies, *xxviii*, 153, 168, 303, 312, 313; resistance, 279, 282, 313, 400; employment, 360-361

Matiwane's Kop, N Natal b/s near Ladysmith, origin, 79; influx, 336, 337; employment, 360-361; diet, 364; removal strategies, 143, 153-154, 169; resistance, *xxx*, 279, 304

Matlala, N Tvl people near Pietersburg, resistance, 314

Matoks, N Tvl reserve area near Pietersburg, reprieved 1952, *see* Sekgosese case study for resistance 250-255, *also* 281-282, 288, 309, 313

Mayen Reserve, N Cape, removal, 147

Mbazwana, NE Natal r/area in Makhathini Flats *q.v.*, KwaZulu, described, 349

Mdantsane, Ciskei r/township near

East London, E Cape, in 1960s, 344; removal to, 57, 118, 161, deception on, *xxxi*, 168-169; conditions, 162, 364, 398; employment, 352-353, 356, 358; unemployment, 359, 360

mechanisation on farms, *see* rural removal factors

memoranda/petitions, 296; texts, 159, 207-215, 242-249, 267, 269, 273-274, 296-300, as letter, 218-219; preparing and use, *see* negotiation tactics (resistance)

Meran, N Natal b/s near Wasbank, cleared 1968, 79

Mfengu Reserves and people, *see Tsitsikama*

Mgwali, E Cape b/s near Stutterheim, removal pressures, 140, 159, 160, 286, 287, 289, 290, 296, 303, 304, 321-325; silence on, 184; resistance, *xxx*, 159, 279, 324-325

migrant labour, to 1948, 76, 80-82, 84; controls from 1948, 107-109, 355-358, 378-379; residence rights, 164-166; forced by removal, 32, 33, 46; swing from, *xxii*, 34, 289, 381; in resistance, 265, 289, 317; split families, 216, 357-358, 378; remittances, 326, 379

military action, to 1910, 70-75, 78, 80, 146, 147, 176, 194; described, 128, 149, 196-197; low profile, 151, 158; censorship, 141; *and see* strategic control

mining interests (white) to 1913, land/land rental 74, labour 80-82; to 1948, 83, 84; in removal 115

minority rule, early days, 70-72, 74, 75-76, 78; by exclusion, 16-19, 25, 88, 103-104, 107, 110-114, 124-125; removal for, 59-60, 66, 103-104, 155, 367-368; removal under, 46, 105-106, 130, 386, 391; and land, 139; and ANC, 98, 103; by proclamation, 88; without Cape vote, 89 *and see* vote; *and see* accountability, apartheid, bantustans, control, cooption, division missions, *see* land tenure

Mitchells Plain, W Cape r/township near Cape Town for coloureds, 58

Mkhize, Saul, Driefontein resistance leader, on removal, 294, 295; on lawyers, 288; killing of, 170, 175, 295, 313; *and see Driefontein*

Mlungisi, E Cape township at Queenstown, housing, 162

Modderdam, W Cape in/s near Cape Town cleared 1977, demolition notices, 143; violent removal, 147; escape from, 281

Mogopa (Zwartrand), W Tvl b/s near Ventersdorp cleared 1984, threatened, 45, 385; removal/resistance, *xxvi, xxviii, xxx*, 291

Mokerong 1, NW Tvl reserve area in Lebowa near Botswana border, possibly reprieved, 387

Mondlo, N Natal r/camp on Trust land 1962, now KwaZulu r/township, near Vryheid, early days, 116, 344; in/s nearby, 392

Monsterlus, N Tvl c/s on Trust land, now Hlogotlou r/township, Lebowa, removal to, 317

Morsgat, W Tvl r/camp on Trust land, now Bop. r/township called Madikwe, early days, 116, 344, 346

Mosita, N Cape b/s near Vryburg, removal, 147

Motlatla, W Tvl b/s near Lichtenburg, resistance, 301-302

Moutse, N Tvl area in Lebowa near

Dennilton, due for KwaNdebele, 179, 370
Mozambique and border, security etc., 47, 151, 388; workers, 117
Mphakane, N Tvl b/s near Pietersburg, cleared 1977-80, removal, 239, 240
Mphophomeni, Natal r/township in KwaZulu near Pietermaritzburg, removals to, 118
Mpondos (SE Ngunis), strong chiefdom, 75; Tomlinson proposal, 37-38
Mudiboon, W Tvl b/s near Rustenburg cleared 1966, moved, 283
Munnik, N Tvl white farm near Soekmekaar, cleared, 239 *and see Klipplaatdrift*, the Makgatos' destination
Mzimhlope, Natal c/s in Qudeni area of KwaZulu near Kranskop, described, 341, 348; employment, 353, 354, 356; *and see box* 148-150

Naboomspruit, N Tvl township at, 'surplus' removed, 33
Namibia, removal to, 280; fighting, 59, 388
Natal, to 1913, 75-79 (incl. map); removals, *xxiii*, 9, 44-46, 53 (map 52), 1960-1983 10, threatened (1983), *xxi*, 9-10, 11, varying b/s figures 13; KwaZulu consolidation, *xxiii*, 37-39 (map 40-41), resistance on Ingwavuma *q.v.*, 43; labour tenancy in, 31, 53, 123; ban on Indians, 99; emergency camps, 332; resistance, 53, 296; no reprieves, 312; SPP surveys, 329, 330; *and see* 330; *and see* KwaZulu places listed in index
Natal Agricultural Union/Natal Landbou Unie (NAUNLU), opinions through, 31, 43, 63-64, 109, 120, 123
National Party (white), 1948 policy, 95, 99, 100; constraints on, (1948) 95-98, 386; bantustan policy, 16, 155, 185; consolidation dilemma, 43; and CP, 43-44, 382; economic advantages to, 102-103; on coloured labour preference, 395
national states, *see* bantustans
Native Farmers' Association, land purchases, 74-75
Native Life in South Africa, quoted, 86-87
Native Representatives (and Council) created (1936), 89; scrapped (1959), 112
Ndebele people, bantustan for, *xxxi*, 38, 179, 372; 'independence' for, 178, 369-370; ethnic troubles, 23, 35, 179, 185, 371-372; 'voluntary' influx, 179, 182, 369; *and see* KwaNdebele
Ndonyane, Natal b/s in Klipriver district N of Ladysmith, resistance, 279
negotiation/consultation (for removal), 153-156, 158, 390-391, 321-325, 396; gives time, 285; in secret, 291; refused, 191-193; *and see* coopted agents, state comment/texts
negotiation (resistance), 302-303, 318-319, 395-396; at work, *see* accountability, negotiation tactics (resistance); problems, *see* resistance problems; advantages, *see* delay, reprieve; confidentiality, 302, 303
negotiation tactics (resistance), reactions to promises, 193, 245, 248, 251, 254, 256; to lapses/evasions,

222, 223, 243, 244, 276, 277; to error/confusion, 243, 247, 268-269, 276, 277, 324-325; to lies/rumours, 209-211, 211-213; to compensation, 252, 253, 303-304; care and planning, 251, 253; limitations, 208, 209, 211, 252; creative approach, 209, 243, 248, 249, 251-252, 277, 296-300; researching home and site, *see* sites evaluated; roles, powers, aims, 209, 213-214, 216-217, 248; making proposals, 246-247, 249, 277; chiefs for cover, 250-251; keeping the national context, 210, 213-215, 218, 245, 266, 276-277; historical perspective, 208, 218, 238, 240, 250, 254, 265, 267, 273-274, 276-277, 297-298; stating rights/demands, 215, 244, 246-247, 260; meetings requiring notice, 263; agendas, 242, 263, 293; cool spokesmen, 250; making full records/affidavits, etc., 209-210, 224-227, 243-244, 248, 251, 270-271 *and see* records/minutes; giving written record to the authorities, 251, 302 *and see* memoranda/petitions; dissociating from unauthorised spokesmen, 248, 291; unity, keeping accountable to group, 213, 290, 302; decisions from whole group, 213, 294; no secrets, 254, 290; guarding against cooption, 209, 211, 318-319; with outsiders, using parliamentary questions 274, some bantustans 248, 257, publicising arguments, *see* publicity, resistance support

Nelspruit, E Tvl township at, cleared, 33

Newcastle, N Natal area, cleared for mining, 115

New Crossroads, W Cape African r/township near Cape Town, under threat, 58, split with (Old) Crossroads *q.v.*, 284, 315

Newlands, E Cape mission/tribal area near East London, under threat, 290

Nguni people, shifts in 19th C, 126; Tomlinson on, 37

Nondweni, N Natal c/s near Nqutu in KwaZulu, conditions, 350

non-negotiation/'authority' (for removal), 'ordered by parliament', 143, 144, 321, 385; 'refusing a lawful order', 242; 'your chief awaits you', 256, 263; 'trespass', 230, 262; 'agreed in consultation', *see* state comment/texts; citing group areas, betterment, consolidation, ethnicity, infrastructural work, squatters, slum clearance/health hazard, *all q.v. and* housing ('housing shortage'), proclamation ('deproclamation'), influx control ('illegals', 'aliens'); rejecting appeal/'closed case'/ignoring people, 191-194, 200, 215, 219, 241, 271, 366; responses to, 61, 100, 131, 143, 145, 191-192, 235, 255, 265, 276-277

non-negotiation (resistance), in 1940s, 96; 1950s, 103; refer officials to others, 252; dissociating from 'spokesmen', 248, 291, 325; refusing notices/to demolish, 223, 224, 262; refusing cooption, 209, 211; refusing compensation, 252, 253; accepting arrest, fines, 194, 279; blocking entry/house numbering, 194, 195, 252-253, 257; leaving authority structure, 216-217; refus-

ing visit to site, 293, 295, 301; refusing information, 255, 264; collecting transferred pensions, 223; defying authorities, 193, 220, 230, 263; flight, 256, 257-259, 281; returning home/rebuilding, 33, 203, 220, 253-265 *passim*, 277, 279, 281, 283
non-resistance, 280, 282-283, 284-289 *passim*, case study 232-238; before 1920, 86-87, 91-92; conditional, 303; and pensions, 302
North Sotho people, 370, 372 *and see* Lebowa, their ethnic bantustan
Northern Cape, removals, *xxiii*, 55, (1960-1983) 10, threatened (1983) 11; reserves for military bases, 47; resistance, case study 201-221; conditions, 55, 375, 376; white interests, 389; *and see* places in index
Northern Cape Administration Board (NCAB), *see* case study 201-221
notice, 132-136; promises with, 190; response ignored, 191-194; none /inadequate, 6, 222-223, 269-271; bypassed, 142-143; to tenants first, 172; household heads evaded, 173; texts, 132, 134 (as undertaking), 135, 173. 222, 270, 272
Ntabethemba, N Ciskei r/area near Queenstown, E Cape, conditions, 301 *and see* Herschel (origin of people)
Nxesha (Mngqesha), E Cape dumping ground, now Dimbaza in Ciskei, 346 *and see* Dimbaza
Nyanga, W Cape African township near Cape Town, threatened, *xxvi*, 58
Nyanga Bush, W Cape in/s near Cape Town, problems, 58, 308, 311; accountability, 302; 1981 removal from, 312, 395

Old Crossroads, see Crossroads
Onderstepoort, Bop. c/s near Sun City, Central Tvl area, *xxviii, xxx,* 168, 313
Onverwacht (Botshabelo), OFS Trust c/s near Bloemfontein, for Qwaqwa, forced influx to, *xxxi, xxxiii,* 55, 161, 186, 202, 292, 371; hidden dump, 7-8, 30, 55, 301; employment, 353, 354, 356
Orange Free State (OFS), to 1913, 72-74, 80, 82; 1940s, 98-99; removals, *xxiii*, 54-55, (1960-1983) 10, threatened (1983) 11, 30, 33, 36, 85-87, 161, 338; origins of ethnic unit, 37-38, map 40-41, ethnic rifts, 292; Indians banned, 99; labour tenancy abolished, 123; erosion, 375; SPP survey, 329; *and see* Qwaqwa, places in index
OFS Agricultural Union, opinions, 97, 98
overcrowding, in reserves/bantustans, 8, 16-18, 31, 34-35, 55, 55-56, 92-94, 123-124, 179, 182-183, 292, 327, 336-338, 375, 376; for jobs, legality, 34-35; and conflict, 263, 373; with freeze, 267; reason for removal, 63
Oxton, Ciskei transit camp and c/s near Queenstown, E Cape, delayed in transit, *xxxi*, 57, misled 301 *and see* Glen Grey (place of origin)

Pachsdraai, W Tvl Trust r/site near Zeerust for Bop., *xxvi*, 291 *and see* Mogopa (people moved to site)
Pact government (1924-1933), policy, 87-88
Pampierstad, Bop. r/township orig. Trust near Jan Kempdorp, N Cape, 1968-80 removals to, 118,

202, 207; resistance, *xxxii, xxxiii*, case study 201-221; conditions, 328, 364; employment, 352; unemployment, 216, 360
parliament, authorising removal, 132, 189-190; limitations, 139; invoked, 143, 145; African representation, 89,112; and removed people, 200 *and see* PFP
party political interests, Inkatha in resistance, 312; CNIP in membership, 38, 308, 375; CP on consolidation, 42, 43-44, 388
passes/pass laws, *see* identity documents, influx control
peasantry (African), *see* farming (African in 'white' areas)
Peddie, Ciskei village and c/s near King William's Town, E Cape, removal to, *xxxi*, 373
Pedi people, *see* North Sotho
pensions, removal pressure, 223, 227, 160; in RSA for African 'aliens', 20; on transfer, 20; private pensions, 20; unpaid, 174-175, 232; vital income, 326, 328, 362-363, 379; in bantustans, 20, 177, 174-175, 326
persuasion, 168-169, 301; 'voluntary', 151-152, 154, 157; about the site, 203-206, 250, 254, 293-295, 301; *and see* cooption methods, deception, promises broken, state comment/texts, state misinformation
petitions, *see* memoranda/petitions
Phatudi, Dr Cedric N, Chief Minister of Lebowa, *q.v.*
Phoenix, Natal Indian group area township near Durban, described, 102, 339, 373; employment, 352, 355; unemployment, 359
Pienaar, E Tvl in/s at Kabokweni *q.v.* in Kangwane near White River,

335-336; employment, 352-353, 356
Plaatje, Sol, on effect of 1913 Land Act, 85-87
planning committees, 153-154, 156, 158, 322-323; indictment of, 159, 324-325; *and see* cooption
police action, role in removals, 146-150, 190, 254-255, 295; removal pressure, *xxvi*, 32-33, 55, 102, 107, 130, 149, 185, 195, 220, 222, 224, 226-227, 256, 258, 263, 292; violence, 58, 147-148, 170, 176, 194-197, 253, 256, 258, 396; low profile, 158
political parties, *see* Ciskei National Independence Party, Conservative Party, Inkatha, National Party, Progressive Federal Party, South African Party, United Party, party political interests, publicity/political pressure
'political' removals, Transkei refugees, 38, 57, 186; banishment, 140
population, land quotas for, 16-17; 1980 figures, 17; African distribution (1950-1980), 18; reserves (1950), 110; Africans in rural/ bantustan areas (1950-1980), 31; shift to bantustans 17, between bantustans, 38, 55, 57, 125-127, 179, 185-186, 369-372; density, 17, 55, 58; divisions racial, 95, ethnic, 23, urban/rural, 103, 106, 107, group areas, 99, reinforced, 101, 339; *and see* apartheid, ethnicity, group areas, influx control, overcrowding, rural population, urban population
Pondoland, annexed by Cape 1894, now Transkei area, betterment riots, 45; Tomlinson proposal,

37-38; *and see* Mpondos, *Transkei*
Pongola, N Natal part of Makhathini Flats in KwaZulu, for site, perhaps for excision, 295
Port Elizabeth, E Cape, vested interest, 312; work at, 355; *and see Soweto, Walmer Township*
Port Natal Administration Board (PNAB), 172-173
Potgietersrus, N Tvl township at, 'surplus' removed, 33
Potsdam, r/area near East London, *xxxi*
poverty/suffering, after Anglo-Boer War, 82; forcing moves (1940s), 94, (1980s) 335; need local work, 34; from migrancy/commuting, 355-357, 357-358; after removal, 292, 326-327, 328, 344-346, 348-350, 378, 379-380; *and see* diet/starvation, family/dependants, pensions, resistance problems, unemployment
Pretoria, Tvl, labour for, 34-35; removal from, 174; and KwaNdebele, 179; also meaning 'the SA government'
private locations, 75
proclamation/deproclamation, defined, *xii*; and township removal, 33-34, 51-52, 393; to alter tribal land, 139; rule by, 88; bantustans proclaimed in terms of the National States Constitution Act 21/1971, *see Gazankulu, Kangwane, KwaNdebele, KwaZulu, Lebowa, Qwaqwa*
Progressive Federal Party (white), on illegal land sale, 200; on illegal removal, 223; on black spot removal, 184, 255, 256, 274; on removal policy, *xxviii*, 374, 385, 389

promises broken, 168-169, 288, 301; 'no forced removal', 8, 191, 215, 224; 'alternative plan', 149-150, 209-210; Section 10 rights, 169; compensation, 169; 'freedom', 168-169; 'equivalant land', 190, 197-198; 'rights and houses', 283-284; good housing, 5, 150, 169, 190, 197; rent, 5, 168, 202; good site, 38, 57, 168-169; schools, clinics, 150; 'no more demolition', 242; *and see* persuasion (for removal), state misinformation
Prospect Farm, Natal b/s near Stanger, origin, 79
publicity/political pressure, 45, 46-47, 146-147, 150-151, 155-156, 170, 175-176, 288, 305-306, 317-318, 341-348, 389, 400; wide, vivid, effective, 7, 43, 47, 147-148, 150-151, 170, 175, 200, 223, 273, 289, 343, 345-348, 398-399; none, poor, useless, 47, 147, 195, 200, 288; policy obscured, evaded, defused by, 129, 130, 146, 151, 152, 155-156, 206, 224, 228, 261, 270, 327, 341-343, 345, 348, 350-351, 390; suppressed, *see* information control; state shift on, 146, 147, 150-151; state image-making through coopted agents, negotiation (for removal), persuasion, reprieves, terminology, state comment/texts, *all q.v.*; image for removals *see* slum clearance/health hazard, 'voluntary' removal
Pudumong (Pudimoe), Bop. r/township near Vryburg, N Cape, resisting move to, 201-221 (Huhudi, since reprieved); removal to, *xxxii*, 203, 218; advertised, 203-206

Putfontein, W Tvl b/s near Lichtenburg, cleared, 386

Qudeni, Natal r/area in KwaZulu, removal to, 148-150 *and see* Mzimhlope
Queenstown, E Cape, and unemployment, 351; *and see* related places in index
quota land, *see* land
Qwaqwa, OFS bantustan self-governing from 1 Nov. 74 under Proclamation 203/1974, land area, population density (1980), 17; origins as a unit, 37-38, map 40-41, 73; removal to, 54, 185-186, 292; dense r/areas, 8, 55 *and see* Onverwacht, 338; more land, 292; ethnic issues, 186, 292 *and see* South Sotho

raids, pass raids, 32-33, 58, 107, 176; ethnic raids, 185, 292; demolition raids, 58, 104, 147-148, 176; other intimidatory raids, 202, 217; *and see* demolition, ethnicity, influx control, intimidation/threat
records/minutes, minutes/affidavits, etc., 209-210, 224-227, 243-244, 248, 251, 270-271, 324-325; hold on negotiation, 242-249, 251, 302-303; historical argument, 193, 208-209, 218, 238-265 *passim*, 267, 273-274, 276-277, 297-298
recruitment, *see* labour supply
reference books, *see* identity documents
released land, *see* land
relocation (action/reaction after), went home, 33, 253-254, 261, 262-265, 279, 281, 283, 316; trying to reverse removal, 189, 199-201; bitter, 189, 262, 285; conflict, disruption, 33, 59, 127, 130, 190, 292, 350, 361; demoralised, helpless, 6, 214, 232, 237, 285, 326, 328, 345, 365-367, 380; endurance, survival, 55, 326-327, 335, 336, 350, 361-363; local organisation, 350, 365-367, 380; of outsiders, 343, 345, 347; some expectations, 339, 344

relocation sites, types of, 330-332, 334-338 *and see* agricultural settlements, closer settlements, group areas, informal settlements, sites evaluated, state misinformation, townships, transit camps; facilities, 338-351 *and see* facilities/social services; economic conditions, 351-365 *and see* employment (of blacks), unemployment/workseeking, diet/starvation, migrant labour, commuters, pensions, rentals; organisation/attitudes in, 365-367 *and see* relocation (action/reaction after); consolidated, *see* Trust land; and outsiders, 343, 347, 351, 373-374 *and see* information control, isolation, publicity/political pressure; expectations, *see* deception, promises broken, state misinformation; *and see* concentration camps

removal, to 1948, 70-93 *passim*; to 1970, 99-100; 1975-1982 with cost, 14; national overview (1960-1983), 8-13, 67-68, 372-390; regional overviews, 51-58; categories of, *xxii*,

32-51, 373 *and see* betterment, black spots, consolidation, farm evictions, group areas, influx control, infrastructural work, 'political' removals, strategic control, urban removal; views and theories on, 61-67 *and see* 'dumping'; case studies, 189-278 (incl. partial reprieves and places still threatened); policy, *see* removal policy; procedure, 131-137 *and see* expropriation, laws, negotiation /consultation (for removal), notice, removal (illegal); lack of land for, 59, 92-93, 231; pressure, *see* removal power, removal strategies, removal described, coercion/resistance described; resisted, *see* resistance; trends, 383-385, 390-395 *and see* vested interests; rejecting/other plans, 395-400; more than once, 10, 47, 51, 208, 221, 231-232, 240, 281, 289, 336, 373; 'voluntary', 31-32, 59, 122-123 *and see* 'voluntary' removal; texts, *see* notice, records/minutes, state comment/ texts; *and see* relocation sites, removal (threatened), removal (whites)
removal agents, *see* bantustans, Development Boards, planning committees, military action, police action, security police action, GG transport
removal and bantustans, policy/role in removals, *xx*, 28-30, 113-115, 162-163, 176-188, 322-323, 369, 376-377, 383-385; attitudes to removals, 45, 46, 51, 156, 158, 177, 178, 183, 228, 239, 240, 241, 244, 370-371; aiding RSA removals, 153-154, 158, 187, 190, 197, 224, 228, 370, 371-372 *and see* planning committees; case studies of removal into, 189-201, 221-232, 232-238; threatened/attempted removal into, 201-221, 238-266, 266-278; other removal into, 5-6, 8, 33, 34, 38, 44-45, 46, 47, 55-57, 67, 115-118, 122, 123, 128-130, 146-147, 148, 150, 161, 162-163, 172-173, 174, 177, 178, 182, 183; bantustans forcing removal into, 140, 159; forcing removal within bantustans, 45-46, 47-48, 67, 186-187, 187-188; forcing removal between, 35, 38, 55, 57, 125-127, 179, 185-186, 369-370; *and see* black spots, Trust land for removal by consolidation
removal (before and after), Tsitsikama-Elukhanyweni, 189-190, 197-199, 200-201; Valspan-Pampierstad, 202, 215-216; Klipfontein-Glenmore, 221, 222, 232; Colchester-Glenmore, 3, 4-5, 6; Kwapitela-Compensation, 232-233, 234-235, 236, 237-238; Mphakane-Mahodi, 239, 254-255; Klipplaatdrift-Kromhoek, 239, 240, 245-246, 251, 261, 263-265; Di Takwanen-Deerward, 55, 285
removal described, urban, 147, 148, 207; rural, 6, 128-130, 149-150, 195-197, 224-225, 225-226, 235-236, 256-259
removal (illegal), unnecessary, 138; law against interdicts, 139-140; easy to get round, 223, 226, 230-231; protest at, 223
removal policy, and apartheid, *xx*, 310, 338, 383-385; 'surplus' to bantustans, 28-30, 327 *and see* 'dumping'; outlined, 16, 67, 155,

367-368, 369-372; disguising, 8, 151-158, 342-343, 350-351, 367-368, 369-372; no change/reformulated, *xxviii*, 158, 163-164, 390-395; problems for, 387-390
removal powers: law, 138-146 *and see* consolidation, group areas, influx control, information control, law, minority rule, security police action; police, 146-150, 158 *and see* police action; military, 146-150, 158 *and see* military action, strategic control; local control, iniative, 130, 370 *and see* removal and bantustans, removal agents, removal strategies
removal strategies, 146-176, 285-286; law/'authority', 138-146, case study 221-232 *and see* non-negotiation/'authority' (for removal); intimidation, 160, case study 189-201 *and see* intimidation/threat; downgrading, 160, case study 201-221 *and see* downgrading; freezing development, 161-163, case study 201-221 *and see* housing (urban); division, 166-168, case study 266-278 *and see* division, gradual removal; blocking protest/support, 139-140, 215, 227, 285, 290 *and see* information control, leadership/group structures, publicity, resistance support; cooption, 168 *and see* cooption; persuasion/deception, 168-169, 187 *and see* deception, persuasion, promises broken, state misinformation; delay, 132, 136, 166, case study 232-238; exploiting uncertainty, confusion, rumour, 6, 101, 128, 132, 143, 145, 293-294; surprise, rapid action, 6, 128, 132, 196, 225-226, 235-236, 269-271,

285, 303 *and see* raids; defusing publicity, 150-158 *and see* publicity, state comment/texts, state misinformation
removal (threatened), 11-12; 1983 outlook, 58-60; case studies, 201-221, 266-278; for bantustans, 28-30; with continuing influx control *q.v.*; from black spots *q.v.*, 44-45, 53, 57, 293-295; from farm evictions, 55, 57; regional picture, 51, 53, 55, 57, 58; with group areas 36, betterment 46, consolidation, 44, 53; slowing mass removal, 383-384; tighter influx controls, 384-385; no basic policy change, 385; shift from land to people consolidation, 386-387
removal (whites), 1950-70 urban, 99-100; 1975-82 consolidation, 14, 43-44, 53, 179, cash delayed, 39; stressed to justify other removal, 154-155, 171; better publicity for, 46-47; distorted comparison with blacks, 14
rentals, to 1913, 73-80 *passim*, 91; removal pressure, *xxxii-xxxiii*, 203, 217; removal lure, 5, 168, 202; high in r̃/townships, 57-58, 202, creating in/ss 336
reprieve, 155-156, 309-310, 315; partial, *xxi*, *xxx-xxxii*, 57, 162, 172, 206, 220, 284, 315, 390; case study, 238-266; with consolidation changes, 15, 316, 386-387; reversible, 314, 390 *and see* publicity (defusing); with delay, 303; confusion on, 389; with pressure, 398-399
Reserve Four, Natal tribal land N of Richards Bay, 'negotiation' under threat, 153, 156, 158; resistance, 279

Reserve Six, Natal tribal land near Richards Bay, cleared 1976, bribery, 168
reserves, to 1913, 71-72, 80-82, Tvl and OFS 72-75, Cape and Natal 75-79; 1913-1950, 83-94; after 1950, restructuring 109-111, consolidated 38 *and see* bantustans, betterment, land
resettlement camps, *see* relocation sites
resistance, 130-131, 279-320, 389-390; to 1910, to colonial pressure, 72, 73, 75, 76; to individual tenure, 75-76, 81-82; 1940s, 96; 1950-60s, 32, 103-104; political, economic, 35, 83, 96, 103, 111, 382; case studies, 189-232, 238-278; boxes, 207-215, 218-219, 226-227, 242-247, 247-249, 250-255, 283-284, 293-295, 296-300, 321-325; effects, 314-317, 273, 376; determinants, 282-289 *and see* resistance assets, resistance problems; styles of, 280-282; organisation, 289-292 *and see* resistance organisation; strategies, 295-314 *and see* resistance strategies; evaluating, 314-317; outsiders, 304-313, 317-320 *and see* resistance support
resistance assets, 282-283, 317-318; old community, 238, 273-274, 282, 297-298; a lot/nothing to lose, 221, 238, 245-246, 250, 251-252, 283, 293, 296-300, 301, 335 (on influx control) *and see* sites evaluated; experience/political grasp, 283, 284, 398; example, contacts, 213-214, 283, 288, 301-302, 317 *and see* contact among communities; information, 317 *and see* resistance support

resistance organisation, 265-266, 289-295, 316-317, 320, 397-398; determinants, 282-289; general meetings, 193-194, 221, 250, 253, 266, 273, 290, 294; committees, 193, 216, 218, 262, 266, broad representation 272; funded, 273; removal strategies identified, 217-218, 288; own aims, strategies identified, 216-217, 290; other issues adopted, 217, 277, 284, 304; protest marches, rallies, campaigns, 217, 259, 260, 310; planning, self-reliance, agendas, 215, 216, 242, 250, 260, 263, 293; *and see* unity, contact among communities, leadership/group structures, negotiation (resistance), resistance problems
resistance problems, 289-295; suppression, *see* removal powers; isolation, 130, 195, 235, 281, 282, 288, 289, 300, 397; poverty, 130, 193, 196, 259, 262-263, 289; ignorance, 61-62, 130, 158, 160, 288-289, 317; no support/publicity, 47, 195, 235, 281, 288; fear, 33, 128, 193-194, 196, 207 *and see* fear/mistrust; bad leadership, 239-240, 255, 265; political weakness, 46, 130, 209, 211, 289; work-seeking, 215-216, 289; insecurity, confusion, rumour, 160, 215, 232, 293-294; depending on legal action, 225-230; submission to 'authority', 131, 234-235, 265; cooption, 159, 250, 252, 254, 286, 287, 324-325; clashing strategies, 265; support deterred, 12, 141, 235, 259; organisation lacking, 282, 288-289; poor relationships, 291; no national overview, 292; division, 304-305, 308, 311 *and see*

division
resistance (protection during), none in law/policy, 289; in publicity, 289, 305; in contacts, 292; by group concern, 287
resistance strategies, *xx*, 280-282, 295-314; statements to authorities, 296 *and see* memoranda/petitions; visiting site (or not), 300-301 *and see* sites evaluated; joint resistance, 301-302 *and see* contact among communities, isolation; negotiation, 302-303 *and see* negotiation (resistance); compensation, 303-304 *and see* compensation; mobilising on other issues, 304, 318 *and see* resistance organisation; using outsiders, 304-313 *and see* resistance support; 'no outsiders', 252, 281-282, 309; legal action, 252, 281, 308-309 *and see* resistance support
resistance support 281, 288, 304-313, 317-320, 398; lawyers, *xxv*, 130, 143, 144, 195, 221, 222, 225, 252, 281, 288, 308-309 *and see* court action; visitors, secular groups, *xxiv, xxxii*, 216, 235, 273, 281, 305-308, 309-310, 317-319, 389, 399 *and see* AFRA, Black Sash, PFP, publicity; churches, *xxi, xxv*, 252, 260, 262, 288, 310-311, 317, 397; bantustans, 241, 244, 311-312; commercial interests, 219-220, 307, 312-313, 389; support obstructed, 12, 26, 141, 144, 235, 241, 244; support wanted, 159, 218-219, 235, 284, 288; support avoided, 252, 288, 309
retrenchment, *see* employment (of blacks)
Richmond Farm, Natal in/s near Durban, 'hanging' notice, 133-134

Riebeeck East, E Cape African and coloured township at, removal, 355
Riekert Commission RP 32/1979 on the utilisation of manpower, 311
Riemvasmaak, NW Cape reserve near Upington, cleared 1973, strategic removal, 280; pressure, 288
Rikhoto case, 164-166, 393-394 *and see* urban residence rights (African)
Rockville, Central Tvl in/s at Soweto, raids, 176
Rooigrond, Bop. c/s near Mafikeng, N Cape/Tvl area, removal/resistance, 281, 291; trickery, 301; no wood, 341; employment, 353, 354, 356, 357; opinions, 366
Rooijantjiesfontein, W Tvl b/s near Gerdau, cleared, 386
Roosboom, Natal b/s near Ladysmith, origin, 79; removal pressure, 63-64; labour pool, 66
Rumpff Commission on Ingwavuma, 43
rural population, Africans in 1940s, 97; after 1952, 106; black increase (*'beswarting'*), 31, 120-122; black decline, 17, 18, 30-32; white decline, 120; 1960s b/s removal, 116-117, other removal, 30-32, 53; tightening control, 26 *and see* farm evictions
rural removal factors, mechanisation, 31, 119-120; farm size, 119-120; wage labour, 30, 31, 120, 122; job conditions, 32, 122-123; tensions, *'beswarting'*, 31, 120-122, 316; *and see* farm evictions, isolation, wages

Sada, E Cape Trust camp, now Ciskei r/township near Whittlesea, 1960s

origin, 57, exposé 57, 327; conditions, 320, 328, 340-341; diet, 363, 364; employment, 352, 356, 358, 362; and influx control, 33; opinions, 365-366, 367
Sahlumbe, Natal c/s in KwaZulu near Weenen, early days, 344-345; employment, 353, 356, 357; unemployment, 359-360; pensions, 362-363; diet, 363; organisation, 366; opinion, 367
St Lucia, see Lake St Lucia
St Wendolins, Natal b/s near Durban, partly reprieved, 172-173, joint resistance, 279
sanitation, *see* water/sanitation
Savannah Park, part of St Wendolins *q.v.*, 172
scheduled land, defined, *xi*, 85; removal process, 132; harder to clear, 138; issue on the sale of, 200; *and see* reserves, black spots
schools, *see* education
Sebe, Chief Lennox, Life President of Ciskei *q.v.*
secrecy, *see* negotiation/consultation, negotiation tactics (resistance); by law, 14-15, 141, 374
Section 10 rights, *xxvii*, 19, 105; in Orderly Movement Bill, 25; 'Rikhoto' rights, 164-166; loss by removal, *xxxiii*, 118, 169; 1983 limit, 393-394; division on, 166; policy against, 124; eroded, 206; objection on, 223; removal if none, *xxxii*, 107 *and see* influx control; reprieve through, 162; *and see* urban residence rights (African)
security police action, 140; deception by, 235; pressure by, 264, 290; intimidation, 12, 140, 160, 220, 256 *and see* intimidation/threat
Sekgosese, N Tvl b/s near Bandelierkop comprising Trust, reserve and freehold land, case study, 238-266; resistance, 287, 290, 397; possible Soekmekaar link, 281, 313; cost factor, 303
Sekhukuniland, N Tvl area, 45
'separate development', early form, 78, 95-127; *wnd see* apartheid disguised
Shantytown, Central Tvl in/s near Johannesburg, 96
sharecroppers, defined, *xv*; origins, 73, 74, 75; opposed, 80; barred, 84; removed, 85-87
Shepstone, Sir Theophilus, Secretary for Native Affairs, Natal, 1853-1875, 78
shops/cost of living: living expenses, 236, 237, 246, 328, 337, 350, 362, 378 *and see* diet, education, rentals; access to shops, 35, 202, 339, 340, 347, 349
Sinthumule/Kutama, N Tvl b/ss near Louis Trichardt, cost factor, 303; part reprieve, 387; site evaluated, 212-213, 235, 245-246, 248, 251, 277, 295, 300-301; non-negotiation on, 293, 295, 301; *and see* persuasion
Skosana, Simon, Chief Minister of KwaNdebele *q.v.*
slum clearance/'health hazard', 35, 36, 129, 138, 228, 230-231, 270; *and see* downgrading (for removal)
smallholders (African), *see* farming (African in 'white' areas)
Soekmekaar, N Tvl, attacked 281, 313
Sophiatown, Central Tvl African freehold area near Johannesburg cleared 1954, 100, 332
South African Broadcasting Corporation (SABC), and removals, 345, 374; and decentralisation, 376

South African Council of Churches (SACC), *xxv*, 260, 262
South African Defence Force (SADF), censorship, 141; supplying water, 376; cost, 388 *and see* military action, strategic control
South African Foundation, 307 *and see* vested interests, publicity/political pressure (state image-making)
South African Party, 83
Southern Free State Administration Board, 161
South Ndebele people, *see* Ndebele
South Sotho people, Tomlinson proposals, 37-38; harassed, 55, 186, 292; removed, *xxxiii*, 202; *and see* Qwaqwa (allotted bantustan)
Soweto, central Tvl city-township near Johannesburg, early days, 332; placing, 373
Soweto, E Cape in/s at Port Elizabeth, 176
Spitskop, W Cape village near Agulhas, 47
SPP survey, *xx-xxvi*, *xxx*, 328, 329-330, 332, 334
squatter camps, *see* informal settlements
squatters, defined, *xiv*; farm removal, (1964-1969) 122, 146-147, 148-150; urban removal, 32-33, 34, 57, 58, 104, 107, 147, 148, 176, 395; in bantustans, 35, 187-188, 392; in threatened groups, *xxvi*, 133; and compensation, 137; *and see* informal settlements, notice
state comment/texts, geographical apartheid, 70, 185, 385; group areas, 13, 36, 100, 101; black spots, 115, 116, 125, 167, 171, 184, 234, 275, 321-323; consolidation, 38, 42, 43, 44, 115-116, 125, 182-183, 185, 386; ethnicity, 'separate development', 65, 112, 114, 126, 171, 185, 321, 327, 370; political, physical exclusion, 17, 114; 'bantustan affairs', 15, 184, 186, 201; 'independence' (incl. land package), 178, 182-183, 205; 'constellation of states', 370; reserves, 93, 112; Africans outside bantustans, 28-30, 105-106, 117-118, 120, 124, 223, 394; labour, 24, 106, 112, 114, 122, 206; local jobs, 182, 321, 351, 390; decentralisation, 112, 386; 'legals', 'illegals', 24, 105-106, 129, 163, 268, 275-276; influx control under white rule, 105-106; 'surplus' people, dumping, 28-30, 114, 138, 157, 206, 223, 341, 390; relocation, removal (esp. forced), 28-30, 129, 130, 152, 153, 157, 169-170, 171, 173, 206, 276, 321-323, 327, 390, 391, 396; 'voluntary' removal, *xxx*, *xxxii*, 8, 30, 59, 128-130, 147, 157, 161, 173, 179, 182, 185, 215, 224, 228, 280, 294, 369, 372; removal figures, 9, 13, 14, 36, 45, 57, 58, 59, 99, 100, 117, 122, 128, 129, 147, 161, 163, 179, 182, 183, 185, 372; removal to bantustans, 28-30, 114, 206, 223, 274, 275-276; bantustans receiving people, 51, erosion, 93, 182-183; negotiation removal, 171, 187; slums, health hazard, 129, 270; strategic removal, 60; Board role, 228; police violence, 170, 175; demolition, 270 *and see* notice; home and facilities, 204, 268; site and facilities, 204-206, 321-325, 341, 342-343, 346, 390; congestion, erosion, 93, 182-183; negotiation-/consultation, 145, 153-154, 167,

171, 224, 274, 275, 277, 322-323, 390, 391; official mouthpiece, 144, 156, 158, 167, 323; persuasion 128, 130, 154, 157, 171; cooperation, 151-152, 155, 321, 323; respect, 138, 144, 171, 191, 224, 323; 'removing structures not people', 270; 'return to chief/place of origin', 268, 275; 'can't intervene', 275, 276, 321; 'unchangeable plans', 143-145, 191; 'deciding on merit', 206, 274; 'reconsidering', 247; 'not even a Fingo', 201; 'law and order', 101, 126, 147; official obstruction, 165, 201; transport, 36, 182, 205-206; compensation, 129, 322; lack of information, 13, 15; publicity on removal, 151, 200, 225; criticism on removal, 152, 387, 389; resistance, 39, 128, 129, 130, 147, 258, 261; white removal too, 14, 38, 154-155, 171; reform, 152, 390, 391; removal continuing, 152, 173; expense of policy, 12, 14, 27, 39, 42, 162, 163, 387, 388

state land (formerly crown land), proclaimed, 78, 91-92; Africans on, 74, 79, 85; rental, sale, 80; excluded from reserves, 90

state misinformation, 12-15; 'few families resisting', 261/258-259, 261; 'more water on site', 261/245-246, 248, 251, 261; Board just 'observing' removal, 228/ and 'using persuasion' (contradiction),130/129-130, 224, 226; 'commitment to cooperation', 191/191-192; 'nobody forced onto trucks, treated in an undignified way', 224/226-227; 'force not being used', 225/224, 226-227; 'notice of compensation amounts', 236/236-237; 'permanent home', 193/193, 240/240; 'equivalent agricultural land', 190/191, 197-198; 'permanent homes built', 190/197; 'the people favour move', 224/223, 224, 225, 226-227, 230231; 'letter of consent', 226 /226; 'demolishing *unoccupied* structures', 270 /269-271; 'affadavits agreeing to move', 294/294, 160; land for tenants, 291/291; negotiation with the people, 322-323 /324-325; the people want to go, 323-324/324-325; *and see* deception

Steadville, N Natal township near Ladysmith, under threat, 267; encouraging local stand, 272, 305; no vacancies, 276, 279

steering committees, *see* planning committees

Steincoalspruit, N Natal b/s in the Klip River area, origin, 79; resistance, 279

Stendhal, Natal mission near Weenen, removal, *xxx*

Stinkwater, W Tvl Trust camp, now Bop. r/site near Pretoria, 116, 346, 367

Stockenstrom, E Cape area, for Ciskei, 38

strategic control, pre-1913, 70, 73, 75, 76, 78, 82; removals for (1960-1983), 10; removals planned for (1983), 11, 43, 46-47, 53, 60, 68, 151, 238, 240, 280; township design for, 101, 393; public relations, 60, 151

Stutterheim, E Cape, influx in area, 337-338; township (Mlungisi) housing, part-reprieve, 162

'surplus' people, for removal, *xxii*, 28-30, 34, 105, 114, 157, 206, 222, 223, 381; on white farms, 31, 110, 119-120, 122-123, case study 221-232; in towns, 98, 104, 117,

206; tussle over, 98; permanent in bantustans, *see* 'dumping', state comment/texts

survival, *see* relocation (action/reaction after)

Suzman, Helen, *see* Progressive Federal Party

Swamp, The, Natal b/s near Himeville, versions of removal, 12-13, 129; delay tactics, 136; unsupported, 310

Swartruggens, W Tvl area, 43-44

Swaziland/Swazis, Tomlinson proposal, 37-38; and Kangwane, Ingwavuma, 43, 184, 282; strategic border, 47; ethnicity trouble, 293; police escort for, 295

Taung, N Cape reserve, now in Bop., 55

tenants, and removal, 133, 166, 172-173, 207, case study 221-232, 291-292; division on, 166-168, 172, case study 266-278; compensation 137, 310-311; in in/ss, 35; under Orderly Movement Bill, 26; *and see* cash tenants (on white farms), labour tenants, sharecroppers

terminology, euphemism, *xxvii-xxix* 8, 28-30, 68, 115, 128, 138, 154, 157, 327; clashes on, 153-154; shifting definitions, 15

Thaba 'Nchu, OFS reserve area, now Bop., near Bloemfontein, early days, 73-74; harassment, 55, 186, 292; land, ethnic shifts, 292; vested interests, 313

Thembalihle, Natal b/s near Estcourt, origin, 79; 'negotiation', 158; intimidation, 160

Thornhill, Ciskei transit camp and c/s near Tarkastad, E Cape, delayed in transit, 57; tricked, 301; conditions, 335

titledeeds, *see* landowners

Tlhaping-Tlaro/Ganyesa, N Cape reserves, now Bop., 55

Tomlinson Commission RP 61/1955 on the socio-economic development of the Bantu areas, purpose, 111-112; reaction, 112; on consolidation, 37-38, 115-116

T(h)ongaland, see Makhathini Flats, N Natal

townships, defined, *xii*; r/sites defined, 331-332; facilities, 332, 339-341, SPP survey 334; showpiece, 347, 348; economic matters, 351-353, 354-355, 356, 358, 359, 360; strategic control, 101, 393; RSA urban, *see* group areas, housing (urban), proclamation/deproclamation, places in index

transit camps, 332, 344; many are c/ss, *q.v.* for description

Transkei, bantustan independent of E Cape since 26 Oct. 76 under Status Acts 3/1976 and 100/1976, origin as ethnic unit, 37-38, approved 38, map 40-41; land area, population density (1980), 17; riots (as Pondoland), 45; to 'independence', 124-125; exodus, 38, 57, 186, 301; bad land refused, 38; removal opposed, 177, 312, 376-377; removal to, *xxxiii*, 33, 55, 57, 162, 163, 202, 395; removal in, 377; transport control, 394

transport, state undertakings, 36, 182, 205-206, 343; objection 246; after removal, 36, 66, 336, 339, 346, 355-357; roads, streets, 340, 342, 343, 347; in removal, *see* GG transport; *and see* commuters

Transvaal, removals overview, *xxiv*, 51-53, province with most, 9, estimate 1960-1983 10, threatened (1913) 11, from townships, 33, 163, to labour pools 35, ethnic, 35, 125-127, by consolidation, *xxiv*, 38, 43-44 (maps 37, 40-41), betterment 45-46, black spot and farm evictions 46; strategic borders, 47; to 1913, 72-75, 80; maps (1982), 48-50; labour tenancy abolished, 123; E Rand housing (1983), 163; ethnic rifts, 292; N Tvl reprieves, 387; SPP surveys 329, 330; *and see* places in index incl. Bophuthatswana, Gazankulu, Kangwane, KwaNdebele, Lebowa, Venda

tribalism, *see* chiefs/headmen

tribal tenure, *see* land tenure

Trust (the SA Development Trust, a function of the Dept. of Cooperation and Development created by Act 18/1936), 74, 89; 1960s purchases, 116; 1980-1984 budget, 39; land quota delayed, 92; control of r/areas, 38, 176, 177, 183; and white farmers, 109; and Driefontein, 293; *and see* consolidation

Trust land, defined, *xi*; consolidating people through, 38, 116, 176, 177, 183; and displaced people, 331, 337-338; white opposition to, 43-44, 53, 116, 179; removal from, 199; *and see* places in index

Tsitsikama (Mfengu Reserves), E Cape Trust areas near Humansdorp cleared 1977/78, case study of removal, 189-201; force used, 61, 128; GG 'foreigners', 136; court action, 143, resistance, 316

Tsonga people, Tomlinson proposal, 37-38; ethnic clash, *xxx*, 53, 125-127; *and see Gazankulu* (allotted bantustan)

Tswana people, Tomlinson proposal, 37-38; ethnic isolation, 35, 185, 371, 372; in removal, *xxix*, *xxxiii*, 202, 284; tenants harassed, 292; *and see Bophuthatswana* (allotted bantustan)

Turfloop University, 260

Tyefu, irrigation scheme in Ciskei near Grahamstown, E Cape, deception, 169; expansion, 187

Uitvlugt, Central Tvl r/area in KwaNdebele near Marble Hall, *xxx*

Umbulwane, N Natal b/s near Ladysmith under threat, resistance, *xxxi*, case study 266-278, 279, 305; and bulldozing, 133, 288; 'consultation', 153-154; influx, 336

Umlazi, Natal township in KwaZulu near Durban, 187-188

Umtata, E Cape town, now capital of Transkei, 395

unemployment/work seeking, defined, 359; 1940s, 96; forcing moves, 35, (pre-1950) 94, 97, 279, 282, 283, 335, 385 *and see* 'voluntary' removal; criterion for removal, 28-30, 166; trapped, 32, 55, 375, 378; on relocation, 189, 214, 216, 232, 292, 358-361; 'farm work only', 32; insurance for 'aliens', 20-21; and cooption, 289; *and see* poverty/suffering

Unibel, W Cape in/s near Cape Town cleared 1977/78, removal, 147; escape from, 281

United Democratic Front (UDF), *xxvi*,

399-400
unity, *xx*, 290-292; and local development, 216, 248, 249, 251-252, 274, 284; broadest base, 217, 250, 266, 259-260, 272, 284, 287, 289, 293; pledged stand, 193, 217, 251-266 *passim*, 274, 276-277, 279, 284, 294, 298; sharing decisions, views, 215 (thwarted), 216, 250, 294, 295; and assets, 308; and outsiders, 304-305, 308, 309; and coopted people, 159, 252, 282, 313; *and see* accountability, contact among communities, leadership/group structures, resistance organisation
unrest, *see* resistance
Upington, N Cape r/area, 280
urban areas, *see* group areas, industry, influx control, informal settlements, housing (urban), townships, urban population, urban residence rights (African)
Urban Foundation, *see* commercial interests
urban population, increase, 96, 97, 103, 384, 385, 393; racial segregation, 95, 99-103; displaced to bantustans, 375-376
urban removals, *xxxi*, 32-36, Tvl 51, OFS 54-55, N Cape 55, E Cape 55, 57, W Cape 57-58; 1950-1970, 99-100; 1960-1983 figures, 10; under threat (1983), 11, 394-395; resistance, 55, case study 201-221; tactics, *xxxi*, 160; *and see* group areas, influx control, informal settlements, proclamation/deproclamation, state comment/texts
urban residence rights (African), 1923 segregation, 99; outlined, 104-105 *and see* Section 10 rights; of families, 117-118, 393-394; eroded,

stripped, 27, 34, 118; migrants' claim, 164-166; in Orderly Movement Bill, 25-26; for 'aliens', 19; cost of 'residence control', 162-163
Utrecht, N Natal area, cleared, 115; army removal, 148-150

Vaalboschhoek, N Cape Trust r/area now Bop., near Taung, 349; move to/from, 55
Vaalharts, irrigation scheme in N Cape area, 208
Vaalkop, N Natal c/s near Ladysmith in Limehill complex *q.v.*, *xxx*
Valspan, N Cape township at Jan Kempdorp, resisting, 283; case study, 201-221; isolated, 55, 281, 292; vested interest, 312; reprieve, *xxxi, xxxii, xxxiii*
Van der Walt Commission on consolidation, 42-43, 387 *and see* Le Roux Committee
Venda, bantustan independent of N Tvl from 13 Sept. 79 under Status Act 107/1979, origin as ethnic unit, 37; map, 40-41; clash on consolidation, *xxx*, 43; land area, population density (1980), 17; 1982 map, 48; 'independence' rewarded, 22; removal to, *xxix*, 47, 162-163; removal from, 126; removal within, 187; repression etc., 127, 376; unemployment, 378
Venda people, ethnic clash, 53; Tomlinson on, 37, 126; *and see* Venda (allotted bantustan)
Ventersdorp, W Tvl, *see Mogopa*
vested interests, clashing pre-1940, 82-83, in 1940s, 96-98; personal (for career, profit, etc.), 98, 102, 111, 113; South African Foundation, 307; *and see* commercial,

farming, industrial, mining, party political interests *and* cooption methods
Viljoen Committee on private sector involvement in housing 1981, 393
Viljoen, Dr Gerrit, Minister of Education and of Cooperation and Development *q.v.*
violence (resistance), 148, 248-249, 258, 264, 282, 313-314; in 1940s, 96
violence (state), 146-148; case study, 189-201; described, 58, 128, 149-150, 170, 176, 220, 253, 256-259, 271, 283, 285, 286, 313, 396; pre-1910 land wars, 73, 75; *and see* death/injury, demolition, raids
Vivo, Lebowa r/area, *see Kromhoek*
'voluntary' removal, by displacement etc., 334-338; by state pressure, 179, 207, 370-372 *and see* removal strategies; by unemployment, 31-32, 122-123, 179, 215-216 *and see* unemployment/workseeking; image for state publicity, 150-158, 385 *and see* publicity; planned image, 383-384; 'consent', 133-134, 225-227, 228-230; *and see* state comment/texts, state misinformation, terminology
vote, Cape African, 76, 83-84, 88, 89; African exclusion, 19, 25, 110, 112, 382; voteless in removal, 46, 130, 176, 289; in new constitution, 25, 319, 382; bantustan, 18-19, 205; *and see* citizenship
Vryburg, N Cape area, *see* Huhudi case study 201-221; under threat, 55; army removal, 147; assurances, 303; vested interest, 312
Vryheid, Natal area cleared, 115

Waaihoek, N Natal r/township near Ladysmith, *xxx*
wages, on farms, 31, 32, 97, 122-123, 179, 379; in rural sites, 354-355; industrial, *xxvii*, 352-353; clash on, 96; and white workers, 97; dependency on, 75-76, 80-81, avoided, 78-79 *and see* unemployment/workseeking
Wakkerstroom, E Tvl town, 294 *and see Driefontein, Daggakraal, KwaNgema*
Walmer Township, E Cape African township in Port Elizabeth, removals from, 1981, 312
Warmbaths, Central Tvl area, 30
water/sanitation, state undertakings, 204, 205, (1983) 342, 348; water, 55, 336, 339-340, 341, 344, 345, 346, 348, 349, 376; sanitation, 331, 340, 341, 344, 345, 346, 348, 378; *and see* state misinformation
Weenen, Natal transit camp at, 332; forced evictions, 136, 146-147; 'surplus', 31; resistance, 280-281
Welcomewood, Ciskei c/s near King William's Town, E Cape, 280
Werkgenot, W Cape in/s near Cape Town, cleared 1977/78, 147, 281
Western Cape, removals, *xxiii, xxvii*, 57-58, (1960-1983) 10, threatened (1983), *xxxiii*, 11, 394-395, Transkei resistance, 377; coloured labour preference, *xxiii*, 24, 57, 395; housing, 393; notice to employers, 24
Western Cape Administration Board (WCAB), 23-24, 58, 165
White City Location, N Natal township near Ladysmith, 267
White River, N Tvl, 52, 353
Wiehahn Commission on labour legislation, RP 47/1979,

38-82-87/1980, 27-28/1981, 311
Windermere, W Cape in/s near Cape Town upgraded in 1950s, 96
Winterton, Natal transit camp, Drakensberg area, 322
Winterveld, Bop., in/s near Pretoria, Central Tvl, commuters, 35; ethnic pressure, *xxxi*, 35, 185, 371; pensions, 174-175
Witzieshoek, OFS, now Phuthaditjaba, capital of Qwaqwa, early reserve, 73; influx, 338
Woodstock Dam, Natal, near Bergville, resistance, 282, 302; support, 310-311
Wyks, The, N Cape Trust r/areas, now Bop., 55

Xhosa people, 75; removal, *xxix*, *xxxiii*, 202, 377; *and see Ciskei, Transkei* (allotted bantustans)

YB, Bop. police, harassing, 185, 292, 371

Zeerust, W Tvl, 43-44
Zimbabwe border, 47
Zulu people, early days, 75, 78-79; Tomlinson on, 37-38; ethnic stress, 184, 293; resistance, 53, 296; *and see KwaZulu* (allotted bantustan)
Zwartrand, Tvl b/s, *see Mogopa*
Zweledinga, Ciskei transit camp near Balfour, E Cape, delay on, 57; being cleared (1985), *xxxi*
Zwide, E Cape African township at Port Elizabeth, 162